4/23

PRICE GUIDE & BIBLIOGRAPHY TO CHILDREN'S & ILLUSTRATED BOOKS

by

Edward S. Postal

M&P Press
Laguna Beach, Ca
1995

Typesetting by Sexton Design, Irvine CA
Printing by We Do Graphics, Orange CA

Library of Congress Catalog Card Number - 94-80238
ISBN: 0-9644800-1-8
1 2 3 4 5 6 7 8 9 0
Printed in the U.S.A.

*To Bonnie, Brook, Tedy, Zoe and Stevie
the kids we all love*

ACKNOWLEDGMENTS

The author wishes to thank the many people and companies who have given much time and information.

A special thanks to

The Fullerton Children's Library

E. Lee Baumgarten

Prince & The Pauper Bookstore

and to most of all my wife Bonnie Macmillan

INTRODUCTION

After talking to many book dealers over the last few years, I realized that there was something lacking in the way of reference material. There were many price guides out, but none included early reprints and most only had a few entries by any one illustrator. After doing much research, I found that it is impossible to have enough detailed information if your category for your price guide is too broad. Usually the larger area a guide includes, the less detailed information it has.

This is the reason that I decided to include only 26 of the top illustrators of illustrated books, so that almost every book that these artists illustrated could be included. The toughest task was to decide who to include and who to leave out. I tried to pick the illustrators that were widely collected and known. I know that there are many important illustrators that should be in here but we had to draw the line somewhere. There will probably be another volume next year with 26 different illustrators. Please feel free to let me know your wishes for artists to be included.

This guide is a result of a year and a half of visiting hundreds of book stores all over the world, reading hundreds of catalogues, price guides, and ads for illustrated books. I hope that it helps whether you are a collector, book store, antique dealer, or whatever your interest in books are.

Edward S. Postal

Contents

KEY TO ABBREVIATIONS

AEG	= All edges gilt
DJ	= Dust jacket
IBDS	= Illustrated boards
TEG	= Top edge gilt
TICP	= Tipped in color plates
<color>/gilt	= color of cloth & gilt
	design or lettering on cover
	or spine

abbreviations of cities where published

Akr	Akron
Bos	Boston
Cam	Cambridge
Chi	Chicago
Cle	Cleveland
Col	Columbus
Edi	Edinburgh
Gar	Garden city
Har	Hartford
Ind	Indianapolis
Jol	Joliet
KC	Kansas City
Lon	London
LA	Los Angeles
NY	New York
NP	No Place
Phi	Philadelphia
Rac	Racine
SF	San Francisco
Scot	Scotland
Spr	Springfield
Syr	Syracuse
Tor	Toronto
Wil	Wilmington

GUIDELINES FOR USE

CONDITION

The prices in this guide are for books in vg (very good) condition. Any defects such as excessive cover wear, torn or missing pages or plates, loose or broken hinges, scribbling or crayon marks, as well as any other major defects affects the value greatly, sometimes as much as 90% less than these prices. On the other hand, books that are extremely fine to as new, are worth substantially more than these prices, sometimes as much as double.

CONVENTION FOR PUBLICATION DATES

Where or if a publication date appears in a book, it can be a very important factor. The standard manner in which this guide and most use for determining dates are the following:

1890　　= Date on Title page

(1890)　= Date on Copyright page only

[1890]　= Date does not appear on either the title page or the copyright page, and the date in brackets represents either the actual or approximate publication date.

DUST JACKETS

We have noted whether a dust jacket was issued with a book only when we were definitely sure of that fact, even though the majority of books were issued with them. The prices listed in this guide are for books without dust jackets. Any book published before 1920 with its original dust jacket is worth substantially more than these prices. The amount could be anywhere from 20% to 400% more depending the scarcity, condition and desirability of the dj.

FIRST THUS

This is probably the most useless and misused term in the book business. I have seen dealers use the term for reprints by A.L Burt, Grosset & Dunlap, as well as for a book that was issued with 14 color plates and was reissued with only 9. It is a term that really should not be used when referring to illustrated books. Instead the terms such as "First Rackham illustrated" should be used or even better mention the publisher, date using the conventions mentioned above.

PRICES

In this guide there is a price range. This does not mean that the low price is for a book in poor condition and the high price is for a book in fine condition. (see condition above). The price range takes into account geographical differences of the demand, as well as different philosophy among different dealers. The prices that we have included in this guide have come from dealer catalogues, auction prices, physically visiting hundreds of bookstores, and receiving quotes for many of these books.

Use this book as a guide not a bible. If you bring a book to sell to a general used bookstore, and the price in this guide is $75-$100 and the bookstore offers you only $10 for the book, they are not necessarily trying to cheat you. The condition may not be such as they can use, or they may not have a market for that book. On the other hand if a book with that price range in this guide is offered by a bookstore or dealer for substantially more, again it does not necessarily mean that they are too expensive. The condition may be far superior than the average book, or they may specialize in illustrated books and have to keep a large inventory on hand to satisfy the demand of their clientele.

PUBLISHERS

We have given the publishers name and city whenever possible. It is much more important in determining value than just the city, and you should always give the publisher when describing a book.

REPRINTS

Most price guides only list first editions. We feel that there is still a very great demand for illustrated books even if they are not first editions. Because there are crossover interests with both the art and antique fields for plates by these illustrators, an early reprint from Parrish, Dulac, or most any of the illustrators in this guide, does not have the great discrepancy between the reprint and the first edition as modern first editions do.

Many publishers such as Scribners published these books many many times. If we have listed a date after the first publication date, the prices are basically the same for any reprint in the same time period.

For example: Treasure Island illustrated by N.C. Wyeth was first published in 1911. In our price guide we might have only one price for a reprint from 1917. The price would be the same whether it is 1913 or 1925.

ERRORS AND OMISSIONS

We have tried to list every book illustrated by the artists that we have selected for inclusion in our guide. If we have missed any book that any of these artists have illustrated, we are sorry, and if you would please bring it to our attention, we will include it in future editions. Unfortunately we have not been able to view every book personally, and had to rely on catalogues, and other reference for some of our information. We apologize for any errors or omissions, and would greatly appreciate any input for future editions.

ILLUSTRATORS

Cicely Mary Barker

Title	Author	Publisher	City
Autumn Song With Music	Linnell/Olive	Blackie & Sons	Lon
Autumn Song With Music	Linnell/Olive	Blackie & Sons	Lon
Book Of Flower Fairies	Barker/Cicely Mary	Blackie & Sons	Lon
Book Of Flower Fairies	Barker/Cicely Mary	Blackie & Sons	Lon
Children's Book Of Hymns (The)	Barker/Cicely Mary	Blackie & Sons	Lon
Children's Book Of Hymns (The)	Barker/Cicely Mary	Blackie & Sons	Lon
Fairies Of The Flowers & Trees	Barker/Cicely Mary	Blackie & Sons	Lon
Flower Fairies Of Autumn	Barker/Cicely Mary	Blackie & Sons	Lon
Flower Fairies Of Spring		Blackie & Sons	Lon
Flower Fairies Of Spring		Blackie & Sons	Lon
Flower Fairies Of Summer	Barker/Cicely Mary	Blackie & Sons	Lon
Flower Fairy Alphabet (A)	Barker/Cicely Mary	Blackie & Sons	Lon
Flower Songs Of The Seasons	Barker/Cicely Mary	Blackie & Sons	Lon
Laugh & Learn	Humphreys/Jennett	Blackie & Sons	Lon
Little Book Of Old Rhymes (A)	Barker/Cicely Mary	Blackie & Sons	Lon
Lord Of The Rushie River (The)	Barker/Cicely Mary	Blackie & Sons	Lon
Rhymes New & Old	Barker/Cicely Mary	Blackie & Sons	Lon
Spring Songs With Music....	Linnell/Olive	Blackie & Sons	Lon
Summer Songs With Music...	Linnell/Olive	Blackie & Sons	Lon

(1895-1973) Croydon, England

Year	Color	Tipped	B&W	Price Range	Pages	Size	TEG	AEG	DJ	Comments
[1920]	12	Ticp		75 — 125	50	4to				
[1930]	12	Ticp		50 — 75	50	4to				
[1927]				150 — 250	92	8vo			DJ	
[1940]	72			50 — 75		8vo			DJ	
	12	Ticp		50 — 75	84					
	12	Ticp		15 — 20						Reprint
				50 — 75	92	8vo				Green/Gilt
[1927]	24			75 — 125		12mo				
[1930]				50 — 75					DJ	
	24			75 — 125		8vo				
(1923)	24			75 — 125	25	12mo				
(1934)	24			75 — 125	24	12mo			DJ	
[1915]	12	Ticp		100 — 150		4to				
[1936]	8			50 — 75	255	8vo				
	12			30 — 50					DJ	
[1938]	12		2	50 — 75	48	12mo				
[1936]	12			60 — 80						
[1920]	12	Ticp		75 — 125		4to			DJ	
[1920]	12	Ticp		75 — 125		4to			DJ	

Howard Chandler Christy

Title	Author	Publisher	City
American Girl (The)	Christy/Howard Chandler	Moffat	NY
An Old Sweetheart Of Mine	Riley/James W.	Bobbs-Merrill	Ind
An Old Sweetheart Of Mine	Riley/James W.	Bobbs-Merrill	Ind
An Old Sweetheart Of Mine	Riley/James W.	Grosset&Dunlap	NY
Cavalier (The)	Cable/G.	Scribner	NY
Christy Girl (The)	Christy/Howard Chandler	Bobbs-Merrill	Ind
Courtship Of Miles Standish	Longfellow/Henry W.	Bobbs-Merrill	Ind
Dolly Dialogues	Hope/Anthony	Russell	
Dorothy Vernon/Hoddon Hall	Major/C.	Macmillan	NY
Drawings	Christy/Howard Chandler	Moffat	NY
Drawings	Christy/Howard Chandler	Review Of Reviews	NY
Evangeline	Longfellow/Henry W.	Bobbs-Merrill	Ind
Fifth String (The)	Sousa/John Phillips	Bowen/Merrill	Ind
Home Again	Riley/James W.	Bobbs-Merrill	Ind
Home Again With Me	Riley/James W.	Bobbs-Merrill	Ind
House Of A Thousand Candles	Nicholson/M.	Bobbs-Merrill	Ind
Lady Of The Lake	Scott/Sir Walter	Bobbs-Merrill	Ind
Liberty Belles		Bobbs-Merrill	Ind
Lion & The Unicorn (The)	Davis/Richard Harding	Scribner	NY
Maid-At-Arms	Chambers/R.	Harper	NY
Man In The Lower Ten	Rinehart/M.R.	Bobbs-Merrill	Ind
Ne'er Do Well (The)	Beach/R.	Harper	NY
Old Gentlemen Of The Black Stock (The)	Page/Thomas Nelson	Scribner	NY
Our Girls	Christy/Howard Chandler	Moffat	NY
Out To Old Aunt Mary's	Riley/James W.	Bobbs-Merrill	Ind
Princess (The)	Tennyson/Alfred	Bobbs-Merrill	Ind
Riley's Roses	Riley/James W.	Bobbs-Merrill	Ind
Rose (The)	Riley/James W.	Bobbs-Merrill	Ind
Songs Of Sentiment	Christy/Howard Chandler	Moffat	NY
Thirty Favorite Paintings		Collier	NY
Under The Rose	Isham/Frederick S.	Bobbs-Merrill	Ind
Wanted A Matchmaker	Ford/Paul L.	Dodd	NY
Wanted, A Chaperone	Ford/Paul L.	Dodd	NY

(1873-1952) Morgan County, OH

Year	Color	Tipped	B&W	Price Range	Pages	Size	TEG	AEG	DJ	Comments
1906	16			100 — 150	157	8vo				
(1902)			19	25 — 50		8vo				
(1902)			19	250 — 350		4to				400 Signed By Riley
(1902)				15 — 25		8vo				
1901				40 — 60	311	8vo				Red Cloth
(1906)	16			75 — 100		8vo				
(1903)	8			25 — 50	152	8vo			DJ	
1901			18	30 — 45	202	8vo	Teg			
1902				20 — 30		8vo				Blue Cloth
1905			28	125 — 175		Folio				
1913				75 — 100		Folio				
(1905)	6			30 — 50	132	4to				Red/Gilt
(1902)				10 — 20	124	8vo	Teg			
(1908)				40 — 75		8vo				
(1908)				35 — 60		4to				
(1905)	7			15 — 30	382	8vo				
(1910)	13			40 — 75		4to				Green/Gilt
(1912)	8			125 — 175		Folio				Brown/Gilt
1899			6	15 — 30	204	8vo				
1902				20 — 35		8vo				Green/Gilt
(1909)				35 — 50	372	8vo				
1911			8	20 — 35	402	12mo				
1900	7			30 — 45	170	12mo	Teg			
1907	16			75 — 100	160	8vo				
(1904)				25 — 40		8vo				
(1911)	14			75 — 100		4to				Brown/Gilt
(1909)	8			75 — 100		4to				Green/Gilt
(1916)			16	30 — 45		4to				
1910	12			75 — 100		8vo				Grey/Gilt
1909				300 — 500	62	Folio				
(1903)	4			15 — 25	427	12mo				Green Cloth
1900			5	25 — 40	112	8vo	Teg			Green/Gilt
1902	6			25 — 50	109	8vo	Teg			

Palmer Cox

Title	Author	Publisher	City
Another Brownie Book	Cox/Palmer	Unwin	Lon
Another Brownie Book	Cox/Palmer	Century	NY
Brownie Clown Of Brownie Town	Cox/Palmer	Century	NY
Brownie Year Book	Cox/Palmer	McLoughlin	NY
Brownies & Other Stories	Cox/Palmer	Donohue	Chi
Brownies & Prince Florimel (The)	Cox/Palmer	Century	NY
Brownies Abroad (The)	Cox/Palmer	Unwin	Lon
Brownies Abroad (The)	Cox/Palmer	Century	NY
Brownies Around The World (The)	Cox/Palmer	Unwin	Lon
Brownies Around The World (The)	Cox/Palmer	Century	NY
Brownies At Home (The)	Cox/Palmer	Unwin	Lon
Brownies At Home (The)	Cox/Palmer	Century	NY
Brownies In Fairyland (The)	Cox/Palmer	Century	NY
Brownies In Fairyland (The)	Cox/Palmer	Harms	NY
Brownies In The Philippines (The)	Cox/Palmer	Unwin	Lon
Brownies In The Philippines (The)	Cox/Palmer	Century	NY
Brownies Many More Nights (The)	Cox/Palmer	Century	NY
Brownies Through The Union (The)	Cox/Palmer	Unwin	Lon
Brownies Through The Union (The)	Cox/Palmer	Century	NY
Brownies' Latest Adventure (The)	Cox/Palmer	Unwin	Lon
Brownies' Latest Adventure (The)	Cox/Palmer	Century	NY
Brownies: Their Book	Cox/Palmer	Century	NY
Brownies: Their Book	Cox/Palmer	Century	NY
Brownies: Their Book	Cox/Palmer	Unwin	Lon
Captivating Stories Of Animals	Veale/E.	Juvenile Publishing	
Children's Funny Book	Cox/Palmer	Lothrop	Bos
Comic Yarns In Verse	Cox/Palmer	Hubbard	Phi
Frontier Humor	Cox/Palmer	Hubbard	Phi
Golden Gate (The)	Dodge/Mary M.		Chi
Hans Von Pelter's Trip To Gotham		Art Printing	NY
How Columbus Found America		Art Printing	NY
Jolly Chinee	Cox/Palmer	Conkey	
Juvenile Budget	Cox/Palmer	Donohue	Chi
Palmer Cox Brownie Printer (The)		Century	NY
Palmer Cox's Funny Animals	Cox/Palmer	Donohue	Chi
Queer People	Cox/Palmer	Unwin	Lon
Queer People	Cox/Palmer	Hubbard	Phi
Queer People With Paws And Claws....	Cox/Palmer	Hubbard	Phi
Queer People With Wings And Stings....	Cox/Palmer	Hubbard	Phi
Queerie Queers	Cox/Palmer	Larkin	
Squibs Of California		Mutual	Har
That Stanley		Art Printing	NY

(1840-1924) Granby, Canada

Year	Color	Tipped	B&W	Price Range	Pages	Size	TEG	AEG	DJ	Comments
(1890)				175 — 225	144	4to				
(1890)				175 — 225	144	4to				
[1908]				175 — 225	103	8vo				
[1895]	12			175 — 225	26	4to				
				40 — 70		8vo				
(1918)				100 — 130	246	8vo				Tan Cloth
(1899)				150 — 185	144	4to				Red Cloth
(1899)				175 — 225	144	4to				
(1894)				150 — 200		4to				
(1894)				175 — 225	144	4to			DJ	
(1893)				175 — 225	144	4to				
(1893)				175 — 225	144	4to				
(1925)				125 — 150	118	8vo				
1894				175 — 225						
(1904)				175 — 225	144	4to				
(1904)				175 — 225	144	4to				
(1913)				150 — 200						
(1895)				175 — 225	144	4to				
(1895)				175 — 225	144	4to				
(1910)				175 — 225		4to				
(1910)				175 — 225		4to				
(1887)				225 — 300	144	4to				Green Ibds
(1887)				125 — 175	144	4to				Early Reprint
1888				175 — 225	144	4to				Green Ibds
(1908)				75 — 125		4to				Yellow Cloth
(1879)				75 — 100	30	8vo				
(1889)				75 — 100	517	8vo				Blue Cloth
(1895)				50 — 75	343	24mo				
(1903)				35 — 50	228	16mo				
1876				100 — 150						
1877				50 — 100						
(1900)				75 — 100		4to				
				30 — 50		4to				
1906				75 — 100	108	12mo				
	1			30 — 50		4to				Ibds
1896				125 — 175		4to				
1899				125 — 175						
(1888)				100 — 150	119	4to				Ibds
(1888)				100 — 150		4to				
(1887)				125 — 150		8vo				Ibds
1874				100 — 150						
1878				50 — 100						

Walter Crane

Title	Author	Publisher	City
Absurd Abc (The)		Routledge	Lon
Adventures Of Her Baby (The)	Molesworth/Mrs.	Macmillan	NY
Adventures Of Her Baby (The)	Molesworth/Mrs.	Macmillan	Lon
Aladdin's Picture Book	Crane/Walter	Routledge	Lon
An Artist's Reminiscences	Crane/Walter	Methuen	Lon
An Old Fashioned Story	Molesworth/Mrs.	Macmillan	NY
Annie & Jack In London		Routledge	Lon
Art & Formation Of Taste	Crane/Walter & Lucy	Macmillan	Lon
Art Of Walter Crane	Konody/P.G.	G. Bell	Lon
Baby's Bouquet	Crane/Walter	Routledge	Lon
Baby's Bouquet	Crane/Walter	Warne	Lon
Baby's Opera	Crane/Walter	Routledge	Lon
Baby's Opera	Crane/Walter	Warne	Lon
Baby's Own Aesop	Crane/Walter	Routledge	Lon
Baby's Own Aesop	Crane/Walter	Warne	Lon
Bases Of Design	Crane/Walter	G. Bell	Lon
Blue Beard's Picture Book	Crane/Walter	Routledge	Lon
Book Of Christmas Verse	Beeching/H.C.	Methuen	Lon
Book Of Christmas Verse	Beeching/H.C.	Methuen	Lon
Book Of Wedding Days	Reid/K.E.J.	Longmans	Lon
Bric-A-Brac Stories	Harrison/B.	Scribner	NY
Carrots: Just A Little Boy	Molesworth/Mrs.	Macmillan	Lon
Carrots: Just A Little Boy	Molesworth/Mrs.	Macmillan	NY
Chattering Jack		Routledge	Lon
Children Of The Castle (The)	Molesworth/Mrs.	Macmillan	Lon
Children's Musical Cinderella		Routledge	Lon
Children's Plutarch (The)	Gould/E.J.	Watts	Lon
Children's Plutarch (The)	Gould/E.J.	Harper	NY
Christmas Child (A)	Molesworth/Mrs.	Macmillan	NY
Christmas Posy (A)	Molesworth/Mrs.	Macmillan	Lon
Christmas-Tree Land	Molesworth/Mrs.	Macmillan	Lon
Cinderella's Picture Book	Crane/Walter	J. Lane	Lon
Cinderella's Picture Book	Crane/Walter	Dodd	NY
Claims Of Decorative Art (The)		Lawrence & Bullen	Lon
Columbia's Courtship	Crane/Walter	Prang Co.	
Cuckoo Clock & The Tapestry Room	Molesworth/Mrs.	Macmillan	Lon
Cuckoo Clock & The Tapestry Room	Molesworth/Mrs.	Macmillan	Lon
Dale Readers Book 2 (The)	Dale/Nellie	Philip	Lon
Don Quixote	Parry/Judge	Blackie & Sons	Lon
Don Quixote	Parry/Judge	J. Lane	NY

(1845-1915) England

Year	Color	Tipped	B&W	Price Range	Pages	Size	TEG	AEG	DJ	Comments
[1870]				250 — 350						
1881			13	150 — 175	171	4to				Red/Gilt
1886			12	100 — 125	180	8vo				Red Cloth
(1875)				125 — 150		4to				
			123	100 — 150						
1923				25 — 35	340	8vo				Blue Cloth
[1860]				40 — 60	8					8 Chromoliths
1882				125 — 175		8vo				
1902	16			300 — 400	147	Folio	Teg			
[1878]	11			200 — 250	56	8vo				
[1890]	11			50 — 100	56	4to				
[1877]				175 — 225	54	8vo				
1900				100 — 125	54	8vo				
1887				125 — 150	56	12mo				
				75 — 100	56	12mo				
1898				150 — 200	365	8vo	Teg			Blue/Gilt
1875				150 — 200		4to				
1895			10	75 — 100	174	8vo	Teg			
1895			10	300 — 500	174	8vo				Maroon Cloth Special Edition Of 50
1889				250 — 300	108	4to				Red/Silver
1885			24	125 — 150	299	8vo				
1921			7	35 — 50						
1929				25 — 35	241	8vo				Lt. Blue Cloth
[1880]				75 — 100						Mounted On Linen
1890			7	75 — 100		8vo				
1879	8			100 — 150	30	8vo				Wraps
1906			6	100 — 125						
1910			3	75 — 100		8vo				
1880			7	125 — 150	223	12mo				
1888			8	75 — 100						
1884			7	100 — 125	223	12mo				Red Cloth
(1897)	8			125 — 150		4to				
				30 — 50		4to				Orange Cloth
1892				100 — 150						
(1892)	12			200 — 250		4to				Blue/Gilt
(1877)			8	125 — 175	242	8vo				
1919			8	50 — 75	242	8vo				Blue/Gilt
1907				50 — 75						
1900	11			175 — 225	245	8vo				
1900	11			100 — 125		8vo				

Walter Crane

Title	Author	Publisher	City
Don Quixote	Parry/Judge	Dodd	NY
Faerie Queen (The)	Spenser/Edmund	George Allen	Lon
Fairy Ship		J. Lane	Lon
Fairy Tales Of ...	D'Aulnoy	Lawrence	Lon
First Of May (The)	Wise/J.R.	Southeran	Lon
First Of May (The)	Wise/J.R.	Southeran	Lon
Flora's Feast	Crane/Walter	Cassell	Lon
Floral Fantasy In An Old English Garden	Crane/Walter	Harper	Lon
Flower Wedding (A)	Crane/Walter	Cassell	Lon
Flowers From Shakespeare's Garden	Crane/Walter	Cassell	Lon
Folk & Fairy Tales	Harrison/Burton	Marcus Ward	Lon
Forty Thieves	Crane/Walter	Routledge	Lon
Four Winds Farm	Molesworth/Mrs.	Macmillan	Lon
Golden Primer	Meiklejohn	Meiklejohn	Lon
Goody Two Shoes	Crane/Walter	J. Lane	Lon
Grammer In Rhyme	Crane/Walter	Routledge	Lon
Grandmother Dear	Molesworth/Mrs.	Macmillan	Lon
Grimm's Fairy Tales	Grimm Brothers	Worthington	
Happy Prince (The)	Wilde/Oscar	D. Nutt	Lon
Hind In The Wood (The)		Routledge	Lon
History Of Reynard The Fox	Ellis/F.S.	D. Nutt	Lon
History Of Reynard The Fox	Ellis/F.S.	D. Nutt	Lon
Household Stories	Brothers Grimm	American Publishing	Har
Household Stories	Brothers Grimm	Macmillan	Lon
Household Stories	Brothers Grimm	Macmillan	Lon
Household Stories	Brothers Grimm	Macmillan	NY
Ideals In Art	Crane/Walter	G. Bell	Lon
India Impressions	Crane/Walter	Macmillan	NY
King Albert's Book		Daily Telegraph	Lon
King Arthur's Nights	Gilbert/Henry	Nelson	NY
King Arthur's Nights	Gilbert/Henry	Jack	Edi
Knights Of The Round Table (The)	Gilbert/Henry	Jack	Edi
Legends For Lionel	Crane/Walter	Cassell	Lon
Line & Form	Crane/Walter	G. Bell	Lon
Little Miss Peggy	Molesworth/Mrs.	Macmillan	Lon
Little Miss Peggy	Molesworth/Mrs.	Macmillan	Lon
Little Queen Anne & Her Majesty's Letters	Crane/Walter	Marcus Ward	Lon
Magic Of Kindness (The)	Mayhew Brothers	Cassell	Lon
Masque Of Days (A)	Crane/Walter	Cassell	Lon
Merry Wives Of Windsor (The)	Shakespeare/William	Dent	Lon
Mrs.. Mundi At Home		Marcus Ward	Lon
Necklace Of Princess Fiorimonde (The)	De Morgan/Mary	Macmillan	Lon

(1845-1915) England

Year	Color	Tipped	B&W	Price Range	Pages	Size	TEG	AEG	DJ	Comments
1926	11			75 — 100	245	4to				Ibds
1895				150 — 200						
(1890)				75 — 125	12	4to				Wraps
1892				175 — 225	535	8vo	Teg			
1881			56	100 — 150						
1881			56	350 — 500				Aeg		300 Signed By Crane
1889	40			200 — 250	40	4to				Ibds
1899	46			125 — 225	48	4to				
1905	40			200 — 250	40	8vo				
1906	40			150 — 200		4to				Ibds
1885			24	150 — 250						
1873	8			100 — 150	8	4to				Wraps
1887			6	75 — 100	180	8vo				Blue Cloth
1884	32			125 — 150						
(1901)	18			175 — 200		4to				Red Cloth
(1868)				75 — 100		4to				Wraps
(1878)			7	75 — 100						
(1888)				75 — 100		4to				Ibds
1888			3	300 — 400	116	8vo				Grey Cloth
[1875]	5			100 — 150		4to				
1895				175 — 225						
1897				100 — 125	289	8vo				
[1894]				75 — 100	269	8vo				
1882			1	175 — 250	269	8vo		Aeg		
1914			0	75 — 100		8vo		Aeg		
1941	1		8	25 — 35		8vo				
1905				75 — 100		8vo				
1907			16	100 — 125	325	8vo				Green/Gilt
[1914]			1	50 — 100	187	4to				
(1911)	16			125 — 150	367	8vo	Teg			
1911	16			175 — 225	367	8vo	Teg			
1915	8			100 — 150						
1887	40			150 — 200		4to				Ibds
1900				125 — 175	282	8vo	Teg			Blue/Gilt
1887			12	75 — 100	195	12mo				Red Cloth
1912			12	40 — 60	195	8vo				Blue/Gilt
1885				150 — 250						
1869			8	50 — 75						
1901	40			200 — 300	40	4to				
1896			8	100 — 150						
1875			24	75 — 100						
1880			0	175 — 225	184	8vo		Aeg		

Walter Crane

Title	Author	Publisher	City
New Forest, Its History & Scenery (The)	Wise/John	Smith,Elder	Lon
Of The Decorative Illustration Of Books...	Crane/Wlater	Bell	Lon
Old Garden (The)	Deland/Margaret	McIlvaine	Lon
Old Garden (The)	Deland/Margaret	Houghton,Mifflin	Bos
Pan Pipes	Marzials/Theo	Routledge	Lon
Pan Pipes	Marzials/Theo	Routledge	Lon
Pan Pipes	Marzials/Theo	Warne	Lon
Pothooks & Preseverance	Crane/Walter	Marcus Ward	Lon
Queen Summer	Crane/Walter	Cassell	Lon
Quiver Of Love (The)	Loftie/W.J.	Marcus Ward	Lon
Rectory Children (The)	Molesworth/Mrs.	Macmillan	Lon
Renascene: A Book Of Verse	Crane/Walter	Elkin Mathews	Lon
Robin Hood & His Merry Men	Gilbert/Henry	Jack	Edi
Robin Hood & The Men Of Greenwood	Gilbert/Henry	Stokes	NY
Robin Hood & The Men Of Greenwood	Gilbert/Henry	Jack	Edi
Robin Hood & The Men Of Greenwood	Gilbert/Henry	Nelson	Lon
Romance/Three R's	Crane/Walter	Marcus Ward	Lon
Rosebud And Other Tales (The)	Kelly/Arthur	Unwin	Lon
Rosy	Molesworth/Mrs.	Macmillan	Lon
Rosy	Molesworth/Mrs.	Macmillan	Lon
Rumbo Rhymes	Calmour/Alfred C.	Harper	Lon
Shepheard's Calander	Spenser/Edmund	Harper	Lon
Sirens Three	Crane/Walter	Macmillan	Lon
Sixpenny Toybooks		Warne	Lon
Sixpenny Toybooks		Routledge	Lon
Slatendpencilvania	Crane/Walter	Marcus Ward	Lon
Stories From Memel For The Young	Havilland/Agnes De	Hunt	Lon
Story Of Glittering Plain (The)	Morris/William	Kelmscott Press	
Story Of Greece (The)	MacGregor/Mary	Jack	Edi
Studies & Stories	Molesworth/Mrs.	A.D. Innes	Lon
Tapestry Room (The)	Molesworth/Mrs.	Macmillan	Lon
Tapestry Room (The)	Molesworth/Mrs.	Macmillan	Lon
Tempest (The)	Shakespeare/William	Dent	Lon
Treatment/Drapery In Art	Rhead/G.W.	G. Bell	Lon
Triplets	Crane/Walter	Routledge	Lon
Turtle Dove's Nest (The)		Routledge	Lon
Two Gentlemen Of Verona	Shakespeare/William	Dent	Lon
Two Little Waifs	Molesworth/Mrs.	Macmillan	NY
Us:An Old Fashioned Story	Molesworth/Mrs.	Macmillan	Lon
Us:An Old Fashioned Story	Molesworth/Mrs.	Macmillan	NY
Valentine & Orson	Crane/Walter	Routledge	Lon

(1845-1915) England

Year	Color	Tipped	B&W	Price Range	Pages	Size	TEG	AEG	DJ	Comments
1863			63	150 — 200						
1896				100 — 150		8vo				
1893				125 — 175	114	8vo				
1894				75 — 100	114	8vo				
[1884]				100 — 150	51	4to				Early Reprint
1883				175 — 225	51	4to				Tan Ibds
				100 — 150	51	4to				
1886	24			200 — 250		8vo				Ibds
1891	40			250 — 300	40	4to	Teg			Ibds
1876				200 — 300				Aeg		Also Illus. By Kate Greenaway
1889			7	75 — 100						
1891				100 — 150						
1915	8			75 — 100						
[1912]	16			100 — 125		8vo	Teg			
1912	16			125 — 150	360	8vo				
	16			75 — 100		8vo	Teg			
1886				175 — 250		8vo				Ibds
1909	20			175 — 225	78	4to				
1882			8	75 — 100	204	8vo				Blue Cloth
1896			7	30 — 50	204	8vo				
1911	23			150 — 175	101	8vo				Ibds
1898			12	150 — 175	118	8vo				Ibds
1886			41	175 — 200		4to				Grey Bds
[1865]				50 — 75						Numerous Titles
[1867				50 — 75						Numerous Titles
1885				125 — 150		8vo				Ibds
1864			6	100 — 125						
1894			23	100 — 150						
1913	19			125 — 150						
1893				125 — 150	256	8vo				
1879			7	75 — 100		8vo				Red Cloth
1906			7	25 — 50	237	8vo				
1892			8	100 — 150						
1904			32	75 — 125	119	8vo				
1894				350 — 400		4to				500 Signed,
1890				50 — 75						
1894			8	300 — 500						Only 650 Copies Printed
(1883)			7	100 — 125	216	8vo				Red Cloth
1886			7	100 — 125	240	8vo				Red/Gilt
			7	75 — 100	240	8vo				
(1873)	8			125 — 150		4to				

Walter Crane

Title	Author	Publisher	City
Vision Of Dante (The)	Harrison/Elizabeth	Kindergarten College	Chi
Walter Crane Reader (The)	Dale/Nellie	Dent	Lon
Walter Crane's Picture Book	Crane/Walter	Cupples & Leon	NY
Walter Crane's Picture Book	Crane/Walter	J. Lane	Lon
Walter Crane's Picture Book	Crane/Walter	Dodd	NY
Wayfarer's Love	Various	Constable	Lon
Wm. Morris To Whistler	Crane/Walter	G. Bell	Lon
Wonder Book & Tanglewood Tales	Hawthorne/Nathaniel	Houghton,Mifflin	Bos
Wonder Book For Boys & Girls	Hawthorne/Nathaniel	Osgood	Lon
Wonder Book For Boys & Girls	Hawthorne/Nathaniel	Houghton,Mifflin	Bos
Wonder Book For Boys & Girls	Hawthorne/Nathaniel	Riverside Press	Cam
Wonder Book For Boys & Girls	Hawthorne/Nathaniel	Houghton,Mifflin	Bos

(1845-1915) England

Year	Color	Tipped	B&W	Price Range	Pages	Size	TEG	AEG	DJ	Comments
1895			3	75 — 100						
1899				40 — 60						
(1903)				75 — 125	145	4to				Ibds
[1895]				200 — 300	35	4to				
				75 — 100	35	4to				
1904				50 — 75		8vo				Green/Gilt
1911				75 — 100	277	12mo				Blue Cloth
1898				175 — 225	421	8vo	Teg			Red Cloth
1892	19			170 — 220	210	8vo				
1893	19			140 — 180	210	4to			DJ	
1893	60			250 — 350	210	8vo	Teg		DJ	Ltd To 250
1905			60	40 — 65						

William Wallace (W.W.) Denslow

Title	Author	Publisher	City
20 Years Of Hus'ling	Johnson	Thompson	
Arkansas Planter	Read/Opie	Rand McNally	NY
Ben King's Verse	Waterman (Ed)		Chi
Billy Bounce	Denslow/W.W.	Dillingham	NY
Colonial Dame	Fesenden/L.D.	Rand Mcnally	NY
Denslow's Animal Fair	Denslow/W.W.	Dillingham	NY
Denslow's Five Little Pigs	Denslow/W.W.	Dillingham	NY
Denslow's Mother Goose	Denslow/W.W.	McClure	NY
Denslow's Mother Goose	Denslow/W.W.	Chambers	Lon
Denslow's Scarecrow & The Tin-Man	Denslow/W.W.	Dillingham	NY
Denslow's Scarecrow & The Tin-Man	Denslow/W.W.	Donohue	Chi
Denslow's Scarecrow & The Tin-Man & Other Stories	Denslow/W.W.	Dillingham	NY
Denslow's Scarecrow & The Tin-Man & Other Stories	Denslow/W.W.	Donohue	Chi
Denslow's Scarecrow & The Tin-Man & Other Stories	Denslow/W.W.	Unwin	Lon
Denslow's Tom Thumb	Denslow/W.W.	Dillingham	NY
Denslow's Zoo	Denslow/W.W.	Dillingham	NY
Dot & Tot In Merryland	Baum/L. Frank	Bobbs-Merrill	Ind
Dot & Tot In Merryland	Baum/L. Frank	Geo Hill	Chi
Father Goose His Book	Baum/L. Frank	Geo Hill	Chi
Father Goose His Book	Baum/L. Frank	Geo Hill	Chi
Father Goose His Book	Baum/L. Frank	Donohue	Chi
Father Goose His Book	Baum/L. Frank	Donohue	Chi
House That Jack Built	Denslow/W.W.	Dillingham	NY
Humpty Dumpty		Dillingham	NY
Jack & The Beanstalk	Denslow/W.W.	Dillingham	NY
Jeweled Toad (The)	Johnston/I.M.	Bobbs-Merrill	Ind
Little Red Riding Hood	Denslow/W.W.	Dillingham	NY
Mary Had A Little Lamb	Denslow/W.W.	Dillingham	NY
Me & Lawson	Webb/R.	Dillingham	NY
New Wizard Of Oz (The)	Baum/L. Frank	Bobbs-Merrill	Ind
New Wizard Of Oz (The)	Baum/L. Frank	Bobbs-Merrill	Ind
New Wizard Of Oz (The)	Baum/L. Frank	Bobbs-Merrill	Ind
Night Before Christmas	Denslow/W.W.	Dillingham	NY
Night Before Christmas	Denslow/W.W.	Donohue	Chi
Old Mother Hubbard	Denslow/W.W.	Dillingham	NY
One Ring Circus	Denslow/W.W.	Dillingham	NY
Pearl & The Pumpkin	West/P.	Dillingham	NY
Pearl & The Pumpkin	West/P.	Donohue	Chi
Pictures From The Wonderful Wizard Of Oz	Russell/Thomas	Ogilvie	Chi

(1856-1915) Philadelphia, PA

Year	Color	Tipped	B&W	Price Range	Pages	Size	TEG	AEG	DJ	Comments
1900			28	100 — 150	664	8vo				
(1896)				75 — 100	315	8vo	Teg			
1894			1	75 — 100		8vo				
(1906)	16			300 — 400	279	8vo				Orange Cloth
1897				50 — 75		8vo				
1904				175 — 225		4to				
(1903)				100 — 125						
1901				400 — 600	96	4to				Ibds
1902				250 — 300		4to				
[1904]				200 — 300	12	8vo				
[1913]				50 — 100	12	8vo				
[1904]				150 — 200	74	8vo				
[1913]				50 — 100	74	8vo				
[1904]				150 — 200	74	8vo				
(1903)				100 — 150	12	8vo				
(1903)				75 — 125	12	8vo				
(1903)				200 — 300	226	8vo				
1901				600 — 800	226	8vo				
(1899)				200 — 700		4to				Other Printings Of 1st Edition
(1899)				2000 —4000		4to				1st Edition 1st Printing
[1913]				100 — 150		4to				
1910				150 — 200		4to			DJ	
(1903)				150 — 200	12	4to				
(1903)				200 — 300	74	4to				
(1903)				150 — 200	12	4to				
(1907)	8			225 — 275	211	4to				Ibds
(1903)				125 — 175		4to				
(1903)				125 — 175		4to				
(1905)			4	75 — 100	78	8vo				
(1903)	16			400 —1200	261	8vo				
(1903)	8			50 — 75		8vo				
(1939)	8	Ticp		100 — 150	208	8vo				
(1902)				300 — 500	64	4to				
[1902]				150 — 200		4to			DJ	
(1903)				125 — 150	12	4to				
(1903)				200 — 250	12	4to				Ibds
(1904)	16			200 — 250	240	8vo				
[1911]	16			125 — 150	239	8vo				
[1904]				300 — 400		8vo				

William Wallace (W.W.) Denslow

Title	Author	Publisher	City
Romance Of A Child	Loti/P.	Rand McNally	NY
Simple Simon	Denslow/W.W.	Dillingham	NY
Songs Of Father Goose	Baum/L. Frank	Bobbs-Merrill	Ind
Songs Of Father Goose	Baum/L. Frank	Geo Hill	Chi
Story Of Louise	Welch/D.		NY
Waters Of Caney Fork	Read/Opie	Rand McNally	NY
When I Grow Up	Denslow/W.W.	Century	NY
Wonderful Wizard Of Oz	Baum/L. Frank	Geo Hill	Chi

(1856-1915) Philadelphia, PA

Year	Color	Tipped	B&W	Price Range	Pages	Size	TEG	AEG	DJ	Comments
1897				50 — 75		8vo				
(1904)				100 — 150		4to				
(1909)				125 — 175	83	4to				Ibds
1900				400 — 600	84	4to				Ibds
1901				50 — 75	194	12				
1898				40 — 60		8vo				
1909	24			175 — 225	104	4to				
1900	24			5000 —10000	261	8vo				

Edmund Dulac

Title	Author	Publisher	City
Bells & Other Poems	Poe/Edgar Allen	Hodder & Stoughton	NY
Bells (The)	Poe/Edgar Allan	Hodder & Stoughton	NY
Comus	Milton/John		
Daughters Of The Stars	Crary/M.	Hatchard	Lon
Dreamer Of Dreams	Queen Marie	Hodder & Stoughton	Lon
Edmund Dulac's Fairy Book	Dulac/Edmund	Doran	NY
Fairies I Have Met	Stawell/R.	J. Lane	Lon
Fairies I Have Met	Stawell/R.	Hodder & Stoughton	Lon
Fairy Garland (A)	Dulac/Edmund	Cassell	Lon
Fairy Garland (A)	Dulac/Edmund	Cassell	Lon
Fairy Garland (A)	Dulac/Edmund	Cassell	Lon
Fairy Garland (A)	Dulac/Edmund	Scribner	NY
Fairy Tales Of Allied Nations	Dulac/Edmund	Hodder & Stoughton	Lon
Four Plays/Dancers	Yeats/W.B.	Macmillan	NY
Gods & Mortals In Love	Williamson/H.	Country Life	Lon
Golden Cockerel (The)	Pushkin/Alexander	Limited Editions Club	Lon
Golden Cockerel (The)	Pushkin/Alexander	Heritage	NY
Green Lacquer Pavillion	Beauclerk/H.	Doran	NY
Green Lacquer Pavillion	Beauclerk/H.	Collins	Lon
Jane Eyre	Bronte/Emily	Dutton	NY
King Albert's Book		Daily Telegraph	Lon
Kingdom Of The Pearl	Rosenthal/L.	Brentano's	NY
Love Of The Foolish Angel	Beauclerk/H.	Collins	Lon
Lyrics Pathetic & Humerous	Dulac/Edmund	Warne	Lon
Magic Horse	Housman/Laurence	Hodder & Stoughton	Lon
Marriage Of Cupid & Psyche			
Masque Of Comus (The)		Limited Editions Club	Cam
Masque Of Comus (The)		Heritage Press	NY
My Day With The Fairies	Stawell/R.	Hodder & Stoughton	Lon
My Day With The Fairies	Stawell/R.	Hodder & Stoughton	Lon
Nightingale (The)	Anderson/Hans Christian	Hodder & Stoughton	Lon
Picture Book/French Red Cross	Dulac/Edmund	Hodder & Stoughton	Lon
Poetical Works Of Poe	Poe/Edgar Allen	Doran	NY
Princess Badoura	Housman/Laurence	Hodder & Stoughton	Lon
Queen Bee (The)	Smith/C.M.	Nelson	Lon
Queen's Book Of The Red Cross		Hodder & Stoughton	Lon
Rubaiyat (The)	Fitzgerald/E.	Hodder & Stoughton	Lon
Rubaiyat (The)	Fitzgerald/E.	Hodder & Stoughton	Lon
Rubaiyat (The)	Fitzgerald/E.	Doran	NY
Rubaiyat (The)	Fitzgerald/E.	Doran	NY
Rubaiyat (The)	Fitzgerald/E.	Doubleday	NY
Rubaiyat (The)	Fitzgerald/E.	Doubleday	NY

(1882-1953) Toulouse, France

Year	Color	Tipped	B&W	Price Range	Pages	Size	TEG	AEG	DJ	Comments
	25			200 — 400						
(1912)	28			250 — 300		4to	Teg			Green/Gilt
(1954)				40 — 75						
1939	3			100 — 150	190	4to				
(1915)	6	Ticp		250 — 300	181	8vo			DJ	Grey Gilt
(1916)	16	Ticp		250 — 300	174	4to				
(1907)	8			250 — 300	117	8vo				
[1910]	8			225 — 275	117	4to				
(1928)	12	Ticp		150 — 200	251	4to				
(1928)	12	Ticp		600 — 800	251	4to				1000 Signed By Dulac
(1928)	12	Ticp		500 — 650	251	4to				
(1929)	12	Ticp		100 — 150	251	4to			DJ	Blue Cloth
[1916]	16	Ticp		250 — 350	174	4to				
1921				100 — 150		8vo				
(1935)	9			75 — 100						
				350 — 400	41	4to				1500 Signed By Dulac
				40 — 60	41	4to				Blue Cloth Boxed
(1926)			10	50 — 75	319	8vo				Tan Cloth
1926			10	75 — 100	319	12mo				Tan/Gilt
				125 — 175						
[1914]	1	Ticp		50 — 100	187	4to				Also Plates By Others
[1920]	10	Ticp		375 — 475		4to				
1929				75 — 100	251	8vo				Blue/Gilt
1908	24			300 — 400		4to				Ibds
(1911)	12			200 — 250		8vo				
				200 — 300						1500 Signed By Dulac
1954				125 — 175		4to				Limited To 1500
1954				35 — 45						In Slipcase
[1913]	8	Ticp		225 — 325	169	4to				Red/Gilt
[1915]	8	Ticp		150 — 200	169	8vo				Grey Cloth
[1911]	12	Ticp		225 — 275	125	4to				Blue/Gilt
[1915]	19	Ticp		200 — 300	135	4to				Yellow Cloth
[1921]	28			225 — 300		4to				
[1913]	10	Ticp		250 — 350	113	4to	Teg			
1907	2			100 — 150		8vo				
(1939)	1			50 — 75	255	4to				With Other Illustrators
[1909]	20	Ticp		200 — 300		4to				
[1914]	16			100 — 150		4to				Blue/Gilt
[1920]	20	Ticp		100 — 130		8vo				
1928	12			20 — 50	197	8vo			DJ	
1932	12			40 — 55	197	8vo				
1933	12			75 — 100	197	4to				Orange Cloth

21

Edmund Dulac

Title	Author	Publisher	City
Rubaiyat (The)	Fitzgerald/E.	Doubleday	NY
Rubaiyat (The)	Fitzgerald/E.	Garden City	Gar
Shirley	Bronte/Charlotte	Dent	Lon
Sinbad The Sailor		Hodder & Stoughton	Lon
Sinbad The Sailor & Other Stories		Hodder & Stoughton	Lon
Sleeping Beauty & Other Fairy Tales	Quiller-Couch/Arthur	Garden City	Gar
Sleeping Beauty & Other Fairy Tales	Quiller-Couch/Arthur	Hodder & Stoughton	Lon
Sleeping Beauty & Other Fairy Tales	Quiller-Couch/Arthur	Doran	NY
Sleeping Beauty & Other Fairy Tales	Quiller-Couch/Arthur	Doubleday	NY
Snow Queen & Other Stories	Anderson/Hans Christian	Hodder & Stoughton	Lon
Stealers Of Light		Hodder & Stoughton	Lon
Stories From ...	Anderson/Hans Christian	Hodder & Stoughton	NY
Stories From ...	Anderson/Hans Christian	Hodder & Stoughton	NY
Stories From ...	Anderson/Hans Christian	Doran	NY
Stories From ...	Anderson/Hans Christian	Doubleday	NY
Stories From Arabian Nights	Housman/Laurence	Hodder & Stoughton	Lon
Stories From Arabian Nights	Housman/Laurence	Scribner	NY
Stories From Arabian Nights	Housman/Laurence	Hodder & Stoughton	Lon
Stories From Arabian Nights	Housman/Laurence	Hodder & Stoughton	Lon
Stories From Arabian Nights	Housman/Laurence	Doran	NY
Stories From Arabian Nights	Housman/Laurence	Garden City	Gar
Stories From Arabian Nights	Housman/Laurence	Doubleday	NY
Tanglewood Tales	Hawthorne/Nathaniel	Hodder & Stoughton	Lon
Tempest (The)	Shakespeare/William	Hodder & Stoughton	Lon
Treasure Island	Stevenson/Robert Louis	Doran	NY
Treasure Island	Stevenson/Robert Louis	Garden City	Gar
Treasure Island	Stevenson/Robert Louis	Doubleday	NY

(1882-1953) Toulouse, France

Year	Color	Tipped	B&W	Price Range	Pages	Size	TEG	AEG	DJ	Comments
1934	12			75 — 100	197	4to				
1937	11			20 — 40						
1905				125 — 175		8vo	Teg			2 Volumes
[1914]	23	Ticp		300 — 375	223	4to				
[1914]	23	Ticp		250 — 350	221	4to				
(1915)	8			35 — 65	196	8vo				Reprint From 1930's
[1910]	30	Ticp		250 — 350	129	4to	Teg			
[1910]	16	Ticp		125 — 225		4to				
	16	Ticp		125 — 225		4to				
	12			100 — 150						
1916	2	Ticp		125 — 150	190	4to				Blue/Gilt
(1911)	28	Ticp		350 — 500	250	4to				Orange/Gilt
[1915]	14			125 — 175	195	8vo				Blue/Gilt
	16	Ticp		200 — 250	250	4to				
	16	Ticp		125 — 150	250	4to				
(1907)	50	Ticp		300 — 400	133	4to				
(1907)	50	Ticp		175 — 225	133	4to		Aeg		
[1911]	24			100 — 150		84				
[1920]	20	Ticp		100 — 125	319	4to				
[1920]	16	Ticp		125 — 175	237	4to				
[1932]	8			50 — 75		8vo				
	16	Ticp		125 — 175	237	4to				
(1938)	14	Ticp		150 — 200	245	4to				
[1908]	40	Ticp		350 — 500	144	4to				Blue/Gilt
[1927]	12	Ticp		125 — 175	287	8vo				Green/Gilt
[1939]				40 — 60	287	8vo				
	12	Ticp		125 — 175	287	8vo				Green/Gilt

Harrison Fisher

Title	Author	Publisher	City
Alternative (The)	McCutcheon/George	Dodd	NY
American Beauties	Fisher/Harrison	Bobbs-Merrill	Ind
American Beauties	Fisher/Harrison	Grosset&Dunlap	NY
American Belles	Fisher/Harrison	Dodd	NY
American Girl	Fisher/Harrison	Scribner	NY
Bachelor Belles	Fisher/Harrison	Grosset&Dunlap	NY
Bachelor Belles	Fisher/Harrison	Dodd	NY
Beauties	Wells/Carolyn	Dodd	NY
Beverly Of Graustark	McCutcheon/George	Dodd	NY
Beverly Of Graustark	McCutcheon/George	Dodd	NY
Black Friday	Isham/F.S.	Bobbs-Merrill	Ind
Bred In The Bone	Page/Thomas Nelson	Scribner	NY
Butterfly Man	McCutcheon/George	Dodd	NY
Checked Love Affair	Ford/Paul L.	Dodd	NY
Cost (The)	Phillips/David G.	Grosset&Dunlap	NY
Cost (The)	Phillips/David G.	Bobbs-Merrill	Ind
Day Of The Dog	McCutcheon/George	Dodd	NY
Dream Of Fair Women	Fisher/Harrison	Grosset&Dunlap	NY
Dream Of Fair Women	Fisher/Harrison	Bobbs-Merrill	Ind
Fair Americans	Fisher/Harrison	Scribner	NY
Francezka	Seawell/M.E.	Bobbs-Merrill	Ind
Garden Of Girls (A)	Fisher/Harrison	Dodd	NY
Garden Of Girls (A)	Fisher/Harrison		Tor
Girl's Life & Other Pictures (A)	Fisher/Harrison		
Golden Horshoe (The)	Aitken/Robert	Grosset&Dunlap	NY
Half A Rogue	MacGrath/Harold	Bobbs-Merrill	Ind
Harrison Fisher Book	Fisher/Harrison	Scribner	NY
Hiawatha	Longfellow/Henry W.	Bobbs-Merrill	Ind
Husbands Of Edith	McCutcheon/George	Dodd	NY
In The Bishop's Carriage	Michelson/M.	Bobbs-Merrill	Ind
Jane Cable	McCutcheon/George	Dodd	NY
Jewel Weed	Winter/A.A.	Bobbs-Merrill	Ind
King Albert's Book		Daily Telegraph	Lon
Little Gift Book	Fisher/Harrison	Scribner	NY
Maidens Fair	Fisher/Harrison	Dodd	NY
Man From Brodneys	McCutcheon/George	Dodd	NY
Market Place (The)	Frederic/H.	Stokes	NY
My Lady Peggy Goes To Town	Mathews/F.A.	Bowen	Ind
Nedra	McCutcheon/George	Dodd	NY
One Way Out	Von Hutten/B.	Dodd	NY
Pictures In Color	Fisher/Harrison	Scribner	NY
Pioneer (The)	Bonner/G.	Bobbs-Merrill	Ind

(1877-1934) Brooklyn, NY

Year	Color	Tipped	B&W	Price Range	Pages	Size	TEG	AEG	DJ	Comments
1909				20 — 30	119	8vo				
(1909)	32			200 — 250	93	4to				Red Cloth
(1909)	21			150 — 200	94	4to				
1911	16			200 — 250		Folio				
1909	12	Ticp		250 — 350		Folio				
(1908)	19			50 — 75						
1908	22			175 — 225		4to				
1913	16	Ticp		225 — 300		4to				Ibds
1904	5			15 — 30	357	8vo				
1906	5			10 — 25	357	8vo				
(1904)			6	25 — 30	409	8vo				
1904			8	25 — 35	274	8vo	Teg			
1910	4			25 — 30	121	8vo	Teg			Lavender Cloth
1903			5	30 — 45	112	8vo	Teg			
(1904)			8	15 — 25	402	8vo				
1904			8	35 — 50						
1904	5			35 — 50	137	8vo				Red/Gilt
(1907)	21			125 — 175	148	8vo				
(1909)	22			180 — 250		8vo				
1911	22			180 — 220		4to				
(1902)			7	30 — 45	466	8vo				
1910	16	Ticp		300 — 450		Folio				Ibds
1910	16	Ticp		200 — 250		4to				
	16			250 — 350		Folio				
(1907)	1			20 — 30	348	8vo				Green Cloth
(1906)				15 — 25		8vo				
1907	9			160 — 230		4to				
(1906)	16			80 — 120	189	4to				
1908	5			25 — 30	126	12mo				
(1904)			6	20 — 30	280	8vo				
1906	5			20 — 30	336	8vo				
(1910)			5	20 — 30	434	12mo				
[1914]	1	Ticp		50 — 100	187	4to				Also Plates By Others
1913	32			180 — 260		8vo				
1912	16	Ticp		300 — 450		4to				
1908	4			20 — 35	355	8vo				
1899			8	30 — 40		12mo				
1901				20 — 30	338	8vo	Teg			
1905	4			20 — 40	339	8vo				
1906	4			30 — 40		8vo				Lavender Cloth
1910	16			350 — 500		Folio				
(1905)			6	30 — 40	392	8vo				

Harrison Fisher

Title	Author	Publisher	City
Purple Parasol	McCutcheon/George	Dodd	NY
Salomy Jane	Harte/Bret	Houghton,Mifflin	Bos
Splendid Idle Forties	Atherton/G.	Macmillan	NY
Their Hearts Desire	Perry/F.F.	Dodd	NY
Thirty Favorite Paintings		Collier	NY
Three Men On Wheels	Jerome/J.K.	Dodd	NY

(1877-1934) Brooklyn, NY

Year	Color	Tipped	B&W	Price Range	Pages	Size	TEG	AEG	DJ	Comments
1905	5			30 — 40	108	8vo				
1910				50 — 75	78	8vo				Blue Cloth
1902			8	30 — 45	389	8vo				
1909	6			65 — 80	152	8vo	Teg			
1909				300 — 500	62	Folio				
1900				35 — 50	301	8vo	Teg			Green Cloth

Henry Justice (H.J.) Ford

Title	Author	Publisher	City
Aesop's Fables For Little Readers	Freshfield/Mrs. Arthur	Unwin	Lon
All Sorts Of Stories Book (The)	Lang/L.B.	Longmans	Lon
Animal Story Book (The)	Lang/Andrew	Longmans	Lon
Arabian Nights Entertainments (The)	Lang/Andrew	Longmans	Lon
Blue Fairy Book (The)	Lang/Andrew	Longmans	Lon
Blue Fairy Book (The)	Lang/Andrew	Longmans	Lon
Blue Fairy Book (The)	Lang/Andrew	Longmans	Lon
Blue Poetry Book (The)	Lang/Andrew	Longmans	Lon
Book Of Princes & Princesses (The)	Lang/Mrs.	Longmans	Lon
Book Of Princes & Princesses (The)	Lang/Mrs.	Longmans	NY
Book Of Romance (The)	Lang/Andrew	Longmans	Lon
Book Of Saints & Heroes (The)	Lang/Mrs.	Longmans	Lon
Brown Fairy Book (The)	Lang/Andrew	Longmans	Lon
Brown Fairy Book (The)	Lang/Andrew	Longmans	Lon
Crimson Fairy Book (The)	Lang/Andrew	Longmans	Lon
Crimson Fairy Book (The)	Lang/Andrew	Longmans	Lon
David Blaize & The Blue Door	Benson/Edward F.	Doubleday	NY
Disentanglers	Lang/Andrew	Longmans	Lon
Early Italian Love Stories		Longmans	Lon
Green Fairy Book (The)	Lang/Andrew	Longmans	Lon
Green Fairy Book (The)	Lang/Andrew	Longmans	Lon
Green Fairy Book (The)	Lang/Andrew	Longmans	Lon
Grey Fairy Book (The)	Lang/Andrew	Longmans	Lon
Grey Fairy Book (The)	Lang/Andrew	Longmans	Lon
Kenilworth	Scott/Sir Walter	Jack	Lon
Kenilworth	Scott/Sir Walter	McKay	Phi
Lilac Fairy Book (The)	Lang/Andrew	Longmans	Lon
Lilac Fairy Book (The)	Lang/Andrew	Longmans	Lon
Lilac Fairy Book (The)	Lang/Andrew	Longmans	Lon
Olive Fairy Book (The)	Lang/Andrew	Longmans	Lon
Olive Fairy Book (The)	Lang/Andrew	Longmans	Lon
Orange Fairy Book (The)	Lang/Andrew	Longmans	Lon
Pilgrim's Progress	Bunyan/John	Macmillan	NY
Pilot & Other Stories	Greene/H.P.	Macmillan	NY
Pink Fairy Book (The)	Lang/Andrew	Longmans	Lon
Pink Fairy Book (The)	Lang/Andrew	Longmans	Lon
Red Book Of Animal Stories (The)	Lang/Andrew	Longmans	Lon
Red Book Of True Stories (The)	Lang/Andrew	Longmans	Lon
Red Fairy Book (The)	Lang/Andrew	Longmans	Lon
Red Fairy Book (The)	Lang/Andrew	Longmans	Lon
Red Romance Book (The)	Lang/Andrew	Longmans	Lon

(1860-1941) London, England

Year	Color	Tipped	B&W	Price Range	Pages	Size	TEG	AEG	DJ	Comments
[1888]				150 — 200	71	4to				
1911	5			100 — 150	377	12mo		Aeg		
1896				100 — 150	400	8vo		Aeg		Blue/Gilt
1898				150 — 175	424	12mo		Aeg		Blue/Gilt
1890				50 — 100	390	8vo		Aeg		
1903				50 — 100	390	8vo		Aeg		
				150 — 200		8vo		Aeg		
1891				150 — 200	243	12mo		Aeg		Blue/Gilt
1908	8			175 — 225	361	8vo		Aeg		
1908	8			125 — 150	361	8vo				
1902	8			175 — 225	384	8vo		Aeg		
1912	12			150 — 175	351	8vo	Teg			Blue/Gilt
1904	8		22	200 — 250	350	8vo		Aeg		
1908	8			150 — 200	350	8vo		Aeg		Brown/Gilt
1903	8			200 — 250	371	8vo		Aeg		
1914	8			50 — 75		8vo				
				75 — 100						
1902			7	100 — 150	418	8vo		Aeg		
1899				100 — 125	144	4to				
1892				175 — 225	366	8vo		Aeg		
1898				75 — 100	366	8vo				
1916			366	50 — 75		8vo				
1924				25 — 50	366	8vo				
1900			32	175 — 225	387	8vo		Aeg		
1924				25 — 50		8vo				
(1920)	12			100 — 125	551	4to	Teg			
				50 — 75		4to				
1910	6			200 — 250	369	8vo		Aeg		
1914	6			50 — 75	369	8vo				
1919	6			50 — 75	369	8vo				
1907	8			175 — 225	336	8vo		Aeg		
1925	8			50 — 75		8vo				
1906	8			175 — 225	358	8vo		Aeg		
				50 — 75						
1916	8			125 — 175	227	8vo				
1897				175 — 225	360	8vo		Aeg		
1906				50 — 75	360	8vo				
1899				75 — 125	379	8vo		Aeg		
1895			19	150 — 200	419	12mo		Aeg		
1890				175 — 225	367	8vo		Aeg		
1917				30 — 60		8vo				
1905	8			200 — 250	366	8vo		Aeg		

Henry Justice (H.J.) Ford

Title	Author	Publisher	City
Red True Story Book (The)	Lang/Andrew	Longmans	Lon
Strange Story Book (The)	Lang/Andrew	Longmans	Lon
Tales Of Troy & Greece	Lang/Andrew	Longmans	Lon
Trusty John & Other Stories	Lang/Andrew	Longmans	Lon
Violet Fairy Book (The)	Lang/Andrew	Longmans	Lon
Violet Fairy Book (The)	Lang/Andrew	Longmans	Lon
Yellow Fairy Book (The)	Lang/Andrew	Longmans	Lon
Yellow Fairy Book (The)	Lang/Andrew	Longmans	Lon
Yellow Fairy Book (The)	Lang/Andrew	Longmans	Lon

(1860-1941) London, England

Year	Color	Tipped	B&W	Price Range	Pages	Size	TEG	AEG	DJ	Comments
1895				75 — 125	419	8vo				
1913	12			200 — 250	312	8vo	Teg			
1907			16	150 — 175	302	8vo	Teg			
1906	1		14	75 — 100	258	8vo				Maroon Cloth
1901	8			200 — 275	388	8vo		Aeg		
1933	8		25	25 — 50	388	8vo				
1894			22	175 — 225	321	8vo		Aeg		
1895			22	100 — 150	321	8vo		Aeg		
1897			22	100 — 150	321	8vo		Aeg		

Charles Dana Gibson

Title	Author	Publisher	City
80 Drawings Of The Weaker Sex	Gibson/Charles D.	Scribner	NY
About Paris	Davis/Richard Harding	Harper	NY
Americans	Gibson/Charles D.	Russell	
Booming Of Acre Hill	Bangs/John K.	Harper	NY
College Girls	Goodloe/A.C.	Scribner	NY
Corner In Women (A)	Masson/T.	Moffat	NY
Drawings	Gibson/Charles D.	Russell	
Education Of Mr. Pipp	Gibson/Charles D.	Russell	
Everyday People	Gibson/Charles D.	Scribner	NY
Gibson Book (The)	Gibson/Charles D.	Scribner	NY
Her First Appearance	Davis/Richard Harding	Harper	NY
Japonette	Chambers/R.	Appleton	NY
King Albert's Book		Daily Telegraph	Lon
London	Gibson/Charles D.	Scribner	NY
Mrs. John Vernon	Addison/J.	Badger	Bos
Our Neighbors	Gibson/Charles D.	Scribner	NY
Pictures Of People	Gibson/Charles D.	Russell	
Portrait Of An Era	Downey/Fairfax	Scribner	NY
Prisoner Of Zenda (The)	Hope/Anthony	Grosset&Dunlap	NY
Prisoner Of Zenda (The)	Hope/Anthony	Holt	NY
Sketches In Egypt	Gibson/Charles D.	Doubleday	NY
Social Ladder	Gibson/Charles D.	Russell	
Streets Of Ascalon	Chambers/R.	Appleton	NY
Thirty Favorite Paintings		Collier	NY
Van Bibber & Others	Davis/Richard Harding	Harper	NY
Widow & Her Friends (A)	Gibson/Charles D.	Harper	NY

(1867-1944) Roxbury, MA

Year	Color	Tipped	B&W	Price Range	Pages	Size	TEG	AEG	DJ	Comments
1903				100 — 150		Folio				Ibds
1895			30	20 — 30	219	12mo				
1903				75 — 100		4to	Teg			
1900				20 — 30	265	12mo	Teg			
1895			11	20 — 30	288	8vo				
1905				20 — 40	332	8vo	Teg			
1897				120 — 150		Folio	Teg			Ibds
1899				120 — 150		Folio	Teg			Ibds
1904				120 — 150		Folio				
1906				150 — 200		Folio	Teg			2 Volumes Red Cloth
1901				15 — 25	53	8vo	Teg			Blue/Gilt
1912			21	20 — 30	384	8vo				
[1914]			1	50 — 100	187	4to				
1897				125 — 175		Folio				
1909				15 — 20	205	12mo				
1905				120 — 150	68	Folio				
1896			86	100 — 165		Folio				
(1936)				20 — 50	391	4to			DJ	
(1898)			4	10 — 15	307	8vo				
1898			4	15 — 25		8vo				
1899				80 — 100	115	8vo				
1902				120 — 150		Folio	Teg			
1912			14	25 — 35	440	8vo				
1909				300 — 500	62	Folio				
1892			4	20 — 30	249	12mo				
1901				120 — 150	78	Folio				

Kate Greenaway

Title	Author	Publisher	City
A Apple Pie	Greenaway/Kate	Routledge	Lon
A Apple Pie	Greenaway/Kate	Warne	Lon
A Apple Pie	Greenaway/Kate	Saalfield	Akr
Almanack And Diary For 1929		Warne	Lon
Almanack For 1883		Routledge	Lon
Almanack For 1884	Greenaway/Kate	Routledge	Lon
Almanack For 1885	Greenaway/Kate	Routledge	Lon
Almanack For 1886	Greenaway/Kate	Routledge	Lon
Almanack For 1887	Greenaway/Kate	Routledge	Lon
Almanack For 1888	Greenaway/Kate	Routledge	Lon
Almanack For 1889	Greenaway/Kate	Routledge	Lon
Almanack For 1890	Greenaway/Kate	Routledge	Lon
Almanack For 1891	Greenaway/Kate	Routledge	Lon
Almanack For 1892	Greenaway/Kate	Routledge	Lon
Almanack For 1893	Greenaway/Kate	Routledge	Lon
Almanack For 1894	Greenaway/Kate	Routledge	Lon
Almanack For 1895	Greenaway/Kate	Routledge	Lon
Almanack For 1897	Greenaway/Kate	Dent	Lon
Almanack For 1924		Warne	Lon
Almanack For 1925		Warne	Lon
Almanack For 1926		Warne	Lon
Almanack For 1927		Warne	Lon
Amateur Theatricals	Pollock/Walter H.	Macmillan	Lon
Ann & Other Poems	Taylor/Jane	Routledge	Lon
April Baby's Book Of Tunes (The)	Russell/Mary	Macmillan	Lon
April Baby's Book Of Tunes (The)		Macmillan	Lon
Around The House		Worthington	
Aunt Louisa's		Warne	Lon
Baby's Birthday Book		Marcus Ward	Lon
Birthday Book For Children	Barker/Mrs. S.	Routledge	Lon
Birthday Book For Children	Barker/Mrs. S.	Warne	Lon
Calendar For 1884		Routledge	Lon
Calendar Of The Seasons		Ward	Lon
Century Of Kate Greenaway (A)	Moore/Anne C.	Warne	NY
Cruise In The Acorn	Jerrold/A.	Marcus Ward	Lon
Dame Wiggins Of Lee	Ruskin/John (Ed)	George Allen	Kent
Dame Wiggins Of Lee	Ruskin/John (Ed)	George Allen	Kent
Dame Wiggins Of Lee	Ruskin/John (Ed)	Dutton	NY
Day In A Child's Life (A)	Foster/Myles B.	Routledge	Lon
Diamonds & Toads		Warne	Lon
Diamonds & Toads		McLoughlin	NY
English Spelling Book (The)	Greenaway/Kate	Routledge	Lon

(1846-1901) Hoxton, England

Year	Color	Tipped	B&W	Price Range	Pages	Size	TEG	AEG	DJ	Comments
[1886]				200 — 250	44	4to				Green Ibds
[1890]				75 — 100					DJ	
1907	11			75 — 100						Muslin
1929				100 — 150		32mo				
1883				100 — 150	12	32mo				
1884				100 — 150	20	16mo				
1885				100 — 150	12	32mo				
1886				100 — 150	12	32mo				
1887				100 — 150		32mo				
1888				100 — 150	22	32mo				
1889				100 — 150		32mo				
1890				100 — 150	24	32mo				
1891				100 — 150		32mo				
1892				100 — 150		32mo				
1893				100 — 150		32mo				
1894				100 — 150	12	32mo				
1895				100 — 150		32mo				
1897				100 — 150		32mo				
1924				100 — 150		32mo			DJ	
1925				100 — 150		32mo			DJ	
1926				100 — 150		32mo				
1927				100 — 150		32mo			DJ	
1879				100 — 150		12mo				
[1882]				200 — 225	64	8vo				
1900	16			175 — 225	75	12mo				Tan Cloth
1900				150 — 200		8vo				
1888				100 — 125	96	4to				Ibds
[1871]				150 — 250		4to		Aeg		
				125 — 150		16mo				
[1880]	12			200 — 275	128	16mo				Green/Gilt
[1900]	12			100 — 125	128	16mo				
1884				50 — 75						
1882				75 — 100						
1946	2			15 — 30	16					
1875	6	Ticp		300 — 350	140	8vo				
1885			4	150 — 200	8	12mo				
1897			4	100 — 125	8	12mo				
			4	75 — 100	8	12mo				
[1881]				175 — 225	29	4to				Ibds
[1869]				200 — 250						Aunt Louisa's Toy Books
[1875]	6			175 — 200		4to				Linen Wraps
[1885]				200 — 250	108	12mo				

Kate Greenaway

Title	Author	Publisher	City
Esther...	Butt/G.	Marcus Ward	Lon
Fairy Gifts	Knox/Kathleen	Dutton	NY
Fairy Gifts	Knox/Kathleen	Griffith & Farran	Lon
Fancy Dresses Described	Holt/A.		Lon
Flowers & Fancies	Ranking/B.M.	Marcus Ward	Lon
Fors Clavigera	Ruskin/John	George Allen	Lon
Fors Clavigera	Ruskin/John	George Allen	Lon
Greenaway's Babies	Greenaway/Kate	Saalfield	Akr
Guernsey Lily	Coolidge/Samuel	Roberts	Bos
Heartsease Or The Brothers Wife	Yonge/Charlotte	Macmillan	NY
Heartsease Or The Brothers Wife	Yonge/Charlotte	Macmillan	Lon
Heartsease Or The Brothers Wife	Yonge/Charlotte	Macmillan	Lon
Heir Of Redclyffe (The)	Yonge/Charlotte	Macmillan	Lon
Heir Of Redclyffe (The)	Yonge/Charlotte	Macmillan	Lon
Heir Of Redclyffe (The)	Yonge/Charlotte	Macmillan	Lon
Illustrated Children's Birthday Book	Weatherby/F.E.	Mack	Lon
Kate Greenaway	Spielmann/M.H.	A&C Black	Lon
Kate Greenaway Pictures		Warne	Lon
Kate Greenaway's Alphabet	Greenaway/Kate	Routledge	Lon
Kate Greenaway's Birthday Book	Greenaway/Kate	Routledge	Lon
Kate Greenaway's Book Of Games	Greenaway/Kate	Routledge	Lon
Kate Greenaway's Book Of Games	Greenaway/Kate	Warne	Lon
Kate Greenaway's Carols		Routledge	Lon
Kate Greenaway's Painting Book		Warne	Lon
Kate Greenaway: 16 Examples In Colour	Spielmann/M.H.	A&C Black	Lon
Kate Greenaway: 16 Examples In Colour	Spielmann/M.H.	A&C Black	Lon
Language Of Flowers	Greenaway/Kate	Routledge	Lon
Language Of Flowers	Greenaway/Kate	Warne	Lon
Library (The)	Lang/Andrew	Macmillan	Lon
Little Ann & Other Poems	Taylor/Jane & Ann	Routledge	Lon
Little Ann & Other Poems	Taylor/Jane & Ann	Warne	Lon
Little Folks		Cassell	Lon
Little Folks Painting Book (The)	Weatherly/George	Cassell	Lon
Madame D'Aulnoy's Fairy Tales	Greenaway/Kate	Gall & Inglis	Edi
Marigold Garden	Greenaway/Kate	Routledge	Lon
Marigold Garden	Greenaway/Kate	Warne	Lon
Miniature Under The Window		McLoughlin	NY
Mother Goose	Greenaway/Kate	Routledge	Lon
Mother Goose		McLoughlin	NY
Mother Goose	Greenaway/Kate	Warne	Lon
Orient Line Guide	Loftie/W.J.	Sampson Low	Lon
Painting Book (A)	Greenaway/Kate	Routledge	Lon

(1846-1901) Hoxton, England

Year	Color	Tipped	B&W	Price Range	Pages	Size	TEG	AEG	DJ	Comments
1878	4	Ticp		200 — 250		4to				
(1874)				125 — 175		16mo				
1874				125 — 175		16mo				
[1882]				125 — 175	105	12mo				
1882	4			200 — 250	186	24mo				
[1895]				125 — 150						Reprint
1883				200 — 300						
1907				100 — 150	12	12mo				
1881				125 — 175	238	8vo				Brown/Gilt
(1902)				100 — 125						
1879			3	125 — 175	478	8vo				
1897			3	50 — 75	478					
1881				75 — 100	524	12mo				Blue/Gilt
1881				100 — 150	524	12mo				
1902				50 — 75	524	12mo				
1882				75 — 100		16mo				With Other Illustrators
1905	53		90	75 — 150		8vo				
1921				150 — 200						
[1885]				150 — 200	32	42mo				Ibds
[1880]				175 — 250		24mo				
[1889]	24			200 — 250	64	4to				
[1890]	24			100 — 150	64	4to				
[1883]				100 — 150						
				75 — 125	62					
1910	16	Ticp		100 — 150		4to				
1911	16	Ticp		75 — 125		4to				
[1884]				125 — 175	80	16mo				
[1900]				75 — 125						
1881				200 — 300						
[1883]				150 — 200	64	8vo				Ibds
[1900]				100 — 150	64	8vo				
(1877)				75 — 100						
1879				125 — 175		8vo				
1871				150 — 175		8vo				
[1885]				225 — 275	60	4to				Green Ibds
[1900]				100 — 150	60	4to				
[1883]				125 — 175						
[1881]	48			175 — 225	48	12mo			DJ	
[1882]				150 — 175	48	4to				Ibds
[1900]				75 — 100	52	12mo				
1888				100 — 150		8vo				
[1884]				200 — 275	80	8vo				

Kate Greenaway

Title	Author	Publisher	City
Pied Piper Of Hamlin(The)	Browning/Robert	Routledge	Lon
Pied Piper Of Hamlin(The)	Browning/Robert	Warne	Lon
Poor Nelly	Hunt/Mrs. Bonavia	Cassell	Lon
Puck & Blossom	Mulholland/Rosa	Ward	Lon
Queen Of Pirate Isle	Harte/Bret	Chatto/Windus	Lon
Queen Of Pirate Isle	Harte/Bret	Houghton,Mifflin	Bos
Queen Victoria's Jubilee Garland	Greenaway/Kate	Routledge	Lon
Quiver Of Love (The)	Loftie/W.J.	Marcus Ward	Lon
Rhymes For The Young Folks	Allingham/William	Cassell	Lon
Royal Progress Of King Pepito (The)	Cresswell/Beatrice	Spck	Lon
Topo	Brunefille/G.	Marcus Ward	Lon
Trot's Journey	Greenaway/Kate	Worthington	
Under The Window	Greenaway/Kate	Routledge	Lon
Under The Window	Greenaway/Kate	McLoughlin	NY
Under The Window	Greenaway/Kate	Routledge	NY
Under The Window	Greenaway/Kate	Warne	Lon

(1846-1901) Hoxton, England

Year	Color	Tipped	B&W	Price Range	Pages	Size	TEG	AEG	DJ	Comments
[1888]	35			200 — 250	64	4to				Orange Ibds
[1903]	35			100 — 150	64	4to				
1878				150 — 175		16mo				
1875	6	Ticp		200 — 250	128					
[1886]				200 — 250	58	4to		Aeg		Tan Cloth
1887				150 — 200	58	4to		Aeg		
[1887]	4			300 — 350		8vo		Aeg		
1876				200 — 300				Aeg		Also Illus. By Walter Crane
(1887)				150 — 200		8vo				
[1889]	12			175 — 225		4to				Ibds
1878			44	200 — 250	140	12mo		Aeg		Green Cloth
(1882)				100 — 125	79	8vo				
[1878]				200 — 250	64	8vo				Green Ibds
[1879]				175 — 225	63	8vo				Green Ibds
[1879]				150 — 175	64	8vo				
[1900]				100 — 150	63	8vo				

Johnny Gruelle

Title	Author	Publisher	City
All About Cinderella	Gruelle/Johnny	Cupples & Leon	NY
All About Cinderella	Gruelle/Johnny	Cupples & Leon	NY
All About Hansel & Gretel		Cupples & Leon	NY
All About Hansel & Gretel		Cupples & Leon	NY
All About Little Black Sambo	Bannerman/Helen	Cupples & Leon	NY
All About Little Black Sambo	Bannerman/Helen	Cupples & Leon	NY
All About Little Red Hen		Cupples & Leon	NY
All About Little Red Hen		Cupples & Leon	NY
All About Little Red Riding Hood	Gruelle/Johnny	Cupples & Leon	NY
All About Little Red Riding Hood	Gruelle/Johnny	Cupples & Leon	NY
All About Mother Goose		Cupples & Leon	NY
All About Mother Goose		Cupples & Leon	NY
All About Story Book (The)		Cupples & Leon	NY
Bam Bam Clock	McEvoy/J.P.	Volland	Chi
Bam Bam Clock	McEvoy/J.P.	Algonquin	
Beloved Belindy	Gruelle/Johnny	Donohue	Chi
Beloved Belindy	Gruelle/Johnny	Volland	Chi
Beloved Belindy	Gruelle/Johnny	Volland	Chi
Beloved Belindy	Gruelle/Johnny	Johnny Gruelle Co.	NY
Cheery Scarcrow	Gruelle/Johnny	Donohue	Chi
Cheery Scarcrow	Gruelle/Johnny	Volland	Chi
Cheery Scarcrow	Gruelle/Johnny	Volland	Chi
Eddie Elephant	Gruelle/Johnny	Donohue	Chi
Eddie Elephant	Gruelle/Johnny	Volland	Chi
Eddie Elephant	Gruelle/Johnny	Volland	Chi
Friendly Fairies	Gruelle/Johnny	Donohue	Chi
Friendly Fairies	Gruelle/Johnny	Volland	Chi
Friendly Fairies	Gruelle/Johnny	Volland	Chi
Friendly Fairies	Gruelle/Johnny	Johnny Gruelle Co.	NY
Funny Little Book	Gruelle/Johnny	Donohue	Chi
Funny Little Book	Gruelle/Johnny	Volland	Chi
Funny Little Book	Gruelle/Johnny	Volland	Chi
Gingerbread Man (The)	Lawrence/Josephine	Whitman	Rac
Grimm's Fairy Tales	Grimm Brothers	Cupples & Leon	NY
Johnny Gruelle's Golden Book	Gruelle/Johnny	Donohue	Chi
Johnny Mouse/Wishing Stick	Gruelle/Johnny	Bobbs-Merrill	Ind
Little Brown Bear	Gruelle/Johnny	Volland	Chi
Little Brown Bear	Gruelle/Johnny	Volland	Chi
Little Brown Bear	Gruelle/Johnny	Donohue	Chi
Little Sunny Stories	Gruelle/Johnny	Donohue	Chi
Little Sunny Stories	Gruelle/Johnny	Volland	Chi
Little Sunny Stories	Gruelle/Johnny	Volland	Chi

(1880-1938) Arcalo, IL

Year	Color	Tipped	B&W	Price Range	Pages	Size	TEG	AEG	DJ	Comments
(1916)				75 — 125		16mo			DJ	
(1929)				25 — 35		16mo			DJ	
(1917)	8			75 — 125	48	16mo			DJ	
(1929)	8			25 — 35	48	16mo				
(1917)	8			125 — 175	48	16mo			DJ	
(1929)	8			50 — 75	48	16mo			DJ	
(1917)				75 — 125		16mo			DJ	
(1929)				25 — 35		16mo			DJ	
(1916)				75 — 100		16mo			DJ	
(1929)				25 — 35		16mo			DJ	
(1916)	8			75 — 125	48	16mo			DJ	
(1929)	8			25 — 35	48	16mo			DJ	
(1929)				100 — 150	63	4to				
(1920)				75 — 100	38	12mo				
(1936)				35 — 50						
(1926)				50 — 75	95	8vo			DJ	30's Reprint
(1926)				150 — 200	95	8vo			DJ	
(1926)				100 — 150	95	8vo			DJ	Volland Reprint
(1940)				50 — 75	95	8vo			DJ	
(1929)	6			40 — 60		12mo			DJ	30's Reprint
(1929)	6			100 — 125		12mo			DJ	
(1929)	6			75 — 100		12mo			DJ	Volland Reprint
(1921)				40 — 60		8vo				30's Reprint
(1921)				100 — 125		8vo				
(1921)				75 — 100		8vo				Volland Reprint
(1919)				45 — 60	86	8vo				30's Reprint
(1919)				125 — 175	86	8vo				
(1919)				100 — 125	86	8vo				Volland Reprint
(1940)				35 — 50		8vo				
(1918)				35 — 50		12mo				30's Reprint
(1918)				100 — 125		12mo				
(1918)				75 — 100		12mo				Volland Reprint
1930				25 — 35						
(1914)	11			150 — 200	419	4to				
[1940]				75 — 150	79	4to				
(1922)				75 — 100	89	8vo				
(1920)				75 — 100		12mo				
(1920)				50 — 75		12mo				Volland Reprint
(1920)				35 — 50						30's Reprint
(1919)				35 — 50						30's Reprint
(1919)				75 — 100						
(1919)				65 — 85		8vo				Volland Reprint

Johnny Gruelle

Title	Author	Publisher	City
Little Sunny Stories	Gruelle/Johnny	Laidlaw	
Magical Land Of Noom (The)	Gruelle/Johnny	Donohue	Chi
Magical Land Of Noom (The)	Gruelle/Johnny	Volland	Chi
Magical Land Of Noom (The)	Gruelle/Johnny	Volland	Chi
Man In Moon Stories...	Lawrence/Josephine	Cupples & Leon	NY
Man In Moon Stories...	Lawrence/Josephine	Whitman	Rac
Marcella Stories	Gruelle/Johnny	Donohue	Chi
Marcella Stories	Gruelle/Johnny	Volland	Chi
Marcella Stories	Gruelle/Johnny	Volland	Chi
Mr. Twee Deedle	Gruelle/Johnny	Cupples & Leon	NY
Mr. Twee Deedle	Gruelle/Johnny	McKay	Phi
My Own Set Of Sunny Books		Donohue	Chi
My Very Own Fairy Stories	Gruelle/Johnny	Donohue	Chi
My Very Own Fairy Stories	Gruelle/Johnny	Volland	Chi
My Very Own Fairy Stories	Gruelle/Johnny	Volland	Chi
My Very Own Fairy Stories	Gruelle/Johnny	Johnny Gruelle Co.	NY
Nobody's Boy	Malot/Hector	Cupples & Leon	NY
Orphant Annie Story Book	Gruelle/Johnny	Bobbs-Merrill	Ind
Paper Dragon	Gruelle/Johnny	Volland	Chi
Paper Dragon	Gruelle/Johnny	Volland	Chi
Quacky Doodles/Danny Doodles	Hubbell/Rose Strong	Volland	Chi
Raggedy Andy Stories	Gruelle/Johnny	Donohue	Chi
Raggedy Andy Stories	Gruelle/Johnny	Volland	Chi
Raggedy Andy Stories	Gruelle/Johnny	Volland	Chi
Raggedy Andy Stories	Gruelle/Johnny	Johnny Gruelle Co.	NY
Raggedy Andy's Number Book	Gruelle/Johnny	Donohue	Chi
Raggedy Andy's Number Book	Gruelle/Johnny	Volland	Chi
Raggedy Ann & Andy/Camel	Gruelle/Johnny	Donohue	Chi
Raggedy Ann & Andy/Camel	Gruelle/Johnny	Volland	Chi
Raggedy Ann & Andy/Camel	Gruelle/Johnny	Volland	Chi
Raggedy Ann & Andy/Camel	Gruelle/Johnny	Johnny Gruelle Co.	NY
Raggedy Ann Cut Out Paper Doll	Gruelle/Johnny	Whitman	Rac
Raggedy Ann In Cookie Land	Gruelle/Johnny	Donohue	Chi
Raggedy Ann In Cookie Land	Gruelle/Johnny	Volland	Chi
Raggedy Ann In Cookie Land	Gruelle/Johnny	Volland	Chi
Raggedy Ann In Cookie Land	Gruelle/Johnny	Johnny Gruelle Co.	NY
Raggedy Ann In Golden Meadow	Gruelle/Johnny	Whitman	Rac
Raggedy Ann In The Deep Woods	Gruelle/Johnny	Donohue	Chi
Raggedy Ann In The Deep Woods	Gruelle/Johnny	Volland	Chi
Raggedy Ann In The Deep Woods	Gruelle/Johnny	Volland	Chi
Raggedy Ann In The Deep Woods	Gruelle/Johnny	Johnny Gruelle Co.	NY
Raggedy Ann Stories	Gruelle/Johnny	Donohue	Chi

(1880-1938) Arcalo, IL

Year	Color	Tipped	B&W	Price Range	Pages	Size	TEG	AEG	DJ	Comments
(1924)				35 — 50						
(1922)	12			75 — 100	157	4to				30's Reprint
(1922)	12			175 — 250	157	4to				
(1922)	12			100 — 150	157	4to				Volland Reprint
(1922)	8			125 — 175	121	4to				
1930	8			35 — 50						
(1929)				75 — 100	94	8vo			DJ	30's Reprint
(1929)				175 — 225	94	8vo			DJ	
(1929)				125 — 175	94	8vo			DJ	Volland Reprint
(1913)				150 — 175						
				50 — 75						
[1940]				100 — 150						Boxed Set Of 4 Sunny Books
(1917)				50 — 75	95	12mo			DJ	30's Reprint
(1917)				125 — 175	95	12mo			DJ	
(1917)				100 — 125	95	12mo			DJ	Volland Reprint
(1940)				35 — 50						
1916	4			60 — 80	372	8vo				Green Cloth P-O
(1921)				100 — 125	85	8vo			DJ	
(1926)				75 — 100	96	8vo				
(1926)				50 — 75	96	8vo				Early Reprint
(1916)				150 — 200		8vo				
(1920)				50 — 75		8vo			DJ	30's Reprint
(1920)				150 — 200		8vo			DJ	
(1920)				100 — 150		8vo			DJ	Volland Reprint
(1940)				35 — 50		8vo			DJ	
(1924)				20 — 30						30's Reprint
(1924)				50 — 75						
(1924)				50 — 75		8vo			DJ	30's Reprint
(1924)				125 — 150		8vo			DJ	
(1924)				100 — 125		8vo			DJ	Volland Reprint
(1940)				35 — 50		8vo				
1935				35 — 50						
(1931)				50 — 75		8vo			DJ	
(1931)				125 — 150		8vo			DJ	
(1931)				100 — 125		8vo			DJ	Volland Reprint
(1940)				35 — 50		8vo			DJ	
1935				75 — 100	56	Folio				
(1930)				50 — 75	95	8vo			DJ	30's Reprint
(1930)				125 — 150	95	8vo			DJ	
(1930)				100 — 125	95	8vo			DJ	Volland Reprint
(1940)				35 — 50	95	8vo			DJ	
(1918)				50 — 75		8vo			DJ	30's Reprint

Johnny Gruelle

Title	Author	Publisher	City
Raggedy Ann Stories	Gruelle/Johnny	Volland	Chi
Raggedy Ann Stories	Gruelle/Johnny	Volland	Chi
Raggedy Ann Stories	Gruelle/Johnny	Johnny Gruelle Co.	NY
Raggedy Ann's Alphabet Book	Gruelle/Johnny	Donohue	Chi
Raggedy Ann's Alphabet Book	Gruelle/Johnny	Volland	Chi
Raggedy Ann's Lucky Pennies	Gruelle/Johnny	Donohue	Chi
Raggedy Ann's Lucky Pennies	Gruelle/Johnny	Volland	Chi
Raggedy Ann's Lucky Pennies	Gruelle/Johnny	Volland	Chi
Raggedy Ann's Magical Wishes	Gruelle/Johnny	Donohue	Chi
Raggedy Ann's Magical Wishes	Gruelle/Johnny	Volland	Chi
Raggedy Ann's Magical Wishes	Gruelle/Johnny	Volland	Chi
Raggedy Ann's Wishing Pebble	Gruelle/Johnny	Donohue	Chi
Raggedy Ann's Wishing Pebble	Gruelle/Johnny	Volland	Chi
Raggedy Ann's Wishing Pebble	Gruelle/Johnny	Volland	Chi
Raggedy Ann's Wishing Pebble	Gruelle/Johnny	Johnny Gruelle Co.	NY
Raggedy Ann/Left Handed Pin	Gruelle/Johnny	Whitman	Rac
Rhymes For Kindly Children	Snyder/Fairmont	Volland	Chi
Rhymes For Kindly Children	Fairmont/Ethel	Volland	Chi
Rhymes For Kindly Children	Fairmont/Ethel	Wise-Parslow	NY
Stories That Never Grow Old		Cupples & Leon	NY
Sunny Bunny	Putnam/Nina Wilcox	Volland	Chi
Sunny Bunny	Putnam/Nina Wilcox	Volland	Chi
Sunny Bunny	Putnam/Nina Wilcox	Algonquin	NY
Sunny-Book Readers		Laidlaw	
Wooden Willie	Gruelle/Johnny	Donohue	Chi
Wooden Willie	Gruelle/Johnny	Volland	Chi
Wooden Willie	Gruelle/Johnny	Volland	Chi

(1880-1938) Arcalo, IL

Year	Color	Tipped	B&W	Price Range	Pages	Size	TEG	AEG	DJ	Comments
(1918)				125 — 175		8vo			DJ	
(1918)				100 — 125		8vo			DJ	Volland Reprint
(1940)				35 — 50		8vo			DJ	
(1925)				20 — 35						30's Reprint
(1925)				35 — 50						
(1932)				50 — 75		8vo			DJ	
(1932)				125 — 150		8vo			DJ	
(1932)				100 — 125		8vo			DJ	Volland Reprint
(1928)				35 — 50	94	8vo			DJ	30's Reprint
(1928)				100 — 150	94	8vo			DJ	
(1928)				75 — 100	94	8vo			DJ	Volland Reprint
(1925)				35 — 50		8vo			DJ	30's Reprint
(1925)				75 — 100		8vo			DJ	
(1925)				65 — 85		8vo			DJ	Volland Reprint
(1940)				35 — 50						
1935				50 — 75						
(1916)				100 — 150		8vo			DJ	
(1928)				75 — 100		8vo			DJ	
(1937)				50 — 75		8vo				
(1918)				75 — 100						
(1918)				125 — 150	42	8vo				
(1918)				100 — 125	42	8vo				Volland Reprint
(1918)				40 — 60		12mo				Thirties Reprint
1924				25 — 35						
(1927)				35 — 50	95	8vo			DJ	30's Reprint
(1927)				100 — 125	95	8vo			DJ	
(1927)				75 — 100	95	8vo			DJ	Volland Reprint

Bessie Collins Pease Gutmann

Title	Author	Publisher	City
Alice In Wonderland	Carroll/Lewis	Dodge	NY
Alice In Wonderland	Carroll/Lewis	Coker	Lon
Alice In Wonderland	Carroll/Lewis	Lippincott	Phi
Biography Of Our Baby	Cooke/E.V.	Dodge	NY
Child's Garden Of Verses	Stevenson/Robert Louis	Dodge	NY
Child's Garden Of Verses	Stevenson/Robert Louis	Dodge	NY
Chronicles/Little Tot	Cooke/E.V.	Dodge	NY
Diary Of A Mouse	Dunham/E.	Dodge	NY
Through The Looking Glass	Carroll/Lewis	Dodge	NY
Told To The Little Tot	Cooke/E.V.	Dodge	NY

(1876-1960) Philadelphia, PA

Year	Color	Tipped	B&W	Price Range	Pages	Size	TEG	AEG	DJ	Comments
(1907)	10			150 — 200	165	8vo				Blue Cloth
[1915]	8			100 — 150	164	4to				Ibds Bessie C. Pease
1923	10			150 — 200	164	8vo				
(1906)				175 — 225		8vo				White/Gilt Bessie C. Pease
(1905)	14		21	100 — 150	113	8vo				Blue Cloth Bessie C. Pease
(1908)	14		21	75 — 100	110	8vo				
(1905)	3			150 — 175	119	8vo				Bessie C. Pease
(1907)				75 — 125		8vo				
(1909)	10			125 — 175	185	8vo				
(1906)	10			125 — 175	132	8vo	Teg			Bessie C. Pease

Maud Humphrey

Title	Author	Publisher	City
Babes Of The Nations	Thomas/Edith M.	Stokes	NY
Babes Of The Year	Humphrey/Maud	Stokes	NY
Baby Sweethearts	Cone/H.G.	Stokes	NY
Baby's Record		Stokes	NY
Bonnie Little People	Cone/H.G.	Stokes	NY
Book Of Fairy Tales	Humphrey/Maud	Stokes	NY
Book Of Pets	Tucker/E.S.	Gardner	
Bride's Book (The)		Stokes	NY
Children Of Spring		Stokes	NY
Children Of The Revolution	Humphrey/Maud	Stokes	NY
Children Of The Revolution		Stokes	NY
Children Of Winter		Stokes	NY
Cosy Corner Stories		Hays	
Cosy Time Story Book		Hays	
Fun On The Playground		Sully	
Gallant Little Patriots	Humphrey/Maud	Stokes	NY
Golf Girl	Humphrey/Maud	Stokes	NY
Grandma's Rhymes & Chimes		Roberts	Bos
Light Princess		Putnam	
Little Colonial Dame	Sage/A.C.	Stokes	NY
Little Continentals		Stokes	NY
Little Grownups	Tucker/E.S.	Stokes	NY
Little Heroes & Heroines	Humphrey/Maud	Stokes	NY
Little Homespun	Ogden/R.	Stokes	NY
Little Ones	Tucker/E.S.	Stokes	NY
Little Soldiers & Sailors	Humphrey/Maud	Stokes	NY
Little Women	Alcott/Louisa May	Holiday	
Littlest Ones (The)	Tucker/Elizabeth	Stokes	NY
Make-Belive Men & Women	Tucker/Elizabeth	Stokes	NY
Mother Goose	Humphrey/Maud	Stokes	NY
Old Youngsters	Tucker/Elizabeth S.	Stokes	NY
One,Two Three Four		Stokes	NY
Oriana		Estes & Lauriat	Bos
Playtime Story Book		Hayes	
Poems By Dobson, Locker & Praed	Dobson/L.	Stokes	NY
Prince & Fido		De Wolfe Fiske	Bos
Rosebud Stories	Humphrey/Maud	Holiday	
Sleepy-Time Stories	Booth/Maud B.	Putnam	NY
Sleepy-Time Stories	Booth/Maud B.	Putnam	NY
Songs/Jingles/Rhymes	Thomas/E.	Stokes	NY
Sunshine For Little Children		Sunshine	
The Light Princess	MacDonald/George	Putnam	NY

(1868-?) England

Year	Color	Tipped	B&W	Price Range	Pages	Size	TEG	AEG	DJ	Comments
1889	12			400 — 600		8vo				
1888	12			300 — 500	25	8vo				
1890	12			400 — 600		Folio				
1898	12			350 — 500		4to				Green/Silver
1890	6			400 — 550	12	4to				
1892	12			500 — 700	30	4to				
1897	12			400 — 600		4to				
1900				250 — 300						
1888				400 — 500						
1900	12			400 — 500	24	4to				
1900				500 — 700						
1888				400 — 500						
				100 — 150						
				100 — 150						
1891				50 — 75						
1899	12			450 — 650		4to				
(1899)				300 — 400		4to				
1889				50 — 75						
1893				200 — 300						
(1898)			16	50 — 70		4to				
1900				400 — 600						
1897	12			400 — 600		4to				
1899	6			200 — 350		4to				
(1897)			15	100 — 140	127					
1898	12			350 — 500		4to				
(1899)	6			250 — 300	19	4to				
1906				75 — 100						
1898	12			300 — 400		4to				
(1897)	6			380 — 500		4to				
1891	24			500 — 700		4to				
(1897)	6			300 — 400	18	4to				
[1890]	4			200 — 300		4to				
1888				40 — 60						
1891				40 — 60						
1892	6			300 — 450		4to				
(1885)			2	100 — 150		8vo				
1906	6			150 — 200		8vo				
1899			17	100 — 165	182	12mo	Teg			
1911			17	40 — 60						
(1894)				250 — 350	251	4to				
1888				150 — 200						
(1893)			9	140 — 175	305	8vo				Tan Cloth

Maud Humphrey

Title	Author	Publisher	City
Tiny Folk/Wintery Days	Thomas/E.	Stokes	NY
Tiny Todlers	Humphrey/Maud	Dean	Lon
Tiny Todlers	Humphrey/Maud	Stokes	NY
Treasury Of Stones,Jingles & Rhymes		Stokes	NY
Vacation Joys		Donohue	Chi
Wildflowers Of America		Buer	
Young American Speaker		Donohue	Chi

(1868-?) England

Year	Color	Tipped	B&W	Price Range	Pages	Size	TEG	AEG	DJ	Comments
1889	6			500 — 650		4to				
[1890]			6	450 — 500						
1890				650 — 800						
1894				250 — 350						
1889				50 — 75						
				40 — 60						
1890				75 — 100						

John R. Neill

Title	Author	Publisher	City
Adventures Of A Brownie		Reilly & Britton	Chi
Adventures Of A Brownie/			
Swiss Family Robinson		Reilly & Britton	Chi
Adventures Of As Brownie (The)		Reilly & Britton	Chi
Aladdin & The Wonderful Lamp/			
Robin Hood		Reilly & Britton	Chi
Alice In Wonderland/			
Through The Looking Glass		Reilly & Britton	Chi
Alice's Adventures In Wonderland		Reilly & Britton	Chi
Anderson's Fairy Tales		Cupples & Leon	NY
Anderson's Fairy Tales;The Ugly Duckling		Reilly & Britton	Chi
Black Beauty		Reilly & Britton	Chi
Black Beauty	Sewell/Anna	Reilly & Britton	Chi
Black Beauty/Little Lame Prince		Reilly & Britton	Chi
Captain Salt In Oz	Thompson/Ruth P.	Reilly & Lee	Chi
Captain Salt In Oz	Thompson/Ruth P.	Reilly & Lee	Chi
Childrens Stories That Never Grow Old	Benoit/C.F.	Reilly & Britton	Chi
Christmas Carol/Jessica's First Prayer		Reilly & Britton	Chi
Cinderella		Reilly & Lee	Chi
Cinderella Or The Little Glass Slipper		Reilly & Britton	Chi
Cinderella/Three Bears		Reilly & Britton	Chi
Clover's Princess	Douglas/A.M.	Altemus	Phi
Cowardly Lion Of Oz (The)	Thompson/Ruth P.	Reilly & Lee	Chi
Cowardly Lion Of Oz (The)	Thompson/Ruth P.	Reilly & Lee	Chi
Cowardly Lion Of Oz (The)	Thompson/Ruth P.	Reilly & Lee	Chi
Curious Cruise/Captain Santa	Thompson/Ruth P.	Reilly & Lee	Chi
Dick Whittington & His Cat		Reilly & Britton	Chi
Dorothy & The Wizard Of Oz	Baum/L. Frank	Reilly & Britton	Chi
Dorothy & The Wizard Of Oz	Baum/L. Frank	Reilly & Britton	Chi
Dorothy & The Wizard Of Oz	Baum/L. Frank	Reilly & Lee	Chi
Dorothy & The Wizard Of Oz	Baum/L. Frank	Reilly & Lee	Chi
Dorothy & The Wizard Of Oz	Baum/L. Frank	Reilly & Lee	Chi
Emerald City Of Oz (The)	Baum/L. Frank	Reilly & Britton	Chi
Emerald City Of Oz (The)	Baum/L. Frank	Reilly & Britton	Chi
Emerald City Of Oz (The)	Baum/L. Frank	Reilly & Lee	Chi
Emerald City Of Oz (The)	Baum/L. Frank	Reilly & Lee	Chi

(1878-1943) Philadephia, PA

Year	Color	Tipped	B&W	Price Range	Pages	Size	TEG	AEG	DJ	Comments
(1912)				40 — 75	57	16mo				
(1908)				75 — 100		12mo			DJ	Children's Red Book Series
(1908)				75 — 100		12mo			DJ	Children's Stories That Never Grow Old Series
(1908)				75 — 100		12mo			DJ	Children's Red Book Series
(1908)				100 — 125		12mo			DJ	Children's Red Book Series
(1908)				100 — 125		12mo			DJ	Children's Stories That Never Grow Old Series
1923				40 — 60	180	8vo				
(1908)				75 — 100		12mo			DJ	Children's Stories That Never Grow Old Series
(1908)				75 — 100		12mo			DJ	Children's Stories That Never Grow Old Series
1908				50 — 75		8vo				
(1908)				75 — 100		12mo			DJ	Children's Red Book Series
(1936)				200 — 300	306	4to			DJ	
(1936)				40 — 60	306	4to			DJ	Reprint
(1908)				75 — 100	312	12mo				
(1908)				75 — 100		12mo			DJ	Children's Red Book Series
[1920]				100 — 150						
(1908)				75 — 100		12mo			DJ	Children's Stories That Never Grow Old Series
(1908)				75 — 100		12mo			DJ	Children's Red Book Series
(1904)			6	50 — 75	95	16mo				
(1923)	12			300 — 400	291	4to			DJ	
(1923)	12			100 — 150	291	4to			DJ	Reprint With Color Plates
(1923)				40 — 60	291	4to			DJ	Reprint Without Color Plates
(1926)				200 — 300	124	8vo				
(1908)				75 — 100		12mo			DJ	Children's Stories That Never Grow Old Series
(1908)	16			500 — 750	256	4to			DJ	
(1908)	16			125 — 200		4to			DJ	Reprint W/ Color Plates
(1908)	16			75 — 125		4to			DJ	Reprint With Color Plates
(1908)				40 — 60		4to			DJ	Reprint Without Color Plates
(1908)	1			75 — 100		4to			DJ	"Popular Edition"
(1910)	16			500 — 750	296	4to			DJ	
(1910)	16			175 — 250		4to			DJ	Reprint With Color Plates
(1910)	12			100 — 125		4to			DJ	Reprint With Color Plates
(1910)				40 — 60		4to			DJ	Reprint w/o Color Plates

John R. Neill

Title	Author	Publisher	City
Evangeline	Longfellow/Henry W.	Reilly & Britton	Chi
Fairy Tales By..	Anderson/Hans C.	Cupples & Leon	NY
Foolish Fox (The)		Altemus	Phi
From Pillar To Post	Bangs/John K.	Century	NY
Giant Horse Of Oz (The)	Thompson/Ruth P.	Reilly & Lee	Chi
Giant Horse Of Oz (The)	Thompson/Ruth P.	Reilly & Lee	Chi
Giant Horse Of Oz (The)	Thompson/Ruth P.	Reilly & Lee	Chi
Gingerbread Man	Baum/L. Frank	Reilly & Britton	Chi
Glinda Of Oz	Baum/L. Frank	Reilly & Lee	Chi
Glinda Of Oz	Baum/L. Frank	Reilly & Lee	Chi
Glinda Of Oz	Baum/L. Frank	Reilly & Lee	Chi
Gnome King Of Oz (The)	Thompson/Ruth P.	Reilly & Lee	Chi
Gnome King Of Oz (The)	Thompson/Ruth P.	Reilly & Lee	Chi
Grim's Fairy Tales;Hansel & Gretel		Reilly & Britton	Chi
Handy Mandy In Oz	Thompson/Ruth P.	Reilly & Lee	Chi
Handy Mandy In Oz	Thompson/Ruth P.	Reilly & Lee	Chi
Hansel & Gretel/Snow White & Red Rose		Reilly & Britton	Chi
Hiawatha	Longfellow/Henry W.	Reilly & Britton	Chi
Hungry Tiger Of Oz (The)	Thompson/Ruth P.	Reilly & Lee	Chi
Hungry Tiger Of Oz (The)	Thompson/Ruth P.	Reilly & Lee	Chi
Hungry Tiger Of Oz (The)	Thompson/Ruth P.	Reilly & Lee	Chi
J. Cole		Reilly & Britton	Chi
Jack & The Bean-Stalk		Reilly & Britton	Chi
Jack & The Beanstalk/Robinson Crusoe		Reilly & Britton	Chi
Jack Pumpkinhead Of Oz	Thompson/Ruth P.	Reilly & Lee	Chi
Jack Pumpkinhead Of Oz	Thompson/Ruth P.	Reilly & Lee	Chi
John Dough & The Cherub	Baum/L. Frank	Reilly & Britton	Chi
John Dough & The Cherub	Baum/L. Frank	Reilly & Britton	Chi
John Dough & The Cherub	Baum/L. Frank	Reilly & Lee	Chi
Kabumpo In Oz	Thompson/Ruth P.	Reilly & Lee	Chi
Kabumpo In Oz	Thompson/Ruth P.	Reilly & Lee	Chi
Kabumpo In Oz	Thompson/Ruth P.	Reilly & Lee	Chi
King Arthur & His Knights	Allen/Phillip S.	Rand McNally	NY
King Arthur & His Knights	Allen/Phillip S.	Rand McNally	NY
Land Of Oz (The)	Baum/L. Frank	Reilly & Britton	Chi
Land Of Oz (The)	Baum/L. Frank	Reilly & Britton	Chi
Land Of Oz (The)	Baum/L. Frank	Reilly & Britton	Chi
Land Of Oz (The)	Baum/L. Frank	Reilly & Lee	Chi

(1878-1943) Philadephia, PA

Year	Color	Tipped	B&W	Price Range	Pages	Size	TEG	AEG	DJ	Comments
(1909)				75 — 100	172	8vo				
(1923)	2			50 — 75	180	8vo				Blue/Gilt
(1904)	22			50 — 75	92	16mo				
1916				50 — 75	339	8vo				
(1928)	12			200 — 250	281	4to			DJ	
(1928)	12			125 — 175	283	4to			DJ	Reprint W/Color Plates
(1928)				40 — 60	283	4to			DJ	Reprint Without Color Plates
(1917)	1			200 — 300	62	4to				
(1920)	12			250 — 350	279	4to			DJ	
(1920)	12			100 — 150	279	4to			DJ	Reprint W/Color Plates
(1920)				40 — 60	279	4to			DJ	Reprint Without Color Plates
(1927)	12			400 — 600	282	4to			DJ	
(1927)				40 — 60	282	4to			DJ	Reprint Without Color Plates
(1908)				75 — 100		12mo			DJ	Children's Stories That Never Grow Old Series
(1937)				150 — 200	246	4to			DJ	
(1937)				40 — 60	246	4to			DJ	Reprint
(1908)				75 — 100		12mo			DJ	Children's Red Book Series
(1909)				75 — 100		8vo				
(1926)				200 — 300	261	4to			DJ	
(1926)				150 — 200	261	4to			DJ	Reprint W/Color Plates
(1926)				40 — 60	261	4to			DJ	Reprint Without Color Plates
(1908)				75 — 100		12mo			DJ	Children's Stories That Never Grow Old Series
(1908)				75 — 100		12mo			DJ	Children's Stories That Never Grow Old Series
(1908)				150 — 200		12mo			DJ	Children's Red Book Series
(1929)	12			250 — 350	252	4to			DJ	
(1929)				40 — 60	252	4to			DJ	Reprint w/o Color Plates
(1906)				600 — 800	315	4to			DJ	
(1906)				200 — 300	315	4to			DJ	Early Reprint
(1906)				150 — 175	315	4to			DJ	R&L Reprint Ca 1920's
(1922)	12			200 — 300	297	4to			DJ	
(1922)	12			125 — 175	297	4to			DJ	Reprint W/Color Plates
(1922)				40 — 60	297	4to			DJ	Reprint Without Color Plates
(1924)			8	30 — 60	455	8vo				
(1936)			8	20 — 30	455	8vo				
(1904)	16			400 — 600	287	4to			DJ	R&B reprint still has marvelous Land Of Oz on title page
(1904)	16			175 — 250	287	4to			DJ	Has Land Of Oz on title page
(1904)	12			100 — 150	287	4to			DJ	Same as above w/12 Plates
(1904)	12			75 — 125	287	4to			DJ	R&L Reprint W/Color Plates

John R. Neill

Title	Author	Publisher	City
Land Of Oz (The)	Baum/L. Frank	Reilly & Lee	Chi
Land Of Oz (The)	Baum/L. Frank	Reilly & Lee	Chi
Little Black Sambo		Reilly & Britton	Chi
Little Black Sambo/Uncle Tom's Cabin		Reilly & Britton	Chi
Little Lamb Prince (The)		Reilly & Britton	Chi
Little Red Riding Hood		Reilly & Britton	Chi
Little Red Riding Hood/Sleeping Beauty		Reilly & Britton	Chi
Little Wizard Series	Baum/L. Frank	Reilly & Britton	Chi
Little Wizard Series	Baum/L. Frank	Reilly & Lee	Chi
Little Wizard Stories Of Oz	Baum/L. Frank	Reilly & Britton	Chi
Little Wizard Stories Of Oz	Baum/L. Frank	Reilly & Britton	Chi
Lost King Of Oz (The)	Thompson/Ruth P.	Reilly & Lee	Chi
Lost King Of Oz (The)	Thompson/Ruth P.	Reilly & Lee	Chi
Lost King Of Oz (The)	Thompson/Ruth P.	Reilly & Lee	Chi
Lost Princess Of Oz (The)	Baum/L. Frank	Reilly & Britton	Chi
Lost Princess Of Oz (The)	Baum/L. Frank	Reilly & Britton	Chi
Lost Princess Of Oz (The)	Baum/L. Frank	Reilly & Lee	Chi
Lost Princess Of Oz (The)	Baum/L. Frank	Reilly & Lee	Chi
Lost Princess Of Oz (The)	Baum/L. Frank	Reilly & Lee	Chi
Lucky Bucky In Oz	Neill/John R.	Reilly & Lee	Chi
Lucky Bucky In Oz	Neill/John R.	Reilly & Lee	Chi
Magic Bed (The)	Hartwell	Altemus	Phi
Magic Cloak	Baum/L. Frank	Reilly & Lee	Chi
Magic Jaw Bone	James/Hart	Altemus	Phi
Magic Of Oz (The)	Baum/L. Frank	Reilly & Lee	Chi
Magic Of Oz (The)	Baum/L. Frank	Reilly & Lee	Chi
Magic Of Oz (The)	Baum/L. Frank	Reilly & Lee	Chi
Magician/One Day	Jenks/Tudor	Altemus	Phi
Marvelous Land Of Oz (The)	Baum/L. Frank	Reilly & Britton	Chi
Mother Goose Nursery Tales		Altemus	Phi
Mother Goose Rhymes & Jingles		Reilly & Britton	Chi
Night Before Christmas (The)		Reilly & Britton	Chi

(1878-1943) Philadephia, PA

Year	Color	Tipped	B&W	Price Range	Pages	Size	TEG	AEG	DJ	Comments
(1904)				40 — 60	287	4to			DJ	R&L reprint without color plates
(1904)	1			75 — 125	287	4to			DJ	"Popular Edition"
(1908)				150 — 200		12mo			DJ	Children's Stories That Never Grow Old Series
(1908)				150 — 200		12mo			DJ	Children's Red Book Series
(1908)				75 — 100		12mo			DJ	Children's Stories That Never Grow Old Series
(1908)				100 — 125		12mo			DJ	Children's Stories That Never Grow Old Series
(1908)	16			100 — 125	57	12mo			DJ	Children's Red Book Series
(1913)				150 — 200	29	12mo				6 Different Books Priced Seperately
(1913)				100 — 125	29	12mo				6 Different Books Priced Seperately
(1914)				350 — 450	196	12mo			DJ	
(1914)				200 — 300	196	12mo			DJ	Reprint
(1925)	12			200 — 300	280	4to			DJ	
(1925)	12			125 — 175	280	4to			DJ	Reprint W/Color Plates
(1925)				40 — 60	280	4to			DJ	Reprint Without Color Plates
(1917)	12			500 — 600	312	4to			DJ	
(1917)	12			150 — 250	312	4to			DJ	R&B Reprint
(1917)	12			100 — 150	312	4to			DJ	R&L Reprint W/Color Plates
(1917)				40 — 60	312	4to			DJ	R&L reprint without color plates
(1917)	1			75 — 125	312	4to			DJ	
(1942)				250 — 350	289	4to			DJ	
(1942)				40 — 60	289	4to			DJ	Reprint
(1906)				50 — 75	109	12mo				
(1916)				500 — 750	58	4to			DJ	
(1906)				50 — 75	107	12mo				
(1919)	12			400 — 600	266	4to			DJ	
(1919)	12			150 — 200	266	4to			DJ	Reprint W/Color Plates
(1919)				40 — 60	266	4to			DJ	Reprint Without Color Plates
(1905)				75 — 100	107	24mo				
(1904)	16			800 —1000	287	4to			DJ	
(1904)				75 — 100	91	16mo				Green Cloth
(1908)				75 — 100		12mo			DJ	Children's Stories That Never Grow Old Series
(1908)				75 — 100		12mo			DJ	Children's Stories That Never Grow Old Series

John R. Neill

Title	Author	Publisher	City
Night Before Christmas (The)/			
Mother Goose Rhymes		Reilly & Britton	Chi
Nursery Tales		Altemus	Phi
Ojo In Oz	Thompson/Ruth P.	Reilly & Lee	Chi
Ojo In Oz	Thompson/Ruth P.	Reilly & Lee	Chi
Ojo In Oz	Thompson/Ruth P.	Reilly & Lee	Chi
Oz Toy Book (The)		Reilly & Britton	Chi
Ozma Of Oz	Baum/L. Frank	Reilly & Britton	Chi
Ozma Of Oz	Baum/L. Frank	Reilly & Britton	Chi
Ozma Of Oz	Baum/L. Frank	Reilly & Lee	Chi
Ozoplanning With The Wizard Of Oz	Thompson/Ruth P.	Reilly & Lee	Chi
Ozoplanning With The Wizard Of Oz	Thompson/Ruth P.	Reilly & Lee	Chi
Patchwork Girl Of Oz (The)	Baum/L. Frank	Reilly & Britton	Chi
Patchwork Girl Of Oz (The)	Baum/L. Frank	Reilly & Britton	Chi
Patchwork Girl Of Oz (The)	Baum/L. Frank	Reilly & Lee	Chi
Peter & The Princess	Grabo/Carl H.	Reilly & Lee	Chi
Peter Rabbit/Dick Whittington		Reilly & Britton	Chi
Pirates In Oz	Thompson/Ruth P.	Reilly & Lee	Chi
Pirates In Oz	Thompson/Ruth P.	Reilly & Lee	Chi
Purple Prince Of Oz (The)	Thompson/Ruth P.	Reilly & Lee	Chi
Purple Prince Of Oz (The)	Thompson/Ruth P.	Reilly & Lee	Chi
Purple Prince Of Oz (The)	Thompson/Ruth P.	Reilly & Lee	Chi
Rab & His Friends		Reilly & Britton	Chi
Rab & His Friends/J.Cole		Reilly & Britton	Chi
Raven (The)	Poe/Edgar Allen		
Rescue Syndicate	Jenks/Tudor	Altemus	Phi
Rinkitink In Oz	Baum/L. Frank	Reilly & Britton	Chi
Rinkitink In Oz	Baum/L. Frank	Reilly & Britton	Chi
Rinkitink In Oz	Baum/L. Frank	Reilly & Lee	Chi
Rinkitink In Oz	Baum/L. Frank	Reilly & Lee	Chi
Rip Van Winkle		Reilly & Britton	Chi
Road To Oz (The)	Baum/L. Frank	Reilly & Britton	Chi
Road To Oz (The)	Baum/L. Frank	Reilly & Britton	Chi
Road To Oz (The)	Baum/L. Frank	Reilly & Lee	Chi
Robber Kitten		Altemus	Phi
Robinson Crusoe:His Man Friday		Reilly & Britton	Chi
Royal Book Of Oz (The)	Baum - Thompson/Ruth	Reilly & Lee	Chi

(1878-1943) Philadephia, PA

Year	Color	Tipped	B&W	Price Range	Pages	Size	TEG	AEG	DJ	Comments
(1908)				75 — 100		12mo			DJ	Children's Red Book Series
(1904)				50 — 75		12mo				
(1933)	12			200 — 300	304	4to			DJ	
(1933)				40 — 60	304	4to			DJ	Reprint Without Color Plates
(1933)	12			100 — 150	304	4to			DJ	Reprint W/Color Plates
(1915)				600 — 800	16	4to				Cut Out Book Made Without Baums Approval
(1907)				500 — 750	270	4to			DJ	
(1907)				150 — 200	270	4to			DJ	R&B Reprint
(1907)				75 — 100	270	4to			DJ	R&L Reprint
(1939)				175 — 250	272	4to				
(1939)				40 — 60	272	4to				Reprint
(1913)				400 — 600	340	4to			DJ	
(1913)				350 — 400	341	4to				R&B Reprint
(1913)				100 — 150	341	4to				R&L Reprint
(1920)	8			175 — 250	243	4to				
(1908)				75 — 100		12mo			DJ	Children's Red Book Series
(1931)	12			200 — 300	280	4to			DJ	
(1931)				40 — 60	280	4to			DJ	Reprint Without Color Plates
(1932)	12			250 — 350	281	4to			DJ	
(1932)				40 — 60	281	4to			DJ	Reprint Without Color Plates
(1932)	12			125 — 150	281	4to			DJ	Reprint With Color Plates
(1908)				75 — 100		12mo			DJ	Children's Stories That Never Grow Old Series
(1908)				75 — 100		12mo			DJ	Children's Red Book Series
(1910)				50 — 75						
(1905)				50 — 75	110	24mo				
(1916)	12			500 — 700	314	4to			DJ	
(1916)	12			200 — 300	314	4to			DJ	R&B Reprint
(1916)	12			100 — 150	314	4to			DJ	R&L Reprint W/Color Plates
(1916)				40 — 60	314	4to			DJ	R&L Reprint Without Color
(1908)				75 — 100		12mo			DJ	Children's Stories That Never Grow Old Series
(1909)				400 — 600	261	4to			DJ	
(1909)				125 — 175	261	4to			DJ	R&B Reprint
(1909)				40 — 60	261	4to			DJ	R&L Reprint
(1904)				40 — 60	96	16mo				
(1908)				75 — 100		12mo			DJ	Children's Stories That Never Grow Old Series
(1921)	12			250 — 350	312	4to			DJ	Baums Name But Actually Written By Thompson

John R. Neill

Title	Author	Publisher	City
Royal Book Of Oz (The)	Baum - Thompson/Ruth	Reilly & Lee	Chi
Royal Book Of Oz (The)	Baum - Thompson/Ruth	Reilly & Lee	Chi
Scalawagons Of Oz (The)	Neill/John R.	Reilly & Lee	Chi
Scalawagons Of Oz (The)	Neill/John R.	Reilly & Lee	Chi
Scarecrow & The Tin Woodman Of Oz (The)	Baum/L. Frank	Rand McNally	Chi
Scarecrow Of Oz (The)	Baum/L. Frank	Reilly & Britton	Chi
Scarecrow Of Oz (The)	Baum/L. Frank	Reilly & Britton	Chi
Scarecrow Of Oz (The)	Baum/L. Frank	Reilly & Lee	Chi
Scarecrow Of Oz (The)	Baum/L. Frank	Reilly & Lee	Chi
Sea Fairies	Baum/L. Frank	Reilly & Britton	Chi
Sea Fairies	Baum/L. Frank	Reilly & Britton	Chi
Silver Princess In Oz	Thompson/Ruth P.	Reilly & Lee	Chi
Silver Princess In Oz	Thompson/Ruth P.	Reilly & Lee	Chi
Sky Island	Baum/L. Frank	Reilly & Britton	Chi
Sky Island	Baum/L. Frank	Reilly & Britton	Chi
Sky Island	Baum/L. Frank	Reilly & Lee	Chi
Sleeping Beauty		Reilly & Britton	Chi
Snow White & Rose Red		Reilly & Britton	Chi
Snowbound	Whittier/John G.	Reilly & Britton	Chi
Speedy In Oz	Thompson/Ruth P.	Reilly & Lee	Chi
Speedy In Oz	Thompson/Ruth P.	Reilly & Lee	Chi
Story Of Peter Rabbit	Potter/Beatrix	Reilly & Britton	Chi
Story Of Peter Rabbit (The)		Reilly & Britton	Chi
Swiss Family Robinson (The)		Reilly & Britton	Chi
Tale Of Peter Rabbit (The)	Potter/Beatrix	Altemus	Phi
Three Bears (The)		Reilly & Britton	Chi
Through The Looking Glass; Humpty Dumpty		Reilly & Britton	Chi
Tik-Tok Of Oz	Baum/L.Frank	Reilly & Britton	Chi
Tik-Tok Of Oz	Baum/L.Frank	Reilly & Britton	Chi
Tik-Tok Of Oz	Baum/L.Frank	Reilly & Lee	Chi
Tik-Tok Of Oz	Baum/L.Frank	Reilly & Lee	Chi
Tin Woodsman Of Oz (The)	Baum/L.Frank	Reilly & Britton	Chi
Tin Woodsman Of Oz (The)	Baum/L.Frank	Reilly & Lee	Chi
Tin Woodsman Of Oz (The)	Baum/L.Frank	Reilly & Lee	Chi

(1878-1943) Philadephia, PA

Year	Color	Tipped	B&W	Price Range	Pages	Size	TEG	AEG	DJ	Comments
(1921)	12			100 — 150	312	4to			DJ	Reprint W/Color Plates
(1921)				40 — 60	312	4to			DJ	Reprint Without Color Plates
(1941)				250 — 350	309	4to			DJ	
(1941)				40 — 60	309	4to			DJ	Reprint
(1939)	16			25 — 50	64	12mo				With Princess Ozma Of
										Oz Little Wizard Series
(1915)	12			400 — 600	288	4to			DJ	
(1915)	12			125 — 175	288	4to			DJ	R&B Reprint
(1915)	12			100 — 150	288	4to			DJ	R&L Reprint W/Color Plates
(1915)				40 — 60	288	4to			DJ	R&L Reprint Without Color Plates
(1911)			12	400 — 600	240	4to			DJ	
(1911)			12	100 — 150	240	4to			DJ	Reprint
(1938)				200 — 300	255	4to			DJ	
(1938)				40 — 60	255	4to			DJ	Reprint
(1912)	12			500 — 750	288	4to			DJ	Blue Cloth
(1912)	12			150 — 250	288	4to			DJ	R&B Reprint
(1912)				100 — 150	288	4to			DJ	R&L Reprint Ca 1920"S
(1908)				100 — 125		12mo			DJ	Children's Stories That
										Never Grow Old Series
(1908)				75 — 100		12mo			DJ	Children's Stories That
										Never Grow Old Series
(1909)			12	40 — 60	123	8vo				
(1934)	12			200 — 300	298	4to			DJ	
(1934)				40 — 60		4to			DJ	Reprint Without Color Plates
(1911)				100 — 125		16mo			DJ	
(1908)				125 — 150		12mo			DJ	Children's Stories That
										Never Grow Old Series
(1908)				75 — 100		12mo			DJ	Children's Stories That
										Never Grow Old Series
(1904)	31			100 — 150	31	16mo				
(1908)				75 — 100		12mo			DJ	Children's Stories That
										Never Grow Old Series
(1908)				100 — 125		12mo			DJ	Children's Stories That
										Never Grow Old Series
(1914)	12			500 — 700	272	4to			DJ	
(1914)	12			150 — 200	272	4to			DJ	R&B Reprint W/Color Plates
(1914)	12			100 — 150	272	4to			DJ	R&L Reprint W/Color Plates
(1914)				40 — 60	272	4to			DJ	R&L Reprint Witout Color Plates
(1918)	12			400 — 600	288	4to			DJ	
(1918)				50 — 75	288	4to			DJ	"Popular Edition"
(1918)	12			100 — 150	288	4to			DJ	R&L Reprint W/Color Plates

John R. Neill

Title	Author	Publisher	City
Tin Woodsman Of Oz (The)	Baum/L.Frank	Reilly & Lee	Chi
Ugly Duckling/Rip Van Winkle		Reilly & Britton	Chi
Uncle Tom's Cabin; The Story Of Topsy		Reilly & Britton	Chi
Uncrowned King	Wright/H.B.	Book Supply Co.	
Wishing Horse Of Oz (The)	Thompson/Ruth P.	Reilly & Lee	Chi
Wishing Horse Of Oz (The)	Thompson/Ruth P.	Reilly & Lee	Chi
Wonder City Of Oz (The)	Neill/John R.	Reilly & Lee	Chi
Wonder City Of Oz (The)	Neill/John R.	Reilly & Lee	Chi
Yellow Knight Of Oz (The)	Thompson/Ruth P.	Reilly & Lee	Chi
Yellow Knight Of Oz (The)	Thompson/Ruth P.	Reilly & Lee	Chi
Yellow Knight Of Oz (The)	Thompson/Ruth P.	Reilly & Lee	Chi

(1878-1943) Philadephia, PA

Year	Color	Tipped	B&W	Price Range	Pages	Size	TEG	AEG	DJ	Comments
(1918)				40 — 60	288	4to			DJ	No Color Plates
(1908)				75 — 100		12mo			DJ	Children's Red Book Series
(1908)				100 — 125		12mo			DJ	Children's Stories That Never Grow Old Series
1910			5	50 — 75	118	16mo				
(1935)	12			250 — 350		4to			DJ	
(1935)				40 — 60		4to			DJ	Reprint Without Color Plates
(1940)				250 — 350	318	4to			DJ	
(1940)				40 — 60	318	4to			DJ	Reprint
(1930)	12			350 — 500	275	4to			DJ	
(1930)	12			100 — 150	275	4to			DJ	Reprint With Color Plates
(1930)				40 — 60	275	4to			DJ	Reprint Without Color Plates

Peter Newell

Title	Author	Publisher	City
Afield & Afloat	Stockton/F.	Scribner	NY
Alice's Adventures In Wonderland	Carroll/Lewis	Harper	NY
Alice's Adventures In Wonderland	Carroll/Lewis	Harper	NY
Bikey The Skycycle	Bangs/John K.	Riggs	
Book Of Clever Beasts (The)	Reed/M.	Putnam	NY
Cobb's Anatomy	Cobb/Irwin S.	Doran	NY
Cobb's Bill Of Fare	Cobb/Irwin S.	Doran	NY
Creature Songs...	Garnett/L.A.	Ditson	NY
Enchanted Typewriter (The)	Bangs/John K.	Harper	NY
Fables For The Frivolous	Carryl/Guy W.	Harper	NY
Far From The Maddening Girls	Carryl/Guy W.	McClure	NY
Favorite Fairy Tales		Harper	NY
Favorites Of Fairyland	Harris/A.V.	Harper	NY
Great Stone Of Sardis	Stockton/F.	Harper	NY
Hole Book (The)	Newell/Peter	Harper	NY
Hole Book (The)	Newell/Peter	Harper	NY
House Boat On The Styx	Bangs/John K.	Harper	NY
Hunting Of The Snark (The)	Carroll/Lewis	Harper	NY
Kingdom Of Why	Stone/S.B.	Bobbs-Merrill	Ind
Merry-Go-Round	Wells/Carolyn	Russell	
Monster... (The)	Crane/S.	Harper	NY
Mother Goose For Grownups	Carryl/Guy W.	Harper	NY
Mother Goose's Menagerie	Wells/Carolyn	Noyes	
Mr. Munchausen	Bangs/John K.	Noyes,Platt	Bos
Nautical Lays Of A Landsman	Irwin/Wallace	Dodd	NY
Parson's Devil	Johnson/C.		Spr
Peace At Any Price	Browne/P.E.	Appleton	NY
Peter Newell's Mother Goose	Bailey/C.S.	Holt	NY
Peter Newell's Pictures & Rhymes	Newell/Peter	Harper	NY
Pictures & Rhymes	Newell/Peter	Harper	NY
Pursuit Of The Houseboat	Bangs/John K.	Harper	NY
Rise & Fall Of Prohibition (The)		Macmillan	NY
Rocket Book (The)	Newell/Peter	Harper	NY
Rocket Book (The)	Newell/Peter	Harper	NY
Runaway Equator	Bell/L.	Stokes	NY
Scars & Stripes	Browne/P.E.	Doran	NY
Shadow Show (A)	Newell/Peter	Century	NY
Slant Book (The)	Newell/Peter	Harper	NY
Slant Book (The)	Newell/Peter	Harper	NY
Story Teller's Pack	Stockton/F.	Copp	
Their First Formal Call	Cooke/G.M.	Harper	NY
Through The Looking Glass	Carroll/Lewis	Harper	NY

(1862-1924) Bushnell, IL

Year	Color	Tipped	B&W	Price Range	Pages	Size	TEG	AEG	DJ	Comments
1900			12	40 — 60	422	8vo	Teg			
(1901)			40	125 — 150	193	8vo	Teg		DJ	
(1901)	1			30 — 50	193	8vo				1930 Reprint Blue Cloth
1902			8	35 — 50	321	8vo				Blue/Gilt
1904	1		8	50 — 75	231	8vo				
(1912)			17	35 — 45	141	8vo				
(1913)			15	35 — 45	148	8vo				
(1912)			10	125 — 175	30	4to				Green/Gilt
1899			0	25 — 50	171	12mo				
1898			6	75 — 100	120	8vo	Teg			
1904			8	50 — 75	185	8vo				
1907			16	150 — 200	355	8vo	Teg			
1911			4	75 — 100	130	8vo				
1898			52	50 — 75	230	8vo				
(1908)	24			175 — 225		4to			DJ	
				75 — 100		4to			DJ	Early Reprint
1896			23	25 — 50	171	16mo				
1903	1		39	125 — 150	248	8vo	Teg			Ibds
(1913)			9	100 — 150		8vo				
1901			11	100 — 150	152	12mo				
1899			25	150 — 200	188	8vo				Orange Gilt
1900			3	100 — 125	125	8vo	Teg			
1901	12			175 — 225	111	8vo				
1901	15			60 — 80	180	8vo				
1904				45 — 60	135	8vo				
(1927)			4	50 — 100	296	8vo				Green Cloth
1916			6	75 — 100		8vo				
1905			20	75 — 100	265	8vo				
1899			50	150 — 200		8vo				
(1899)				100 — 150		8vo				
1897			24	25 — 40	204	16mo				
1923			4	50 — 75						
(1912)	23			175 — 225	48	8vo			DJ	
				75 — 100		8vo			DJ	Early Reprint
(1911)			16	100 — 125	118	8vo				
(1917)			1	25 — 35	208	8vo				
1896	36			250 — 300	72	8vo				
(1910)				150 — 200	47	8vo			DJ	
				75 — 100		8vo				Early Reprint
1897				50 — 75		8vo				
1906			14	50 — 100	55	8vo				
1902			40	150 — 200	211	8vo	Teg			

Peter Newell

Title	Author	Publisher	City
Tommy Toodles	Lee/Al	Harper	NY
Topsys & Turveys	Newell/Peter	Century	NY
Topsys & Turveys #2	Newell/Peter	Century	NY
Whilomville Stories	Crane/S.	Harper	NY
Wind In The Rose Bush	Wilkins/M.E.	Doubleday	NY

(1862-1924) Bushnell, IL

Year	Color	Tipped	B&W	Price Range	Pages	Size	TEG	AEG	DJ	Comments
1896			26	150 — 200	192	8vo				Blue Cloth
1893	31			225 — 300		4to				
1894				200 — 225		8vo				
1900			34	175 — 225	198	8vo				Green/Gilt
1903			8	50 — 75	237	8vo				Green/Gilt

Kay Nielsen

Title	Author	Publisher	City
East Of The Sun West Of Moon	Asbjornsen	Hodder & Stoughton	Lon
East Of The Sun West Of Moon	Asbjornsen	Doran	NY
East Of The Sun West Of Moon	Asbjornsen	Garden City	Gar
East Of The Sun West Of Moon	Asbjornsen	Doran	NY
East Of The Sun West Of Moon	Asbjornsen	Doubleday	NY
Fairy Tales	Anderson/Hans Christian	Doran	NY
Fairy Tales	Anderson/Hans Christian	Hodder & Stoughton	Lon
Fairy Tales	Anderson/Hans Christian	Hodder & Stoughton	Lon
Fairy Tales	Anderson/Hans Christian	Garden City	Gar
Fairy Tales	Anderson/Hans Christian	Doubleday	NY
Hansel & Gretel	Grimm Brothers	Doran	NY
Hansel & Gretel	Grimm Brothers	Doran	NY
Hansel & Gretel	Grimm Brothers	Hodder & Stoughton	Lon
Hansel & Gretel	Grimm Brothers	Doubleday	NY
In Powder & Crinoline	Quiller-Couch/Arthur	Hodder & Stoughton	Lon
King Albert's Book		Daily Telegraph	Lon
Red Magic	Wilson/R.	J. Cape	Lon
Twelve Dancing Princesses	Quiller-Couch/Arthur	Doran	NY
Twelve Dancing Princesses	Quiller-Couch/Arthur	Doran	NY
Twelve Dancing Princesses	Quiller-Couch/Arthur	Doubleday	NY

(1886-1957) Copenhagen, Denmark

Year	Color	Tipped	B&W	Price Range	Pages	Size	TEG	AEG	DJ	Comments
[1914]	25	Ticp		500 — 700	206	4to				
[1914]	25	Ticp		250 — 350	205	4to				
[1930]	8			50 — 100	204	8vo				
	25	Ticp		100 — 150	204	4to				1920's Reprint
	8			75 — 100	204	8vo				
(1924)	12	Ticp		275 — 450	281	4to				
[1924]	12	Ticp		600 — 800	197	4to		Aeg		
[1924]	12	Ticp		1000 —1250	197	4to				500 Signed By Nielsen
[1932]	8			70 — 100	272	4to				
	8			75 — 125	272	4to				
(1925)	12	Ticp		250 — 350	310	4to				
(1925)	12	Ticp		125 — 175	310	4to				Early Reprint
[1925]	12	Ticp		750 —1000	310	4to				600 Signed By Nielson
				100 — 125		4to				
[1913]	24	Ticp		700 — 900	164	4to				
[1914]	1	Ticp		50 — 100	187	4to				Also Plates By Dulac,Rackham,Parrish
(1930)	8			400 — 600	368	8vo				
[1913]	16	Ticp		300 — 400	244	8vo				
	10	Ticp		150 — 200					DJ	
1930				75 — 125	244	4to				

Rose O'Neill

Title	Author	Publisher	City
Biography Of A Boy	Bacon/J.D.	Harper	NY
Boss Of The Little Arcady	Wilson/H.	L.L. & S.	
Clever Betsy	Burnham/C.L.	Houghton,Mifflin	Bos
For Love Of Mary Ellen	Brainerd/E.H.	Harper	NY
Garda	O'Neill/Rose	Doubleday	NY
Goblin Woman	O'Neill/Rose	Doubleday	NY
Hickory Limb(The)	Fillmore/Parker H.	J. Lane	Lon
Jell-O Girl Entertains (The)	O'Neill/Rose	Jell-O Co.	
Kewpie Kutouts (The)	O'Neill/Rose	Stokes	NY
Kewpie Primer	O'Neill/Rose	Stokes	NY
Kewpies & Dotty Darling (The)	O'Neill/Rose	Stokes	NY
Kewpies & Dotty Darling (The)	O'Neill/Rose	Dent	Lon
Kewpies & Runaway Baby	O'Neill/Rose	Doubleday	NY
Kewpies: Their Book (The)	O'Neill/Rose	Stokes	NY
Lady In The White Vail	O'Neill/Rose	Harper	NY
Lions Of The Lord	Wilson/H.L.	Lothrop	
Little Question Of Ladies' Rights	Fillmore/P.H.	J. Lane	Lon
Loves Of Edwy	O'Neill/Rose	Lothrop	Bos
Master-Mistress	O'Neill/Rose	Knopf	NY
Round Rabbit (The)	Lee/A.	Copeland/Day	Bos
Seeker (The)	Wilson/H.L.	Doubleday	NY
Sing A Song Of Safety	Marks/Gerald		
Tomorrow's House	O'Neill/G.	Dutton	NY
Very Little Person	Vorse/M.H.	Houghton,Mifflin	Bos

(1874-1944) Wilkes-Barre, PA

Year	Color	Tipped	B&W	Price Range	Pages	Size	TEG	AEG	DJ	Comments
1910			14	50 — 75	322	8vo				Blue Cloth
1905			4	30 — 50	371	8vo				Green Cloth
1910			3	30 — 50	402	8vo				Red/Gilt
1912			4	30 — 50	43	12mo				Tan Cloth
1929				40 — 60	305	8vo			DJ	Blue Cloth
1930				40 — 60	345	8vo				
1910			4	40 — 60	70	8vo				Green Cloth
[1920]				100 — 125	15	12mo				
(1914)				700 — 900		4to				
(1916)				150 — 200	118	8vo				
(1912)				200 — 300	88	4to				
1916				175 — 225	88	4to				
1928				175 — 225	111	8vo				
(1913)				225 — 325	80	4to				
1909			5	75 — 100	350	8vo				Blue Cloth
(1903)			6	40 — 60	520	8vo				
1916				50 — 75		12mo				
(1904)				50 — 75	432	8vo				Tan Cloth
1922			9	50 — 75	227	8vo				
1898			6	150 — 250	52	12mo				Brown Cloth
1904				25 — 40	341	8vo				Green Cloth
1937				30 — 50	71					
1930				40 — 60	159	8vo				Purple Cloth
1911				40 — 60	163	8vo				Green/Gilt

Maxfield Parrish

Title	Author	Publisher	City
American Pictures & Painters	Bryant/Lorinda M.	J. Lane	Lon
Annual Of Advertising Art		Publishers Printing Co.	
Annual Of Advertising Art		Publishers Printing Co.	
Annual Of Advertising Art		Publishers Printing Co.	
Annual Of Advertising Art		Publishers Printing Co.	
Arabian Nights (The)	Wiggin/Kate Douglas (Ed)	Scribner	NY
Arabian Nights (The)	Wiggin/Kate Douglas (Ed)	Scribner	NY
Arabian Nights (The)	Wiggin/Kate Douglas (Ed)	Scribner	NY
Arabian Nights (The)	Wiggin/Kate Douglas (Ed)	Scribner	NY
Bolanyo	Read/Opie	Way/Williams	Chi
Children's Book (The)	Scudder/Horace E.	Houghton,Mifflin	Bos
Dream Days	Grahame/Kenneth	J. Lane	Lon
Emerald Story Book (The)	Skinner/Ada & Eleanor	Duffield	NY
Free To Serve	Raynor/Emma	Copeland/Day	Bos
Garden Of Years	Carryl/Guy W.	Putnam	NY
Golden Age (The)	Grahame/Kenneth	J. Lane	NY
Golden Age (The)	Grahame/Kenneth	J. Lane	Lon
Golden Treasury Of Songs..	Palgrave/Francis Turner	Duffield	NY
Golden Treasury Of Songs..	Palgrave/Francis Turner	Duffield	NY
Golden Treasury Of Songs..	Palgrave/Francis Turner	Scribner	NY
Graphic Arts & Crafts Yearbook	Meadon/Joseph (Ed)	Republican Publishing	
Hiawatha	Longfellow/Henry W.	Harrap	Lon
History & Ideals Of Amer. Artt	Neuhaus/Eugene	Stanford University Press	
Italian Villas & Their Gardens	Wharton/Edith	Century	NY
King Albert's Book		Daily Telegraph	Lon
Knave Of Hearts (The)	Saunders/Louise	Scribner	NY
Knave Of Hearts (The)	Saunders/Louise	Scribner	NY
Knickerbocker's History Of NY	Irving/Washington	Russell	NY
Knickerbocker's History Of NY	Irving/Washington	Dodd	NY
Lure Of The Garden	Hawthorne/Hildegarde	Century	NY
Mother Goose In Prose	Baum/L. Frank	Way/Williams	Chi
Mother Goose In Prose	Baum/L. Frank	Bobbs-Merrill	Ind
Mother Goose In Prose	Baum/L. Frank	Way/Williams	Chi
Mural Painting In America	Blashfield/Edwin H.	Scribner	NY
Peterkin	Jackson/Gabrielle E.	Duffield	NY
Poems Of Childhood	Field/Eugene	Lane	Lon
Poems Of Childhood	Field/Eugene	Scribner	NY
Poems Of Childhood	Field/Eugene	Scribner	NY
Romantic America	Schauffer/Robert Haven	Century	NY

(1870-1966) Philadelphia, PA.

Year	Color	Tipped	B&W	Price Range	Pages	Size	TEG	AEG	DJ	Comments
1917			3	40 — 80						
1921			5	50 — 75						
1923			2	40 — 60						
1924			3	40 — 60						
1925			3	40 — 60						
(1937)	12			50 — 90	340	4to				
1909	12			125 — 200	339	4to	Teg			
1919	12			100 — 175	339	4to				
1935	12			50 — 90	340	4to				
1897				150 — 200	309	12mo	Teg			2 Color Cover
1907	1			75 — 100						Color Cover
[1902]			9	75 — 150	228	8vo	Teg			
1917	1			75 — 150						
1897				100 — 150	434	8vo				Color Cover
1904	1			45 — 75		8vo	Teg			
(1904)			18	75 — 125	252	8vo	Teg			
1900			18	100 — 200	252	8vo	Teg			
1911	8			150 — 225	373	4to				
1941	4			50 — 80						
				100 — 125						
1907	2			40 — 60						
[1911]				175 — 225		4to				Cover By Parrish, Frontis By Wyeth
1931			2	20 — 35						
1904	15		11	200 — 300	270	4to				
[1914]	1	Ticp		50 — 100	187	4to				Also Plates By Dulac, Rackham,Neilsen
1925	23			750 —1000	46	Folio				Hardbound With Slipcase Ad $200
1925	23			600 — 800		4to				Spiral
1900			8	125 — 200	299	4to	Teg			
1915	8	Ticp		175 — 250		4to				
1911	1			50 — 125	259	4to	Teg			
(1897)			12	4000 —5000	265	4to				
(1905)			13	500 — 750	265	8vo				
1901				500 — 750	265	4to				
1913			2	25 — 50						
1912	1			75 — 125	75	8vo				Cover Illus In Color
1904	8			150 — 225		4to			DJ	
1904	8			150 — 225	199	4to	Teg			
1929	8			100 — 150	199	4to	Teg			
1913	1			75 — 100	339	4to	Teg			

Maxfield Parrish

Title	Author	Publisher	City
Ruby Story Book (The)		Duffield	NY
Saphire Story Book (The)		Duffield	NY
Song Of Hiawatha	Longfellow/Henry W.	Houghton,Mifflin	Bos
Thirty Favorite Paintings		P.F. Collier	NY
Thirty Favorite Paintings		Collier	NY
Topaz Story Book (The)	Skinner/Ada & Eleanor	Duffield	NY
Troubadour Tales	Stein/Evaleen	Bobbs-Merrill	Ind
Troubadour Tales	Stein/Evaleen	Bobbs-Merrill	Ind
Turquoise Cup	Smith/Arthur Coslett	Scribner	NY
Turquoise Cup	Smith/Arthur Coslett	Scribner	NY
Turquoise Story Book (The)	Skinner/Ada & Eleanor	Duffield	NY
Water Color Rendering Sugg.		J.H. Jansen	
Whist Reference Book	Butler	John C. Yorston	Phi
Wonder Book & Tangelwood Tales	Palgrave/Francis Turner	Duffield	NY
Wonder Book & Tangelwood Tales	Palgrave/Francis Turner	Duffield	NY

(1870-1966) Philadelphia, PA.

Year	Color	Tipped	B&W	Price Range	Pages	Size	TEG	AEG	DJ	Comments
1921	1			75 — 125						
1919	1			75 — 125						
1911				200 — 400	242	8vo	Teg			Color Cover
1908	1			100 — 150						
1909				300 — 500	62	Folio				
1917	1			75 — 125	381	12mo				
(1903)	1			75 — 100		8vo				
1929	1			25 — 40		8vo				
1903	1			50 — 80	209	8vo				
1910	1			25 — 40		8vo				
1918	1			90 — 140		8vo				
1917			7	150 — 200						
1897	1			175 — 250						
1910	10			125 — 200	358	4to				
1928	10			100 — 150	358	4to				

William Adrew (Willy) Pogany

Title	Author	Publisher	City
44 Turkish Tales	Kunos/I.	Harrap	Lon
Adventures Of A Dodo	Farrow/G.E.	Unwin	Lon
Adventures Of Odysseus	Colum/Pedraic	Macmillan	NY
Adventures Of Odysseus	Colum/Pedraic	Macmillan	NY
Alice/Wonderland	Carroll/Lewis	Dutton	NY
Atta Troll	Heine/H.	Sidgwick	Lon
Atta Troll	Heine/H.	Huebsch	
Bible Stories/Read And Tell	Olcott/F.J.	Houghton,Mifflin	Bos
Blue Lagoon	Stacpoole/H.	Unwin	Lon
Children In Japan	Bartruse/G.	McBride	
Children Of Odin (The)	Colum/Pedraic	Macmillan	NY
Children Of Odin (The)	Colum/Pedraic	Macmillan	NY
Cinderella	Elias/E.	McBride	
Everyday Classics	Baker/Franklin T.	Macmillan	NY
Fairies & Christmas Child	Gask/L.	Crowell	NY
Fairy Flowers	Newman/I.	Holt	NY
Fairy Flowers	Newman/I.	H. Milford	
Fairy Tales From Many Lands	Gask/Lillian		Lon
Faust	Goethe	Hutchinson	Lon
Faust	Goethe	Musson	Tor
Folk Tales Of Many Lands	Gask/Lillian	Crowell	NY
Folk Tales Of Many Lands	Gask/Lillian	Harrap	Lon
Folk Tales Of Many Lands	Gask/Lillian	Harrap	Lon
Frenzied Prince	Colum/Pedraic	McKay	Phi
G.W. Lincoln Goes Around The World	Thomas	Nelson	
Gingerbread Man	Fable/L.	McBride	
Golden Book Of Sonnets	Robertson/W.G.	Harrap	Lon
Golden Cockerel	Pogany/E.	Nelson	
Goldon Fleece (The)	Colum/Pedraic	Macmillan	NY
Goldon Fleece (The)	Colum/Pedraic	Macmillan	NY
Gulliver's Travels	Colum/Pedraic	Macmillan	NY
Gulliver's Travels	Colum/Pedraic	Harrap	Lon
Home Book Of Verse For Young Folks	Stevenson/Burton E.	Holt	NY
Hungarian Fairy Book	Pogany/N.	Unwin	Lon
Hungarian Fairy Book	Pogany/Nandor	Stokes	NY
Kasidah Of Haji Abdu El-Yezdi	Burton/R.	McKay	Phi
King Of Ireland's Son	Colum/Pedraic	Holt	NY
King Of Ireland's Son	Colum/Pedraic	Harrap	Lon
King Of Ireland's Son	Colum/Pedraic	Macmillan	NY
Legend Of The Tulip	Newman/I.	Whitman	Rac
Light Of Asia (The)	Arnold/Sir Edward	McKay	Phi
Little Mother Goose		McBride	

(1882-1955) Szeged, Hungry

Year	Color	Tipped	B&W	Price Range	Pages	Size	TEG	AEG	DJ	Comments
(1913)	16	Ticp		150 — 200	363	8vo	Teg			
(1907)			70	150 — 200	245	8vo				
(1927)	8			25 — 50	254	12mo				
1918	8			50 — 75	254	12mo				
(1929)				100 — 150	192	8vo				
1913				90 — 130	185	12mo				
1914			3	75 — 100		12mo				
1916	8			50 — 75	465	8vo				
1910	13	Ticp		150 — 180	326	8vo				
1915	16			130 — 180		8vo				
(1929)	4			25 — 35	282	8vo				
1920	4			35 — 50	282	8vo				
1915	16			175 — 200		4to				Red Bds
1923				25 — 50						
(1910)	8			140 — 185	261	8vo				
(1926)	15	Ticp		130 — 180	196	8vo				
(1926)	15	Ticp		160 — 200	160	4to				
1933	4		18	25 — 30		8vo			DJ	
(1908)	31			150 — 200	205	4to	Teg			Red Cloth
[1908]				350 — 500	210	4to	Teg			100 Signed By Pogany
(1910)	8			75 — 100		8vo				
1910	8			100 — 125	287	8vo				
1929	4		18	20 — 40	256	8vo				
(1943)			10	75 — 100	196	4to			DJ	
				50 — 75						
1915	8			100 — 130	32	4to				
1903				100 — 125		8vo				
1938	12			80 — 110	46	Folio			DJ	Red Gilt
(1921)			8	50 — 60	290	8vo				Orange Cloth
				15 — 25	290	8vo				Reprint
1917	12			75 — 100	296	8vo				
1919	12			50 — 75	296	8vo				Red Cloth
(1922)				25 — 50						Blue Cloth
(1913)	1			130 — 165	287	8vo				
	1			75 — 100		8vo				
(1931)	12			65 — 100	129	4to				
1916	4			75 — 100	316	8vo				
1920	4			75 — 100	316	8vo				
1921	4			50 — 75		8vo				
(1928)	4			30 — 40		8vo				
(1932)			12	75 — 100	182	4to				Blk Cloth
1915	16			165 — 190	30	4to				

William Adrew (Willy) Pogany

Title	Author	Publisher	City
Little Taylor Of The Winding Way	Crownfield/Gertrude	Macmillan	NY
Lohengrin	Rolleston/T.	Harrap	Lon
Lohengrin	Wagner/Richard	Crowell	NY
Magyar Fairy Tales	Pogany/N.	Dutton	NY
More Tales From Arabian Nights	Olcott/F.J.	Holt	NY
My Poetry Book	Ferris	Winston	NY
My Poetry Book	Ferris	Hufford	Lon
Peterkin	Pogany/Will	McKay	Phi
Pogany's Mother Goose	Pogany/Will	Nelson	Lon
Polly Garden	Banks	Macmillan	NY
Rime/Ancient Mariner	Coleridge/S.T.	Harrap	Lon
Rime/Ancient Mariner	Coleridge/S.T.	Crowell	NY
Rime/Ancient Mariner	Coleridge/S.T.	Doubleday	NY
Romance/Lohengrin	Capes/B.	Dean	Lon
Rubaiyat Of Omar Khayyam	Fitzgerald/E.	Harrap	Lon
Rubaiyat Of Omar Khayyam	Fitzgerald/E.	Crowell	NY
Rubaiyat Of Omar Khayyam	Fitzgerald/E.	Crowell	NY
Rubaiyat Of Omar Khayyam	Fitzgerald/E.	Crowell	NY
Rubaiyat Of Omar Khayyam	Fitzgerald/E.	Crowell	NY
Songs Of Bilitis	Louys/P	Macy	
Sonnets From The Portuguese	Browning/Elizabeth Barrett	Crowell	NY
Sonnets From The Portuguese	Browning/Elizabeth Barrett	Crowell	NY
Stories To Tell The Littlest Ones	Bryant/Sara C.	Houghton,Mifflin	Bos
Stories To Tell The Littlest Ones	Bryant/Sara C.	Harrap	Lon
Stories To Tell The Littlest Ones	Bryant/Sara C.	Harrap	Lon
Story Of Hiawatha (The)	Elias/Edith L.	Harrap	Lon
Stray Birds	Tagore/Rabindranth	Macmillan	Lon
Tales/Persian Genii	Olcott/F.J.	Harrap	Lon
Tanglewood Tales	Hawthorne/Nathaniel	Unwin	Lon
Tannhauser	Wagner/Richard	Harrap	Lon
Tannhauser	Wagner/Richard	Brentano's	NY
Tisza Tales	Schwimmer/R.	Doubleday	NY
Treasury Of Verse	Edgar/Madalen G.	Crowell	NY
Treasury Of Verse For Little Children	Edgar/Madalen G.	Crowell	NY
Treasury Of Verse For Little Children	Edgar/Madalen G.	Macmillan	NY
Uncle Davie's Children	Daulton	Macmillan	NY
Welsh Fairy Book	Jenkyn-Thomas	Unwin	Lon
Witch's Kitchen	Young/G.	Crowell	NY
Witch's Kitchen	Young/G.	Harrap	Lon
Wonder Book	Hawthorne/Nathaniel	Jacobs	

(1882-1955) Szeged, Hungry

Year	Color	Tipped	B&W	Price Range	Pages	Size	TEG	AEG	DJ	Comments
				75 — 100						
(1913)	8			150 — 200		4to				Brown Gilt
(1913)				100 — 150		4to	Teg			
(1930)				100 — 150	268	8vo				Green Gilt
1915	12			75 — 135	274	8vo				
(1934)	6			25 — 35		8vo				Blue Gilt
1934				25 — 35		8vo				Blue Cloth
(1912)	16	Ticp		180 — 220		4to				Grey Gilt
1940	14			80 — 100	75	4to				
(1928)				130 — 170	152	4to	Teg			Blue Gilt
				75 — 100						
(1910)	20	Ticp		200 — 250		Folio	Teg			
(1910)	20	Ticp		150 — 200		4to				
1928				75 — 100						
1905			14	125 — 150	271					Blue Gilt
(1909)	24	Ticp		175 — 225			Teg			
(1909)	24	Ticp		125 — 175	96	4to	Teg			
(1930)	12		45	35 — 60			Teg			
(1930)	24	Ticp		600 — 800		4to				Leather 750 Signed
[1933]	16	Ticp		50 — 75		8vo				
				125 — 150						
(1936)	8	Ticp		50 — 75	96	8vo				
(1945)	8	Ticp		40 — 60	85	4to				
(1916)	6			50 — 75	178					
1918	6			75 — 100	178	12mo				
1919	5		7	25 — 50	178	12mo				
[1914]				75 — 100		12mo				
1917	1			30 — 40	84	8vo				
1919	4			70 —	225	8vo				
[1910]	4		24	100 — 130	320	12mo				Red Cloth
(1911)	16	Ticp		175 — 250		4to				Grey/Gilt
				75 — 100						
1928	8			85 — 100	225	4to			DJ	Blue Gilt
(1908)	8			100 — 135		8vo	Teg			
1923				10 — 20						Reprint
				30 — 50	256	4to				
				75 — 100						
(1907)	1		9	150 — 200	312					Blue Cloth
(1912)	8			120 — 160		8vo				
1910	8			150 — 180		4to				
(1909)	4			100 — 150	320	8vo				

Beatrix Potter

Title	Author	Publisher	City
Appley Dapply's Nursery Rhymes	Potter/Beatrix	Warne	NY
Appley Dapply's Nursery Rhymes	Potter/Beatrix	Warne	Lon
Appley Dapply's Nursery Rhymes	Potter/Beatrix	Warne	Lon
Cecily Parsley's Nursery Rhymes	Potter/Beatrix	Warne	NY
Cecily Parsley's Nursery Rhymes	Potter/Beatrix	Warne	Lon
Fairy Caravan (The)	Potter/Beatrix	McKay	Phi
Ginger & Pickles	Potter/Beatrix	Warne	NY
Ginger & Pickles	Potter/Beatrix	Warne	NY
Ginger & Pickles	Potter/Beatrix	Warne	Lon
Jemima Puddle Duck's Painting Book	Potter/Beatrix	Warne	Lon
Peter Rabbit's Almanac For 1929	Potter/Beatrix	Warne	NY
Peter Rabbit's Almanac For 1929	Potter/Beatrix	Warne	Lon
Peter Rabbit's Painting Book	Potter/Beatrix	Warne	Lon
Peter Rabbit's Painting Book	Potter/Beatrix	Warne	Lon
Pie & The Patty Pan (The)	Potter/Beatrix	Warne	Lon
Pie & The Patty Pan (The)	Potter/Beatrix	Warne	Lon
Pie & The Patty Pan (The)	Potter/Beatrix	Warne	NY
Roly Poly Pudding (The)	Potter/Beatrix	Warne	NY
Roly Poly Pudding (The)	Potter/Beatrix	Warne	NY
Roly Poly Pudding (The)	Potter/Beatrix	Warne	Lon
Story Of A Fierce Bad Rabbit (The)	Potter/Beatrix	Warne	Lon
Story Of A Fierce Bad Rabbit (The)	Potter/Beatrix	Warne	Lon
Story Of A Fierce Bad Rabbit (The)	Potter/Beatrix	Warne	NY
Story Of A Fierce Bad Rabbit (The)	Potter/Beatrix	Warne	Lon
Story Of Miss Moppet (The)	Potter/Beatrix	Warne	Lon
Story Of Miss Moppet (The)	Potter/Beatrix	Warne	Lon
Story Of Miss Moppet (The)	Potter/Beatrix	Warne	Lon
Story Of Miss Moppet (The)	Potter/Beatrix	Warne	Lon
Story Of Miss Moppet (The)	Potter/Beatrix	Warne	NY
Tailor Of Gloucester	Potter/Beatrix	Warne	Lon
Tailor Of Gloucester	Potter/Beatrix	Warne	NY
Tailor Of Gloucester	Potter/Beatrix	Warne	Lon
Tailor Of Gloucester	Potter/Beatrix	Privately Printed	Lon
Tale Of Benjamin Bunny (The)	Potter/Beatrix	Warne	NY
Tale Of Benjamin Bunny (The)	Potter/Beatrix	Warne	NY
Tale Of Benjamin Bunny (The)	Potter/Beatrix	Warne	Lon
Tale Of Flopsy Bunnies (The)	Potter/Beatrix	Warne	Lon
Tale Of Flopsy Bunnies (The)	Potter/Beatrix	Warne	NY
Tale Of Flopsy Bunnies (The)	Potter/Beatrix	Warne	Lon
Tale Of Flopsy Bunnies (The)	Potter/Beatrix	Warne	Lon
Tale Of Jemima Puddle Duck (The)	Potter/Beatrix	Warne	NY
Tale Of Jemima Puddle Duck (The)	Potter/Beatrix	Warne	Lon

(1864-1943) London, England

Year	Color	Tipped	B&W	Price Range	Pages	Size	TEG	AEG	DJ	Comments
(1917)	15			50 — 75	53	16mo			DJ	
[1917]	15			300 — 400	53	16mo			DJ	
[1919]	15			150 — 200	53	16mo				
(1922)	15			150 — 300	54	16mo				
[1922]	15			500 — 750	54	16mo			DJ	
(1929)	6			125 — 175	225	8vo		Aeg		
[1920]	10			100 — 150	52	12mo				
(1909)	10			150 — 200	52	12mo				
1909	10			350 — 450	52	12mo				
[1925]	8			100 — 150	8	8vo				
[1928]	13			150 — 200	44	16mo			DJ	
[1928]	13			150 — 200	44	16mo			DJ	
[1911]	12			100 — 150	12	8vo			DJ	
[1917]	8			50 — 75	8	8vo				
(1933)				25 — 50	76	12mo				
1905	10			225 — 350	52	12mo			DJ	
1905	10			200 — 250	52	16mo				
(1908)	18			200 — 300	70	8vo				
[1920]	18			50 — 75	70	8vo				
1908	18			300 — 400	70	8vo				
[1906]	14			400 — 500		16mo				Wallet Form
[1914]	15			300 — 400	54	16mo			DJ	Tan Boards
[1914]	15			200 — 300	54	16mo			DJ	
[1933]	15			100 — 150	54	16mo			DJ	
[1906]	14			400 — 600		16mo				Wallet Form
[1913]	15			350 — 450	54	16mo			DJ	Book Form
[1925]	15			250 — 350	54	16mo				Grey Boards
[1933]	15			100 — 125	54	16mo			DJ	
[1933]	15			100 — 125	54	16mo			DJ	
(1903)	27			500 — 650	85	16mo				
[1903]	27			350 — 500	96	16mo				Green Boards
[1909]	27			75 — 100	96	16mo				Early Reprint
1902	16			1000 —2000	96	16mo				Pink Boards
(1932)				50 — 75	85	16mo				
[1908]	27			250 — 300	86	16mo				Green Boards
1904	27			400 — 500	86	16mo			DJ	
(1937)	27			25 — 50	59	16mo				
[1909]	27			200 — 300	86	16mo				
[1915]	27			50 — 75	86	16mo				
1909	27			300 — 500	86	16mo			DJ	
(1908)	27			125 — 175	86	16mo				
[1920]	27			50 — 75	86	16mo				

Beatrix Potter

Title	Author	Publisher	City
Tale Of Jemima Puddle Duck (The)	Potter/Beatrix	Warne	Lon
Tale Of Johnny Town Mouse (The)	Potter/Beatrix	Warne	Lon
Tale Of Johnny Town Mouse (The)	Potter/Beatrix	Warne	Lon
Tale Of Johnny Town Mouse (The)	Potter/Beatrix	Warne	NY
Tale Of Little Pig Robinson (The)	Potter/Beatrix	Warne	Lon
Tale Of Little Pig Robinson (The)	Potter/Beatrix	Warne	Lon
Tale Of Little Pig Robinson (The)	Potter/Beatrix	McKay	Phi
Tale Of Mr. Jeremy Fisher (The)	Potter/Beatrix	Warne	NY
Tale Of Mr. Jeremy Fisher (The)	Potter/Beatrix	Warne	NY
Tale Of Mr. Jeremy Fisher (The)	Potter/Beatrix	Warne	Lon
Tale Of Mr. Jeremy Fisher (The)	Potter/Beatrix	Warne	Lon
Tale Of Mr. Tod (The)	Potter/Beatrix	Warne	NY
Tale Of Mr. Tod (The)	Potter/Beatrix	Warne	Lon
Tale Of Mrs. Tiggy Winkle (The)	Potter/Beatrix	Warne	NY
Tale Of Mrs. Tiggy Winkle (The)	Potter/Beatrix	Warne	Lon
Tale Of Mrs. Tittlemouse (The)	Potter/Beatrix	Warne	NY
Tale Of Mrs. Tittlemouse (The)	Potter/Beatrix	Warne	NY
Tale Of Mrs. Tittlemouse (The)	Potter/Beatrix	Warne	Lon
Tale Of Peter Rabbit (The)	Potter/Beatrix	Platt & Munk	NY
Tale Of Peter Rabbit (The)	Potter/Beatrix	Privately Printed	Lon
Tale Of Peter Rabbit (The)	Potter/Beatrix	Warne	Lon
Tale Of Peter Rabbit (The)	Potter/Beatrix	Warne	NY
Tale Of Peter Rabbit (The)	Potter/Beatrix	Warne	NY
Tale Of Peter Rabbit (The)	Potter/Beatrix	Altemus	Phi
Tale Of Pigling Bland (The)	Potter/Beatrix	Warne	NY
Tale Of Pigling Bland (The)	Potter/Beatrix	Warne	NY
Tale Of Pigling Bland (The)	Potter/Beatrix	Warne	Lon
Tale Of Squirrel Nutkin (The)	Potter/Beatrix	Warne	NY
Tale Of Squirrel Nutkin (The)	Potter/Beatrix	Warne	NY
Tale Of Squirrel Nutkin (The)	Potter/Beatrix	Warne	NY
Tale Of Squirrel Nutkin (The)	Potter/Beatrix	Warne	Lon
Tale Of Timmy Tiptoes (The)	Potter/Beatrix	Warne	NY
Tale Of Timmy Tiptoes (The)	Potter/Beatrix	Warne	Lon
Tale Of Timmy Tiptoes (The)	Potter/Beatrix	Warne	Lon
Tale Of Tom Kitten (The)	Potter/Beatrix	Warne	Lon
Tale Of Tom Kitten (The)	Potter/Beatrix	Warne	NY
Tale Of Tom Kitten (The)	Potter/Beatrix	Warne	Lon
Tale Of Two Bad Mice (The)	Potter/Beatrix	Warne	Lon
Tale Of Two Bad Mice (The)	Potter/Beatrix	Warne	NY
Tale Of Two Bad Mice (The)	Potter/Beatrix	Warne	Lon
Tale/Beatrix Potter	Lane/Margaret	Warne	Lon
Tom Kitten's Painting Book		Warne	Lon

(1864-1943) London, England

Year	Color	Tipped	B&W	Price Range	Pages	Size	TEG	AEG	DJ	Comments
1908	27			350 — 450	86	16mo				
(1918)	27			200 — 300	86	16mo				
(1918)	27			100 — 150	86	16mo				Early Reprint
(1946)				25 — 50	59	16mo				
(1930)	6			100 — 150	96	16mo				Blue Cloth
(1930)	6			225 — 275	96	8vo			DJ	
(1930)	6			200 — 250	142	8vo				
(1934)				25 — 50	85	16mo				
[1908]	27			250 — 350	86	16mo				
[1915]	27			75 — 100	86	16mo				
1906	27			450 — 600	86	16mo				
[1912]	15			200 — 250	94	16mo				
1912	15			280 — 350	94	16mo				
[1915]	27			75 — 100	86	16mo				Early Reprint
1905	27			450 — 600	86	16mo			DJ	
(1938)				20 — 30	59	16mo				
[1915]	27			100 — 150	86	16mo				
1910	27			300 — 375	86	16mo		Aeg		
(1938)				25 — 35	26	8vo				Blue Cloth
[1901]	1		41	3000 —5000	86	16mo				Green Boards
[1902]	30			700 —1000	98	16mo				Brown Boards Or Green Cloth
[1902]	30			500 — 800	98	16mo				
[1906]				50 — 100	98	16mo				
1904	30			350 — 500	136	16mo				
(1941)				25 — 50	94	16mo				
[1913]	15			200 — 250	94	16mo				
1913	15			275 — 325	94	16mo				
(1903)	27			250 — 350	86	16mo				
(1905)	27			150 — 200	86	16mo				Brown Boards
(1931)				25 — 50	81	16mo				
1903	27			350 — 500	86	16mo			DJ	
(1911)	27			200 — 300	86	16mo				
[1919]	27			100 — 150	86	16mo				
1911	27			350 — 500	86	16mo				
(1935)				30 — 50		16mo				
[1909]	27			100 — 150	86	16mo				Maroon Boards
1907	27			300 — 500	86	16mo				
(1932)				25 — 50	84	16mo			DJ	
[1908]	27			150 — 300	86	16mo				Greenish-Brown Boards
1904	27			300 — 450	86	16mo				
(1946)			20	50 — 75	162	8vo			DJ	
[1917]	8			500 — 700		8vo			DJ	

Howard Pyle

Title	Author	Publisher	City
Abraham Lincoln	Coffin/Charles C.	Harper	NY
American Art By American Authors		Collier	NY
American Illustrators	Smith/F. Hopkinson	Scribner	NY
Around Old Chester	Deland/Margaret	Harper	NY
Art In America	Benjamin/S.G.W.	Harper	NY
Art Of The American Wood Engraver (The)	Hamerton/Philip	Scribner	NY
Art Year Book		New England Institute	Bos
Autocrat At The Breakfast Table (The)	Holmes/Oliver W.	Houghton,Mifflin	Bos
Bibliomanis Or Book Madness	Dibdin/Thomas F.	Bibliophile Society	Bos
Blue Flower (The)	Van Dyke/Henry	Scribner	NY
Blue Flower (The)	Van Dyke/Henry	Scribner	NY
Book Of American Spirit	Pyle/Howard	Harper	NY
Book Of American Spirit	Pyle/Howard	Harper	NY
Book Of Pirates	Pyle/Howard	Harper	NY
Book Of Pirates	Pyle/Howard	Harper	NY
Book Of The Ocean (The)	Ingersoll/Ernest	Century	NY
Bucaneers (The)	Seitz/Don	Harper	NY
Building The Nation	Coffin/Charles C.	Harper	NY
Captain Ravenshaw	Stephens/Robert N.	L.C. Page	Bos
Captain's Well (The)	Whittier/John G.	New York Ledger	NY
Champions Of The Round Table (The)	Pyle/Howard	Scribner	NY
Chivalry	Cabell/James B.	Harper	NY
Chronicle Of The Drum (The)	Thackeray/William M.	Scribner	NY
City Ballads	Carleton/Will	Harper	NY
Closing Scene (The)	Read/Thomas B.	Lippincott	Phi
David Balfour	Stevenson/Robert Louis	Scribner	NY
Dorothy Q.	Holmes/Oliver W.	Houghton,Mifflin	Bos
Dulcibel	Peterson/Henry	Winston	NY
Eclogues Of Vergil (The)	Bowen/Baron	Privately Printed	Bos
Etchings	Bicknell/W.H.W.	Bibliophile Society	Bos
Etchings	Bicknell/W.H.W.	Bibliophile Society	Bos
Farm Ballads	Carleton/Will	Harper	NY
First Book Of The Dofobs (The)		Society Of The Dofobs	Chi
First Christmas Tree (The)	Van Dyke/Henry	Scribner	NY
First Lessons In Our Country's History	Swinton/William	American Book Co.	NY
Flute & Violin & Other Kentucky Tales	Allen/James L.	Harper	NY
Founders Of Our Country	Coe/Fanny	American Book Co	NY
Gallantry	Cabbell/James B.	Harper	NY
Garden Behind The Moon (The)	Pyle/Howard	Scribner	NY
George Washington	Wilson/Woodrow	Harper	NY
Ghost Of Captain Brand (The)		Rogers	Wil
Giles Corey, Yeoman	Wilkins/Mary E.	Harper	NY

(1853-1911) Wilmington, DE

Year	Color	Tipped	B&W	Price Range	Pages	Size	TEG	AEG	DJ	Comments
1893				30 — 50						
1915				40 — 60						
1892				75 — 100						
1915				20 — 30						
1880				75 — 100						
1894				50 — 75						
1884				100 — 150						
1894			15	125 — 150		8vo	Teg			2 Vols
1903				50 — 75						
1902	3			25 — 50		8vo	Teg			Blue Gilt
1909	3			15 — 25		8vo	Teg			Blue Gilt
(1923)	23			100 — 125	344	4to				Early Reprint
1923	23			140 — 185	344	4to				
(1921)	1		11	50 — 75	209	4to				Reprint
1921	11			150 — 185	247	4to				
1898				50 — 75						
1912			1	50 — 75	52	8vo	Teg			
1883				25 — 35						
1901				20 — 30						
1890				50 — 75						
1905			50	175 — 225		8vo				
1909	12			90 — 125	224	8vo	Teg			
1882				25 — 35						
1886				25 — 35						
1887				25 — 35						
1895				25 — 50						
1893				75 — 100	131	8vo				Gray Cloth
1907	3			50 — 75	402	12mo	Teg			Grey Cloth
1904				100 — 150						
1903				75 — 100						
1913				50 — 75						
1882				25 — 35						
1907				100 — 125						
1897			4	35 — 50		8vo	Teg			
1894				20 — 30						
1891				20 — 40						
1912				15 — 20						
1907	4	Ticp		100 — 145	334	8vo	Teg			Grey Cloth
1895			10	125 — 175	192	12mo				Green/Gilt
1897			20	50 — 75	333	8vo	Teg			
1896				50 — 75						
1893				25 — 50						

Howard Pyle

Title	Author	Publisher	City
Good For The Soul	Deland/Margaret	Harper	NY
Great Men's Sons	Brooks/Elbridge	Putnam	NY
Harper's Book Of Little Plays	Briscoe/Margaret	Harper	NY
Harper's Fourth Reader		Harper	NY
Harper's Popular Cyclopaedia/ U.S. History	Lossing/Benson	Harper	NY
History Of American Art (A)	Hartmann/Sadakichi	L.C. Page	Bos
History Of New York...... (A)	Knickerbocker/Diedrich	Grolier Club	NY
History Of The American People (A)	Wilson/Woodrow	Harper	NY
History Of The American People (A)	Wilson/Woodrow	Harper	NY
History Of The Last Quarter Century (The)	Andrews/E. Benjamin	Scribner	NY
History Of The United States	Andrews/Benjamin	Scribner	NY
History Of The United States	Higginson/Thomas W.	Harper	NY
History Of The United States (A)	Scudder/Horace	Sheldon	NY
History Of The United States (A)	Gordy/Wilbur	Scribner	NY
How To Draw	Barritt/Leon	Harper	NY
Howard Pyle/A Chronicle	Abbott/C.	Harper	NY
Hugh Wynne,Free Quaker	Mitchell/Silas W.	Century	NY
Hugh Wynne,Free Quaker	Mitchell/Silas W.	Century	NY
Illustrated Poems Of			
Oliver Wendell Holmes	Holmes/Oliver W.	Houghton,Mifflin	Bos
In Old New York	Janvier/Thomas	Harper	NY
In Ole Virginia	Page/Thomas N.	Scribner	NY
In The Valley	Frederic/Harold	Scribner	NY
Inca Princess (The)		Lippincott	Phi
Indian History For Young Folks	Drake/Francis	Harper	NY
Island Of Enchantment (The)	Forman/Justus M.	Harper	NY
Janice Meredith	Ford/Paul Leicester	Dodd	NY
Kidnapped	Stevenson/Robert Louis	Scribner	NY
Lady Of Shalott (The)	Tennyson/Alfred	Dodd	NY
Larger History Of The United States (A)	Higginson/Thomas W.	Harper	NY
Library Of Universal Adventure	Howels/W. & Perry/T.	Harper	NY
Lincoln & The Sleeping Sentinel	Chittenden/Charles	Harper	NY
Line Of Love (The)	Cabbell/James B.	Harper	NY
Man With The Hoe & Other Poems (The)	Markham/Edwin	McClure	NY
Men Of Iron	Pyle/Howard	Harper	NY
Men Of Iron	Pyle/Howard	Harper	NY
Merry Adventures Of Robin Hood (The)	Pyle/Howard	Scribner	NY
Merry Adventures Of Robin Hood (The)	Pyle/Howard	Scribner	NY
Merry Adventures Of Robin Hood (The)	Pyle/Howard	Scribner	NY
Merry Men & Other Tales & Fables (The)	Stevfenson/Robert Louis	Scribner	NY
Modern Alladin (A)	Pyle/Howard	Harper	NY
Modern Illustration	Pennell/Joseph	George Bell	Lon

(1853-1911) Wilmington, DE

Year	Color	Tipped	B&W	Price Range	Pages	Size	TEG	AEG	DJ	Comments
1899				25 — 35						
1895				30 — 50						
1910				30 — 50						
1888				20 — 30						
1881				75 — 100						
1901				50 — 75						
1886				50 — 75						(Washington Irving)
1902				75 — 100						
1918				50 — 75						
1896				20 — 30						
1895				20 — 30						
1905				20 — 30						
1884				25 — 35						
1904				20 — 30						
1904				30 — 50						
1925				120 — 150	249	4to				Grey Bds
[1897]				100 — 150		8vo				2 Volumes
1899				75 — 100		8vo				2 Volumes
1885				35 — 50						
1894				20 — 30						
1896				25 — 35						
1890				30 — 50						
1886				15 — 25						
1886				35 — 50						
1905				25 — 35						
1899				35 — 50						
1895				75 — 100						
(1881)				350 — 450	64	8vo		Aeg		Blue Cloth
1886				40 — 60						
1888				50 — 75						
1909				15 — 25						
1905	10			75 — 100	291	8vo	Teg			
1900				75 — 100	114	12mo	Teg			
(1919)	1		16	40 — 60	327	8vo				Red Cloth
1892			15	150 — 200	328	8vo	Teg			Red Cloth
(1911)				10 — 20	176	8vo				
1884				150 — 175	296	4to				
1917			23	75 — 100	296	4to				Brown Cloth
1895				75 — 100						
1892				100 — 130	205	8vo				Blue Gilt
1895				50 — 75						

Howard Pyle

Title	Author	Publisher	City
Modern Pen Drawings	Holme/Charles	The Studio	Lon
New England Bygones	Arr/E.H.	Lippincott	Phi
Odes & Epodes Of Horace (The)	Smith/Clement	Bibliophile Society	Bos
Odysseus, The Hero Of Ithaca	Burt/Mary E.	Scribner	NY
Old Chester Tales	Deland/Margaret	Harper	NY
Old Homestead Poems	Bruce/Wallace	Harper	NY
Old Times In The Colonies	Coffin/Charles C.	Harper	NY
On Hazardous Service	Beymer/William G.	Harper	NY
One-Hoss Shay (The)	Holmes/Oliver W.	Houghton,Mifflin	Bos
One-Hoss Shay (The)	Holmes/Oliver W.	Houghton,Mifflin	Bos
Otto Of The Silver Hand	Pyle/Howard	Scribner	NY
Parasite (The)	Doyle/Arthur C.	Harper	NY
Pen Drawing & Pen Draughtsmen	Pennell/Joseph	Macmillan	Lon
Pepper & Salt	Pyle/Howard	Harper	NY
Pepper & Salt	Pyle/Howard	Harper	NY
Phaeton Rogers	Johnson/Rossiter	Scribner	NY
Price Of Blood (The)	Pyle/Howard	Badger	Bos
Quo Vadis	Sienkiewicz/Henryk	Little Brown	Bos
Recollections Of A Minister To France	Washburne/E.B.	Scribner	NY
Rose Of Paradise (The)	Pyle/Howard	Harper	NY
Ruby Of Kishmoor (The)	Pyle/Howard	Harper	NY
Saint Joan Of Arc	Twain/Mark	Harper	NY
School History Of The United States (A)	Swinton/William	American Book Co.	NY
Silence & Other Stories	Wilkins/Mary	Harper	NY
Sir Christopher...	Goodwin/Maud W.	Little Brown	Bos
Snow Bound	Whittier/John Greenleaf	Houghton,Mifflin	Bos
Some American College Bookplates	Ward/Harry P.		Col
Some Merry Adventures Of Robin Hood	Pyle/Howard	Scribner	NY
Some Merry Adventures Of Robin Hood	Pyle/Howard	Scribner	NY
Soul Of Melicent (The)	Cabbell/James B.	Stokes	NY
St. Joan Of Arc	Twain/Mark	Harper	NY
Star Bearer (The)	Stedman/Edmund C.	Lothrop	Bos
Stolen Treasure	Pyle/Howard	Harper	NY
Stops Of Various Quills	Howells/W.D.	Harper	NY
Storied Holidays	Brooks/Elbridge S.	Lothrop	Bos
Stories Of Later American History	Gordy/Wilbur	Scribner	NY
Story Of Champions Of The Round Table	Pyle/Howard	Scribner	NY
Story Of Jack Ballister's Fortunes (The)	Pyle/Howard	Century	NY
Story Of King Arthur & Knights (The)	Pyle/Howard	Scribner	NY
Story Of King Arthur & Knights (The)	Pyle/Howard	Scribner	NY
Story Of Siegfried (The)	Baldwin/James	Scribner	NY
Story Of Siegfried (The)	Baldwin/James	Scribner	NY

(1853-1911) Wilmington, DE

Year	Color	Tipped	B&W	Price Range	Pages	Size	TEG	AEG	DJ	Comments
1901				50 — 75						
1883				25 — 35						
1901				50 — 75						
1898				20 — 30						
1899			16	25 — 50	360	12mo				Green Cloth
1888				25 — 50						
1881				25 — 50						
1912				20 — 30						
1892				75 — 125						
1905	12			75 — 125		12mo	Teg			
1888			25	175 — 250	173	8vo				Olive Cloth
1895			4	65 — 85	143	12mo				
1889				100 — 150						
(1922)				50 — 75	121	4to				Tan Cloth
1886				275 — 400	121	4to				Tan Gilt
1881				25 — 50						
1899	6			150 — 225	98	12mo				
1897				30 — 50						
1889				30 — 60						
1888			8	75 — 100	231	12mo				Green Gilt
1908	10			80 — 120	74	8vo	Teg			
1919				75 — 100						
1893				20 — 30						
1898				20 — 30						
1901			1	25 — 35	411	12mo				
1906				60 — 80						
1915				50 — 75						
(1911)				20 — 30	176	8vo				
1902				100 — 150						
(1913)	4			90 — 130		8vo				
(1919)	4	Ticp		75 — 125	32	8vo				
[1888]				100 — 125						
1907			8	100 — 125	253	12mo				Orange Cloth
1895				50 — 75		8vo	Teg			
[1887]				150 — 175	271	8vo				
1915				15 — 20						
1905				75 — 100	328	8vo			DJ	Tan Cloth
1895			14	150 — 200	420	8vo				
(1933)	1			40 — 60						
1903				100 — 175	313	8vo				
1882				150 — 200	306	8vo	Teg			Red Gilt
1929				75 — 100						

Howard Pyle

Title	Author	Publisher	City
Story Of Sir Launcelot (The)	Pyle/Howard	Scribner	NY
Story Of The Golden Age	Baldwin/J.	Scribner	NY
Story Of The Golden Age (A)	Baldwin/James	Scribner	NY
Story Of The Grail....(The)	Pyle/Howard	Scribner	NY
Story Of The Grail....(The)	Pyle/Howard	Scribner	NY
Story Of The Revolution (The)	Lodge/Henry C.	Scribner	NY
Struggle For A Continent (The)	Parkman/Francis	Little Brown	Bos
Swinton's Advanced Third Reader		Ivison	Chi
Theatrical Bookplates	Pope/A. Winthrop	Fowler	KC
To Have & To Hold	Johnston/Mary	Houghton,Mifflin	Bos
Tour Around New York (A)	Mines/John F.	Harper	NY
True Story Of George Washington (The)	Brooks/Elbridge	Lothrop	Bos
True Story Of Unites States Of America	Brooks/Elbridge	Lothrop	Bos
Twilight Land	Pyle/Howard	Harper	NY
Twilight Land	Pyle/Howard	Harper	NY
Twilight Land	Pyle/Howard	Harrap	Lon
Under Green Apple Boughs	Campbell/Helen	Fords, Howard	NY
Within The Capes	Pyle/Howard	Int'l Assoc Of NP	
Wonder Clock (The)	Pyle/Howard	Harper	NY
Wonder Clock (The)	Pyle/Howard	Harper	NY
Wonder Clock (The)	Pyle/Howard	Harper	NY
Works Of William Makepeace Thackery	Ritchie/Lady	Harper	NY
Yankee Doodle	Pyle/Howard	Dodd	NY
Youma: The Story Of A West Indian Slave	Hearn/Lafcadio	Harper	NY

(1853-1911) Wilmington, DE

Year	Color	Tipped	B&W	Price Range	Pages	Size	TEG	AEG	DJ	Comments
1907			47	175 — 225	340	8vo				Tan Cloth
1887				180 — 230	286	8vo				
1887				75 — 100						
1910			25	175 — 225	258	4to				Tan Cloth
1927			25	50 — 75	258	4to				
1898				25 — 35						
1902				40 — 60						
1886				15 — 25						
1914				75 — 100						
1900			1	20 — 30	403	8vo				
1893				50 — 75						
1895				15 — 25						
1891				15 — 25						
(1894)				40 — 60	437	8vo				Red Cloth Early Reprint
(1922)				25 — 40	438	8vo				
1895				75 — 100	438	8vo				
1882				35 — 50						
1901				15 — 30						
1888				200 — 300	318	8vo				Gray Cloth
1899				100 — 125	318	4to				
1915				25 — 35						
1910				30 — 50						
1881	8			250 — 300	31	4to				
1890				250 — 350		8vo				

Arthur Rackham

Title	Author	Publisher	City
Aesop's Fables	Aesop	Heinemann	Lon
Aesop's Fables	Aesop	Heinemann	Lon
Aesop's Fables	Aesop	Doubleday,Page	NY
Aesop's Fables	Aesop	Bell & Cockburn	Scot
Aesop's Fables	Aesop	Doubleday	NY
Alice's Adventures In Wonderland	Carroll/Lewis	Heinemann	Lon
Alice's Adventures In Wonderland	Carroll/Lewis	Heinemann	Lon
Alice's Adventures In Wonderland	Carroll/Lewis	Doubleday	NY
Alice's Adventures In Wonderland	Carroll/Lewis	Doubleday	NY
Allies' Fairy Book (The)	Gosse/Edmund	Heinemann	Lon
Allies' Fairy Book (The)	Gosse/Edmund	Heinemann	Lon
Allies' Fairy Book (The)	Gosse/Edmund	Heinemann	Lon
Allies' Fairy Book (The)	Gosse/Edmund	Lippincott	Phi
Argonauts Of The Amazon (The)	Kenyon/C.R.	W.R. Chambers	Lon
Argonauts Of The Amazon (The)	Kenyon/C.R.	Dutton	NY
Art Of Pen Drawing (The)	Montague/G.	B.T. Batsford	Lon
Arthur Rackham A Bibliography	Latimore/Sarah B.	Suttonhouse	LA
Arthur Rackham A Bibliography	Latimore/Sarah B.	Suttonhouse	LA
Arthur Rackham Fairy Book (The)	Rackham/Arthur	Harrap	Lon
Arthur Rackham Fairy Book (The)	Rackham/Arthur	Lippincott	Phi
Arthur Rackham Fairy Book (The)	Rackham/Arthur	Harrap	Lon
Arthur Rackham's Book Of Pictures	Rackham/Arthur	Heinemann	Lon
Arthur Rackham's Book Of Pictures	Rackham/Arthur	Heinemann	Lon
Arthur Rackham's Book Of Pictures	Rackham/Arthur	Century	NY
Arthur Rackham's Book Of Pictures	Rackham/Arthur	Heinemann	Lon
Auld Acquaintance	Savory/Harry	Dent	Lon
Bee-Blowaways (The)	Herbertson/Agnes Grozier	Cassell	Lon
Book Of Betty Barber (The)	Brown/Maggie	Duckworth	Lon
Book Of Betty Barber (The)	Brown/Maggie	Badger	NY
Book Of Queen's Doll House	Benson/A.C.	Methuen	Lon
Book Of Queen's Doll House	Benson/A.C.	Methuen	Lon
Book Of The Titmarsh Club (The)	Rhys/Ernest	J. Davy	Lon
Bracebridge Hall	Irving/Washington	Putnam	Lon & NY
Bracebridge Hall	Irving/Washington	Putnam	Lon & NY
Brains & Bravery	Henty/G.A & Others	Chambers	Lon
Brains & Bravery	Henty/G.A & Others	Chambers	Lon
British Book Illustration	Holme/Geoffrey	The Studio	Lon
Captain Castle	Dawe/Carlton	Smith,Elder	Lon
Castle Inn (The)	Weyman/Stanley	Smith,Elder	Lon
Castle Inn (The)	Weyman/Stanley	Smith,Elder	Lon
Charles O'Malley The Irish Dragoon	Lever/Charles	Nesbit	Lon

(1867-1939) London, England

Year	Color	Tipped	B&W	Price Range	Pages	Size	TEG	AEG	DJ	Comments
1912	13			225 — 300	223	8vo				Green/Gilt
1912	13	Ticp	53	800 —1200	223	4to	Teg			1450 Signed By Rackham
1912	13	Ticp		175 — 225	223	8vo				Green Cloth
1912				150 — 175						Green Cloth
1926	13			50 — 100		8vo				
[1907]	13	Ticp	14	500 — 700	161	4to	Teg			Ltd Edition Of 1130 Not Signed
[1907]				150 — 200		8vo				Green Cloth
[1907]	13		14	125 — 175	161	8vo				Red Cloth
[1907]	13	Ticp	14	400 — 600	161	8vo	Teg			Ltd Edition 550 Copies Signed By Publisher
(1916)	12	Ticp	24	850 —1250	121	8vo	Teg			525 Signed By Rackham
(1918)	12			100 — 125		8vo				
[1916]	12		24	175 — 275	121	8vo			DJ	Blue
[1916]	12			125 — 225	122	8vo			DJ	Green Or Red Cloth
1901			6	175 — 250	337					Blue Or Pinkcloth
1901			6	125 — 175	337		Teg			Blue Cloth
(1927)	1		1	50 — 75	207	8vo				
1936	1		8	100 — 150	111	8vo				Ltd To 550 Copies
1936			9	50 — 75	98	8vo			DJ	Turquoise Cloth
(1933)	8		60	175 — 250	286	8vo			DJ	Red Cloth
(1933)	8		60	100 — 150	286	8vo			DJ	Red Cloth
1933	8		60	1000 —1500	286	8vo	Teg			460 Signed By Rackham
(1913)	44	Ticp	10	300 — 400	43	4to				Grey Cloth
(1913)	44		10	750 —1000	43	4to	Teg			1030 Signed By Rackham
(1913)	44		10	175 — 250	43	4to				Gray Or Brown Clothcloth
	44		10	100 — 150	43	4to				Early Reprint
1907			2	75 — 100		4to				
[1900]			16	100 — 150	33	8vo				
(1910)	6		12	250 — 350	129		Teg			Brown Cloth
[1910]	6		12	250 — 350	129	8vo	Teg			
(1924)			1	50 — 75						
(1924)			1	150 — 200	248	4to				
1925				125 — 175						
1896			5	100 — 150	653	8vo	Teg			2 Volumes Blu Cloth
1896			5	200 — 300	653					Ltd To 100
1903			8	75 — 125	398					Red Or Blue Cloth
1905			8	50 — 75	398					Green Cloth
1923	1		2	75 — 100	175	8vo	Teg			Tan Cloth
1897			1	50 — 75	296					Blue Cloth
[1900]			1	50 — 75	371	8vo				Ribbed Cloth
1898			1	100 — 125	371	8vo				Blue Cloth
[1899]			16	100 — 125	628		Teg			

Arthur Rackham

Title	Author	Publisher	City
Charles O'Malley The Irish Dragoon	Lever/Charles	Service & Paton	Lon
Charles O'Malley The Irish Dragoon	Lever/Charles	Putnam	NY
Children & Pictures (The)	Tennant/Pamela	Heinemann	Lon
Children & Pictures (The)	Tennant/Pamela	Macmillan	NY
Children's Christmas Treasury (The)	Hutton/Edward	Dent	Lon
Children's Christmas Treasury (The)	Hutton/Edward	Dutton	NY
Children's Hour (The)	Caine/Ralph Hall	Newnes	Lon
Children's Treasury Of Great Stories		Daily Express	Lon
Children's Treasury Of Great Stories		Daily Express	Lon
Chimes (The)	Dickens/Charles	Limited Editions Club	Lon
Christmas Carol (A)	Dickens/Charles	Heinemann	Lon
Christmas Carol (A)	Dickens/Charles	Heinemann	Lon
Christmas Carol (A)	Dickens/Charles	Heinemann	Lon
Christmas Carol (A)	Dickens/Charles	Lippincott	Phi
Christmas Carol (A)	Dickens/Charles	Lippincott	Phi
Christmas Carol (A)	Dickens/Charles	Lippincott	Phi
Christmas Carol (A)	Dickens/Charles	Heinemann	Lon
Cinderella	Evans/C.S.	Heinemann	Lon
Cinderella	Evans/C.S.	Heinemann	Lon
Cinderella	Evans/C.S.	Lippincott	Phi
Compleat Angler (The)	Walton/Izaak	Harrap	Lon
Compleat Angler (The)	Walton/Izaak	Harrap	Lon
Compleat Angler (The)	Walton/Izaak	Harrap	Lon
Compleat Angler (The)	Walton/Izaak	McKay	Phi
Comus	Milton/John	Heinemann	Lon
Comus	Milton/John	Heinemann	Lon
Comus	Milton/John	Doubleday,Page	NY
Costume Through The Ages	Rackham/Arthur	Maggs Brothers	Lon
Cotter's Saturday Night (The)	Burns/Robert	Heweston	Lon
Dish Of Apples (A)	Phillpotts/Eden	Hodder & Stoughton	Lon & N
Dish Of Apples (A)	Phillpotts/Eden	Hodder & Stoughton	Lon
Dish Of Apples (A)	Phillpotts/Eden	Hodder & Stoughton	NY
Dolly Dialogues (The)	Hope/Anthony	Westminster Gazette	Lon
Dolly Dialogues (The)	Hope/Anthony	Westminster Gazette	Lon
Dolly Dialogues (The)	Hope/Anthony	Holt	NY
Don Gypsy	Starkie/Walter	John Murray	Lon
Drawings In Pen & Pencil	Sheringham/George	The Studio	Lon
Drawings In Pen & Pencil	Sheringham/George	The Studio	Lon
East Coast Scenery	Tate/William James	Jarrold	Lon
English Book Illustration Of Today	Sketchley/R.E.D.	Kegan	Lon

(1867-1939) London, England

Year	Color	Tipped	B&W	Price Range	Pages	Size	TEG	AEG	DJ	Comments
1897			16	125 — 150	628					Maroon Cloth
1897			16	100 — 125	628					Maroon Cloth
1907			1	100 — 150	223					Pink Cloth
1907			1	100 — 150	223					Rose Cloth
(1905)	15		15	250 — 300	207	4to	Teg			White Cloth
(1905)	15		15	225 — 275	207	4to	Teg			White Cloth
(1906)			1	75 — 100	127	4to				Green Cloth
[1910]	3			125 — 175	447	8vo				Blue Cloth
[1930]	3			50 — 75	447	8vo				Red Cloth
1931			6	350 — 600	128	4to	Teg			1 Of 1500 Signed By Rackham In Slipcase
(1915)	12	Ticp	20	1000 —1250	147	4to	Teg			525 Signed By Rackham
(1915)	12	Ticp	20	150 — 200	147	8vo			DJ	Green Cloth
(1915)	12	Ticp	20	175 — 225	147	8vo	Teg			Brown Antique Leather
(1915)	12	Ticp	20	1000 —1250	147	4to				100 Signed By Rackham
(1915)	12		20	100 — 150	146	8vo			DJ	Red Or Lavender Cloth
(1923)	4			75 — 100		8vo			DJ	
[1923]	12		20	75 — 100	147	8vo			DJ	Reprints
(1919)	1	Ticp		750 —1000	110	4to	Teg			850 Signed By Rackham
(1919)	1			200 — 250	110	4to			DJ	
(1919)	1			175 — 250	110	4to			DJ	
(1931)	12		25	225 — 275	223	4to	Teg		DJ	Blue Cloth
(1931)	12		25	250 — 300	223	4to				Green Or Brown Leather
[1931]	12		25	750 —1000	223	4to	Teg			775 Signed By Rackham
[1931]	12		25	125 — 175	223	4to	Teg		DJ	Blue-Grey Cloth
[1921]	24	Ticp		500 — 800	76	4to	Teg			550 Signed By Rackham
[1921]	24	Ticp		175 — 250	76	4to			DJ	Green Cloth
[1921]	24	Ticp		175 — 225	76	4to				Green/Gilt
1938				125 — 150						
[1908]			1	125 — 150	17	12mo				
(1921)	3	Ticp		600 — 800	75	4to	Teg			600 Signed By Rackham
[1921]	3	Ticp		175 — 225	75	4to			DJ	Grey Cloth
[1921]	3	Ticp		150 — 175	75	4to			DJ	Grey Cloth
1894			4	150 — 250	111	8vo				Yellow Or Red Wrappers
1894			4	125 — 175	111					Blue Or Tan Cloth
1894			1	50 — 100	195	12mo	Teg			Tan Buckram
(1936)				40 — 80	525	8vo			DJ	
1922			1	50 — 75	184	4to	Teg			Gray-Green Cloth
1922			1	150 — 200	184	4to	Teg			Ltd To 250 In Vellum
1899			7	100 — 150	261					
1903			1	75 — 100	175					Green Cloth

Arthur Rackham

Title	Author	Publisher	City
English Book Illustration Of Today	Sketchley/R.E.D.	Kegan	Lon
English Fairy Tales	Steele/Flora Annie	Macmillan	Lon
English Fairy Tales	Steele/Flora Annie	Macmillan	Lon
English Fairy Tales	Steele/Flora Annie	Macmillan	NY
English Fairy Tales	Steele/Flora Annie	Macmillan	NY
English Fairy Tales	Steele/Flora Annie	Macmillan	NY
English Fairy Tales	Steele/Flora Annie	Macmillan	NY
English Illustration:Nineties	Thorpe/James	Faber	Lon
Evelina	Burney/Frances	Newnes	Lon
Evelina	Burney/Frances	Newnes	Lon
Fairy Book (A)	Rackham/Arthur	Doubleday,Page	NY
Fairy Tales By Hans Anderson	Anderson/Hans Christian	Harrap	Lon
Fairy Tales By Hans Anderson	Anderson/Hans Christian	Harrap	Lon
Fairy Tales By Hans Anderson	Anderson/Hans Christian	Harrap	Lon
Fairy Tales By Hans Anderson	Anderson/Hans Christian	McKay	Phi
Fairy Tales Of Brothers Grimm	Grimm Brothers	Freemantle	Lon
Fairy Tales Of Brothers Grimm	Grimm Brothers	Freemantle	Phi
Fairy Tales Of Brothers Grimm	Grimm Brothers	Lippincott	Phi
Fairy Tales Of Brothers Grimm	Grimm Brothers	Partridge	Lon
Fairy Tales Of Brothers Grimm	Grimm Brothers	Constable	Lon
Fairy Tales Of Brothers Grimm	Grimm Brothers	Constable	Lon
Fairy Tales Of Brothers Grimm	Grimm Brothers	Constable	Lon & Ny
Fairy Tales Of Brothers Grimm	Grimm Brothers	Doubleday	NY
Fairy Tales Of Brothers Grimm	Lucas/Mrs. Edgar	Constable	Lon
Fairy Tales Old & New		Cassell	Lon
Faithful Friends	Bingham/Clifton	Blackie & Sons	Lon
Faithful Friends	Bingham/Clifton	Blackie & Sons	Lon
Far Familiar (The)	MacKaye/Percy	Richards	Lon
Featherweights	Byron/May	Hodder & Stoughton	Lon
Feats Of The Fjord	Martineau/Harriet	Dent	Lon
Feats Of The Fjord	Martineau/Harriet	Dutton	NY
Feats Of The Fjord	Martineau/Harriet	Dent	Lon
Feats Of The Fjord	Martineau/Harriet	Dutton	NY
Feats Of The Fjord	Martineau/Harriet	Dent	Lon
Feats Of The Fjord	Martineau/Harriet	Dent	Lon
Feats Of The Fjord	Martineau/Harriet	Dutton	NY
Fourth Annual Of Advertising Art	Art Directors Club	Book Service Co.	NY
Gardens Old & New	Leyland/John	Newnes	Lon

(1867-1939) London, England

Year	Color	Tipped	B&W	Price Range	Pages	Size	TEG	AEG	DJ	Comments
1903			1	100 — 125	175					50 Numbered Copies On Japenese Vellum
1918	16	Ticp		750 — 900	341	4to	Teg			500 Signed By Rackham
1918	16			200 — 250	341	4to				Red Cloth
1918	16			175 — 250	341	8vo				Red Cloth
1918	16	Ticp		250 — 350	341	4to	Teg			White Calf Ltd To 250 Unsigned
1919	16			125 — 175	363	8vo				
1930	4			50 — 75		8vo				
1935				50 — 75						Purple Cloth
[1900]			16	100 — 150	416	8vo				Early Reprint
1898			16	175 — 225	416	8vo	Teg			Blue Cloth
(1923)	11			125 — 175	111	8vo			DJ	Reprint Of Allies Fairy Book
(1932)	8		19	125 — 150	286	4to			DJ	Rose Cloth
(1932)	8		19	150 — 175	286	4to				Full Morocco
[1932]	8		19	900 —1250	286	4to	Teg			525 Signed By Rackham
(1932)	8		19	75 — 100	286	4to			DJ	
[1900]			99	150 — 200	464					Tan Cloth
[1900]			99	125 — 175	464		Teg			
[1900]				75 — 100						
[1904]			12	75 — 125	334			Aeg		Red Or Blue Cloth
[1907]				100 — 125	464					
1909	40	Ticp	45	300 — 400	325	4to				Red Cloth
1909	40	Ticp	45	1000 —1500	325	4to	Teg			750 Signed By Rackham For Great Britain & 50 For NY
1909	40	Ticp	45	350 — 450	325	8vo				
	2			35 — 60		12mo				Blue Cloth
(1905)				100 — 150		8vo		Aeg		Pink Cloth
(1902)	1		6	350 — 450		4to		Aeg		Blue Pictorial Boards
[1913]	5		1	250 — 300		4to				Red Cloth
(1938)			1	75 — 100	79	12mo				Blue Cloth
(1908)	1			150 — 250	10	16mo				
(1910)			11	50 — 75	239	12mo			DJ	Blue/Gilt Everymans Library
(1910)			11	50 — 75	239	12mo			DJ	Blue/Gilt Everymans Library
(1914)				75 — 100						
(1914)	8			75 — 125	128	12mo				Red Or Green Cloth
1899	1		11	150 — 250	237	12mo	Teg			Blue Cloth Or Blue Leather One Of Temple Classics Series
	8			50 — 75	128	12mo				Orange Cloth Reprint
	8			50 — 75	128	12mo				
1925			3	50 — 75	165	4to				
[1900]				175 — 225		Folio		Aeg		3 Volumes

Arthur Rackham

Title	Author	Publisher	City
Goblin Market	Rossetti/Christina	Harrap	Lon
Goblin Market	Rossetti/Christina	Lippincott	Phi
Goblin Market	Rossetti/Christina	Harrap	Lon
Good Night	Gates/Eleanor	Crowell	NY
Greek Heroes (The)	Niebuhr	Cassell	Lon
Greek Heroes (The)	Niebuhr	Cassell	Lon
Greek Heroes (The)	Niebuhr	Cassell	Lon
Grey House On The Hill (The)	Greene/Mrs.	Nelson	Lon
Grey House On The Hill (The)	Greene/Mrs.	Nelson	Lon
Grey Lady (The)	Merriman/Henry S.	Smith,Elder	Lon
Grey Lady (The)	Merriman/Henry S.	Smith,Elder	Lon
Grimm's Fairy Tales	Grimm Brothers	Heinemann	Lon
Gulliver's Travels	Swift/Jonathan	Dent	Lon
Gulliver's Travels	Swift/Jonathan	Dent	Lon
Gulliver's Travels	Swift/Jonathan	Temple Press	Lon
Gulliver's Travels	Swift/Jonathan	Dent	Lon
Gulliver's Travels	Swift/Jonathan	Dent	Lon
Gulliver's Travels	Swift/Jonathan	Dent	Lon
Gulliver's Travels	Swift/Jonathan	Dent	Lon
Gulliver's Travels	Swift/Jonathan	Dutton	NY
Gulliver's Travels	Swift/Jonathan	Temple Press	Lon
Hansel & Grethel & Other Tales	Grimm Brothers	Constable	Lon
Hansel & Grethel & Other Tales	Grimm Brothers	Dutton	NY
Homes & Haunts Of Carlyle (The)		Westminster Gazette	Lon
Illustrated Guide To Wells-Next-The-Sea	Lingwood/Lemmon	Jarrold	Lon
Illustrated Guide To Wells-Next-The-Sea	Lingwood/Lemmon	Jarrold	Lon
Imagina	Ford/Julia E.	Duffield	NY
Imagina	Ford/Julia E.	Dutton	NY
Imagina	Ford/Julia E.	Duffield	NY
In The Evening Of His Days	Friederichs/Hulda	Westminster Gazette	Lon
Ingoldsby Legends (The)	Ingoldsby/Thomas	Heinemann	Lon
Ingoldsby Legends (The)	Ingoldsby/Thomas	Dent	Lon
Ingoldsby Legends (The)	Ingoldsby/Thomas	Dent	Lon
Ingoldsby Legends (The)	Ingoldsby/Thomas	Dent	Lon & NY
Ingoldsby Legends (The)	Ingoldsby/Thomas	Dutton	NY
Ingoldsby Legends (The)	Ingoldsby/Thomas	Heinemann	Lon
Ingoldsby Legends (The)	Ingoldsby/Thomas	Dent	Lon
Irish Fairy Tales	Stephens/James	Macmillan	Lon
Irish Fairy Tales	Stephens/James	Macmillan	Lon

(1867-1939) London, England

Year	Color	Tipped	B&W	Price Range	Pages	Size	TEG	AEG	DJ	Comments
(1933)	4		19	200 — 250	42	8vo			DJ	
[1933]	4		19	150 — 175	42	8vo			DJ	Red Cloth
1933	4		19	750 — 900	42	8vo	Teg			410 Signed By Rackham
(1907)	5			350 — 500	53	8vo				Grey Cloth
1903	4		8	250 — 275	96					Green Buckram
1910	4		8	175 — 225	96	12mo	Teg			Blue/Gilt
	4		8	75 — 125	96	12mo				Brown Cloth
[1903]	8			150 — 175	205	8vo				Pink Cloth
[1905]	8			100 — 125	205	8vo				Red Cloth
1897			12	125 — 150	342	8vo				Gray Cloth
1898			12	75 — 100	342	8vo				
(1925)	40		55	150 — 200	325	4to			DJ	Reprint Of 1909 Book Red Cloth
(1904)	1		11	75 — 125		12mo				From Temple Classics
[1912]	8			100 — 125	128	8vo			DJ	Blue,Green Or Orange Cloth
[1937]	12			40 — 60		8vo				
1900	1		11	150 — 200	363	12mo	Teg			Blue Cloth Or Leather From Temple Classics
1901	1		12	50 — 100		16mo				"Temple Classics For Young People"
1909	12	Ticp		250 — 300	291	8vo	Teg		DJ	Red Cloth
1909	13	Ticp	2	750 —1000	291	4to	Teg			750 Signed By Rackham
1909	12			175 — 225	291	8vo	Teg		DJ	Red Cloth
1939	12			30 — 50		8vo				Blue Cloth
(1920)	20			175 — 250	159	4to				Blue/Gilt
(1920)	20			175 — 225	159	4to				Blue Cloth
1895			1	75 — 100	148		Teg			Blue Cloth
(1894)			49	100 — 150	164	8vo				
(1910)			9	75 — 100	79	8vo				
1914	2			100 — 175	178	8vo				Blue Cloth
1923	2			50 — 75	178	8vo				Blue Cloth
1924	2			50 — 75	178	8vo				
1896			10	200 — 300	150					Gray Cloth
(1909)	24	Ticp	12	125 — 150	549	4to			DJ	Blue Pictorial Cloth
1898	12		90	175 — 225	638	8vo				Green/Gilt
1907	24	Ticp	12	200 — 300	549	4to	Teg		DJ	Green Cloth
1907	24	Ticp	12	750 —1000	549		Teg			560 Signed By Rackham
1907	24	Ticp	12	200 — 250	549	4to	Teg		DJ	Green/Gilt
1919	24	Ticp		100 — 125	549	4to			DJ	
	12		90	125 — 150	638	8vo				Early Reprint
1920	16	Ticp		850 —1000	318	4to	Teg			520 Signed By Rackham
1920	16	Ticp		175 — 250	318	4to	Teg		DJ	Green Cloth

Arthur Rackham

Title	Author	Publisher	City
Irish Fairy Tales	Stephens/James	Macmillan	NY
Irish Fairy Tales	Stephens/James	Macmillan	Lon
Isis Very Much Unveiled	Garrett/Fydell E.	Westminster Gazette	Lon
King Albert's Book		Daily Telegraph	Lon
King Of The Golden River	Ruskin/John	Harrap	Lon
King Of The Golden River	Ruskin/John	Harrap	Lon
King Of The Golden River	Ruskin/John	Lippincott	Phi
Kingdoms Curious	Hamilton/Myra	Heinemann	Lon
Kingsway Shakespeare (The)		Harrap	Lon
Land Of Enchantment (The)		Cassell	Lon
Land Of Enchantment (The)		Cassell	Lon
Legend Of Sleepy Hollow (The)	Irving/Washington	Harrap	Lon
Legend Of Sleepy Hollow (The)	Irving/Washington	Harrap	Lon
Legend Of Sleepy Hollow (The)	Irving/Washington	Harrap	Lon
Legend Of Sleepy Hollow (The)	Irving/Washington	McKay	Phi
Legend Of Sleepy Hollow (The)	Irving/Washington	McKay	Phi
Life Of A Century (The)	Hodder/Edwin	Newnes	Lon
Little Brother & Little Sister	Brothers Grimm	Constable	Lon
Little Brother & Little Sister	Brothers Grimm	Constable	Lon
Little Brother & Little Sister	Brothers Grimm	Dodd	NY
Little Folks Fairy Book (The)	Hamer/Sam H.	Cassell	Lon
Little Folks Picture Album	Hamer/Sam H.	Cassell	Lon
Little Folks Plays (The)	Hill & Browne	Cassell	Lon
Little Folks Plays (The)	Hill & Browne	Cassell	Lon
Little White Bird	Barrie/J.M.	Scribner	NY
Little White Bird	Barrie/J.M.	Scribner	NY
Littledom Castle & Other Tales	Spielmann/Mrs. M.H.	Routledge	Lon
Littledom Castle & Other Tales	Spielmann/Mrs. M.H.	Routledge	Lon
Littledom Castle & Other Tales	Spielmann/Mrs. M.H.	Dutton	NY
London Garland (A)	Henley/W.E.	Macmillan	Lon
London Garland (A)	Henley/W.E.	Macmillan	Lon
Lonesomest Doll (The)	Brown/Abbie F.	Houghton,Mifflin	Bos
Midsummer Night's Dream	Shakespeare/William	Limited Editions Club	Lon
Midsummer Night's Dream	Shakespeare/William	Heinemann	Lon
Midsummer Night's Dream	Shakespeare/William	Heinemann	Lon
Midsummer Night's Dream	Shakespeare/William	Doubleday	NY
Midsummer Night's Dream	Shakespeare/William	Heinemann	Lon
Midsummer Night's Dream	Shakespeare/William	Heinemann	Lon
Modern Book Illustrators & Their Work	Salaman/M.C.	The Studio	Lon
Molly Bawn	Hungerford/Margaret Wolfe	Newnesw	Lon

(1867-1939) London, England

Year	Color	Tipped	B&W	Price Range	Pages	Size	TEG	AEG	DJ	Comments
1920	16	Ticp		175 — 250	318	4to	Teg		DJ	Green Cloth
1924	16			125 — 175	318	4to	Teg		DJ	
[1894]			1	75 — 100	136					Volume 11
[1914]	1	Ticp		50 — 100	187	4to				Also Plates By
										Dulac,Parrish,Neilsen
(1932)	4		15	150 — 200	47	8vo			DJ	
(1932)	4		15	600 — 800	47	8vo	Teg			570 Signed By Rackham
1932	4		15	100 — 150	47	8vo			DJ	Red Cloth
1905			4	175 — 250	247	8vo				Tan Cloth
	2			125 — 150	1331	8vo				
1907			13	175 — 225	114	4to				Green Cloth
1907			36	200 — 250	144	4to				Brown Cloth
(1928)	8		30	200 — 300	102	4to	Teg		DJ	Green Cloth
(1928)	8		30	175 — 250	102	4to				Brown Leather Sept 1928
(1928)	8	Ticp	30	1000 —1300	102	4to	Teg			250signed By Rackham
(1928)	8		30	150 — 200	102	4to	Teg		DJ	Brown Cloth
(1928)	8	Ticp	30	1000 —1300	102	4to				125 Signed By Rackham
1901			6	100 — 125	760			Aeg		
(1917)	12	Ticp	43	200 — 300	250	4to				Green/Gilt
(1917)	13	Ticp	43	750 —2000	250	4to	Teg			525 Signed By Rackham
(1917)	12	Ticp	0	200 — 250	250	8vo				Red Or Blue Cloth
1905			9	125 — 150	190	4to				
1904	1			100 — 125	96					Green Or Brown Cloth
1903	2		2	125 — 150	48					
1906	2		2	75 — 100	48					
1912	2			250 — 300		8vo	Teg			Brown Cloth
1913			2	30 — 50		8vo	Teg			Brown Cloth
(1912)			12	75 — 100	377	8vo				Red Cloth
1903			12	150 — 200	377			Aeg		Red Cloth
1903			12	125 — 150	377	8vo				Red Cloth
1895			1	175 — 225	203		Teg			White Cloth
1895			1	250 — 350	203			Aeg	DJ	Vellum In Green Slipcase
(1928)			4	175 — 250	80	8vo				Tan Cloth
(1939)	6			250 — 350		Folio				Ltd to 1950 copies one of 37
										vol. of set by different artists
1908	40	Ticp	30	225 — 325	134	4to				Tan Cloth
1908	40	Ticp	30	750 —1000	134	4to	Teg			1000 Signed By Rackham
1908	40	Ticp	30	200 — 250	134	4to				
1911	40	Ticp	0	125 — 175	134	4to				
1920	40	Ticp	30	175 — 250	134	4to	Teg			Full Calf
1914	1		4	75 — 125	192	4to				
(1904)			8	300 — 500	220	12mo				

Arthur Rackham

Title	Author	Publisher	City
Money-Spinner (The)	Merriman/Henry S.	Smith,Elder	Lon
Money-Spinner (The)	Merriman/Henry S.	Smith,Elder	Lon
More Tales Of The Stumps	Bleackley/Horace	Ward,Lock	Lon
Mother Goose		Heinemann	Lon
Mother Goose		Heinemann	Lon
Mother Goose		Century	NY
Mother Goose		Heinemann	Lon
Mysteries Of Police & Crime	Griffiths&Gold	Cassell	Lon
Mysteries Of Police & Crime	Griffiths&Gold	Cassell	Lon
New Book Of Sense & Nonsense	Rhys/Ernest	Dent	Lon
New Book Of Sense & Nonsense	Rhys/Ernest	Dutton	NY
New Fiction & Other Papers	The Philistine	Westminster Gazette	Lon
Night Before Christmas (The)	Moore/Clement C.	Harrap	Lon
Night Before Christmas (The)	Moore/Clement C.	Harrap	Lon
Night Before Christmas (The)	Moore/Clement C.	Lippincott	Phi
Night Before Christmas (The)	Moore/Clement C.	Lippincott	Phi
Not All The Truth	Melville/Lewis	Jarrold	Lon
Not All The Truth	Melville/Lewis	Doubleday,Page	NY
Now Then....		Boy Scouts Appeal	Lon
Odd Volume (The)	Matz/B.W.	Simpkin,Marshall	Lon
Old Water Colour Society's Club (The)	Davies/Randall		Lon
Old Water Colour Society's Club (The)	Holme/Charles	The Studio	Lon
Outline Of Literature (The)	Drinkwater/John	Newnes	Lon
Oxted,Limpsfield & Neighbourhood	Fry/Lewis	W.&G. Godwin	Lon
Peer Gynt	Ibsen/Henrik	Harrap	Lon
Peer Gynt	Ibsen/Henrik	Harrap	Lon
Peer Gynt	Ibsen/Henrik	Harrap	Lon
Peer Gynt	Ibsen/Henrik	Lippincott	Phi
Pen,Pencil & Chalk	Holme/Charles	The Studio	Lon
Peradventures Of Private Pagett (The)	Drury/W.P.	Chapman/Hall	Lon
Peradventures Of Private Pagett (The)	Drury/W.P.	Chapman/Hall	Lon
Peter Pan In Kensington Gardens	Barrie/J.M.	Hodder & Stoughton	Lon
Peter Pan In Kensington Gardens	Barrie/J.M.	Hodder & Stoughton	Lon
Peter Pan In Kensington Gardens	Barrie/J.M.	Hodder & Stoughton	Lon
Peter Pan In Kensington Gardens	Barrie/J.M.	Hodder & Stoughton	Lon
Peter Pan In Kensington Gardens	Byron/May	Hodder & Stoughton	Lon
Peter Pan In Kensington Gardens	Byron/May	Scribner	NY
Peter Pan In Kensington Gardens	Barrie/J.M.	Hodder & Stoughton	Lon
Peter Pan In Kensington Gardens	Barrie/J.M.	Hodder & Stoughton	Lon
Peter Pan In Kensington Gardens	Barrie/J.M.	Scribner	NY

(1867-1939) London, England

Year	Color	Tipped	B&W	Price Range	Pages	Size	TEG	AEG	DJ	Comments
1896			12	150 — 250	242	8vo				Red/Gilt
1897			12	100 — 150	242	8vo				Red/Gilt
1902			11	175 — 225	224					Blue Cloth
(1913)	13			200 — 300	159	8vo				Grey Cloth
[1913]	13		85	1000 —1500	159	4to	Teg			1130 Signed By Rackham
1913	13			225 — 325	262	4to				Black Cloth
	13			75 — 100	159	8vo				Reprint
[1901]			14	125 — 150	464					Green Cloth 3 Volumes
[1904]			14	75 — 100	464					Red Cloth 3 Volumes
(1928)			11	50 — 75	298	12mo				Green Or Orange Cloth From Everyman's Library Series
(1928)			11	50 — 75	298	12mo				Green Or Orange Cloth From Everyman's Library Series
1895				75 — 100						
[1931]	4		17	750 — 900	35	8vo	Teg			275 Signed By Rackham
[1931]	4		17	150 — 200	35	8vo	Teg		DJ	
[1931]	4		17	750 — 900	35	8vo				275 Signed By Rackham
[1931]	4		17	150 — 175	35	8vo	Teg		DJ	Green Cloth
1928			1	50 — 75	286	8vo				Blue Cloth
1929			1	60 — 80	286	8vo				Blue Cloth
[1927]			1	150 — 250	95	85				Only 2000 Printed
1908			1	50 — 75	95	4to				
1934			1	75 — 100	77	4to				
1905	40			175 — 225	46					Green Or Grey Cloth
[1930]	1			150 — 200		4to				Red Or Blue Leather 2 Volumes
(1932)			5	100 — 125	144	8vo				
[1936]	12	Ticp		850 —1250	255	4to	Teg			460 Signed By Rackham
[1936]	12			100 — 150	255	4to			DJ	Orange Cloth
[1936]	12			150 — 200	255	4to	Teg			Green Morocco
[1936]	12			100 — 150	255	4to			DJ	Orange Cloth
1911			2	50 — 75						Blue Cloth Or Wraps
(1911)	8			150 — 200	242	12mo				
1904			8	200 — 300	242	12mo				Orange/Red Cloth
(1910)	24			150 — 175	125	8vo				Green Suede
(1910)	24	Ticp		100 — 125	125	8vo	Teg			Red Cloth
(1912)	50	Ticp	12	1250 —1500	125	4to	Teg			New Deluxe Edition
(1912)	50	Ticp	12	250 — 400	125	4to	Teg		DJ	Green Cloth
(1929)	6		15	75 — 100	123	8vo			DJ	Green Cloth
(1929)	6		15	75 — 100	123	8vo			DJ	Green Cloth
1906	50	Ticp		300 — 500	125	4to		Aeg		Brown Cloth
1906	50	Ticp		1250 —2000	125	4to	Teg			500 Signed By Rackham
1906	50	Ticp		250 — 400	125	4to		Aeg		Green Cloth

Arthur Rackham

Title	Author	Publisher	City
Peter Pan In Kensington Gardens	Barrie/J.M.	Scribner	NY
Peter Pan In Kensington Gardens	Barrie/J.M.	Scribner	NY
Peter Pan In Kensington Gardens	Barrie/J.M.	Scribner	NY
Peter Pan In Kensington Gardens	Barrie/J.M.	Scribner	NY
Peter Pan In Kensington Gardens	Barrie/J.M.	Scribner	NY
Peter Pan In Kensington Gardens	Byron/May	Scribner	NY
Peter Pan In Kensington Gardens	Barrie/J.M.	Scribner	NY
Peter Pan Portfolio	Rackham/Arthur	Hodder & Stoughton	Lon
Peter Pan Portfolio	Rackham/Arthur	Brentano's	NY
Pied Piper Of Hamlin (The)	Browning/Robert	Harrap	Lon
Pied Piper Of Hamlin (The)	Browning/Robert	Lippincott	Phi
Pied Piper Of Hamlin (The)	Browning/Robert	Harrap	Lon
Poor Cecco	Bianco/Margery W.	Chatto/Windus	Lon
Poor Cecco	Bianco/Margery W.	Doran	NY
Poor Cecco	Bianco/Margery W.	Doran	NY
Poor Cecco	Bianco/Margery W.	Doubleday	NY
Practice Of Water Colour Painting	Baldry/A.L.	Macmillan	Lon
Princess Mary's Gift Book		Hodder & Stoughton	Lon
Puck Of Pook's Hill	Kipling/Rudyard	Doubleday,Page	NY
Puck Of Pook's Hill	Kipling/Rudyard	Doubleday	NY
Queen Mab's Fairy Realm		Newnes	Lon
Queen Mab's Fairy Realm		Newnes	Lon
Queen's Gift Book		Hodder & Stoughton	Lon
Raggle-Taggle Adventures With A Fiddle	Starkie/Walter	John Murray	Lon
Raggle-Taggle Adventures With A Fiddle	Starkie/Walter	Dutton	NY
Rainbow Book (The)	Spielmann/Mrs. M.H.	Chatto/Windus	Lon
Rainbow Book (The)	Spielmann/Mrs. M.H.		NY
Red Pottage	Cholmondeley/Mary	Newnes	Lon
Red Pottage	Cholmondeley/Mary	Newnes	Lon
Rhinegold & The Valkyrie (The)	Wagner/Richard	Heinemann	Lon
Rhinegold & The Valkyrie (The)	Wagner/Richard	Heinemann	Lon & NY
Rhinegold & The Valkyrie (The)	Wagner/Richard	Doubleday,Page	NY
Rhinegold & The Valkyrie (The)	Wagner/Richard	Garden City	Gar
Ring Of The Niblung (The)	Wagner/Richard	Garden City	Gar
Ring Of The Niblung (The)	Wagner/Richard	Heinemann	Lon
Rip Van Winkle	Irving/Washington	Heinemann	Lon
Rip Van Winkle	Irving/Washington	Doubleday,Page	NY
Rip Van Winkle	Irving/Washington	Heinemann	Lon
Rip Van Winkle	Irving/Washington	Heinemann	Lon
Rip Van Winkle	Irving/Washington	Heinemann	Lon

(1867-1939) London, England

Year	Color	Tipped	B&W	Price Range	Pages	Size	TEG	AEG	DJ	Comments
1907	50	Ticp		175 — 225	125	4to		Aeg		Green/Gilt
1913	24	Ticp		175 — 200	125	8vo				Green Cloth
1926	16			75 — 125	126	8vo				
1929				75 — 125					DJ	Green Cloth
1929	16			75 — 125	126	8vo				
1934	6		15	50 — 75	123	8vo			DJ	
1940	16			50 — 100	126	8vo				
(1912)	12	Ticp		4000 —6000		Folio				Ltd To 500
(1914)	12	Ticp		2500 —3500		Folio				Ltd To 300
[1934]	4		14	200 — 300	44	8vo			DJ	
[1934]	4		14	100 — 200	44	8vo			DJ	
1934	4		14	750 —1000	44	8vo	Teg			410 Signed By Rackham
(1925)	7	Ticp	24	150 — 175	175	4to			DJ	
(1925)	7	Ticp	24	125 — 150	175	4to			DJ	Blue Gilt
1925	7	Ticp	24	6000 —8000	175	4to	Teg			105 Signed By Rackham
				100 — 125						
1911	2			75 — 100	166	4to	Teg			Blue Cloth
[1914]	1	Ticp		50 — 75		4to			DJ	White Or Blue Cloth
1906	4			60 — 100	277	8vo	Teg			Green Cloth
1916	4			25 — 50		8vo				Green Cloth
1901			5	225 — 300	310			Aeg		Blue Cloth
1915			3	100 — 125	98					
[1915]	1		2	50 — 75	160	4to				Blue Cloth
(1933)			2	50 — 75	399	8vo				Green Cloth
(1933)			2	40 — 60	399	8vo				Green Cloth
1909	1			150 — 175	289	8vo	Teg			Red Cloth
	1			125 — 150	289	8vo	Teg			
[1904]			2	200 — 300	202	8vo				Tan Wraps
1904			8	400 — 550	202	8vo				Yellow Wraps
1910	34	Ticp	14	200 — 300	159	4to	Teg			Brown Buckram
1910	34	Ticp	14	750 —1000	159	4to	Teg			1150 Signed By Rackham
1910	34	Ticp	14	150 — 175	159	4to	Teg			Blue Cloth
1939	24			75 — 100		8vo				Blue Cloth
(1939)	48			50 — 100	181	4to			DJ	Blue Cloth
(1939)	48			75 — 125	181	4to			DJ	Blue Cloth
(1916)	24		14	150 — 175	36	8vo			DJ	Brown Boards
(1916)	24		14	125 — 150	36	8vo			DJ	Grey-Blue Cloth
[1917]	24		14	75 — 100	36	8vo			DJ	
1905	51	Ticp		300 — 400	61	4to			DJ	Green/Gilt
1905	51	Ticp		1000 —1500	57	4to				250 Signed By Rackham
										Full Vellum

Arthur Rackham

Title	Author	Publisher	City
Rip Van Winkle	Irving/Washington	Doubleday,Page	NY
Rip Van Winkle	Irving/Washington	Heinemann	Lon
Rip Van Winkle	Irving/Washington	Heinemann	Lon
Rip Van Winkle	Irving/Washington	Doubleday,Page	NY
River & Rainbow	Carroll/Walter	Forsyth	Lon
River & Rainbow	Carroll/Walter	Forsyth	Lon
Road To Fairyland (A)	Fay/Erica	Putnam	Lon
Road To Fairyland (A)	Fay/Erica	Putnam	NY
Romance Of King Arthur...(The)	Pollard/Alfred	Macmillan	Lon
Romance Of King Arthur...(The)	Pollard/Alfred	Macmillan	Lon
Romance Of King Arthur...(The)	Pollard/Alfred	Macmillan	NY
Romance Of King Arthur...(The)	Pollard/Alfred	Macmillan	NY
Romance Of King Arthur...(The)	Pollard/Alfred	Macmillan	NY
Rudyard Kipling	Cooper/Anice P.	Doubleday,Page	NY
Siegfried & Twilight Of The Gods	Wagner/Richard	Heinemann	Lon
Siegfried & Twilight Of The Gods	Wagner/Richard	Heinemann	Lon
Siegfried & Twilight Of The Gods	Wagner/Richard	Heinemann	Lon
Siegfried & Twilight Of The Gods	Wagner/Richard	Doubleday,Page	NY
Siegfried & Twilight Of The Gods	Wagner/Richard	Garden City	Gar
Siegfried & Twilight Of The Gods	Wagner/Richard	Heinemann	Lon
Sketch Book Of Geoffrey Crayon (The)	Irving/Washington	Putnam	NY
Sketch Book Of Geoffrey Crayon (The)	Irving/Washington	Putnam	NY
Sketch Book Of Geoffrey Crayon (The)	Irving/Washington	Putnam	NY
Sleeping Beauty (The)	Evans/C.S.	Heinemann	Lon
Sleeping Beauty (The)	Evans/C.S.	Heinemann	Lon
Sleeping Beauty (The)	Evans/C.S.	Lippincott	Phi
Snickerty Nick	Ford/Julia E.	Moffat	NY
Snickerty Nick & The Giant	Ford/Julia E.	Sutton House	SF
Snickerty Nick & The Giant	Ford/Julia E.	Sutton House	LA
Snowdrop & Other Tales	Grimm Brothers	Dutton	NY
Snowdrop & Other Tales	Grimm Brothers	Constable	Lon
Some British Ballads		Constable	Lon
Some British Ballads		Dodd	NY
Some British Ballads		Heinemann	Lon
Some British Ballads		Constable	Lon
Souvenir Of Sir Henry Irving	Calvert/Walter	Chant,Drane	Lon

(1867-1939) London, England

Year	Color	Tipped	B&W	Price Range	Pages	Size	TEG	AEG	DJ	Comments
1905				200 — 250	57	4to			DJ	Green/Gilt
1909	50	Ticp		125 — 150	61	4to			DJ	
1919	51	Ticp		200 — 300	61	4to	Teg			Green Leather
1919	51	Ticp		200 — 300	61	4to	Teg			Green Leather
(1933)	1		1	125 — 150	11	4to				Brown Spine
(1933)	1		1	75 — 100	11	4to				Black Spine
(1926)	1			100 — 150	219	8vo			DJ	Grey Cloth
(1926)	1			100 — 150	171	8vo			DJ	Red Cloth
1917	16	Ticp	7	750 —1250	517	4to	Teg			500 Signed By Rackham
1917	16	Ticp	7	150 — 175	509	8vo			DJ	Blue Cloth
1917	16	Ticp	7	150 — 175	509	8vo			DJ	Green Cloth
1917	16	Ticp	7	200 — 250	509	8vo				Bound In Whiter Goatskin Ltd To 250 Unsigned
1926			7	40 — 60	517	8vo			DJ	Blue Cloth
1926			1	30 — 50	100	8vo				
(1911)	30	Ticp	9	100 — 150	182	4to				Early Reprint
1911	30	Ticp	9	200 — 350	182	4to	Teg			Brown Buckram
1911	30	Ticp	9	300 — 400	182	4to				Limp Green Suede
1911	30	Ticp	9	175 — 275	182	4to	Teg			
1930	24			75 — 125					DJ	
1911	30	Ticp	9	800 —1000	182	4to	Teg			1150 Signed By Rackham
(1894)			3	125 — 150	609					2 Volumes Red Cloth Holly Edition Ltd To 1000
(1894)			3	250 — 300	609		Teg			2 Volumes Bound In Leather Westminster Edition Limited To 175 Sets
(1894)			4	100 — 125	609		Teg		DJ	2 Volumes White Or Blue Cloth Van Tassel Edition
(1920)	1	Ticp		150 — 200	110	4to			DJ	3 Double Page Silouhette Drawings
(1920)	1	Ticp		750 —1000	110	4to	Teg		DJ	625 Signed By Rackham
(1920)	1	Ticp		150 — 200	110	4to			DJ	
1919	3		10	125 — 175	78	4to			DJ	Blue Cloth
[1935]				35 — 50		4to				
1933	3		8	50 — 75	80	4to			DJ	Orange Cloth
(1920)	20	Ticp		150 — 175	165	4to				Blue Cloth
1920	20	Ticp		150 — 200	165	4to				Blue/Gilt
[1919]	16	Ticp		175 — 225	170	4to	Teg		DJ	Blue/Gilt
[1919]	16	Ticp		150 — 175	170	4to	Teg		DJ	Blue Cloth
[1925]	16	Ticp	1	150 — 175	170	4to			DJ	Light Blue Cloth
1919	16	Ticp		750 —1000	170	4to	Teg			575 Signed By Rackham
(1895)			1	75 — 100	48	8vo				

Arthur Rackham

Title	Author	Publisher	City
Spanish Raggle-Taggle......	Starkie/Walter	John Murray	Lon
Spanish Raggle-Taggle.......	Starkie/Walter	Dutton	NY
Springtide Of Life	Swinburne/Algernon C.	Heinemann	Lon
Springtide Of Life	Swinburne/Algernon C.	Heinemann	Lon
Springtide Of Life	Swinburne/Algernon C.	Heinemann	Lon
Springtide Of Life	Swinburne/Algernon C.	Heinemann	Lon
Springtide Of Life	Swinburne/Algernon C.	Lippincott	Phi
Stories Of King Arthur	Haydon/A.L.	Cassell	Lon
Stories Of King Arthur	Haydon/A.L.	Cassell	Lon
Sun Princess (The)	Millar/H.R.	Shaw	Lon
Sunrise-Land	Berlyn/Mrs. Alfred	Jarrold	Lon
Sunrise-Land	Berlyn/Mrs. Alfred	Jarrold	Lon
Surprising Adventures Of			
Tuppy & Tue (The)	Brown/Maggie	Cassell	Lon
Tales & Talks About Animals		Blackie & Sons	Lon
Tales From Shakespeare	Lamb/Charles & Mary	Dent	Lon
Tales From Shakespeare	Lamb/Charles & Mary	Dent	Lon
Tales From Shakespeare	Lamb/Charles & Mary	Dent	Lon
Tales From Shakespeare	Lamb/Charles & Mary	Dutton	NY
Tales Of A Traveler	Irving/Washington	Putnam	NY
Tales Of A Traveler	Irving/Washington	Putnam	NY
Tales Of Mystery & Imagination	Poe/Edgar Allan	Harrap	Lon
Tales Of Mystery & Imagination	Poe/Edgar Allan	Harrap	Lon
Tales Of Mystery & Imagination	Poe/Edgar Allan	Harrap	Lon
Tales Of Mystery & Imagination	Poe/Edgar Allan	Lippincott	Phi
Tempest (The)	Shakespeare/William	Heinemann	Lon
Tempest (The)	Shakespeare/William	Heinemann	Lon
Tempest (The)	Shakespeare/William	Doubleday,Page	NY
Third Annual Of Advertising Art	Art Directors Club	Book Service Co.	NY
Through A Glass Lightly	Greg/T.T.	Dent	Lon
To The Other Side	Rhodes/Thomas	George Philip	Lon
Two Old Ladies,Two Foolish Fairies			
& A Tom Cat	Brown/Maggie	Cassell	Lon
Two Old Ladies,Two Foolish Fairies			
& A Tom Cat	Brown/Maggie	Cassell	Lon
Two Years Before The Mast	Dana/Richard Henry	Collins	Lon
Two Years Before The Mast	Dana/Richard Henry	Collins	Lon
Two Years Before The Mast	Dana/Richard Henry	Monarch	Lon

(1867-1939) London, England

Year	Color	Tipped	B&W	Price Range	Pages	Size	TEG	AEG	DJ	Comments
(1934)			1	75 — 100	488	8vo				Red Cloth
1934			1	50 — 75	488	8vo				Red Cloth
(1818)	8			250 — 300	132	8vo	Teg			Greeen Leather
(1918)	8			200 — 250	132	4to	Teg		DJ	Green Cloth
(1918)	9	Ticp		750 —1000	132	4to	Teg			765 Signed By Rackham
(1918)	8			50 — 75	132	8vo			DJ	1925 Reprint Dated 1918 Green Cloth No Pictorial End Papers
(1918)	8			100 — 150	132	4to	Teg		DJ	Green Cloth
1910	4		2	175 — 225	94	12mo				Red Cloth
1918	4		2	100 — 125	94	12mo				Red Cloth
[1930]			3	40 — 60		4to			DJ	
1894			71	175 — 225	345	8vo				Grey Cloth
1898			71	100 — 125	345	8vo				Blue Cloth
1904	4		10	250 — 350	190	8vo				Blue Cloth
(1907)	5		3	125 — 150	166	4to		Aeg		
1899	1		11	150 — 200	562	12mo	Teg			Blue Leather Or Blue Cloth One Of Temple Classics Series
1909	12		2	200 — 275	304	8vo	Teg		DJ	Blue Or Purple Cloth
1909	13	Ticp	2	750 —1000	304	4to	Teg			750 Signed By Rackham
1909	12		2	175 — 225	304	8vo	Teg		DJ	
1895			5	100 — 150	628		Teg			2 Volumes Bound In Blue Or White Cloth
1895			5	250 — 350						Ltd To 150
(1935)	12		17	200 — 250	317	4to			DJ	Grey Cloth
(1935)	12		17	250 — 300	317	4to	Teg			Blue Morocco
[1935]	12	Ticp	17	1500 —2500	317	4to	Teg			460 Numbered & Signed
[1935]	12		17	175 — 250	317	4to			DJ	Red Cloth
(1926)	20	Ticp		175 — 250	185	4to			DJ	Olive-Green or Grey-Black Cloth
(1926)	21	Ticp		1000 —1250	185	4to	Teg			520 Signed By Rackham
(1926)	20	Ticp		150 — 200	185	4to			DJ	Olive-Green Or Grey-Black Cloth
1924			1	75 — 100	165	4to				
1897			1	175 — 200	143		Teg			Yellow Silk
1893				300 — 400	106					
1897	4		19	500 — 750	190		Teg			Red, Green Or Blue Cloth 1st Colored Ill By Rackham
1904	4		19	100 — 150	190					
(1904)	8			100 — 150	304					Pink Or Green Cloth
(1904)	8			75 — 100	304					Blue Or Red Cloth
[1904]	8			75 — 100	304					Green/Gilt

Arthur Rackham

Title	Author	Publisher	City
Two Years Before The Mast	Dana/Richard Henry	Winston	NY
Undine	Fouque/De La Motte	Heinemann	Lon
Undine	Fouque/De La Motte	Heinemann	Lon & NY
Undine	Fouque/De La Motte	Doubleday,Page	NY
Undine	Fouque/De La Motte	Heinemann	Lon
Undine	Fouque/De La Motte	Doubleday	NY
University Press Shakespeare	Shakespeare/William	Harrap	Lon
Venture (The) Annual Of Art & Literature		John Baillie	Lon
Venture (The) Annual Of Art & Literature		John Baillie	Lon
Vicar Of Wakefield (The)	Goldsmith/Oliver	Harrap	Lon
Vicar Of Wakefield (The)	Goldsmith/Oliver	Harrap	Lon
Vicar Of Wakefield (The)	Goldsmith/Oliver	Harrap	Lon
Vicar Of Wakefield (The)	Goldsmith/Oliver	McKay	Phi
Vicar Of Wakefield (The)	Goldsmith/Oliver	Lippincott	Phi
Where Flies The Flag	Harbour/Henry	Collins	Lon
Where Flies The Flag	Harbour/Henry	Collins	Lon
Where The Blue Begins	Morley/Christopher	Doubleday,Page	NY
Where The Blue Begins	Morley/Christopher	Heinemann	Lon
Where The Blue Begins	Morley/Christopher	Heinemann	Lon
Where The Blue Begins	Morley/Christopher	Doubleday,Page	NY
Where The Blue Begins	Morley/Christopher	Lippincott	Phi
Wild Life In Hampshire Highlands	Dewar/George A.B.	Dent	Lon
Wind In The Willows (The)	Grahame/Kenneth	Heritage Press	NY
Wind In The Willows (The)	Grahame/Kenneth	Methuen	Lon
Wind In The Willows (The)	Grahame/Kenneth	Methuen	Lon
Wind In The Willows (The)	Grahame/Kenneth	Limited Editions Club	NY
Windmill (The)	Callender/L.	Heinemann	Lon
Windmill (The)	Callender/L.	Heinemann	NY
Wonder Book (A)	Hawthorne/Nathaniel	Hodder & Stoughton	Lon
Wonder Book (A)	Hawthorne/Nathaniel	Hodder & Stoughton	Lon
Wonder Book (A)	Hawthorne/Nathaniel	Doran	NY
Wonderful Visit (The)	Wells/H.G.	Dent	Lon
World In A Garden (A)	Neish/R.	Dent	Lon
Zankiwank & The Bletherwitch	Fitzgerald/S.J.	Dent	Lon
Zankiwank & The Bletherwitch	Fitzgerald/S.J.	Dutton	NY
Zankiwank & The Bletherwitch	Fitzgerald/S.J.	Stokes	NY

(1867-1939) London, England

Year	Color	Tipped	B&W	Price Range	Pages	Size	TEG	AEG	DJ	Comments
1904	8			50 — 75	304					Tan Or Blue Cloth
1909	15	Ticp		250 — 300	136	4to			DJ	Blue Cloth
1909	15	Ticp		750 —1000	136	4to				1000 Signed By Rackham For London 250 For Ny
1909	15	Ticp		200 — 250	136	4to			DJ	
1911	15			100 — 125	136	4to			DJ	Reprinted 1911,12,16,19,20,25
1919	11	Ticp		100 — 150	136	8vo			DJ	
1908				75 — 100						Vol 23 & 24
1903			1	100 — 125	187					Tan Cloth
1905			1	75 — 100	187					Tan Cloth
[1929]	12			175 — 225	231	4to	Teg		DJ	Green Cloth
[1929]	12			200 — 250	231	4to	Teg			Olive Morocco
[1929]	12			750 —1000	231	4to	Teg			775 Signed By Rackham
[1929]	12			125 — 150	231	4to	Teg		DJ	Blue Cloth
1929				75 — 100					DJ	Green Cloth
(1904)	6			150 — 200	286	12mo				Blue Or Red Cloth
[1904]			6	50 — 75		12mo				
(1922)	4			1000 —1250	227	4to	Teg			100 Signed By Rackham & Author
[1922]	4		16	750 —1000	227	4to	Teg		DJ	175 Signed By Rackham
[1925]	4			100 — 125	227	4to	Teg		DJ	Blue Cloth
[1925]	4			100 — 125	227	4to	Teg		DJ	Blue Cloth
[1925]	4			50 — 100	227	4to				Blue Cloth
1899				150 — 200	304		Teg			Green/Gilt
(1940)	12			50 — 75	190	8vo				Box
(1950)	12			40 — 60	178	8vo			DJ	Green Cloth
(1951)	12	Ticp		250 — 500	178	4to	Teg			White Leather Limited To 500
1940	16	Ticp		400 — 600	244	4to	Teg			Limited To 2020 Signed By Bruce Rogers
1923	1			75 — 100	225	4to				Orange Boards
1923	1			125 — 150	225	4to	Teg			Limited To 500
(1922)	24	Ticp		225 — 300	206	4to			DJ	Red Cloth
(1922)	24	Ticp		750 —1000	206	4to	Teg			600 Signed By Rackham
(1922)	24	Ticp		200 — 250	206	4to			DJ	Red Cloth
1895			1	125 — 150	251		Teg			Cover Ill Only Red Cloth
1899				75 — 100						Pink Cloth
1896			17	600 — 750	188	8vo	Teg			Green/Gilt
1896				300 — 450	188	8vo	Teg			Green/Gilt
1896				250 — 350	188	8vo	Teg			Green/Gilt

John Rae

Title	Author	Publisher	City
American Indian Fairy Tales	Larned/W.T.	Volland	Jol
American Indian Fairy Tales	Larned/W.T.	Wise-Parslow	NY
Big Family (The)	Rae/John	Dodd	NY
Buddy Jim	Gordon/Elizabeth	Volland	Jol
Buddy Jim	Gordon/Elizabeth	Wise-Parslow	NY
Christmas Story/St. Mark		Volland	Jol
Countess Diane	Rowland/H.	Dodd	NY
Crossing ...(The)	Churchill/Winston	Macmillan	NY
Epic Of Ebenezzer (The)	Cox/Florence T.	Dodd	NY
Fables In Rhyme For Little Folk	La Fontaine	Volland	Jol
Fables In Rhyme For Little Folk	La Fontaine	Wise-Parslow	NY
Fairy Tales From France	Larned/William T.	Volland	Jol
Girl I Left Behind Me	Mills/W.J.	Dodd	NY
Granny Goose	Rae/John	Volland	Jol
Grasshopper Green & The Meadow Mice	Rae/John	Volland	Jol
Grasshopper Green & The Meadow Mice	Rae/John	Algonquin	NY
Grimm's Animal Stories	Crane/L.	Duffield	NY
Heartbreak Hill	Viele/H.K.	Duffield	NY
Lovely Garden	Snyder/Fairmont	Volland	Jol
Lucky Locket	Rae/John	Volland	Jol
Master Simon's Garden	Meigs/C.	Macmillan	NY
Masterman Ready	Marryat	Harper	NY
More Really-So Stories	Gordon/Elizabeth	Volland	Jol
More Really-So Stories	Gordon/Elizabeth	Wise-Parslow	NY
Mother	Wister/O.	Dodd	NY
Music Master	Klein/C.	Dodd	NY
New Adventures Of Alice	Rae/John	Volland	Jol
Prayers/Little Men & Women	Martin/J.	Harper	NY
Really So Stories	Gordon/Elizabeth	Volland	Jol
Really So Stories	Gordon/Elizabeth	Wise-Parslow	NY
Return Of Peter Grimm	Belasco/David	Dodd	NY
Reynard The Fox	Larned/W.T.	Volland	Jol
Story Of Mince Pie	Gates/J.S.	Dodd	NY
Story/Dogie Told To Me	Barbour/R.H.	Dodd	NY
Sword Of Dundee	Peck/T.	Duffield	NY
Three Little Frogs	Mee/J.	Volland	Jol
Through The Gates/Old Romance	Mills/W.J.	Lippincott	Phi
Under The Southern Cross	Robbins/E.	Stokes	NY
Van Rensselaers/Old Manhattan	Mills/W.J.	Stokes	NY
Why...	Rae/John	Dodd	NY

(1882-1963) Jersey City, NJ

Year	Color	Tipped	B&W	Price Range	Pages	Size	TEG	AEG	DJ	Comments
(1921)				75 — 100	88	8vo				
(1935)				35 — 50	96	4to				
1916				50 — 75	50	4to				
(1922)				40 — 70		8vo				Ibds
(1935)				20 — 35	109	8vo				
(1921)				40 — 60		16mo				
1908	5			35 — 50	149	8vo				
1930			10	25 — 50	296	8vo				Green/Gilt
1912				25 — 35	72	12mo				
(1918)				50 — 75		8vo				
1950				25 — 50		8vo				
(1920)				50 — 75	93	8vo				
1910	11			75 — 100	90	4to	Teg			
(1926)	21			100 — 150	44	4to				
(1922)				40 — 60		12mo				
(1922)				25 — 35		12mo				
1911				75 — 125		8vo				
1908	6			40 — 60		12mo				Grey Cloth
(1919)				50 — 75	38	12mo				
(1928)				50 — 75	120	8vo				Ibds
1929			5	50 — 75	320	8vo				
1928	6			35 — 50	403	4to				
(1929)				65 — 85	95	8vo				Ibds
				25 — 50		8vo				
1907			7	25 — 45	95	8vo				
1909	4			25 — 45	341	8vo				
(1917)	12			100 — 150		8vo				
1912	6	Ticp		50 — 75	96	8vo				
(1924)	11			50 — 75	96	8vo				
(1937)				25 — 50	96	4to				
1912	3			25 — 40	344	12mo				
(1925)				65 — 100		8vo				Ibds
1916	16			50 — 75		8vo				
1914				35 — 50	182	8vo				
1908			7	25 — 35		8vo				
(1924)				40 — 60		8vo				
1903				25 — 40		12mo	Teg			
(1907)	4			25 — 40	234	8vo	Teg			
(1907)	5			25 — 40	215	8vo				
1910				75 — 100		4to				

113

Jessie Wilcox Smith

Title	Author	Publisher	City
An Old-Fashioned Girl	Alcott/Louisa May	Little Brown	Bos
An Old-Fashioned Girl	Alcott/Louisa May	Little Brown	Bos
An Old-Fashioned Girl	Alcott/Louisa May	Sampson.Low	Lon
Art Stories - Book One	Whitford/William G.	Scott,Foresman	Chi
At The Back Of The North Wind	MacDonald/George	McKay	Phi
At The Back Of The North Wind	MacDonald/George	McKay	Phi
Baby's Red Letter Days	Smith/Jessie Wilcox	Just Foods	Syr
Baby's Red Letter Days	Smith/Jessie Wilcox	Just Foods	Syr
Bed-Time Book (The)	Whitney/Helen H.	Chatto/Windus	Lon
Bed-Time Book (The)	Whitney/Helen H.	Duffield	NY
Billy Boy	Long/John L.	Dodd	NY
Billy Boy	Long/John L.	Dodd	NY
Bobs, King Of The Fortunate Isle	Franchot/Annie W.	Dutton	NY
Book Of Lullabies (A)	Smith/Elva S.	Lothrop	Bos
Book Of The Child (The)	Humphrey/Mabel	Stokes	NY
Boys & Girls Of Bookland	Smith/Nora	McKay	Phi
Boys & Girls Of Bookland	Smith/Nora	McKay	Phi
Boys & Girls Of Bookland	Smith/Nora	Cosmopolitan	NY
Brenda's Summer At Rockley	Reed/Helen L.	Little Brown	Bos
Brenda's Summer At Rockley	Reed/Helen L.	Little Brown	Bos
Brenda, Her School & Her Club	Reed/Helen L.	Little Brown	Bos
Bugs & Wings & Other Things	Franchot/Annie W.	Dutton	NY
Child's Book Of Country Stories (A)	Skinner/Ada & Eleanor	Dial Press	NY
Child's Book Of Country Stories (A)	Skinner/Ada & Eleanor	Duffield	NY
Child's Book Of Country Stories (A)	Skinner/Ada & Eleanor	Dial Press	NY
Child's Book Of Famous Stories(A)	Coussens/Penrhyn W.	Garden City	NY
Child's Book Of Modern Stories (A)	Skinner/Ada & Eleanor	Duffield	NY
Child's Book Of Modern Stories (A)	Skinner/Ada & Eleanor	Dial Press	NY
Child's Book Of Old Verses (A)	Smith/Jessie Wilcox	Duffield	NY
Child's Book Of Old Verses (A)	Smith/Jessie Wilcox	Dial Press	NY
Child's Book Of Old Verses (A)	Smith/Jessie Wilcox	Duffield	NY
Child's Book Of Old Verses (A)	Smith/Jessie Wilcox	Dial Press	NY
Child's Book Of Stories (A)	Coussens/Penrhyn	Duffield	NY
Child's Book Of Stories (A)	Coussens/Penrhyn	Chatto/Windus	Lon
Child's Book Of Stories (A)	Coussens/Penrhyn	Duffield	NY
Child's Book Of Stories (A)	Coussens/Penrhyn	Dial Press	NY
Child's Book Of Verses (A)	Smith/Jessie Wilcox	Chatto/Windus	Lon
Child's Garden Of Verses (A)	Stevenson/Robert Louis	Longmans	Lon
Child's Garden Of Verses (A)	Stevenson/Robert Louis	Scribner	NY

(1863-1935) Philadelphia, Pa.

Year	Color	Tipped	B&W	Price Range	Pages	Size	TEG	AEG	DJ	Comments
1902			12	100 — 150	371	8vo				Green Cloth
1904			12	75 — 100	371	8vo			DJ	Green Cloth. Issued Almost Every Year
1907			12	75 — 100	371	8vo				Olive Cloth
[1933]	1			35 — 50	144	8vo				Blue Cloth
(1919)	8			100 — 150	342	4to	Teg		DJ	Printed In Usa On Copyright Page , Brown Cloth
1919	8			125 — 175	342	4to	Teg		DJ	Beige Cloth
(1906)			5	100 — 200	24	8vo				
[1901]			5	200 — 300	24	8vo			DJ	Embossed Cover
1907	6			225 — 275	31	4to				
1907	6			225 — 275	31	4to				
(1906)	1		3	100 — 150	74	8vo			DJ	Blue Cloth
1906	1		3	150 — 200	74	8vo	Teg		DJ	Blue Cloth
(1928)	1			50 — 75	210	8vo			DJ	Blue Cloth
(1925)			1	25 — 50	563	8vo				Purple Cloth
(1903)	3			600 — 750	59	Folio			DJ	Ibds
(1923)	11			100 — 150	100	4to			DJ	Dark Green Cloth
(1923)	11			75 — 100	100	4to			DJ	Brown Paper Covered Boards
1923	11			150 — 175	100	4to			DJ	Gray-Green Cloth
1901			5	175 — 225	376	8vo				Blue Cloth
1904			5	75 — 100	376	8vo			DJ	
1900			5	175 — 225	328	8vo				Green Cloth
(1918)	1			50 — 75	99	8vo			DJ	Green Cloth
(1935)	4			50 — 75	265	4to				
1925	4			175 — 225	265	4to				Red Cloth
1935	4			75 — 100	265	4to			DJ	Red Cloth Issued In Box
(1940)	4			40 — 60	462	4to				
1920	8			175 — 225	340	4to				
1935	8			100 — 125	341	4to			DJ	Green Cloth Issued With Box
(1910)	10			125 — 150	124	4to				Blue Cloth No Pictorial End Papers
(1935)	10			50 — 75	124	4to			DJ	
1910	10			175 — 225	124	4to	Teg			Blue Cloth
1935	10			75 — 100	124	4to			DJ	Blue Cloth Issued With Box
1911	10			250 — 300	463	4to				Blue Cloth
1913	10			125 — 150	142	4to				
1914	10			150 — 175	463	4to				
1935	10			75 — 100	463	4to				Blue Cloth
1912	10			100 — 125	95	4to				
1905	12			125 — 250	125	4to				
1905	12			125 — 250	125	4to	Teg			

Jessie Wilcox Smith

Title	Author	Publisher	City
Child's Garden Of Verses (A)	Stevenson/Robert Louis	Scribner	NY
Child's Garden Of Verses (A)	Stevenson/Robert Louis	Scribner	NY
Child's Garden Of Verses (A)	Stevenson/Robert Louis	Scribner	NY
Child's Prayer (A)	Toogood/Cora C.	McKay	Phi
Child's Prayer (A)	Toogood/Cora C.	McKay	Phi
Child's Stamp Book Of Old Verses (A)	Smith/Jessie Wilcox	Duffield	NY
Children Of Dickens (The)	Crothers/Samuel McChord	Scribner	NY
Children Of Dickens (The)	Crothers/Samuel McChord	Scribner	NY
Children Of Dickens (The)	Crothers/Samuel McChord	Scribner	NY
Children Of Dickens (The)	Crothers/Samuel McChord	Scribner	NY
Chronicles Of Rhoda (The)	Cox/Florence T.	Small,Maynard	Bos
Dancing-Master	Chabot/Adrien	Lippincott	Phi
Dickens's Children	Smith/Jesse Wilcox	Chatto/Windus	Lon
Dickens's Children	Smith/Jesse Wilcox	Scribner	NY
Dickens's Children	Smith/Jesse Wilcox	Scribner	NY
Dickens's Children	Smith/Jesse Wilcox	Chatto/Windus	Lon
Dream Blocks	Higgins/Aileen C.	Duffield	NY
Dream Blocks	Higgins/Aileen C.	Chatto/Windus	Lon
Evangeline	Longfellow/H.W.	Houghton,Mifflin	Bos
Evangeline	Longfellow/H.W.	Houghton,Mifflin	Bos
Evangeline	Longfellow/H.W.	Gay & Bird	Lon
Evangeline	Longfellow/H.W.	Houghton,Mifflin	Bos
Everyday & Now-A-Day Fairy Book (The)	Chapin/Anna Alice	Coker	Lon
Everyday & Now-A-Day Fairy Book (The)	Chapin/Anna Alice	Coker	Lon
Everyday Fairy Book (The)	Chapin/Anna Alice	Harrap	Lon
Everyday Fairy Book (The)	Chapin/Anna Alice	Coker	Lon
Everyday Fairy Book (The)	Chapin/Anna Alice	Coker	Lon
Everyday Fairy Book (The)	Chapin/Anna Alice	Dodd	NY
Everyday Fairy Book (The)	Chapin/Anna Alice	Harrap	Lon
Fairy & Wonder Tales	Patten/William	Collier	NY
Five Senses (The)	Keyes/Angela M.	Moffat,Yard	NY
Folk-Lore, Fables & Fairy Tales		The University Society	NY
Grimm's Fairy Tales	Grimm Brothers	Grosset&Dunlap	NY
Head Of A Hundred (The)	Goodwin/Maud W.	Little Brown	Bos
Head Of A Hundred (The)	Goodwin/Maud W.	Little Brown	Bos
Head Of A Hundred (The)	Goodwin/Maud W.	Little Brown	Bos
Heidi	Spyri/Johanna	McKay	Phi
Heidi	Spyri/Johanna	McKay	Phi
Heidi	Spyri/Johanna	Dial Press	NY
Ideal Heads	Waugh/Ida	Sunshine	Phi

(1863-1935) Philadelphia, Pa.

Year	Color	Tipped	B&W	Price Range	Pages	Size	TEG	AEG	DJ	Comments
1925	9			75 — 100	125	4to				
1944	9			30 — 75	125	4to			DJ	
1945	9			30 — 75	125	4to				
(1925)	1		6	40 — 60	16	8vo			DJ	Blue Cloth
(1925)	1		6	30 — 50	12	8vo				Wrappers
1915	12			125 — 175	30	16mo				
1925	10			100 — 150	259	4to			DJ	
1933	10			35 — 50	259	4to			DJ	
1940	10			25 — 40	259	4to				
1944	10			25 — 35	257	4to				
(1909)	2			75 — 125	287	12mo				Red Cloth
1901			4	150 — 175	139	12mo	Teg			Green Cloth
1912	10			125 — 175	48	4to	Teg			Green Cloth
1912	10			125 — 175	48	4to	Teg			Green Cloth
1912	10			100 — 150	48	4to				Tan Cloth
1913	10			100 — 125	48	4to				
(1908)	15			275 — 375	47	4to			DJ	Beige Cloth
1911	15			200 — 250	47	4to				
1897	5			150 — 200		8vo			DJ	Green Cloth
1897	5			125 — 150		8vo			DJ	Red Cloth
1897	5			150 — 200		8vo				Full Vellum
1916	3			50 — 75		8vo				
[1935]	13			100 — 150	300	4to				
[1935]	8			75 — 100	300	4to				
(1919)	7			100 — 150	159	4to				
[1935]	7			100 — 150	160	4to				
[1935]	7			75 — 100	159	4to				
1915	7			175 — 250	160	4to				Green Cloth
1917	7			150 — 225	159	4to				
(1918)			1	50 — 75	514	12mo				Red Cloth Part Of Junior Classics
1911	5			180 — 250	252	8vo				Tan Cloth
(1927)			1	25 — 50	400	8vo				Maroon Cloth Vol 3 Of The Home University Bookshelf
[1940]				15 — 25	377	8vo			DJ	Color Jacket Only By Smith
1897			2	85 — 100	225	8vo	Teg			Green Gilt
1899			2	70 — 80	225	8vo				Beige/Gilt
1900	1		2	75 — 100	221	8vo				Red Gilt
(1922)	10			100 — 150	380	8vo			DJ	Printed In U.S. Of America On Copyright Page
1922	10			125 — 175	380	8vo	Teg		DJ	Light Blue Cloth
1935	10			75 — 100						
1890			1	50 — 75	92	4to		Aeg		Brown Cloth

Jessie Wilcox Smith

Title	Author	Publisher	City
In The Closed Room	Burnett/Frances Hodgson	Grosset&Dunlap	NY
In The Closed Room	Burnett/Frances Hodgson	Hodder & Stoughton	Lon
In The Closed Room	Burnett/Frances Hodgson	McClure,Phillips	NY
Kitchen Fun	Bell/Louise P.	Harter	Cle
Kitchen Fun	Bell/Louise P.	Perks Publishing	
Listen & Sing	Glenn/Mabelle	Ginn	Bos
Listen & Sing	Glenn/Mabelle	Ginn	Bos
Little Child's Book Of Stories (A)	Skinner/Ada & Eleanor	Dial Press	NY
Little Child's Book Of Stories (A)	Skinner/Ada & Eleanor	Duffield	NY
Little Child's Book Of Stories (A)	Skinner/Ada & Eleanor	Dial Press	NY
Little Folks Illustrated Annual	Pratt/Charles & Ella	Small,Maynard	Bos
Little Mistress Goodhope	Taylor/Mary I.	McClurg	Chi
Little Mistress Goodhope	Taylor/Mary I.	McClurg	Chi
Little Mother Goose (The)	Smith/Jessie Wilcox	Dodd	NY
Little Mother Goose (The)	Smith/Jessie Wilcox	Dodd	NY
Little Mother Goose (The)	Smith/Jessie Wilcox	Musson	Tor
Little Paul's Christ Child	Bull/Kathryn J.	NP	Np
Little Women	Alcott/Louisa May	Little Brown	Bos
Little Women	Alcott/Louisa May	Little Brown	Bos
Little Women	Alcott/Louisa May	Little Brown	Bos
Little Women	Alcott/Louisa May	Little Brown	Bos
Lullaby Book (The)	Shelby/Annie B.	Duffield	NY
Memories And Garden	Saville/Emily A.	Privately Printed	
Mosses From An Old Manse	Hawthorne/Nathaniel	Houghton,Mifflin	Bos
Mosses From An Old Manse	Hawthorne/Nathaniel	Houghton,Mifflin	Bos
Mosses From An Old Manse	Hawthorne/Nathaniel	Houghton,Mifflin	Bos
Mother Goose	Smith/Jessie Wilcox	Dodd	NY
Mother Goose	Smith/Jessie Wilcox	Dodd	NY
Mother Goose	Smith/Jessie Wilcox	Hodder & Stoughton	Lon
Mother Goose	Smith/Jessie Wilcox	Hodder & Stoughton	Lon
New & True	Staver/Mary Wiley	Lee & Shepard	Bos
Now-A-Days Fairy Book (The)	Chapin/Anna A.	Dodd	NY
Now-A-Days Fairy Book (The)	Chapin/Anna A.	Prospect	NY
Now-A-Days Fairy Book (The)	Chapin/Anna A.	Harrap	Lon
Now-A-Days Fairy Book (The)	Chapin/Anna A.	Coker	Lon
Now-A-Days Fairy Book (The)	Chapin/Anna A.	Dodd	NY
An Old-Fashioned Girl	Alcott/Louisa May	Little Brown	Bos
Poems Old & New	Patten/William	Collier	NY
Princess & The Goblin (The)	MacDonald/George	McKay	Phi
Princess & The Goblin (The)	MacDonald/George	McKay	Phi

(1863-1935) Philadelphia, Pa.

Year	Color	Tipped	B&W	Price Range	Pages	Size	TEG	AEG	DJ	Comments
(1904)	4			25 — 50		8vo				Blue Cloth Issued W/Box
1904	8			100 — 150	130	8vo				
1904	8			100 — 150	130	8vo	Teg		DJ	Green Cloth
1932				50 — 75	27	4to				Color Cover By Smith
1946				35 — 50	27	4to				Color Cover By Smith
(1936)	2			35 — 50	140	12mo				Light Green Cloth
(1943)	2			25 — 35	140	8vo				
(1935)	8			50 — 75	258	4to				
1922	8			125 — 150	258	4to				Orange Cloth
1935	8			75 — 100	258	4to			DJ	Orange Cloth Issued With Box
(1918)	1		1	75 — 100	555	8vo			DJ	
(1902)	1		7	100 — 125	186	8vo				Green Cloth
1902	1		7	150 — 175	186	8vo				Blue Buckram
(1918)	12			125 — 160	176	8vo				
(1918)	12			100 — 125	176	8vo				Red Calf Spine
1921	12			75 — 100	176	8vo				
1929			2	50 — 75	18	8vo				Red Wraps
1915	8			125 — 150	617	8vo		Aeg		Green Cloth
1917	8			100 — 125	617	8vo				Green Cloth
1922	8			50 — 75	397	8vo			DJ	Black Cloth
1930	8			25 — 50	397	8vo				
1921	1			50 — 75	183	8vo			DJ	Light Blue Cloth
1924	1			100 — 150	212	8vo			DJ	Gray Cloth
1900			1	750 —1000	345	8vo	Teg			1 Volume Of 22 Limited To 500 . Ill. Signed In Pencil By Smith. Light Blue Crushed Morocco.
1900			1	75 — 100	345	8vo	Teg			Red Cloth
1903			1	50 — 60	34	8vo				
(1912)	12		5	175 — 250	173	4to				Issued With Box Price $2.50
(1916)	12		5	125 — 150	173	4to				Issued With Box Price $5.00
(1938)	12			75 — 100	159	4to				
[1920]	12			125 — 150	159	4to				
1892			4	75 — 100	136	8vo				
(1911)	6			150 — 175	159	4to				
(1913)	6			100 — 125	159	4to				
[1922]	6			100 — 125	159	4to				
[1935]	6			75 — 100	159	4to				
1911	6	Ticp		200 — 300	159	4to			DJ	
1915			12	85 — 100	371	8vo	Teg			
(1918)			1	50 — 75	529	12mo				Red Cloth Part Of Junior Classics
[1923]	4			50 — 75		8vo				
1920	8			150 — 175	203	4to	Teg		DJ	Beige Cloth

Jessie Wilcox Smith

Title	Author	Publisher	City
Princess & The Goblin (The)	MacDonald/George	McKay	Phi
Princess & The Goblin (The)	MacDonald/George	McKay	Phi
Reminiscences/Old Chest Of Drawers	Sill/Sarah Cauffman	Lippincott	Phi
Rhymes & Reminiscences	Saville/Henry M.	Stratford	Bos
Rhymes Of Real Children	Sage/Betty	Duffield	NY
Rhymes Of Real Children	Sage/Betty	D. Nutt	Lon
Rhymes Of Real Children	Sage/Betty	Duffield	NY
Seven Ages Of Childhood (The)	Wells/Carolyn	Donohue	Chi
Seven Ages Of Childhood (The)	Wells/Carolyn	Moffat	NY
Seven Ages Of Childhood (The)	Wells/Carolyn	Duffield	NY
Sonny's Father	Stuart/Ruth M.	Century	NY
Tales & Sketches	Hawthorne/Nathaniel	Houghton,Mifflin	Bos
Tales & Sketches	Hawthorne/Nathaniel	Houghton,Mifflin	Bos
Ten To Seventeen	Bacon/Josephine D.	Harper	NY
Thirty Favorite Paintings		Collier	NY
Truth Dexter	McCall/Sidney	Little Brown	Bos
Truth Dexter	McCall/Sidney	Little Brown	Bos
Tuning Up	Glenn/Mabelle	Ginn	Bos
Tuning Up	Glenn/Mabelle	Ginn	Bos
Twas The Night Before Christmas	Moore/Clement C.	Houghton,Mifflin	Bos
Twas The Night Before Christmas	Moore/Clement C.	Houghton,Mifflin	Bos
Very Little Child's Book Of Stories (A)	Skinner/Ada & Eleanor	Dial Press	NY
Very Little Child's Book Of Stories (A)	Skinner/Ada & Eleanor	Duffield	NY
Very Little Child's Book Of Stories (A)	Skinner/Ada & Eleanor	Dial Press	NY
Water Babies (The)	Kingsley/Charles	Dodd	NY
Water Babies (The)	Kingsley/Charles	Dodd	NY
Water Babies (The)	Kingsley/Charles	Dodd	NY
Water Babies (The)	Kingsley/Charles	Dodd	NY
Water Babies (The)	Kingsley/Charles	Dodd	NY
Water Babies (The)	Kingsley/Charles	Garden City	NY
Water Babies (The)	Kingsley/Charles	Hodder & Stoughton	Lon
Water Babies (The)	Kingsley/Charles	Boots	Lon
Water Babies (The)	Kingsley/Charles	Hodder & Stoughton	Lon
Water Babies (The)	Kingsley/Charles	Boots	Lon
Water Babies (The)	Kingsley/Charles	Dodd	NY
Way To Wonderland (The)	Stewart/Mary	Dodd	NY
Way To Wonderland (The)	Stewart/Mary	Dodd	NY
Way To Wonderland (The)	Stewart/Mary	Hodder & Stoughton	Lon
When Christmas Comes Around	Underwood/Priscilla	Chatto/Windus	Lon

120

(1863-1935) Philadelphia, Pa.

Year	Color	Tipped	B&W	Price Range	Pages	Size	TEG	AEG	DJ	Comments
1920	8			125 — 150	203	4to	Teg		DJ	Printed In Usa On Copyright Page
1920	8			100 — 125	203	4to			DJ	Green Cloth
1900			6	75 — 100	40	8vo		Aeg		Tan Cloth
(1929)	1			50 — 75	139	8vo				Red Cloth
1903	6			250 — 300	32	4to				
1905	6			150 — 200	32	4to				
1906	6			150 — 200	32	4to				
(1909)	7			100 — 125	56	4to				Red Cloth
1909	7			250 — 350	56	4to			DJ	
1921	7			100 — 125						
1910			2	70 — 90	240	12mo	Teg			Light Green Cloth
1900			1	750 —1000	358	8vo	Teg			1 Volume Of 22 Limited To 500 . Ill. Signed In Pencil By Smith. Light Blue Crushed Morocco.
1900			1	75 — 100	358	8vo				Red Cloth
1908			3	40 — 60	261	8vo				
1909	1		1	300 — 500	62	Folio				
1903			1	25 — 50	375	8vo				Blue Cloth
1906			1	15 — 25	375	8vo				Blue Cloth
(1936)	1			35 — 50	176	8vo				Orange Cloth
(1943)	1			25 — 35	176	8vo				
(1912)	12			160 — 220	32	8vo			DJ	
[1914]	12			100 — 150	32	8vo			DJ	Paper Not Cloth Spine
(1935)	8			50 — 75	232	4to				
1923	8			125 — 150	232	4to				Blue Cloth
1935	8			75 — 100	232	4to				Red Cloth Issued With Box
(1916)	8			100 — 175	270	8vo				
(1916)	8			75 — 150	270	8vo				Plain Endpapers
(1916)	12			200 — 300	362	4to				Issued With Box
(1916)	12	Ticp		225 — 325	362	4to				
(1916)	11	Ticp		175 — 250	362	4to				
(1937)	4			35 — 50	362	4to				Blue Cloth
(1938)	12			100 — 150	212	4to				Gray Cloth
[1919]	12	Ticp		150 — 250	240	4to		Aeg		Olive Green Cloth
[1919]	12	Ticp		175 — 250	240	4to			DJ	Blue Cloth
[1925]	12	Ticp		125 — 150	240	4to				Green Cloth
[1936]				25 — 35	270	16mo			DJ	Green Cloth No Color Plates
(1917)	6			170 — 240	194	4to				Brown Cloth
(1917)	6			150 — 200	194	4to				Light Blue Cloth
[1920]	6	Ticp		200 — 250	144	4to				Blue Gilt
1915	6			175 — 200	26	4to				

Jessie Wilcox Smith

Title	Author	Publisher	City
When Christmas Comes Around	Underwood/Priscilla	Duffield	NY
When Mother Lets Us Make Paper Box Furniture	Rich/G. Ellingwood	Dodd	NY
Young Puritans In Captivity (The)	Smith/Mary P. Wells	Little Brown	Bos
Young Puritans In Captivity (The)	Smith/Mary P. Wells	Little Brown	Bos

(1863-1935) Philadelphia, Pa.

Year	Color	Tipped	B&W	Price Range	Pages	Size	TEG	AEG	DJ	Comments
1915	6			175 — 200	26	4to				
1925				50 — 75	111	8vo			DJ	
1899			6	100 — 160	323	8vo				Grey Cloth
1907			6	50 — 75	323	8vo				

Hugh Thomson

Title	Author	Publisher	City
Admirable Crichton	Barrie/J.M.	Hodder & Stoughton	Lon
As You Like It	Shakespeare/William	Hodder & Stoughton	Lon
Chimes (The)	Dickens/Charles	Hodder & Stoughton	Lon
Cranford	Gaskell/Elizabeth C.	Macmillan	NY
Emma	Austen/J.	Macmillan	NY
Evelina	Burney	Macmillan	NY
Henry Esmond	Thackeray/William M.	Macmillan	NY
History/Henry Esmond	Thackeray/William M.	Macmillan	Lon
Hugh Thomson: His Art	Spielmann/M.H.	A&C Black	Lon
Jack The Giant Killer	Thomson/Hugh	Macmillan	Lon
Kentucky Cardinal Aftermath	Allen/J.L.	Macmillan	NY
Maid Marian....	Peacock/T.L.	Macmillan	Lon
Mansfield Park	Austen/J.	Macmillan	Lon
Merry Wives Of Windsor	Shakespeare/William	Stokes	NY
Merry Wives Of Windsor	Shakespeare/William	Heinemann	Lon
My Son & I	Spielman/M.H.	G. Allen	Lon
Northanger Abbey	Austin/J.	Macmillan	Lon
Old English Songs		Macmillan	Lon
Our Village	Mitford/M.R.	Macmillan	Lon
Peg Woffington	Reade/C.	G. Allen	Lon
Peg Woffington	Reade/C.	Doubleday	NY
Pied Piper Of Hamelin	Buchanan/R.	Heinemann	Lon
Pride & Prejudice	Austin/J.	G. Allen	Lon
Quality Street	Barrie/J.M	Hodder & Stoughton	Lon
Rainbow Book (The)	Spielmann/Mrs. M.H.	Chatto/Windus	Lon
Rainbow Book (The)	Spielmann/Mrs. M.H.		NY
Scarlet Letter	Hawthorne/Nathaniel	Methuen	Lon
School For Scandal (The)	Sheridan/Richard B.	Hodder & Stoughton	Lon
School For Scandal (The)	Sheridan/Richard B.	Hodder & Stoughton	Lon
Sense & Sensibility	Austen/Jane	Macmillan	NY
She Stoops To Conquer	Goldsmith/Oliver	Hodder & Stoughton	Lon
Story Of Canterbury Pilgrims (The)	Darton/Frederick J.	Stokes	NY
Story Of Rosina	Dobson/A.	Kegan	Lon
Tales From Maria Edgeworth	Edgeworth/Maria	Stokes	NY
This & That	Molesworth/Mrs.	Macmillan	Lon
Tom Brown's School Days	Hughes/Thomas	Ginn	Bos
Vicar Of Wakefield	Goldsmith/Oliver	Macmillan	Lon

(1860-1920) Coleraine, Ireland

Year	Color	Tipped	B&W	Price Range	Pages	Size	TEG	AEG	DJ	Comments
[1914]	21	Ticp		125 — 165	235	4to				
[1909]	40	Ticp		130 — 165	143	4to				
(1920)	7	Ticp		50 — 75		8vo				Red Gilt
				40 — 60						
				50 — 75						
				40 — 60						
				50 — 75						
1905			50	50 — 75				Aeg		
1931	12			85 — 125	269	8vo				
1898	16			160 — 200		8vo				Wraps
1900				60 — 80	276	8vo	Teg			
1895				50 — 75		8vo		Aeg		Blue Bds
				50 — 75						
(1910)	40			100 — 140		4to	Teg			Red Gilt
1910	40	Ticp		120 — 160	172	4to	Teg			
1908			12	50 — 75	307	8vo	Teg			Red Gilt
1897				50 — 75		8vo		Aeg		Red Cloth
1894				50 — 75	163	8vo		Aeg		Green Gilt
1893				50 — 65		8vo		Aeg		Green Gilt
1899				65 — 80	298	12mo		Aeg		Green Gilt
1899				50 — 75	298	12mo		Aeg		Green Gilt
1893			12	50 — 70	64	8vo				
1894				65 — 90	476	8vo		Aeg		Green Gilt
[1913]	22	Ticp		130 — 170	198	4to				Blue Gilt
1909			21	150 — 175	289	8vo	Teg			Red Cloth
			21	125 — 150	289	8vo	Teg			
(1920)	31			150 — 200	296	4to	Teg			
[1911]	25	Ticp		100 — 145	196	4to	Teg			
[1911]	25	Ticp		200 — 300	196	4to				350 Signed By Thomson
				50 — 75						
(1912)	25	Ticp		120 — 160		4to				
				40 — 60						
1895			28	65 — 80	120	8vo		Aeg		
				40 — 60						
1899			8	50 — 65	212	8vo				Orange Cloth
				50 — 75						
1890				75 — 100	305	8vo		Aeg		

Newell Convers (N.C.) Wyeth

Title	Author	Publisher	City
Adventure Of Tom Sawyer (The)	Twain/Mark	Winston	NY
Anthology Of Children's Literature	Johnson /Edna(Ed)	Houghton,Mifflin	Bos
Anthology Of Children's Literature	Johnson /Edna(Ed)	Houghton,Mifflin	Bos
Anthony Adverse	Allen/Hervey	Farrar & Rinehart	NY
Arizona Nights	White/Stewart E.	Grosset&Dunlap	NY
Arizona Nights	White/Stewart E.	McClure	NY
Bar 20	Mulford/C.	A.L. Burt	NY
Bar 20	Mulford/C.	Outing	
Beth Norvell	Parrish/R.	McClurg	Chi
Black Arrow (The)	Stevenson/Robert Louis	Scribner	NY
Black Arrow (The)	Stevenson/Robert Louis	Scribner	NY
Botany Bay	Nordhoff & Hall	Little Brown	NY
Bounty Trilogy	Nordhoff/& Hall	Little Brown	NY
Boy's King Arthur	Lanier/S.	Scribner	NY
Boy's King Arthur	Lanier/S.	Scribner	NY
Boys Of St. Timothy's	Pier/A.S.	Scribner	NY
Cease Firing	Johnston/Mary	Houghton,Mifflin	Bos
Challenge (The)	Cheney/W.	Bobbs-Merrill	Ind
Courtship Of Miles Standish	Longfellow/Henry W.	Houghton,Mifflin	Bos
Crested Seas (The)	Connolly/J.B.	Scribner	NY
David Balfour	Stevenson/Robert Louis	Scribner	NY
David Balfour	Stevenson/Robert Louis	Scribner	NY
Deerslayer (The)	Cooper/James Fenimore	Scribner	NY
Deerslayer (The)	Cooper/James Fenimore	Scribner	NY
Deerslayer (The)	Cooper/James Fenimore	Scribner	NY
Deerslayer (The)	Cooper/James Fenimore	Scribner	NY
Drums	Boyd/J.	Scribner	NY
Drums	Boyd/James	Scribner	NY
Drums	Boyd/James	Scribner	NY
Even Unto Bethlehem	Van Dyke/Henry	Scribner	NY
Hiawatha	Longfellow/Henry W.	Harrap	Lon
Jinglebob	Rollins/P.A.	Scribner	NY
Kidnapped	Stevenson/Robert Louis	Scribner	NY
Kidnapped	Stevenson/Robert Louis	Scribner	NY
Kidnapped	Stevenson/Robert Louis	Scribner	NY
Langford Of The Three Bars	Boyles/K.	McClurg	Chi
Last Of The Mohicans	Cooper/James Fenimore	Scribner	NY
Last Of The Mohicans	Cooper/James Fenimore	Scribner	NY
Legends Of Charlemagne	Bullfinch/Thomas	Cosmopolitan	NY
Letters Of A Woman Homesteader	Stewart/E.P.	Houghton,Mifflin	Bos
Little Shepherd Of Kingdom Come (The)	Fox/John	Scribner	NY
Little Shepherd Of Kingdom Come (The)	Fox/John	Scribner	NY

(1882-1945) Needham, Ma.

Year	Color	Tipped	B&W	Price Range	Pages	Size	TEG	AEG	DJ	Comments
1931	1			25 — 50		8vo				Ill By Hurd
1940	15			125 — 150		8vo			DJ	
1948	4			50 — 100	1114	8vo			DJ	
1934	2			75 — 100	1224	8vo				2 Volumes Green/Gilt
(1907)				10 — 20	351	12mo				
1907	7			50 — 75	351	8vo				
(1907)				10 — 20	382	12mo				
1907			2	25 — 45	382	8vo				
1907				25 — 40	341	8vo				
1916	14			150 — 175	328	4to	Teg			
1927	10			60 — 90	328	4to			DJ	
1941	1			100 — 150		8vo			DJ	
1940	12			150 — 200	903	8vo			DJ	
1917	14			125 — 150	321	4to	Teg			
1926	14			50 — 75	321	4to				
1904			3	50 — 75	284	12mo				
1912	4			20 — 35	457	8vo				
(1906)			4	20 — 35	386	12mo				Red Cloth
1920	8			100 — 150	148	4to				
1907			2	20 — 40	311	8vo	Teg			
1924	12			100 — 150	356	4to				
1927	12			45 — 75						
1925	12			100 — 150	462	4to				
1925	12			100 — 150	462	4to				
1927	9			45 — 75	462	4to				
1929	10			20 — 50					DJ	
1928	17			100 — 150	409	4to				
1928	17			500 — 750	409	4to			DJ	525 Signed By Wyeth & Boyd
1930	17			50 — 75	409	4to			DJ	
1928	1			30 — 50	101	8vo				Blue/Gilt
[1911]	1			175 — 225		4to				Cover By Parrish
1930	7			100 — 150	263	4to				
(1941)				35 — 50		4to			DJ	
1913	14			150 — 200	289	4to	Teg			
1940				40 — 65		4to				
1907	4			40 — 60	278	8vo				
1919	14			150 — 175	370	4to				
1925				50 — 75		4to				
1924	8			125 — 200	273	4to	Teg			Maroon Cloth
1914			6	40 — 60	282	12mo				
1931	14			125 — 175	322	4to				
1931	16	Ticp		500 — 750	322	4to				512 Signed By Wyeth

Newell Convers (N.C.) Wyeth

Title	Author	Publisher	City
Long Roll (The)	Johnston/Mary	Houghton,Mifflin	Bos
Long Roll (The)	Johnston/Mary	Houghton,Mifflin	Bos
Lost Boy (The)	Van Dyke/Henry	Harper	NY
Men Of Concord	Thoreau/Henry D.	Houghton,Mifflin	Bos
Michael Strogoff	Verne/Jules	Scribner	NY
Militants (The)	Andrews/M.S.	Scribner	NY
My Country	Turkington/Grace	Ginn	Bos
Mysterious Island	Verne/Jules	Scribner	NY
Mysterious Island	Verne/Jules	Scribner	NY
Mysterious Stranger (The)	Twain/Mark	Harper	NY
Mysterious Stranger (The)	Twain/Mark	Harper	NY
Nan Of Music Mountain	Spearman/Frank	Grosset&Dunlap	NY
Nan Of Music Mountain	Spearman/Frank	Scribner	NY
Odyssey Of Homer	Palmer.George H.	Houghton,Mifflin	Bos
Oregon Trail	Parkman/Francis	Little Brown	Bos
Parables Of Jesus	Cadman/S.P.	McKay	Phi
Pike County Ballads (The)	Hay/John	Houghton,Mifflin	Bos
Poems Of American Patriotism	Matthews/B.	Scribner	NY
Ramona	Jackson/Helen Hunt	Little Brown	Bos
Rip Van Winkle	Irving/Washington	McKay	Phi
Rip Van Winkle	Irving/Washington	McKay	Phi
Riverman (The)	White/S.E.	McClure	NY
Robin Hood		McKay	Phi
Robinson Crusoe	Defoe/Daniel	Cosmopolitan	NY
Sally Castleton/Southerner	Marriott/C.	Lippincott	Phi
Sampo (The)	Baldwin/J.	Scribner	NY
Scottish Chiefs	Wiggin/Kate Douglas	Scribner	NY
Scottish Chiefs	Wiggin/Kate Douglas	Scribner	NY
Song Of Hiawatha	Longfellow/Henry W.	Houghton,Mifflin	Bos
Susanna & Sue	Wiggin/Kate Douglas	Houghton,Mifflin	Bos
Throwback (The)	Lewis/A.H.	Outing	
Treasure Island	Stevenson/Robert Louis	Scribner	NY
Treasure Island	Stevenson/Robert Louis	Scribner	NY
Trending Into Maine	Roberts/Kenneth	Little Brown	Bos
Vandermark's Folly	Quick/H.	Bobbs-Merrill	Ind
War	Long/John L.	Bobbs-Merrill	Ind
Westward Ho	Kingsley/Charles	Scribner	NY
Westward Ho	Kingsley/Charles	Scribner	NY
Westward Ho	Kingsley/Charles	Scribner	NY
Westward Ho	Kingsley/Charles	Scribner	NY
Whispering Smith	Spearman/Frank	Scribner	NY
Whispering Smith	Spearman/Frank	Scribner	NY

(1882-1945) Needham, Ma.

Year	Color	Tipped	B&W	Price Range	Pages	Size	TEG	AEG	DJ	Comments
1911	4			20 — 30	683	8vo				
1911	4			20 — 40	683	8vo				Grey Cloth
(1914)				20 — 30		8vo	Teg		DJ	
1936	10			175 — 225	255	4to			DJ	Green/Silver
1927	9			150 — 200	397	4to				
1907			2	25 — 40	379	12mo	Teg			
1923	1			15 — 25						
1918	14			175 — 225	493	4to				
1946	9			30 — 50		4to				
(1916)	7			100 — 150	151	4to	Teg			
(1916)	7			75 — 100	151	4to	Teg			1920 Reprint
(1916)				15 — 25		8vo				
1916	4			20 — 40	430	8vo				Green Cloth
1929	16			150 — 200	314	4to				Red Cloth
1925	5			75 — 100	364	8vo				
1931	8			300 — 400	163	4to				Purple Cloth
(1912)	6			75 — 125	47	8vo				
1922	14			175 — 225		8vo				
1945	4			35 — 50		8vo				
(1921)	8			100 — 150	86	8vo	Teg		DJ	
(1921)	8			75 — 100	86	8vo			DJ	Latter State Top Edge Not Gilt
1908			12	40 — 60	368	8vo				
1917	8			75 — 125	362	8vo	Teg			
1920	13			125 — 150	368	4to	Teg			
1913			6	25 — 50	312					
1912	4			40 — 60	368	8vo				Green Cloth
1921	17			125 — 175	503	4to				
1934	9			65 — 85	503	4to				
1911				200 — 350	242	8vo	Teg			Red Cloth
1909			1	40 — 60	225	8vo	Teg			
1906	4			35 — 50	347	12mo				Green Cloth
(1939)	9			50 — 75	251	4to				
1911	14			175 — 225	273	4to	Teg			
1938	14			75 — 100		8vo				
(1922)				20 — 40	420	12mo				
(1913)	4			50 — 75	371	12				Red Cloth
(1948)	14			20 — 35		4to			DJ	
1920	14			75 — 150	413	4to				
1935	10			30 — 50		4to				
1947				20 — 50					DJ	
1906	4			35 — 55	421	12mo				Red Cloth
1908				15 — 25	421	12mo				

Newell Convers (N.C.) Wyeth

Title	Author	Publisher	City
Whispering Smith	Spearman/Frank	Grosset&Dunlap	NY
White Company (The)	Doyle/Arthur C.	Cosmopolitan	NY
Yearling (The)	Rawlings/M.K.	Scribner	NY
Yearling (The)	Rawlings/M.K.	Scribner	NY
Yearling (The)	Rawlings/M.K.	Scribner	NY
Yearling (The)	Rawlings/M.K.	Scribner	NY

(1882-1945) Needham, Ma.

Year	Color	Tipped	B&W	Price Range	Pages	Size	TEG	AEG	DJ	Comments
				15 — 25						
1922	13			175 — 225	363	4to	Teg			
1938	14			100 — 150	400	4to			DJ	
1940	14			75 — 100	400	4to			DJ	
1942	5			50 — 75	400	4to				
1945	12			25 — 50	400	4to			DJ	Black Cloth

John Neill from Sunny Bunny

*W.W. Denslow from
Denslow's Night Before Christmas*

John Rae from American Indian Fairy Tales

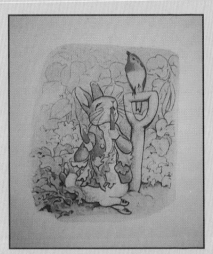

Beatrix Potter from Tale of Peter Rabbit

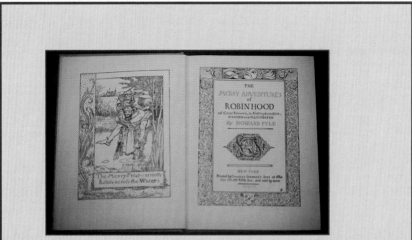

Howard Pyle from the Merry Adventures of Robin Hood

Maxfield Parrish from King Albert's Book

Will Pogany from The Children of Odin

Kate Greenaway from
A Day In A Child's Life

H.J. Ford from The Lilac Fairy Book

N.C. Wyeth from Even Unto Bethlehem

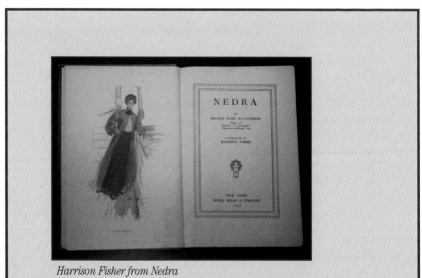

Harrison Fisher from Nedra

Maud Humphrey from Prince & Fido

Walter Crane from Don Quixote

*Jessie Wilcox Smith from
A Child's Garden of Verses*

LISTINGS BY TITLE

Listings By Title

Title	Illustrator
20 Years Of Hus'ling	Denslow/W.W.
44 Turkish Tales	Pogany/Will
80 Drawings Of The Weaker Sex	Gibson/Charles D.

A

A Apple Pie	Greenaway/Kate
A Apple Pie	Greenaway/Kate
A Apple Pie	Greenaway/Kate
About Paris	Gibson/Charles D.
Abraham Lincoln	Pyle/Howard
Absurd Abc (The)	Crane/Walter
Admirable Crichton	Thomson/Hugh
Adv.Of A Brownie/Swiss Family Robinson	Neill/John R.
Adventure Of Tom Sawyer (The)	Wyeth/N.C.
Adventures Of A Brownie (The)	Neill/John R.
Adventures Of A Brownie (The)	Neill/John R.
Adventures Of A Dodo	Pogany/Will
Adventures Of Her Baby (The)	Crane/Walter
Adventures Of Her Baby (The)	Crane/Walter
Adventures Of Odysseus	Pogany/Will
Adventures Of Odysseus	Pogany/Will
Aesop's Fables	Rackham/Arthur
Aesop's Fables	Rackham/Arthur
Aesop's Fables	Rackham/Arthur
Aesop's Fables	Rackham/Arthur
Aesop's Fables	Rackham/Arthur
Aesop's Fables For Little Readers	Ford/H.J.
Afield & Afloat	Newell/Peter
Aladdin & The Wonderful Lamp/Robin Hood	Neill/John R.
Aladdin's Picture Book	Crane/Walter
Alice In Wonderland	Gutmann/Bessie Pease
Alice In Wonderland	Gutmann/Bessie Pease
Alice In Wonderland	Gutmann/Bessie Pease
Alice In Wonderland/Through The Looking Glass	Neill/John R.
Alice's Adventures In Wonderland	Neill/John R.
Alice's Adventures In Wonderland	Newell/Peter
Alice's Adventures In Wonderland	Newell/Peter
Alice's Adventures In Wonderland	Rackham/Arthur
Alice's Adventures In Wonderland	Rackham/Arthur
Alice's Adventures In Wonderland	Rackham/Arthur
Alice's Adventures In Wonderland	Rackham/Arthur
Alice/Wonderland	Pogany/Will

LISTINGS BY TITLE

Author	Publisher	Year	Price Range
Johnson	Thompson	1900	100 — 150
Kunos/I.	Harrap	(1913)	150 — 200
Gibson/Charles D.	Scribner	1903	100 — 150
Greenaway/Kate	Routledge	[1886]	200 — 250
Greenaway/Kate	Warne	[1890]	75 — 100
Greenaway/Kate	Saalfield	1907	75 — 100
Davis/Richard Harding	Harper	1895	20 — 30
Coffin/Charles C.	Harper	1893	30 — 50
	Routledge	[1870]	250 — 350
Barrie/J.M.	Hodder & Stoughton	[1914]	125 — 165
	Reilly & Britton	(1908)	75 — 100
Twain/Mark	Winston	1931	25 — 50
	Reilly & Britton	(1908)	75 — 100
	Reilly & Britton	(1912)	40 — 75
Farrow/G.E.	Unwin	(1907)	150 — 200
Molesworth/Mrs.	Macmillan	1881	150 — 175
Molesworth/Mrs.	Macmillan	1886	100 — 125
Colum/Pedraic	Macmillan	(1927)	25 — 50
Colum/Pedraic	Macmillan	1918	50 — 75
Aesop	Heinemann	1912	225 — 300
Aesop	Heinemann	1912	800 — 1200
Aesop	Doubleday,Page	1912	175 — 225
Aesop	Bell & Cockburn	1912	150 — 175
Aesop	Doubleday	1926	50 — 100
Freshfield/Mrs. Arthur	Unwin	[1888]	150 — 200
Stockton/F.	Scribner	1900	40 — 60
	Reilly & Britton	(1908)	75 — 100
Crane/Walter	Routledge	(1875)	125 — 150
Carroll/Lewis	Dodge	(1907)	150 — 200
Carroll/Lewis	Coker	[1915]	100 — 150
Carroll/Lewis	Lippincott	1923	150 — 200
	Reilly & Britton	(1908)	100 — 125
	Reilly & Britton	(1908)	100 — 125
Carroll/Lewis	Harper	(1901)	125 — 150
Carroll/Lewis	Harper	(1901)	30 — 50
Carroll/Lewis	Heinemann	[1907]	500 — 700
Carroll/Lewis	Heinemann	[1907]	150 — 200
Carroll/Lewis	Doubleday	[1907]	125 — 175
Carroll/Lewis	Doubleday	[1907]	400 — 600
Carroll/Lewis	Dutton	(1929)	100 — 150

LISTINGS BY TITLE

Title	Illustrator
All About Cinderella	Gruelle/Johnny
All About Cinderella	Gruelle/Johnny
All About Hansel & Gretel	Gruelle/Johnny
All About Hansel & Gretel	Gruelle/Johnny
All About Little Black Sambo	Gruelle/Johnny
All About Little Black Sambo	Gruelle/Johnny
All About Little Red Hen	Gruelle/Johnny
All About Little Red Hen	Gruelle/Johnny
All About Little Red Riding Hood	Gruelle/Johnny
All About Little Red Riding Hood	Gruelle/Johnny
All About Mother Goose	Gruelle/Johnny
All About Mother Goose	Gruelle/Johnny
All About Story Book (The)	Gruelle/Johnny
All Sorts Of Stories Book (The)	Ford/H.J.
Allies' Fairy Book (The)	Rackham/Arthur
Allies' Fairy Book (The)	Rackham/Arthur
Allies' Fairy Book (The)	Rackham/Arthur
Allies' Fairy Book (The)	Rackham/Arthur
Almanack And Diary For 1929	Greenaway/Kate
Almanack For 1883	Greenaway/Kate
Almanack For 1884	Greenaway/Kate
Almanack For 1885	Greenaway/Kate
Almanack For 1886	Greenaway/Kate
Almanack For 1887	Greenaway/Kate
Almanack For 1888	Greenaway/Kate
Almanack For 1889	Greenaway/Kate
Almanack For 1890	Greenaway/Kate
Almanack For 1891	Greenaway/Kate
Almanack For 1892	Greenaway/Kate
Almanack For 1893	Greenaway/Kate
Almanack For 1894	Greenaway/Kate
Almanack For 1895	Greenaway/Kate
Almanack For 1897	Greenaway/Kate
Almanack For 1924	Greenaway/Kate
Almanack For 1925	Greenaway/Kate
Almanack For 1926	Greenaway/Kate
Almanack For 1927	Greenaway/Kate
Alternative (The)	Fisher/Harrison
Amateur Theatricals	Greenaway/Kate
American Art By American Authors	Pyle/Howard
American Beauties	Fisher/Harrison
American Beauties	Fisher/Harrison

LISTINGS BY TITLE

Author	Publisher	Year	Price Range
Gruelle/Johnny	Cupples & Leon	(1916)	75 — 125
Gruelle/Johnny	Cupples & Leon	(1929)	25 — 35
	Cupples & Leon	(1917)	75 — 125
	Cupples & Leon	(1929)	25 — 35
Bannerman/Helen	Cupples & Leon	(1917)	125 — 175
Bannerman/Helen	Cupples & Leon	(1929)	50 — 75
	Cupples & Leon	(1917)	75 — 125
	Cupples & Leon	(1929)	25 — 35
Gruelle/Johnny	Cupples & Leon	(1916)	75 — 100
Gruelle/Johnny	Cupples & Leon	(1929)	25 — 35
	Cupples & Leon	(1916)	75 — 125
	Cupples & Leon	(1929)	25 — 35
	Cupples & Leon	(1929)	100 — 150
Lang/L.B.	Longmans	1911	100 — 150
Gosse/Edmund	Heinemann	(1916)	850 — 1250
Gosse/Edmund	Heinemann	(1918)	100 — 125
Gosse/Edmund	Heinemann	[1916]	175 — 275
Gosse/Edmund	Lippincott	[1916]	125 — 225
	Warne	1929	100 — 150
	Routledge	1883	100 — 150
Greenaway/Kate	Routledge	1884	100 — 150
Greenaway/Kate	Routledge	1885	100 — 150
Greenaway/Kate	Routledge	1886	100 — 150
Greenaway/Kate	Routledge	1887	100 — 150
Greenaway/Kate	Routledge	1888	100 — 150
Greenaway/Kate	Routledge	1889	100 — 150
Greenaway/Kate	Routledge	1890	100 — 150
Greenaway/Kate	Routledge	1891	100 — 150
Greenaway/Kate	Routledge	1892	100 — 150
Greenaway/Kate	Routledge	1893	100 — 150
Greenaway/Kate	Routledge	1894	100 — 150
Greenaway/Kate	Routledge	1895	100 — 150
Greenaway/Kate	Dent	1897	100 — 150
	Warne	1924	100 — 150
	Warne	1925	100 — 150
	Warne	1926	100 — 150
	Warne	1927	100 — 150
McCutcheon/George	Dodd	1909	20 — 30
Pollock/Walter H.	Macmillan	1879	100 — 150
	Collier	1915	40 — 60
Fisher/Harrison	Bobbs-Merrill	(1909)	200 — 250
Fisher/Harrison	Grosset&Dunlap	(1909)	150 — 200

137

LISTINGS BY TITLE

Title	Illustrator
American Belles	Fisher/Harrison
American Girl	Fisher/Harrison
American Girl (The)	Christy/Howard Chandler
American Illustrators	Pyle/Howard
American Indian Fairy Tales	Rae/John
American Indian Fairy Tales	Rae/John
American Pictures & Painters	Parrish/Maxfield
Americans	Gibson/Charles D.
An Artist's Reminiscences	Crane/Walter
An Old Fashioned Story	Crane/Walter
An Old Sweetheart Of Mine	Christy/Howard Chandler
An Old Sweetheart Of Mine	Christy/Howard Chandler
An Old Sweetheart Of Mine	Christy/Howard Chandler
An Old-Fashioned Girl	Smith/Jessie Wilcox
An Old-Fashioned Girl	Smith/Jessie Wilcox
An Old-Fashioned Girl	Smith/Jessie Wilcox
An Old-Fashioned Girl	Smith/Jessie Wilcox
Anderson's Fairy Tales	Neill/John R.
Anderson's Fairy Tales;The Ugly Duckling	Neill/John R.
Animal Story Book (The)	Ford/H.J.
Ann & Other Poems	Greenaway/Kate
Annie & Jack In London	Crane/Walter
Annual Of Advertising Art	Parrish/Maxfield
Annual Of Advertising Art	Parrish/Maxfield
Annual Of Advertising Art	Parrish/Maxfield
Annual Of Advertising Art	Parrish/Maxfield
Another Brownie Book	Cox/Palmer
Another Brownie Book	Cox/Palmer
Anthology Of Children's Literature	Wyeth/N.C.
Anthology Of Children's Literature	Wyeth/N.C.
Anthony Adverse	Wyeth/N.C.
Appley Dapply's Nursery Rhymes	Potter/Beatrix
Appley Dapply's Nursery Rhymes	Potter/Beatrix
Appley Dapply's Nursery Rhymes	Potter/Beatrix
April Baby's Book Of Tunes (The)	Greenaway/Kate
April Baby's Book Of Tunes (The)	Greenaway/Kate
Arabian Nights (The)	Parrish/Maxfield
Arabian Nights (The)	Parrish/Maxfield
Arabian Nights (The)	Parrish/Maxfield
Arabian Nights (The)	Parrish/Maxfield
Arabian Nights Entertainments (The)	Ford/H.J.
Argonauts Of The Amazon (The)	Rackham/Arthur

LISTINGS BY TITLE

Author	Publisher	Year	Price Range
Fisher/Harrison	Dodd	1911	200 — 250
Fisher/Harrison	Scribner	1909	250 — 350
Christy/Howard Chandler	Moffat	1906	100 — 150
Smith/F. Hopkinson	Scribner	1892	75 — 100
Larned/W.T.	Volland	(1921)	75 — 100
Larned/W.T.	Wise-Parslow	(1935)	35 — 50
Bryant/Lorinda M.	J. Lane	1917	40 — 80
Gibson/Charles D.	Russell	1903	75 — 100
Crane/Walter	Methuen		100 — 150
Molesworth/Mrs.	Macmillan	1923	25 — 35
Riley/James W.	Bobbs-Merrill	(1902)	25 — 50
Riley/James W.	Bobbs-Merrill	(1902)	250 — 350
Riley/James W.	Grosset&Dunlap	(1902)	15 — 25
Alcott/Louisa May	Little Brown	1902	100 — 150
Alcott/Louisa May	Little Brown	1904	75 — 100
Alcott/Louisa May	Sampson.Low	1907	75 — 100
Alcott/Louisa May	Little Brown	1915	85 — 100
	Cupples & Leon	1923	40 — 60
	Reilly & Britton	(1908)	75 — 100
Lang/Andrew	Longmans	1896	100 — 150
Taylor/Jane	Routledge	[1882]	200 — 225
	Routledge	[1860]	40 — 60
	Publishers Printing Co.	1921	50 — 75
	Publishers Printing Co.	1923	40 — 60
	Publishers Printing Co.	1924	40 — 60
	Publishers Printing Co.	1925	40 — 60
Cox/Palmer	Unwin	(1890)	175 — 225
Cox/Palmer	Century	(1890)	175 — 225
Johnson /Edna(Ed)	Houghton,Mifflin	1940	125 — 150
Johnson /Edna(Ed)	Houghton,Mifflin	1948	50 — 100
Allen/Hervey	Farrar & Rinehart	1934	75 — 100
Potter/Beatrix	Warne	(1917)	50 — 75
Potter/Beatrix	Warne	[1917]	300 — 400
Potter/Beatrix	Warne	[1919]	150 — 200
Russell/Mary	Macmillan	1900	175 — 225
	Macmillan	1900	150 — 200
Wiggin/Kate Douglas (Ed)	Scribner	(1937)	50 — 90
Wiggin/Kate Douglas (Ed)	Scribner	1909	125 — 200
Wiggin/Kate Douglas (Ed)	Scribner	1919	100 — 175
Wiggin/Kate Douglas (Ed)	Scribner	1935	50 — 90
Lang/Andrew	Longmans	1898	150 — 175
Kenyon/C.R.	W.R. Chambers	1901	175 — 250

LISTINGS BY TITLE

Title	Illustrator
Argonauts Of The Amazon (The)	Rackham/Arthur
Arizona Nights	Wyeth/N.C.
Arizona Nights	Wyeth/N.C.
Arkansas Planter	Denslow/W.W.
Around Old Chester	Pyle/Howard
Around The House	Greenaway/Kate
Art & Formation Of Taste	Crane/Walter
Art In America	Pyle/Howard
Art Of Pen Drawing (The)	Rackham/Arthur
Art Of The American Wood Engraver (The)	Pyle/Howard
Art Of Walter Crane	Crane/Walter
Art Stories - Book One	Smith/Jessie Wilcox
Art Year Book	Pyle/Howard
Arthur Rackham A Bibliography	Rackham/Arthur
Arthur Rackham A Bibliography	Rackham/Arthur
Arthur Rackham Fairy Book (The)	Rackham/Arthur
Arthur Rackham Fairy Book (The)	Rackham/Arthur
Arthur Rackham Fairy Book (The)	Rackham/Arthur
Arthur Rackham's Book Of Pictures	Rackham/Arthur
Arthur Rackham's Book Of Pictures	Rackham/Arthur
Arthur Rackham's Book Of Pictures	Rackham/Arthur
Arthur Rackham's Book Of Pictures	Rackham/Arthur
As You Like It	Thomson/Hugh
At The Back Of The North Wind	Smith/Jessie Wilcox
At The Back Of The North Wind	Smith/Jessie Wilcox
Atta Troll	Pogany/Will
Atta Troll	Pogany/Will
Auld Acquaintance	Rackham/Arthur
Aunt Louisa's	Greenaway/Kate
Autocrat At The Breakfast Table (The)	Pyle/Howard
Autumn Song With Music	Barker/Cicely Mary
Autumn Song With Music	Barker/Cicely Mary

B

Title	Illustrator
Babes Of The Nations	Humphrey/Maud
Babes Of The Year	Humphrey/Maud
Baby Sweethearts	Humphrey/Maud
Baby's Birthday Book	Greenaway/Kate
Baby's Bouquet	Crane/Walter
Baby's Bouquet	Crane/Walter
Baby's Opera	Crane/Walter
Baby's Opera	Crane/Walter

Listings By Title

Author	Publisher	Year	Price Range
Kenyon/C.R.	Dutton	1901	125 — 175
White/Stewart E.	Grosset&Dunlap	(1907)	10 — 20
White/Stewart E.	McClure	1907	50 — 75
Read/Opie	Rand Mcnally	(1896)	75 — 100
Deland/Margaret	Harper	1915	20 — 30
	Worthington	1888	100 — 125
Crane/Walter & Lucy	Macmillan	1882	125 — 175
Benjamin/S.G.W.	Harper	1880	75 — 100
Montague/G.	B.T. Batsford	(1927)	50 — 75
Hamerton/Philip	Scribner	1894	50 — 75
Konody/P.G.	G. Bell	1902	300 — 400
Whitford/William G.	Scott,Foresman	[1933]	35 — 50
	New England Institute	1884	100 — 150
Latimore/Sarah B.	Suttonhouse	1936	100 — 150
Latimore/Sarah B.	Suttonhouse	1936	50 — 75
Rackham/Arthur	Harrap	(1933)	175 — 250
Rackham/Arthur	Lippincott	(1933)	100 — 150
Rackham/Arthur	Harrap	1933	1000 — 1500
Rackham/Arthur	Heinemann	(1913)	300 — 400
Rackham/Arthur	Heinemann	(1913)	750 — 1000
Rackham/Arthur	Century	(1913)	175 — 250
Rackham/Arthur	Heinemann		100 — 150
Shakespeare/William	Hodder & Stoughton	[1909]	130 — 165
MacDonald/George	McKay	(1919)	100 — 150
MacDonald/George	McKay	1919	125 — 175
Heine/H.	Sidgwick	1913	90 — 130
Heine/H.	Huebsch	1914	75 — 100
Savory/Harry	Dent	1907	75 — 100
	Warne	[1871]	150 — 250
Holmes/Oliver W.	Houghton,Mifflin	1894	125 — 150
Linnell/Olive	Blackie & Sons	[1920]	75 — 125
Linnell/Olive	Blackie & Sons	[1930]	50 — 75
Thomas/Edith M.	Stokes	1889	400 — 600
Humphrey/Maud	Stokes	1888	300 — 500
Cone/H.G.	Stokes	1890	400 — 600
	Marcus Ward		125 — 150
Crane/Walter	Routledge	[1878]	200 — 250
Crane/Walter	Warne	[1890]	50 — 100
Crane/Walter	Routledge	[1877]	175 — 225
Crane/Walter	Warne	1900	100 — 125

LISTINGS BY TITLE

Title	Illustrator
Baby's Own Aesop	Crane/Walter
Baby's Own Aesop	Crane/Walter
Baby's Record	Humphrey/Maud
Baby's Red Letter Days	Smith/Jessie Wilcox
Baby's Red Letter Days	Smith/Jessie Wilcox
Bachelor Belles	Fisher/Harrison
Bachelor Belles	Fisher/Harrison
Bam Bam Clock	Gruelle/Johnny
Bam Bam Clock	Gruelle/Johnny
Bar 20	Wyeth/N.C.
Bar 20	Wyeth/N.C.
Bases Of Design	Crane/Walter
Beauties	Fisher/Harrison
Bed-Time Book (The)	Smith/Jessie Wilcox
Bed-Time Book (The)	Smith/Jessie Wilcox
Bee-Blowaways (The)	Rackham/Arthur
Bells & Other Poems	Dulac/Edmund
Bells (The)	Dulac/Edmund
Beloved Belindy	Gruelle/Johnny
Beloved Belindy	Gruelle/Johnny
Beloved Belindy	Gruelle/Johnny
Beloved Belindy	Gruelle/Johnny
Ben King's Verse	Denslow/W.W.
Beth Norvell	Wyeth/N.C.
Beverly Of Graustark	Fisher/Harrison
Beverly Of Graustark	Fisher/Harrison
Bible Stories/Read And Tell	Pogany/Will
Bibliomanis Or Book Madness	Pyle/Howard
Big Family (The)	Rae/John
Bikey The Skycycle	Newell/Peter
Billy Bounce	Denslow/W.W.
Billy Boy	Smith/Jessie Wilcox
Billy Boy	Smith/Jessie Wilcox
Biography Of A Boy	O'neill/Rose
Biography Of Our Baby	Gutmann/Bessie Pease
Birthday Book For Children	Greenaway/Kate
Birthday Book For Children	Greenaway/Kate
Black Arrow (The)	Wyeth/N.C.
Black Arrow (The)	Wyeth/N.C.
Black Beauty	Neill/John R.
Black Beauty	Neill/John R.
Black Beauty/Little Lame Prince	Neill/John R.

LISTINGS BY TITLE

Author	Publisher	Year	Price Range
Crane/Walter	Routledge	1887	125 — 150
Crane/Walter	Warne		75 — 100
	Stokes	1898	350 — 500
Smith/Jessie Wilcox	Just Foods	(1906)	100 — 200
Smith/Jessie Wilcox	Just Foods	[1901]	200 — 300
Fisher/Harrison	Grosset&Dunlap	(1908)	50 — 75
Fisher/Harrison	Dodd	1908	175 — 225
McEvoy/J.P.	Volland	(1920)	75 — 100
McEvoy/J.P.	Algonquin	(1936)	35 — 50
Mulford/C.	A.L. Burt	(1907)	10 — 20
Mulford/C.	Outing	1907	25 — 45
Crane/Walter	G. Bell	1898	150 — 200
Wells/Carolyn	Dodd	1913	225 — 300
Whitney/Helen H.	Chatto/Windus	1907	225 — 275
Whitney/Helen H.	Duffield	1907	225 — 275
Herbertson/Agnes Grozier	Cassell	[1900]	100 — 150
Poe/Edgar Allen	Hodder & Stoughton		200 — 400
Poe/Edgar Allan	Hodder & Stoughton	(1912)	250 — 300
Gruelle/Johnny	Donohue	(1926)	50 — 75
Gruelle/Johnny	Volland	(1926)	150 — 200
Gruelle/Johnny	Volland	(1926)	100 — 150
Gruelle/Johnny	Johnny Gruelle Co.	(1940)	50 — 75
Waterman (Ed)		1894	75 — 100
Parrish/R.	McClurg	1907	25 — 40
McCutcheon/George	Dodd	1904	15 — 30
McCutcheon/George	Dodd	1906	10 — 25
Olcott/F.J.	Houghton,Mifflin	1916	50 — 75
Dibdin/Thomas F.	Bibliophile Society	1903	50 — 75
Rae/John	Dodd	1916	50 — 75
Bangs/John K.	Riggs	1902	35 — 50
Denslow/W.W.	Dillingham	(1906)	300 — 400
Long/John L.	Dodd	(1906)	100 — 150
Long/John L.	Dodd	1906	150 — 200
Bacon/J.D.	Harper	1910	50 — 75
Cooke/E.V.	Dodge	(1906)	175 — 225
Barker/Mrs. S.	Routledge	[1880]	200 — 275
Barker/Mrs. S.	Warne	[1900]	100 — 125
Stevenson/Robert Louis	Scribner	1916	150 — 175
Stevenson/Robert Louis	Scribner	1927	60 — 90
	Reilly & Britton	(1908)	75 — 100
Sewell/Anna	Reilly & Britton	1908	50 — 75
	Reilly & Britton	(1908)	75 — 100

LISTINGS BY TITLE

Title	Illustrator
Black Friday	Fisher/Harrison
Blue Beard's Picture Book	Crane/Walter
Blue Fairy Book (The)	Ford/H.J.
Blue Fairy Book (The)	Ford/H.J.
Blue Fairy Book (The)	Ford/H.J.
Blue Flower (The)	Pyle/Howard
Blue Flower (The)	Pyle/Howard
Blue Lagoon	Pogany/Will
Blue Poetry Book (The)	Ford/H.J.
Bobs, King Of The Fortunate Isle	Smith/Jessie Wilcox
Bolanyo	Parrish/Maxfield
Bonnie Little People	Humphrey/Maud
Book Of American Spirit	Pyle/Howard
Book Of American Spirit	Pyle/Howard
Book Of Betty Barber (The)	Rackham/Arthur
Book Of Betty Barber (The)	Rackham/Arthur
Book Of Christmas Verse	Crane/Walter
Book Of Christmas Verse	Crane/Walter
Book Of Clever Beasts (The)	Newell/Peter
Book Of Fairy Tales	Humphrey/Maud
Book Of Flower Fairies	Barker/Cicely Mary
Book Of Flower Fairies	Barker/Cicely Mary
Book Of Lullabies (A)	Smith/Jessie Wilcox
Book Of Pets	Humphrey/Maud
Book Of Pirates	Pyle/Howard
Book Of Pirates	Pyle/Howard
Book Of Princes & Princesses (The)	Ford/H.J.
Book Of Princes & Princesses (The)	Ford/H.J.
Book Of Queen's Doll House	Rackham/Arthur
Book Of Queen's Doll House	Rackham/Arthur
Book Of Romance (The)	Ford/H.J.
Book Of Saints & Heroes (The)	Ford/H.J.
Book Of The Child (The)	Smith/Jessie Wilcox
Book Of The Ocean (The)	Pyle/Howard
Book Of The Titmarsh Club (The)	Rackham/Arthur
Book Of Wedding Days	Crane/Walter
Booming Of Acre Hill	Gibson/Charles D.
Boss Of The Little Arcady	O'Neill/Rose
Botany Bay	Wyeth/N.C.
Bounty Trilogy	Wyeth/N.C.
Boy's King Arthur	Wyeth/N.C.
Boy's King Arthur	Wyeth/N.C.

LISTINGS BY TITLE

Author	Publisher	Year	Price Range
Isham/F.S.	Bobbs-Merrill	(1904)	25 — 30
Crane/Walter	Routledge	1875	150 — 200
Lang/Andrew	Longmans	1890	50 — 100
Lang/Andrew	Longmans	1903	50 — 100
Lang/Andrew	Longmans		150 — 200
Van Dyke/Henry	Scribner	1902	25 — 50
Van Dyke/Henry	Scribner	1909	15 — 25
Stacpoole/H.	Unwin	1910	150 — 180
Lang/Andrew	Longmans	1891	150 — 200
Franchot/Annie W.	Dutton	(1928)	50 — 75
Read/Opie	Way/Williams	1897	150 — 200
Cone/H.G.	Stokes	1890	400 — 550
Pyle/Howard	Harper	(1923)	100 — 125
Pyle/Howard	Harper	1923	140 — 185
Brown/Maggie	Duckworth	(1910)	250 — 350
Brown/Maggie	Badger	[1910]	250 — 350
Beeching/H.C.	Methuen	1895	75 — 100
Beeching/H.C.	Methuen	1895	300 — 500
Reed/M.	Putnam	1904	50 — 75
Humphrey/Maud	Stokes	1892	500 — 700
Barker/Cicely Mary	Blackie & Sons	[1927]	150 — 250
Barker/Cicely Mary	Blackie & Sons	[1940]	50 — 75
Smith/Elva S.	Lothrop	(1925)	25 — 50
Tucker/E.S.	Gardner	1897	400 — 600
Pyle/Howard	Harper	(1921)	50 — 75
Pyle/Howard	Harper	1921	150 — 185
Lang/Mrs.	Longmans	1908	175 — 225
Lang/Mrs.	Longmans	1908	125 — 150
Benson/A.C.	Methuen	(1924)	50 — 75
Benson/A.C.	Methuen	(1924)	150 — 200
Lang/Andrew	Longmans	1902	175 — 225
Lang/Mrs.	Longmans	1912	150 — 175
Humphrey/Mabel	Stokes	(1903)	600 — 750
Ingersoll/Ernest	Century	1898	50 — 75
Rhys/Ernest	J. Davy	1925	125 — 175
Reid/K.E.J.	Longmans	1889	250 — 300
Bangs/John K.	Harper	1900	20 — 30
Wilson/H.	L.L. & S.	1905	30 — 50
Nordhoff & Hall	Little Brown	1941	100 — 150
Nordhoff & Hall	Little Brown	1940	150 — 200
Lanier/S.	Scribner	1917	125 — 150
Lanier/S.	Scribner	1926	50 — 75

LISTINGS BY TITLE

Title	Illustrator
Boys & Girls Of Bookland	Smith/Jessie Wilcox
Boys & Girls Of Bookland	Smith/Jessie Wilcox
Boys & Girls Of Bookland	Smith/Jessie Wilcox
Boys Of St. Timothy's	Wyeth/N.C.
Bracebridge Hall	Rackham/Arthur
Bracebridge Hall	Rackham/Arthur
Brains & Bravery	Rackham/Arthur
Brains & Bravery	Rackham/Arthur
Bred In The Bone	Fisher/Harrison
Brenda's Summer At Rockley	Smith/Jessie Wilcox
Brenda's Summer At Rockley	Smith/Jessie Wilcox
Brenda, Her School & Her Club	Smith/Jessie Wilcox
Bric-A-Brac Stories	Crane/Walter
Bride's Book (The)	Humphrey/Maud
British Book Illustration	Rackham/Arthur
Brown Fairy Book (The)	Ford/H.J.
Brown Fairy Book (The)	Ford/H.J.
Brownie Clown Of Brownie Town	Cox/Palmer
Brownie Year Book	Cox/Palmer
Brownies & Other Stories	Cox/Palmer
Brownies & Prince Florimel (The)	Cox/Palmer
Brownies Abroad (The)	Cox/Palmer
Brownies Abroad (The)	Cox/Palmer
Brownies Around The World (The)	Cox/Palmer
Brownies Around The World (The)	Cox/Palmer
Brownies Around The World (The)	Cox/Palmer
Brownies At Home (The)	Cox/Palmer
Brownies At Home (The)	Cox/Palmer
Brownies In Fairyland (The)	Cox/Palmer
Brownies In Fairyland (The)	Cox/Palmer
Brownies In The Philippines (The)	Cox/Palmer
Brownies In The Philippines (The)	Cox/Palmer
Brownies Many More Nights (The)	Cox/Palmer
Brownies Through The Union (The)	Cox/Palmer
Brownies Through The Union (The)	Cox/Palmer
Brownies' Latest Adventure (The)	Cox/Palmer
Brownies' Latest Adventure (The)	Cox/Palmer
Brownies: Their Book	Cox/Palmer
Brownies: Their Book	Cox/Palmer
Brownies: Their Book	Cox/Palmer
Bucaneers (The)	Pyle/Howard
Buddy Jim	Rae/John

LISTINGS BY TITLE

Author	Publisher	Year	Price Range
Smith/Nora	McKay	(1923)	100 — 150
Smith/Nora	McKay	(1923)	75 — 100
Smith/Nora	Cosmopolitan	1923	150 — 175
Pier/A.S.	Scribner	1904	50 — 75
Irving/Washington	Putnam	1896	100 — 150
Irving/Washington	Putnam	1896	200 — 300
Henty/G.A & Others	Chambers	1903	75 — 125
Henty/G.A & Others	Chambers	1905	50 — 75
Page/Thomas Nelson	Scribner	1904	25 — 35
Reed/Helen L.	Little Brown	1901	175 — 225
Reed/Helen L.	Little Brown	1904	75 — 100
Reed/Helen L.	Little Brown	1900	175 — 225
Harrison/B.	Scribner	1885	125 — 150
	Stokes	1900	250 — 300
Holme/Geoffrey	The Studio	1923	75 — 100
Lang/Andrew	Longmans	1904	200 — 250
Lang/Andrew	Longmans	1908	150 — 200
Cox/Palmer	Century	[1908]	175 — 225
Cox/Palmer	McLoughlin	[1895]	175 — 225
Cox/Palmer	Donohue		40 — 70
Cox/Palmer	Century	(1918)	100 — 130
Cox/Palmer	Unwin	(1899)	150 — 185
Cox/Palmer	Century	(1899)	175 — 225
Cox/Palmer	Unwin	(1894)	150 — 200
Cox/Palmer	Century	(1894)	175 — 225
Cox/Palmer	Century	(1922)	75 — 125
Cox/Palmer	Unwin	(1893)	175 — 225
Cox/Palmer	Century	(1893)	175 — 225
Cox/Palmer	Century	(1925)	125 — 150
Cox/Palmer	Harms	1894	175 — 225
Cox/Palmer	Unwin	(1904)	175 — 225
Cox/Palmer	Century	(1904)	175 — 225
Cox/Palmer	Century	(1913)	150 — 200
Cox/Palmer	Unwin	(1895)	175 — 225
Cox/Palmer	Century	(1895)	175 — 225
Cox/Palmer	Unwin	(1910)	175 — 225
Cox/Palmer	Century	(1910)	175 — 225
Cox/Palmer	Century	(1887)	225 — 300
Cox/Palmer	Century	(1887)	125 — 175
Cox/Palmer	Unwin	1888	175 — 225
Seitz/Don	Harper	1912	50 — 75
Gordon/Elizabeth	Volland	(1922)	40 — 70

LISTINGS BY TITLE

Title	Illustrator
Buddy Jim	Rae/John
Bugs & Wings & Other Things	Smith/Jessie Wilcox
Building The Nation	Pyle/Howard
Butterfly Man	Fisher/Harrison

C

Calendar For 1884	Greenaway/Kate
Calendar Of The Seasons	Greenaway/Kate
Captain Castle	Rackham/Arthur
Captain Ravenshaw	Pyle/Howard
Captain Salt In Oz	Neill/John R.
Captain Salt In Oz	Neill/John R.
Captain's Well (The)	Pyle/Howard
Captivating Stories Of Animals	Cox/Palmer
Carrots: Just A Little Boy	Crane/Walter
Carrots: Just A Little Boy	Crane/Walter
Castle Inn (The)	Rackham/Arthur
Castle Inn (The)	Rackham/Arthur
Cavalier (The)	Christy/Howard Chandler
Cease Firing	Wyeth/N.C.
Cecily Parsley's Nursery Rhymes	Potter/Beatrix
Cecily Parsley's Nursery Rhymes	Potter/Beatrix
Century Of Kate Greenaway (A)	Greenaway/Kate
Challenge (The)	Wyeth/N.C.
Champions Of The Round Table (The)	Pyle/Howard
Charles O'Malley The Irish Dragoon	Rackham/Arthur
Charles O'Malley The Irish Dragoon	Rackham/Arthur
Charles O'Malley The Irish Dragoon	Rackham/Arthur
Chattering Jack	Crane/Walter
Checked Love Affair	Fisher/Harrison
Cheery Scarcrow	Gruelle/Johnny
Cheery Scarcrow	Gruelle/Johnny
Cheery Scarcrow	Gruelle/Johnny
Child's Book Of Country Stories (A)	Smith/Jessie Wilcox
Child's Book Of Country Stories (A)	Smith/Jessie Wilcox
Child's Book Of Country Stories (A)	Smith/Jessie Wilcox
Child's Book Of Famous Stories(A)	Smith/Jessie Wilcox
Child's Book Of Modern Stories (A)	Smith/Jessie Wilcox
Child's Book Of Modern Stories (A)	Smith/Jessie Wilcox
Child's Book Of Old Verses (A)	Smith/Jessie Wilcox
Child's Book Of Old Verses (A)	Smith/Jessie Wilcox
Child's Book Of Old Verses (A)	Smith/Jessie Wilcox

LISTINGS BY TITLE

Author	Publisher	Year	Price Range
Gordon/Elizabeth	Wise-Parslow	(1935)	20 — 35
Franchot/Annie W.	Dutton	(1918)	50 — 75
Coffin/Charles C.	Harper	1883	25 — 35
McCutcheon/George	Dodd	1910	25 — 30
	Routledge	1884	50 — 75
	Ward	1882	75 —100
Dawe/Carlton	Smith,Elder	1897	50 — 75
Stephens/Robert N.	L.C. Page	1901	20 — 30
Thompson/Ruth P.	Reilly & Lee	(1936)	200 —300
Thompson/Ruth P.	Reilly & Lee	(1936)	40 — 60
Whittier/John G.	New York Ledger	1890	50 — 75
Veale/E.	Juvenile Publishing	(1908)	75 —125
Molesworth/Mrs.	Macmillan	1921	35 — 50
Molesworth/Mrs.	Macmillan	1929	25 — 35
Weyman/Stanley	Smith,Elder	[1900]	50 — 75
Weyman/Stanley	Smith,Elder	1898	100 —125
Cable/G.	Scribner	1901	40 — 60
Johnston/Mary	Houghton,Mifflin	1912	20 — 35
Potter/Beatrix	Warne	(1922)	150 —300
Potter/Beatrix	Warne	[1922]	500 —750
Moore/Anne C.	Warne	1946	15 — 30
Cheney/W.	Bobbs-Merrill	(1906)	20 — 35
Pyle/Howard	Scribner	1905	175 —225
Lever/Charles	Nesbit	[1899]	100 —125
Lever/Charles	Service & Paton	1897	125 —150
Lever/Charles	Putnam	1897	100 —125
	Routledge	[1880]	75 —100
Ford/Paul L.	Dodd	1903	30 — 45
Gruelle/Johnny	Donohue	(1929)	40 — 60
Gruelle/Johnny	Volland	(1929)	100 —125
Gruelle/Johnny	Volland	(1929)	75 —100
Skinner/Ada & Eleanor	Dial Press	(1935)	50 — 75
Skinner/Ada & Eleanor	Duffield	1925	175 —225
Skinner/Ada & Eleanor	Dial Press	1935	75 —100
Coussens/Penrhyn W.	Garden City	(1940)	40 — 60
Skinner/Ada & Eleanor	Duffield	1920	175 —225
Skinner/Ada & Eleanor	Dial Press	1935	100 —125
Smith/Jessie Wilcox	Duffield	(1910)	125 —150
Smith/Jessie Wilcox	Dial Press	(1935)	50 — 75
Smith/Jessie Wilcox	Duffield	1910	175 —225

Listings By Title

Title	Illustrator
Child's Book Of Old Verses (A)	Smith/Jessie Wilcox
Child's Book Of Stories (A)	Smith/Jessie Wilcox
Child's Book Of Stories (A)	Smith/Jessie Wilcox
Child's Book Of Stories (A)	Smith/Jessie Wilcox
Child's Book Of Stories (A)	Smith/Jessie Wilcox
Child's Book Of Verses (A)	Smith/Jessie Wilcox
Child's Garden Of Verses(A)	Gutmann/Bessie Pease
Child's Garden Of Verses(A)	Gutmann/Bessie Pease
Child's Garden Of Verses (A)	Smith/Jessie Wilcox
Child's Garden Of Verses (A)	Smith/Jessie Wilcox
Child's Garden Of Verses (A)	Smith/Jessie Wilcox
Child's Garden Of Verses (A)	Smith/Jessie Wilcox
Child's Garden Of Verses (A)	Smith/Jessie Wilcox
Child's Prayer (A)	Smith/Jessie Wilcox
Child's Prayer (A)	Smith/Jessie Wilcox
Child's Stamp Book Of Old Verses (A)	Smith/Jessie Wilcox
Children & Pictures (The)	Rackham/Arthur
Children & Pictures (The)	Rackham/Arthur
Children In Japan	Pogany/Will
Children Of Dickens (The)	Smith/Jessie Wilcox
Children Of Dickens (The)	Smith/Jessie Wilcox
Children Of Dickens (The)	Smith/Jessie Wilcox
Children Of Dickens (The)	Smith/Jessie Wilcox
Children Of Odin (The)	Pogany/Will
Children Of Odin (The)	Pogany/Will
Children Of Spring	Humphrey/Maud
Children Of The Castle (The)	Crane/Walter
Children Of The Revolution	Humphrey/Maud
Children Of The Revolution	Humphrey/Maud
Children Of Winter	Humphrey/Maud
Children's Book (The)	Parrish/Maxfield
Children's Book Of Hymns (The)	Barker/Cicely Mary
Children's Book Of Hymns (The)	Barker/Cicely Mary
Children's Christmas Treasury (The)	Rackham/Arthur
Children's Christmas Treasury (The)	Rackham/Arthur
Children's Funny Book	Cox/Palmer
Children's Hour (The)	Rackham/Arthur
Children's Musical Cinderella	Crane/Walter
Children's Plutarch (The)	Crane/Walter
Children's Plutarch (The)	Crane/Walter
Children's Treasury Of Great Stories	Rackham/Arthur
Children's Treasury Of Great Stories	Rackham/Arthur

LISTINGS BY TITLE

Author	Publisher	Year	Price Range
Smith/Jessie Wilcox	Dial Press	1935	75 — 100
Coussens/Penhryn	Duffield	1911	250 — 300
Coussens/Penhryn	Chatto/Windus	1913	125 — 150
Coussens/Penhryn	Duffield	1914	150 — 175
Coussens/Penhryn	Dial Press	1935	75 — 100
Smith/Jessie Wilcox	Chatto/Windus	1912	100 — 125
Stevenson/Robert Louis	Dodge	(1905)	100 — 150
Stevenson/Robert Louis	Dodge	(1908)	75 — 100
Stevenson/Robert Louis	Longmans	1905	125 — 250
Stevenson/Robert Louis	Scribner	1905	125 — 250
Stevenson/Robert Louis	Scribner	1925	75 — 100
Stevenson/Robert Louis	Scribner	1944	30 — 75
Stevenson/Robert Louis	Scribner	1945	30 — 75
Toogood/Cora C.	McKay	(1925)	40 — 60
Toogood/Cora C.	McKay	(1925)	30 — 50
Smith/Jessie Wilcox	Duffield	1915	125 — 175
Tennant/Pamela	Heinemann	1907	100 — 150
Tennant/Pamela	Macmillan	1907	100 — 150
Bartruse/G.	McBride	1915	130 — 180
Crothers/Samuel McChord	Scribner	1925	100 — 150
Crothers/Samuel McChord	Scribner	1933	35 — 50
Crothers/Samuel McChord	Scribner	1940	25 — 40
Crothers/Samuel McChord	Scribner	1944	25 — 35
Colum/Pedraic	Macmillan	(1929)	25 — 35
Colum/Pedraic	Macmillan	1920	35 — 50
	Stokes	1888	400 — 500
Molesworth/Mrs.	Macmillan	1890	75 — 100
Humphrey/Maud	Stokes	1900	400 — 500
	Stokes	1900	500 — 700
	Stokes	1888	400 — 500
Scudder/Horace E.	Houghton,Mifflin	1907	75 — 100
Barker/Cicely Mary	Blackie & Sons		50 — 75
Barker/Cicely Mary	Blackie & Sons		15 — 20
Hutton/Edward	Dent	(1905)	250 — 300
Hutton/Edward	Dutton	(1905)	225 — 275
Cox/Palmer	Lothrop	(1879)	75 — 100
Caine/Ralph Hall	Newnes	(1906)	75 — 100
	Routledge	1879	100 — 150
Gould/E.J.	Watts	1906	100 — 125
Gould/E.J.	Harper	1910	75 — 100
	Daily Express	[1910]	125 — 175
	Daily Express	[1930]	50 — 75

LISTINGS BY TITLE

Title	Illustrator
Childrens Stories That Never Grow Old	Neill/John R.
Chimes (The)	Rackham/Arthur
Chimes (The)	Thomson/Hugh
Chivalry	Pyle/Howard
Christmas Carol (A)	Rackham/Arthur
Christmas Carol (A)	Rackham/Arthur
Christmas Carol (A)	Rackham/Arthur
Christmas Carol (A)	Rackham/Arthur
Christmas Carol (A)	Rackham/Arthur
Christmas Carol (A)	Rackham/Arthur
Christmas Carol (A)	Rackham/Arthur
Christmas Carol/Jessica's First Prayer	Neill/John R.
Christmas Child (A)	Crane/Walter
Christmas Posy (A)	Crane/Walter
Christmas Story/St. Mark	Rae/John
Christmas-Tree Land	Crane/Walter
Christy Girl (The)	Christy/Howard Chandler
Chronicle Of The Drum (The)	Pyle/Howard
Chronicles Of Rhoda (The)	Smith/Jessie Wilcox
Chronicles/Little Tot	Gutmann/Bessie Pease
Cinderella	Neill/John R.
Cinderella	Pogany/Will
Cinderella	Rackham/Arthur
Cinderella	Rackham/Arthur
Cinderella	Rackham/Arthur
Cinderella Or The Little Glass Slipper	Neill/John R.
Cinderella's Picture Book	Crane/Walter
Cinderella's Picture Book	Crane/Walter
Cinderella/Three Bears	Neill/John R.
City Ballads	Pyle/Howard
Claims Of Decorative Art (The)	Crane/Walter
Clever Betsy	O'neill/Rose
Closing Scene (The)	Pyle/Howard
Clover's Princess	O'Neill/John R.
Cobb's Anatomy	Newell/Peter
Cobb's Bill Of Fare	Newell/Peter
College Girls	Gibson/Charles D.
Colonial Dame	Denslow/W.W.
Columbia's Courtship	Crane/Walter
Comic Yarns In Verse	Cox/Palmer
Compleat Angler (The)	Rackham/Arthur
Compleat Angler (The)	Rackham/Arthur

LISTINGS BY TITLE

Author	Publisher	Year	Price Range
Benoit/C.F.	Reilly & Britton	(1908)	75 — 100
Dickens/Charles	Limited Editions Club	1931	350 — 600
Dickens/Charles	Hodder & Stoughton	(1920)	50 — 75
Cabell/James B.	Harper	1909	90 — 125
Dickens/Charles	Heinemann	(1915)	1000 — 1250
Dickens/Charles	Heinemann	(1915)	150 — 200
Dickens/Charles	Heinemann	(1915)	175 — 225
Dickens/Charles	Lippincott	(1915)	1000 — 1250
Dickens/Charles	Lippincott	(1915)	100 — 150
Dickens/Charles	Lippincott	(1923)	75 — 100
Dickens/Charles	Heinemann	[1923]	75 — 100
	Reilly & Britton	(1908)	75 — 100
Molesworth/Mrs.	Macmillan	1880	125 — 150
Molesworth/Mrs.	Macmillan	1888	75 — 100
	Volland	(1921)	40 — 60
Molesworth/Mrs.	Macmillan	1884	100 — 125
Christy/Howard Chandler	Bobbs-Merrill	(1906)	75 — 100
Thackeray/William M.	Scribner	1882	25 — 35
Cox/Florence T.	Small,Maynard	(1909)	75 — 125
Cooke/E.V.	Dodge	(1905)	150 — 175
	Reilly & Lee	[1920]	100 — 150
Elias/E.	McBride	1915	175 — 200
Evans/C.S.	Heinemann	(1919)	750 — 1000
Evans/C.S.	Heinemann	(1919)	200 — 250
Evans/C.S.	Lippincott	(1919)	175 — 250
	Reilly & Britton	(1908)	75 — 100
Crane/Walter	J. Lane	(1897)	125 — 150
Crane/Walter	Dodd		30 — 50
	Reilly & Britton	(1908)	75 — 100
Carleton/Will	Harper	1886	25 — 35
	Lawrence & Bullen	1892	100 — 150
Burnham/C.L.	Houghton,Mifflin	1910	30 — 50
Read/Thomas B.	Lippincott	1887	25 — 35
Douglas/A.M.	Altemus	(1904)	50 — 75
Cobb/Irwin S.	Doran	(1912)	35 — 45
Cobb/Irwin S.	Doran	(1913)	35 — 45
Goodloe/A.C.	Scribner	1895	20 — 30
Fesenden/L.D.	Rand Mcnally	1897	50 — 75
Crane/Walter	Prang Co.	(1892)	200 — 250
Cox/Palmer	Hubbard	(1889)	75 — 100
Walton/Izaak	Harrap	(1931)	225 — 275
Walton/Izaak	Harrap	(1931)	250 — 300

LISTINGS BY TITLE

Title	Illustrator
Compleat Angler (The)	Rackham/Arthur
Compleat Angler (The)	Rackham/Arthur
Comus	Dulac/Edmund
Comus	Rackham/Arthur
Comus	Rackham/Arthur
Comus	Rackham/Arthur
Corner In Women (A)	Gibson/Charles D.
Cost (The)	Fisher/Harrison
Cost (The)	Fisher/Harrison
Costume Through The Ages	Rackham/Arthur
Cosy Corner Stories	Humphrey/Maud
Cosy Time Story Book	Humphrey/Maud
Cotter's Saturday Night (The)	Rackham/Arthur
Countess Diane	Rae/John
Courtship Of Miles Standish	Christy/Howard Chandler
Courtship Of Miles Standish	Wyeth/N.C.
Cowardly Lion Of Oz (The)	Neill/John R.
Cowardly Lion Of Oz (The)	Neill/John R.
Cowardly Lion Of Oz (The)	Neill/John R.
Cranford	Thomson/Hugh
Creature Songs...	Newell/Peter
Crested Seas (The)	Wyeth/N.C.
Crimson Fairy Book (The)	Ford/H.J.
Crimson Fairy Book (The)	Ford/H.J.
Crossing ...(The)	Rae/John
Cruise In The Acorn	Greenaway/Kate
Cuckoo Clock & The Tapestry Room	Crane/Walter
Cuckoo Clock & The Tapestry Room	Crane/Walter
Curious Cruise/Captain Santa	Neill/John R.

D

Title	Illustrator
Dale Readers Book 2 (The)	Crane/Walter
Dame Wiggins Of Lee	Greenaway/Kate
Dame Wiggins Of Lee	Greenaway/Kate
Dame Wiggins Of Lee	Greenaway/Kate
Dancing-Master	Smith/Jessie Wilcox
Daughters Of The Stars	Dulac/Edmund
David Balfour	Pyle/Howard
David Balfour	Wyeth/N.C.
David Balfour	Wyeth/N.C.
David Blaize & The Blue Door	Ford/H.J.
Day In A Child's Life (A)	Greenaway/Kate

LISTINGS BY TITLE

Author	Publisher	Year	Price Range
Walton/Izaak	Harrap	[1931]	750 —1000
Walton/Izaak	McKay	[1931]	125 — 175
Milton/John		(1954)	40 — 75
Milton/John	Heinemann	[1921]	500 —800
Milton/John	Heinemann	[1921]	175 —250
Milton/John	Doubleday,Page	[1921]	175 —225
Masson/T.	Moffat	1905	20 — 40
Phillips/David G.	Grosset&Dunlap	(1904)	15 — 25
Phillips/David G.	Bobbs-Merrill	1904	35 — 50
Rackham/Arthur	Maggs Brothers	1938	125 —150
	Hays		100 —150
	Hays		100 —150
Burns/Robert	Heweston	[1908]	125 —150
Rowland/H.	Dodd	1908	35 — 50
Longfellow/Henry W.	Bobbs-Merrill	(1903)	25 — 50
Longfellow/Henry W.	Houghton,Mifflin	1920	100 —150
Thompson/Ruth P.	Reilly & Lee	(1923)	300 —400
Thompson/Ruth P.	Reilly & Lee	(1923)	100 —150
Thompson/Ruth P.	Reilly & Lee	(1923)	40 — 60
Gaskell/Elizabeth C.	Macmillan		40 — 60
Garnett/L.A.	Ditson	(1912)	125 —175
Connolly/J.B.	Scribner	1907	20 — 40
Lang/Andrew	Longmans	1903	200 —250
Lang/Andrew	Longmans	1914	50 — 75
Churchill/Winston	Macmillan	1930	25 — 50
Jerrold/A.	Marcus Ward	1875	300 —350
Molesworth/Mrs.	Macmillan	(1877)	125 —175
Molesworth/Mrs.	Macmillan	1919	50 — 75
Thompson/Ruth P.	Reilly & Lee	(1926)	200 —300
Dale/Nellie	Philip	1907	50 — 75
Ruskin/John (Ed)	George Allen	1885	150 —200
Ruskin/John (Ed)	George Allen	1897	100 —125
Ruskin/John (Ed)	Dutton		75 —100
Chabot/Adrien	Lippincott	1901	150 —175
Crary/M.	Hatchard	1939	100 —150
Stevenson/Robert Louis	Scribner	1895	25 — 50
Stevenson/Robert Louis	Scribner	1924	100 —150
Stevenson/Robert Louis	Scribner	1927	45 — 75
Benson/Edward F.	Doubleday		75 —100
Foster/Myles B.	Routledge	[1881]	175 —225

LISTINGS BY TITLE

Title	Illustrator
Day Of The Dog	Fisher/Harrison
Deerslayer (The)	Wyeth/N.C.
Deerslayer (The)	Wyeth/N.C.
Deerslayer (The)	Wyeth/N.C.
Deerslayer (The)	Wyeth/N.C.
Denslow's Animal Fair	Denslow/W.W.
Denslow's Five Little Pigs	Denslow/W.W.
Denslow's Mother Goose	Denslow/W.W.
Denslow's Mother Goose	Denslow/W.W.
Denslow's Scarecrow & The Tin-Man	Denslow/W.W.
Denslow's Scarecrow & The Tin-Man	Denslow/W.W.
Denslow's Scarecrow & The Tin-Man & Other Stories	Denslow/W.W.
Denslow's Scarecrow & The Tin-Man & Other Stories	Denslow/W.W.
Denslow's Scarecrow & The Tin-Man & Other Stories	Denslow/W.W.
Denslow's Tom Thumb	Denslow/W.W.
Denslow's Zoo	Denslow/W.W.
Diamonds & Toads	Greenaway/Kate
Diamonds & Toads	Greenaway/Kate
Diary Of A Mouse	Gutmann/Bessie Pease
Dick Whittington & His Cat	Neill/John R.
Dickens's Children	Smith/Jessie Wilcox
Dickens's Children	Smith/Jessie Wilcox
Dickens's Children	Smith/Jessie Wilcox
Dickens's Children	Smith/Jessie Wilcox
Disentanglers	Ford/H.J.
Dish Of Apples (A)	Rackham/Arthur
Dish Of Apples (A)	Rackham/Arthur
Dish Of Apples (A)	Rackham/Arthur
Dolly Dialogues	Christy/Howard Chandler
Dolly Dialogues (The)	Rackham/Arthur
Dolly Dialogues (The)	Rackham/Arthur
Dolly Dialogues (The)	Rackham/Arthur
Don Gypsy	Rackham/Arthur
Don Quixote	Crane/Walter
Don Quixote	Crane/Walter
Don Quixote	Crane/Walter
Dorothy & The Wizard Of Oz	Neill/John R.
Dorothy & The Wizard Of Oz	Neill/John R.
Dorothy & The Wizard Of Oz	Neill/John R.
Dorothy & The Wizard Of Oz	Neill/John R.
Dorothy & The Wizard Of Oz	Neill/John R.
Dorothy Q.	Pyle/Howard

Listings By Title

Author	Publisher	Year	Price Range
McCutcheon/George	Dodd	1904	35 — 50
Cooper/James Fenimore	Scribner	1925	100 — 150
Cooper/James Fenimore	Scribner	1925	100 — 150
Cooper/James Fenimore	Scribner	1927	45 — 75
Cooper/James Fenimore	Scribner	1929	20 — 50
Denslow/W.W.	Dillingham	1904	175 — 225
Denslow/W.W.	Dillingham	(1903)	100 — 125
Denslow/W.W.	McClure	1901	400 — 600
Denslow/W.W.	Chambers	1902	250 — 300
Denslow/W.W.	Dillingham	[1904]	200 — 300
Denslow/W.W.	Donohue	[1913]	50 — 100
Denslow/W.W.	Dillingham	[1904]	150 — 200
Denslow/W.W.	Unwin	[1904]	150 — 200
Denslow/W.W.	Donohue	[1913]	50 — 100
Denslow/W.W.	Dillingham	(1903)	100 — 150
Denslow/W.W.	Dillingham	(1903)	75 — 125
	Warne	[1869]	200 — 250
	McLoughlin	[1875]	175 — 200
Dunham/E.	Dodge	(1907)	75 — 125
	Reilly & Britton	(1908)	75 — 100
Smith/Jesse Wilcox	Chatto/Windus	1912	125 — 175
Smith/Jesse Wilcox	Scribner	1912	125 — 175
Smith/Jesse Wilcox	Scribner	1912	100 — 150
Smith/Jesse Wilcox	Chatto/Windus	1913	100 — 125
Lang/Andrew	Longmans	1902	100 — 150
Phillpotts/Eden	Hodder & Stoughton	(1921)	600 — 800
Phillpotts/Eden	Hodder & Stoughton	[1921]	175 — 225
Phillpotts/Eden	Hodder & Stoughton	[1921]	150 — 175
Hope/Anthony	Russell	1901	30 — 45
Hope/Anthony	Westminster Gazette	1894	150 — 250
Hope/Anthony	Westminster Gazette	1894	125 — 175
Hope/Anthony	Holt	1894	50 — 100
Starkie/Walter	John Murray	(1936)	40 — 80
Parry/Judge	Blackie & Sons	1900	175 — 225
Parry/Judge	J. Lane	1900	100 — 125
Parry/Judge	Dodd	1926	75 — 100
Baum/L. Frank	Reilly & Britton	(1908)	500 — 750
Baum/L. Frank	Reilly & Britton	(1908)	125 — 200
Baum/L. Frank	Reilly & Lee	(1908)	75 — 125
Baum/L. Frank	Reilly & Lee	(1908)	40 — 60
Baum/L. Frank	Reilly & Lee	(1908)	75 — 100
Holmes/Oliver W.	Houghton,Mifflin	1893	75 — 100

157

LISTINGS BY TITLE

Title	Illustrator
Dorothy Vernon/Hoddon Hall	Christy/Howard Chandler
Dot & Tot In Merryland	Denslow/W.W.
Dot & Tot In Merryland	Denslow/W.W.
Drawings	Christy/Howard Chandler
Drawings	Christy/Howard Chandler
Drawings	Gibson/Charles D.
Drawings In Pen & Pencil	Rackham/Arthur
Drawings In Pen & Pencil	Rackham/Arthur
Dream Blocks	Smith/Jessie Wilcox
Dream Blocks	Smith/Jessie Wilcox
Dream Days	Parrish/Maxfield
Dream Of Fair Women	Fisher/Harrison
Dream Of Fair Women	Fisher/Harrison
Dreamer Of Dreams	Dulac/Edmund
Drums	Wyeth/N.C.
Drums	Wyeth/N.C.
Drums	Wyeth/N.C.
Dulcibel	Pyle/Howard

E

Title	Illustrator
Early Italian Love Stories	Ford/H.J.
East Coast Scenery	Rackham/Arthur
East Of The Sun West Of Moon	Nielson/Kay
East Of The Sun West Of Moon	Nielson/Kay
East Of The Sun West Of Moon	Nielson/Kay
East Of The Sun West Of Moon	Nielson/Kay
East Of The Sun West Of Moon	Nielson/Kay
Eclogues Of Vergil (The)	Pyle/Howard
Eddie Elephant	Gruelle/Johnny
Eddie Elephant	Gruelle/Johnny
Eddie Elephant	Gruelle/Johnny
Edmund Dulac's Fairy Book	Dulac/Edmund
Education Of Mr. Pipp	Gibson/Charles D.
Emerald City Of Oz (The)	Neill/John R.
Emerald City Of Oz (The)	Neill/John R.
Emerald City Of Oz (The)	Neill/John R.
Emerald City Of Oz (The)	Neill/John R.
Emerald Story Book (The)	Parrish/Maxfield
Emma	Thomson/Hugh
Enchanted Typewriter (The)	Newell/Peter
English Book Illustration Of Today	Rackham/Arthur
English Book Illustration Of Today	Rackham/Arthur

LISTINGS BY TITLE

Author	Publisher	Year	Price Range
Major/C.	Macmillan	1902	20 — 30
Baum/L. Frank	Bobbs-Merrill	(1903)	200 — 300
Baum/L. Frank	Geo Hill	1901	600 — 800
Christy/Howard Chandler	Moffat	1905	125 — 175
Christy/Howard Chandler	Review Of Reviews	1913	75 — 100
Gibson/Charles D.	Russell	1897	120 — 150
Sheringham/George	The Studio	1922	50 — 75
Sheringham/George	The Studio	1922	150 — 200
Higgins/Aileen C.	Duffield	(1908)	275 — 375
Higgins/Aileen C.	Chatto/Windus	1911	200 — 250
Grahame/Kenneth	J. Lane	[1902]	75 — 150
Fisher/Harrison	Grosset&Dunlap	(1907)	125 — 175
Fisher/Harrison	Bobbs-Merrill	(1909)	180 — 250
Queen Marie	Hodder & Stoughton	(1915)	250 — 300
Boyd/J.	Scribner	1928	100 — 150
Boyd/James	Scribner	1928	500 — 750
Boyd/James	Scribner	1930	50 — 75
Peterson/Henry	Winston	1907	50 — 75
	Longmans	1899	100 — 125
Tate/William James	Jarrold	1899	100 — 150
Asbjornsen	Hodder & Stoughton	[1914]	500 — 700
Asbjornsen	Doran	[1914]	250 — 350
Asbjornsen	Garden City	[1930]	50 — 100
Asbjornsen	Doran		100 — 150
Asbjornsen	Doubleday		75 — 100
Bowen/Baron	Privately Printed	1904	100 — 150
Gruelle/Johnny	Donohue	(1921)	40 — 60
Gruelle/Johnny	Volland	(1921)	100 — 125
Gruelle/Johnny	Volland	(1921)	75 — 100
Dulac/Edmund	Doran	(1916)	250 — 300
Gibson/Charles D.	Russell	1899	120 — 150
Baum/L. Frank	Reilly & Britton	(1910)	500 — 750
Baum/L. Frank	Reilly & Britton	(1910)	175 — 250
Baum/L. Frank	Reilly & Lee	(1910)	100 — 125
Baum/L. Frank	Reilly & Lee	(1910)	40 — 60
Skinner/Ada & Eleanor	Duffield	1917	75 — 150
Austen/J.	Macmillan		50 — 75
Bangs/John K.	Harper	1899	25 — 50
Sketchley/R.E.D.	Kegan	1903	75 — 100
Sketchley/R.E.D.	Kegan	1903	100 — 125

159

LISTINGS BY TITLE

Title	Illustrator
English Fairy Tales	Rackham/Arthur
English Fairy Tales	Rackham/Arthur
English Fairy Tales	Rackham/Arthur
English Fairy Tales	Rackham/Arthur
English Fairy Tales	Rackham/Arthur
English Fairy Tales	Rackham/Arthur
English Illustration:Nineties	Rackham/Arthur
English Spelling Book (The)	Greenaway/Kate
Epic Of Ebenezer (The)	Rae/John
Esther...	Greenaway/Kate
Etchings	Pyle/Howard
Etchings	Pyle/Howard
Evangeline	Christy/Howard Chandler
Evangeline	Neill/John R.
Evangeline	Smith/Jessie Wilcox
Evangeline	Smith/Jessie Wilcox
Evangeline	Smith/Jessie Wilcox
Evangeline	Smith/Jessie Wilcox
Evelina	Rackham/Arthur
Evelina	Rackham/Arthur
Evelina	Thomson/Hugh
Even Unto Bethlehem	Wyeth/N.C.
Everyday & Now-A-Day Fairy Book (The)	Smith/Jessie Wilcox
Everyday & Now-A-Day Fairy Book (The)	Smith/Jessie Wilcox
Everyday Classics	Pogany/Will
Everyday Fairy Book (The)	Smith/Jessie Wilcox
Everyday Fairy Book (The)	Smith/Jessie Wilcox
Everyday Fairy Book (The)	Smith/Jessie Wilcox
Everyday Fairy Book (The)	Smith/Jessie Wilcox
Everyday Fairy Book (The)	Smith/Jessie Wilcox
Everyday People	Gibson/Charles D.

F

Fables For The Frivolous	Newell/Peter
Fables In Rhyme For Little Folk	Rae/John
Fables In Rhyme For Little Folk	Rae/John
Faerie Queen (The)	Crane/Walter
Fair Americans	Fisher/Harrison
Fairies & Christmas Child	Pogany/Will
Fairies I Have Met	Dulac/Edmund
Fairies I Have Met	Dulac/Edmund
Fairies Of The Flowers & Trees	Barker/Cicely Mary

LISTINGS BY TITLE

Author	Publisher	Year	Price Range
Steele/Flora Annie	Macmillan	1918	750 — 900
Steele/Flora Annie	Macmillan	1918	200 — 250
Steele/Flora Annie	Macmillan	1918	175 — 250
Steele/Flora Annie	Macmillan	1918	250 — 350
Steele/Flora Annie	Macmillan	1919	125 — 175
Steele/Flora Annie	Macmillan	1930	50 — 75
Thorpe/James	Faber	1935	50 — 75
Greenaway/Kate	Routledge	[1885]	200 — 250
Cox/Florence T.	Dodd	1912	25 — 35
Butt/G.	Marcus Ward	1878	200 — 250
Bicknell/W.H.W.	Bibliophile Society	1903	75 — 100
Bicknell/W.H.W.	Bibliophile Society	1913	50 — 75
Longfellow/Henry W.	Bobbs-Merrill	(1905)	30 — 50
Longfellow/Henry W.	Reilly & Britton	(1909)	75 — 100
Longfellow/Henry W.	Houghton,Mifflin	1897	150 — 200
Longfellow/Henry W.	Houghton,Mifflin	1897	125 — 150
Longfellow/Henry W.	Gay & Bird	1897	150 — 200
Longfellow/Henry W.	Houghton,Mifflin	1916	50 — 75
Burney/Frances	Newnes	[1900]	100 — 150
Burney/Frances	Newnes	1898	175 — 225
Burney	Macmillan		40 — 60
Van Dyke/Henry	Scribner	1928	30 — 50
Chapin/Anna Alice	Coker	[1935]	100 — 150
Chapin/Anna Alice	Coker	[1935]	75 — 100
Baker/Franklin T.	Macmillan	1923	25 — 50
Chapin/Anna Alice	Harrap	(1919)	100 — 150
Chapin/Anna Alice	Coker	[1935]	100 — 150
Chapin/Anna Alice	Coker	[1935]	75 — 100
Chapin/Anna Alice	Dodd	1915	175 — 250
Chapin/Anna Alice	Harrap	1917	150 — 225
Gibson/Charles D.	Scribner	1904	120 — 150
Carryl/Guy W.	Harper	1898	75 — 100
La Fontaine	Volland	(1918)	50 — 75
La Fontaine	Wise-Parslow	1950	25 — 50
Spenser/Edmund	George Allen	1895	150 — 200
Fisher/Harrison	Scribner	1911	180 — 220
Gask/L.	Crowell	(1910)	140 — 185
Stawell/R.	J. Lane	(1907)	250 — 300
Stawell/R.	Hodder & Stoughton	[1910]	225 — 275
Barker/Cicely Mary	Blackie & Sons		50 — 75

LISTINGS BY TITLE

Title	Illustrator
Fairy & Wonder Tales	Smith/Jessie Wilcox
Fairy Book (A)	Rackham/Arthur
Fairy Caravan (The)	Potter/Beatrix
Fairy Flowers	Pogany/Will
Fairy Flowers	Pogany/Will
Fairy Garland (A)	Dulac/Edmund
Fairy Garland (A)	Dulac/Edmund
Fairy Garland (A)	Dulac/Edmund
Fairy Garland (A)	Dulac/Edmund
Fairy Gifts	Greenaway/Kate
Fairy Gifts	Greenaway/Kate
Fairy Ship	Crane/Walter
Fairy Tales	Nielson/Kay
Fairy Tales	Nielson/Kay
Fairy Tales	Nielson/Kay
Fairy Tales	Nielson/Kay
Fairy Tales	Nielson/Kay
Fairy Tales By Hans Anderson	Rackham/Arthur
Fairy Tales By Hans Anderson	Rackham/Arthur
Fairy Tales By Hans Anderson	Rackham/Arthur
Fairy Tales By Hans Anderson	Rackham/Arthur
Fairy Tales By..	Neill/John R.
Fairy Tales From France	Rae/John
Fairy Tales From Many Lands	Pogany/Will
Fairy Tales Of ...	Crane/Walter
Fairy Tales Of Allied Nations	Dulac/Edmund
Fairy Tales Of Brothers Grimm	Rackham/Arthur
Fairy Tales Of Brothers Grimm	Rackham/Arthur
Fairy Tales Of Brothers Grimm	Rackham/Arthur
Fairy Tales Of Brothers Grimm	Rackham/Arthur
Fairy Tales Of Brothers Grimm	Rackham/Arthur
Fairy Tales Of Brothers Grimm	Rackham/Arthur
Fairy Tales Of Brothers Grimm	Rackham/Arthur
Fairy Tales Of Brothers Grimm	Rackham/Arthur
Fairy Tales Of Brothers Grimm	Rackham/Arthur
Fairy Tales Old & New	Rackham/Arthur
Faithful Friends	Rackham/Arthur
Faithful Friends	Rackham/Arthur
Fancy Dresses Described	Greenaway/Kate
Far Familiar (The)	Rackham/Arthur
Far From The Maddening Girls	Newell/Peter
Farm Ballads	Pyle/Howard

LISTINGS BY TITLE

Author	Publisher	Year	Price Range
Patten/William	Collier	(1918)	50 — 75
Rackham/Arthur	Doubleday,Page	(1923)	125 — 175
Potter/Beatrix	McKay	(1929)	125 — 175
Newman/I.	Holt	(1926)	130 — 180
Newman/I.	H. Milford	(1926)	160 — 200
Dulac/Edmund	Cassell	(1928)	150 — 200
Dulac/Edmund	Cassell	(1928)	600 — 800
Dulac/Edmund	Cassell	(1928)	500 — 650
Dulac/Edmund	Scribner	(1929)	100 — 150
Knox/Kathleen	Dutton	(1874)	125 — 175
Knox/Kathleen	Griffith & Farran	1874	125 — 175
	J. Lane	(1890)	75 — 125
Anderson/Hans Christian	Doran	(1924)	275 — 450
Anderson/Hans Christian	Hodder & Stoughton	[1924]	600 — 800
Anderson/Hans Christian	Hodder & Stoughton	[1924]	1000 — 1250
Anderson/Hans Christian	Garden City	[1932]	70 — 100
Anderson/Hans Christian	Doubleday		75 — 125
Anderson/Hans Christian	Harrap	(1932)	125 — 150
Anderson/Hans Christian	Harrap	(1932)	150 — 175
Anderson/Hans Christian	Harrap	[1932]	900 — 1250
Anderson/Hans Christian	McKay	(1932)	75 — 100
Anderson/Hans C.	Cupples & Leon	(1923)	50 — 75
Larned/William T.	Volland	(1920)	50 — 75
Gask/Lillian		1933	25 — 30
D'Aulnoy	Lawrence	1892	175 — 225
Dulac/Edmund	Hodder & Stoughton	[1916]	250 — 350
Grimm Brothers	Freemantle	[1900]	150 — 200
Grimm Brothers	Freemantle	[1900]	125 — 175
Grimm Brothers	Lippincott	[1900]	75 — 100
Grimm Brothers	Partridge	[1904]	75 — 125
Grimm Brothers	Constable	[1907]	100 — 125
Grimm Brothers	Constable	1909	300 — 400
Grimm Brothers	Constable	1909	1000 — 1500
Grimm Brothers	Doubleday	1909	350 — 450
Lucas/Mrs. Edgar	Constable		35 — 60
	Cassell	(1905)	100 — 150
Bingham/Clifton	Blackie & Sons	(1902)	350 — 450
Bingham/Clifton	Blackie & Sons	[1913]	250 — 300
Holt/A.		[1882]	125 — 175
MacKaye/Percy	Richards	(1938)	75 — 100
Carryl/Guy W.	McClure	1904	50 — 75
Carleton/Will	Harper	1882	25 — 35

163

LISTINGS BY TITLE

Title	Illustrator
Father Goose His Book	Denslow/W.W.
Father Goose His Book	Denslow/W.W.
Father Goose His Book	Denslow/W.W.
Father Goose His Book	Denslow/W.W.
Faust	Pogany/Will
Faust	Pogany/Will
Favorite Fairy Tales	Newell/Peter
Favorites Of Fairyland	Newell/Peter
Featherweights	Rackham/Arthur
Feats Of The Fjord	Rackham/Arthur
Feats Of The Fjord	Rackham/Arthur
Feats Of The Fjord	Rackham/Arthur
Feats Of The Fjord	Rackham/Arthur
Feats Of The Fjord	Rackham/Arthur
Feats Of The Fjord	Rackham/Arthur
Feats Of The Fjord	Rackham/Arthur
Fifth String (The)	Christy/Howard Chandler
First Book Of The Dofobs (The)	Pyle/Howard
First Christmas Tree (The)	Pyle/Howard
First Lessons In Our Country's History	Pyle/Howard
First Of May (The)	Crane/Walter
First Of May (The)	Crane/Walter
Five Senses (The)	Smith/Jessie Wilcox
Flora's Feast	Crane/Walter
Floral Fantasy In An Old English Garden (A)	Crane/Walter
Flower Fairies Of Autumn	Barker/Cicely Mary
Flower Fairies Of Spring	Barker/Cicely Mary
Flower Fairies Of Spring	Barker/Cicely Mary
Flower Fairies Of Summer	Barker/Cicely Mary
Flower Fairy Alphabet (A)	Barker/Cicely Mary
Flower Songs Of The Seasons	Barker/Cicely Mary
Flower Wedding (A)	Crane/Walter
Flowers & Fancies	Greenaway/Kate
Flowers From Shakespeare's Garden	Crane/Walter
Flute & Violin & Other Kentucky Tales	Pyle/Howard
Folk & Fairy Tales	Crane/Walter
Folk Tales Of Many Lands	Pogany/Will
Folk Tales Of Many Lands	Pogany/Will
Folk Tales Of Many Lands	Pogany/Will
Folk-Lore, Fables & Fairy Tales	Smith/Jessie Wilcox
Foolish Fox (The)	Neill/John R.
For Love Of Mary Ellen	O'neill/Rose

164

LISTINGS BY TITLE

Author	Publisher	Year	Price Range
Baum/L. Frank	Geo Hill	(1899)	200 — 700
Baum/L. Frank	Geo Hill	(1899)	2000 —4000
Baum/L. Frank	Donohue	[1913]	100 — 150
Baum/L. Frank	Donohue	1910	150 — 200
Goethe	Hutchinson	(1908)	150 — 200
Goethe	Musson	[1908]	350 — 500
	Harper	1907	150 — 200
Harris/A.V.	Harper	1911	75 — 100
Byron/May	Hodder & Stoughton	(1908)	150 — 250
Martineau/Harriet	Dent	(1910)	50 — 75
Martineau/Harriet	Dutton	(1910)	50 — 75
Martineau/Harriet	Dent	(1914)	75 — 100
Martineau/Harriet	Dutton	(1914)	75 — 125
Martineau/Harriet	Dent	1899	150 — 250
Martineau/Harriet	Dent		50 — 75
Martineau/Harriet	Dutton		50 — 75
Sousa/John Phillips	Bowen/Merrill	(1902)	10 — 20
	Society Of The Dofobs	1907	100 — 125
Van Dyke/Henry	Scribner	1897	35 — 50
Swinton/William	American Book Co.	1894	20 — 30
Wise/J.R.	Southeran	1881	100 — 150
Wise/J.R.	Southeran	1881	350 — 500
Keyes/Angela M.	Moffat,Yard	1911	180 — 250
Crane/Walter	Cassell	1889	200 — 250
Crane/Walter	Harper	1899	125 — 225
Barker/Cicely Mary	Blackie & Sons	[1927]	75 — 125
	Blackie & Sons	[1930]	50 — 75
	Blackie & Sons		75 — 125
Barker/Cicely Mary	Blackie & Sons	(1923)	75 — 125
Barker/Cicely Mary	Blackie & Sons	(1934)	75 — 125
Barker/Cicely Mary	Blackie & Sons	[1915]	100 — 150
Crane/Walter	Cassell	1905	200 — 250
Ranking/B.M.	Marcus Ward	1882	200 — 250
Crane/Walter	Cassell	1906	150 — 200
Allen/James L.	Harper	1891	20 — 40
Harrison/Burton	Marcus Ward	1885	150 — 250
Gask/Lillian	Crowell	(1910)	75 — 100
Gask/Lillian	Harrap	1910	100 — 125
Gask/Lillian	Harrap	1929	20 — 40
	The University Society	(1927)	25 — 50
	Altemus	(1904)	50 — 75
Brainerd/E.H.	Harper	1912	30 — 50

LISTINGS BY TITLE

Title	Illustrator
Fors Clavigera	Greenaway/Kate
Fors Clavigera	Greenaway/Kate
Forty Thieves	Crane/Walter
Founders Of Our Country	Pyle/Howard
Four Plays/Dancers	Dulac/Edmund
Four Winds Farm	Crane/Walter
Fourth Annual Of Advertising Art	Rackham/Arthur
Francezka	Fisher/Harrison
Free To Serve	Parrish/Maxfield
Frenzied Prince	Pogany/Will
Friendly Fairies	Gruelle/Johnny
Friendly Fairies	Gruelle/Johnny
Friendly Fairies	Gruelle/Johnny
Friendly Fairies	Gruelle/Johnny
From Pillar To Post	Neill/John R.
Frontier Humor	Cox/Palmer
Fun On The Playground	Humphrey/Maud
Funny Little Book	Gruelle/Johnny
Funny Little Book	Gruelle/Johnny
Funny Little Book	Gruelle/Johnny

G

Title	Illustrator
Gallant Little Patriots	Humphrey/Maud
Gallantry	Pyle/Howard
Garda	O'Neill/Rose
Garden Behind The Moon (The)	Pyle/Howard
Garden Of Girls (A)	Fisher/Harrison
Garden Of Girls (A)	Fisher/Harrison
Garden Of Years	Parrish/Maxfield
Gardens Old & New	Rackham/Arthur
George Washington	Pyle/Howard
George Washington Lincoln Goes Around The World	Pogany/Will
Ghost Of Captain Brand (The)	Pyle/Howard
Giant Horse Of Oz (The)	Neill/John R.
Giant Horse Of Oz (The)	Neill/John R.
Giant Horse Of Oz (The)	Neill/John R.
Gibson Book (The)	Gibson/Charles D.
Giles Corey, Yeoman	Pyle/Howard
Ginger & Pickles	Potter/Beatrix
Ginger & Pickles	Potter/Beatrix
Ginger & Pickles	Potter/Beatrix
Gingerbread Man	Neill/John R.

LISTINGS BY TITLE

Author	Publisher	Year	Price Range
Ruskin/John	George Allen	[1895]	125 — 150
Ruskin/John	George Allen	1883	200 — 300
Crane/Walter	Routledge	1873	100 — 150
Coe/Fanny	American Book Co	1912	15 — 20
Yeats/W.B.	Macmillan	1921	100 — 150
Molesworth/Mrs.	Macmillan	1887	75 — 100
Art Directors Club	Book Service Co.	1925	50 — 75
Seawell/M.E.	Bobbs-Merrill	(1902)	30 — 45
Raynor/Emma	Copeland/Day	1897	100 — 150
Colum/Pedraic	McKay	(1943)	75 — 100
Gruelle/Johnny	Donohue	(1919)	45 — 60
Gruelle/Johnny	Volland	(1919)	125 — 175
Gruelle/Johnny	Volland	(1919)	100 — 125
Gruelle/Johnny	Johnny Gruelle Co.	(1940)	35 — 50
Bangs/John K.	Century	1916	50 — 75
Cox/Palmer	Hubbard	(1895)	50 — 75
	Sully	1891	50 — 75
Gruelle/Johnny	Donohue	(1918)	35 — 50
Gruelle/Johnny	Volland	(1918)	100 — 125
Gruelle/Johnny	Volland	(1918)	75 — 100
Humphrey/Maud	Stokes	1899	450 — 650
Cabbell/James B.	Harper	1907	100 — 145
O'Neill/Rose	Doubleday	1929	40 — 60
Pyle/Howard	Scribner	1895	125 — 175
Fisher/Harrison	Dodd	1910	300 — 450
Fisher/Harrison		1910	200 — 250
Carryl/Guy W.	Putnam	1904	45 — 75
Leyland/John	Newnes	[1900]	175 — 225
Wilson/Woodrow	Harper	1897	50 — 75
Thomas	Nelson		50 — 75
	Rogers	1896	50 — 75
Thompson/Ruth P.	Reilly & Lee	(1928)	200 — 250
Thompson/Ruth P.	Reilly & Lee	(1928)	125 — 175
Thompson/Ruth P.	Reilly & Lee	(1928)	40 — 60
Gibson/Charles D.	Scribner	1906	150 — 200
Wilkins/Mary E.	Harper	1893	25 — 50
Potter/Beatrix	Warne	(1909)	150 — 200
Potter/Beatrix	Warne	[1920]	100 — 150
Potter/Beatrix	Warne	1909	350 — 450
Baum/L. Frank	Reilly & Britton	(1917)	200 — 300

LISTINGS BY TITLE

Title	Illustrator
Gingerbread Man	Pogany/Will
Gingerbread Man (The)	Gruelle/Johnny
Girl I Left Behind Me	Rae/John
Girl's Life & Other Pictures (A)	Fisher/Harrison
Glinda Of Oz	Neill/John R.
Glinda Of Oz	Neill/John R.
Glinda Of Oz	Neill/John R.
Gnome King Of Oz (The)	Neill/John R.
Gnome King Of Oz (The)	Neill/John R.
Goblin Market	Rackham/Arthur
Goblin Market	Rackham/Arthur
Goblin Market	Rackham/Arthur
Goblin Woman	O'Neill/Rose
Gods & Mortals In Love	Dulac/Edmund
Golden Age (The)	Parrish/Maxfield
Golden Age (The)	Parrish/Maxfield
Golden Book Of Sonnets	Pogany/Will
Golden Cockerel	Pogany/Will
Golden Cockerel (The)	Dulac/Edmund
Golden Cockerel (The)	Dulac/Edmund
Golden Gate (The)	Cox/Palmer
Golden Horshoe (The)	Fisher/Harrison
Golden Primer	Crane/Walter
Golden Treasury Of Songs..	Parrish/Maxfield
Golden Treasury Of Songs..	Parrish/Maxfield
Golden Treasury Of Songs..	Parrish/Maxfield
Goldon Fleece (The)	Pogany/Will
Goldon Fleece (The)	Pogany/Will
Golf Girl	Humphrey/Maud
Good For The Soul	Pyle/Howard
Good Night	Rackham/Arthur
Goody Two Shoes	Crane/Walter
Grammer In Rhyme	Crane/Walter
Grandma's Rhymes & Chimes	Humphrey/Maud
Grandmother Dear	Crane/Walter
Granny Goose	Rae/John
Graphic Arts & Crafts Yearbook	Parrish/Maxfield
Grasshopper Green & The Meadow Mice	Rae/John
Grasshopper Green & The Meadow Mice	Rae/John
Great Men's Sons	Pyle/Howard
Great Stone Of Sardis	Newell/Peter
Greek Heroes (The)	Rackham/Arthur

LISTINGS BY TITLE

Author	Publisher	Year	Price Range
Fable/L.	McBride	1915	100 — 130
Lawrence/Josephine	Whitman	1930	25 — 35
Mills/W.J.	Dodd	1910	75 — 100
Fisher/Harrison			250 — 350
Baum/L. Frank	Reilly & Lee	(1920)	250 — 350
Baum/L. Frank	Reilly & Lee	(1920)	100 — 150
Baum/L. Frank	Reilly & Lee	(1920)	40 — 60
Thompson/Ruth P.	Reilly & Lee	(1927)	400 — 600
Thompson/Ruth P.	Reilly & Lee	(1927)	40 — 60
Rossetti/Christina	Harrap	(1933)	200 — 250
Rossetti/Christina	Lippincott	[1933]	150 — 175
Rossetti/Christina	Harrap	1933	750 — 900
O'Neill/Rose	Doubleday	1930	40 — 60
Williamson/H.	Country Life	(1935)	75 — 100
Grahame/Kenneth	J. Lane	(1904)	75 — 125
Grahame/Kenneth	J. Lane	1900	100 — 200
Robertson/W.G.	Harrap	1903	100 — 125
Pogany/E.	Nelson	1938	80 — 110
Pushkin/Alexander	Limited Editions Club		350 — 400
Pushkin/Alexander	Heritage		40 — 60
Dodge/Mary M.		(1903)	35 — 50
Aitken/Robert	Grosset&Dunlap	(1907)	20 — 30
Meiklejohn	Meiklejohn	1884	125 — 150
Palgrave/Francis Turner	Duffield	1911	150 — 225
Palgrave/Francis Turner	Duffield	1941	50 — 80
Palgrave/Francis Turner	Scribner		100 — 125
Colum/Pedraic	Macmillan	(1921)	50 — 60
Colum/Pedraic	Macmillan		15 — 25
Humphrey/Maud	Stokes	(1899)	300 — 400
Deland/Margaret	Harper	1899	25 — 35
Gates/Eleanor	Crowell	(1907)	350 — 500
Crane/Walter	J. Lane	(1901)	175 — 200
Crane/Walter	Routledge	(1868)	75 — 100
	Roberts	1889	50 — 75
Molesworth/Mrs.	Macmillan	(1878)	75 — 100
Rae/John	Volland	(1926)	100 — 150
Meadon/Joseph (Ed)	Republican Publishing	1907	40 — 60
Rae/John	Volland	(1922)	40 — 60
Rae/John	Algonquin	(1922)	25 — 35
Brooks/Elbridge	Putnam	1895	30 — 50
Stockton/F.	Harper	1898	50 — 75
Niebuhr	Cassell	1903	250 — 275

LISTINGS BY TITLE

Title	Illustrator
Greek Heroes (The)	Rackham/Arthur
Greek Heroes (The)	Rackham/Arthur
Green Fairy Book (The)	Ford/H.J.
Green Fairy Book (The)	Ford/H.J.
Green Fairy Book (The)	Ford/H.J.
Green Fairy Book (The)	Ford/H.J.
Green Lacquer Pavillion	Dulac/Edmund
Green Lacquer Pavillion	Dulac/Edmund
Greenaway's Babies	Greenaway/Kate
Grey Fairy Book (The)	Ford/H.J.
Grey Fairy Book (The)	Ford/H.J.
Grey House On The Hill (The)	Rackham/Arthur
Grey House On The Hill (The)	Rackham/Arthur
Grey Lady (The)	Rackham/Arthur
Grey Lady (The)	Rackham/Arthur
Grim's Fairy Tales;Hansel & Gretel	Neill/John R.
Grimm's Animal Stories	Rae/John
Grimm's Fairy Tales	Crane/Walter
Grimm's Fairy Tales	Gruelle/Johnny
Grimm's Fairy Tales	Rackham/Arthur
Grimm's Fairy Tales	Smith/Jessie Wilcox
Guernsey Lily	Greenaway/Kate
Gulliver's Travels	Pogany/Will
Gulliver's Travels	Pogany/Will
Gulliver's Travels	Rackham/Arthur
Gulliver's Travels	Rackham/Arthur
Gulliver's Travels	Rackham/Arthur
Gulliver's Travels	Rackham/Arthur
Gulliver's Travels	Rackham/Arthur
Gulliver's Travels	Rackham/Arthur
Gulliver's Travels	Rackham/Arthur
Gulliver's Travels	Rackham/Arthur
Gulliver's Travels	Rackham/Arthur

H

Half A Rogue	Fisher/Harrison
Handy Mandy In Oz	Neill/John R.
Handy Mandy In Oz	Neill/John R.
Hans Von Pelter's Trip To Gotham	Cox/Palmer
Hansel & Gretel	Nielson/Kay
Hansel & Gretel	Nielson/Kay
Hansel & Gretel	Nielson/Kay

LISTINGS BY TITLE

Author	Publisher	Year	Price Range
Niebuhr	Cassell	1910	175 — 225
Niebuhr	Cassell		75 — 125
Lang/Andrew	Longmans	1892	175 — 225
Lang/Andrew	Longmans	1898	75 — 100
Lang/Andrew	Longmans	1916	50 — 75
Lang/Andrew	Longmans	1924	25 — 50
Beauclerk/H.	Doran	(1926)	50 — 75
Beauclerk/H.	Collins	1926	75 — 100
Greenaway/Kate	Saalfield	1907	100 — 150
Lang/Andrew	Longmans	1900	175 — 225
Lang/Andrew	Longmans	1924	25 — 50
Greene/Mrs.	Nelson	[1903]	150 — 175
Greene/Mrs.	Nelson	[1905]	100 — 125
Merriman/Henry S.	Smith,Elder	1897	125 — 150
Merriman/Henry S.	Smith,Elder	1898	75 — 100
	Reilly & Britton	(1908)	75 — 100
Crane/L.	Duffield	1911	75 — 125
Grimm Brothers	Worthington	(1888)	75 — 100
Grimm Brothers	Cupples & Leon	(1914)	150 — 200
Grimm Brothers	Heinemann	(1925)	150 — 200
Grimm Brothers	Grosset&Dunlap	[1940]	15 — 25
Coolidge/Samuel	Roberts	1881	125 — 175
Colum/Pedraic	Macmillan	1917	75 — 100
Colum/Pedraic	Harrap	1919	50 — 75
Swift/Jonathan	Dent	(1904)	75 — 125
Swift/Jonathan	Dent	[1912]	100 — 125
Swift/Jonathan	Temple Press	[1937]	40 — 60
Swift/Jonathan	Dent	1900	150 — 200
Swift/Jonathan	Dent	1901	50 — 100
Swift/Jonathan	Dent	1909	250 — 300
Swift/Jonathan	Dent	1909	750 — 1000
Swift/Jonathan	Dutton	1909	175 — 225
Swift/Jonathan	Temple Press	1939	30 — 50
MacGrath/Harold	Bobbs-Merrill	(1906)	15 — 25
Thompson/Ruth P.	Reilly & Lee	(1937)	150 — 200
Thompson/Ruth P.	Reilly & Lee	(1937)	40 — 60
	Art Printing	1876	100 — 150
Grimm Brothers	Doran	(1925)	250 — 350
Grimm Brothers	Doran	(1925)	125 — 175
Grimm Brothers	Hodder & Stoughton	[1925]	750 — 1000

LISTINGS BY TITLE

Title	Illustrator
Hansel & Gretel	Nielson/Kay
Hansel & Gretel/Snow White & Red Rose	Neill/John R.
Hansel & Grethel & Other Tales	Rackham/Arthur
Hansel & Grethel & Other Tales	Rackham/Arthur
Happy Prince (The)	Crane/Walter
Harper's Book Of Little Plays	Pyle/Howard
Harper's Fourth Reader	Pyle/Howard
Harper's Popular Cyclopaedia Of U.S. History	Pyle/Howard
Harrison Fisher Book	Fisher/Harrison
Head Of A Hundred (The)	Smith/Jessie Wilcox
Head Of A Hundred (The)	Smith/Jessie Wilcox
Head Of A Hundred (The)	Smith/Jessie Wilcox
Heartbreak Hill	Rae/John
Heartsease Or The Brothers Wife	Greenaway/Kate
Heartsease Or The Brothers Wife	Greenaway/Kate
Heartsease Or The Brothers Wife	Greenaway/Kate
Heidi	Smith/Jessie Wilcox
Heidi	Smith/Jessie Wilcox
Heidi	Smith/Jessie Wilcox
Heir Of Redclyffe (The)	Greenaway/Kate
Heir Of Redclyffe (The)	Greenaway/Kate
Heir Of Redclyffe (The)	Greenaway/Kate
Henry Esmond	Thomson/Hugh
Her First Appearance	Gibson/Charles D.
Hiawatha	Fisher/Harrison
Hiawatha	Neill/John R.
Hiawatha	Parrish/Maxfield
Hiawatha	Wyeth/N.C.
Hickory Limb(The)	O'Neill/Rose
Hind In The Wood (The)	Crane/Walter
History & Ideals Of Amer. Artt	Parrish/Maxfield
History Of American Art (A)	Pyle/Howard
History Of New York...... (A)	Pyle/Howard
History Of Reynard The Fox	Crane/Walter
History Of Reynard The Fox	Crane/Walter
History Of The American People (A)	Pyle/Howard
History Of The American People (A)	Pyle/Howard
History Of The Last Quarter Century (The)	Pyle/Howard
History Of The United States	Pyle/Howard
History Of The United States	Pyle/Howard
History Of The United States (A)	Pyle/Howard
History Of The United States (A)	Pyle/Howard

LISTINGS BY TITLE

Author	Publisher	Year	Price Range
Grimm Brothers	Doubleday		100 — 125
	Reilly & Britton	(1908)	75 — 100
Grimm Brothers	Constable	(1920)	175 — 250
Grimm Brothers	Dutton	(1920)	175 — 225
Wilde/Oscar	D. Nutt	1888	300 — 400
Briscoe/Margaret	Harper	1910	30 — 50
	Harper	1888	20 — 30
Lossing/Benson	Harper	1881	75 — 100
Fisher/Harrison	Scribner	1907	160 — 230
Goodwin/Maud W.	Little Brown	1897	85 — 100
Goodwin/Maud W.	Little Brown	1899	70 — 80
Goodwin/Maud W.	Little Brown	1900	75 — 100
Viele/H.K.	Duffield	1908	40 — 60
Yonge/Charlotte	Macmillan	(1902)	100 — 125
Yonge/Charlotte	Macmillan	1879	125 — 175
Yonge/Charlotte	Macmillan	1897	50 — 75
Spyri/Johanna	McKay	(1922)	100 — 150
Spyri/Johanna	McKay	1922	125 — 175
Spyri/Johanna	Dial Press	1935	75 — 100
Yonge/Charlotte	Macmillan	1881	75 — 100
Yonge/Charlotte	Macmillan	1881	100 — 150
Yonge/Charlotte	Macmillan	1902	50 — 75
Thackery/William M.	Macmillan		50 — 75
Davis/Richard Harding	Harper	1901	15 — 25
Longfellow/Henry W.	Bobbs-Merrill	(1906)	80 — 120
Longfellow/Henry W.	Reilly & Britton	(1909)	75 — 100
Longfellow/Henry W.	Harrap	[1911]	175 — 225
Longfellow/Henry W.	Harrap	[1911]	175 — 225
Fillmore/Parker H.	J. Lane	1910	40 — 60
	Routledge	[1875]	100 — 150
Neuhaus/Eugene	Stanford University Press	1931	20 — 35
Hartmann/Sadakichi	L.C. Page	1901	50 — 75
Knickerbocker/Diedrich	Grolier Club	1886	50 — 75
Ellis/F.S.	D. Nutt	1895	175 — 225
Ellis/F.S.	D. Nutt	1897	100 — 125
Wilson/Woodrow	Harper	1902	75 — 100
Wilson/Woodrow	Harper	1918	50 — 75
Andrews/E. Benjamin	Scribner	1896	20 — 30
Andrews/Benjamin	Scribner	1895	20 — 30
Higginson/Thomas W.	Harper	1905	20 — 30
Scudder/Horace	Sheldon	1884	25 — 35
Gordy/Wilbur	Scribner	1904	20 — 30

Listings By Title

Title	Illustrator
History/Henry Esmond	Thomson/Hugh
Hole Book (The)	Newell/Peter
Hole Book (The)	Newell/Peter
Home Again	Christy/Howard Chandler
Home Again With Me	Christy/Howard Chandler
Home Book Of Verse For Young Folks	Pogany/Will
Homes & Haunts Of Carlyle (The)	Rackham/Arthur
House Boat On The Styx	Newell/Peter
House Of A Thousand Candles	Christy/Howard Chandler
House That Jack Built	Denslow/W.W.
Household Stories	Crane/Walter
Household Stories	Crane/Walter
Household Stories	Crane/Walter
Household Stories	Crane/Walter
How Columbus Found America	Cox/Palmer
How To Draw	Pyle/Howard
Howard Pyle/A Chronicle	Pyle/Howard
Hugh Thomson: His Art	Thomson/Hugh
Hugh Wynne,Free Quaker	Pyle/Howard
Hugh Wynne,Free Quaker	Pyle/Howard
Humpty Dumpty	Denslow/W.W.
Hungarian Fairy Book	Pogany/Will
Hungarian Fairy Book	Pogany/Will
Hungry Tiger Of Oz (The)	Neill/John R.
Hungry Tiger Of Oz (The)	Neill/John R.
Hungry Tiger Of Oz (The)	Neill/John R.
Hunting Of The Snark (The)	Newell/Peter
Husbands Of Edith	Fisher/Harrison

I

Title	Illustrator
Ideal Heads	Smith/Jessie Wilcox
Ideals In Art	Crane/Walter
Illustrated Children's Birthday Book	Greenaway/Kate
Illustrated Guide To Wells-Next-The-Sea	Rackham/Arthur
Illustrated Guide To Wells-Next-The-Sea	Rackham/Arthur
Illustrated Poems Of Oliver Wendell Holmes	Pyle/Howard
Imagina	Rackham/Arthur
Imagina	Rackham/Arthur
Imagina	Rackham/Arthur
In Old New York	Pyle/Howard
In Ole Virginia	Pyle/Howard
In Powder & Crinoline	Nielson/Kay

Listings By Title

Author	Publisher	Year	Price Range
Thackeray/William	Macmillan	1905	50 — 75
Newell/Peter	Harper	(1908)	175 — 225
Newell/Peter	Harper		75 — 100
Riley/James W.	Bobbs-Merrill	(1908)	40 — 75
Riley/James W.	Bobbs-Merrill	(1908)	35 — 60
Stevenson/Burton E.	Holt	(1922)	25 — 50
	Westminster Gazette	1895	75 — 100
Bangs/John K.	Harper	1896	25 — 50
Nicholson/M.	Bobbs-Merrill	(1905)	15 — 30
Denslow/W.W.	Dillingham	(1903)	150 — 200
Grimm Brothers	American Publishing	[1894]	75 — 100
Grimm Brothers	Macmillan	1882	175 — 250
Grimm Brothers	Macmillan	1914	75 — 100
Grimm Brothers	Macmillan	1941	25 — 35
	Art Printing	1877	50 — 100
Barritt/Leon	Harper	1904	30 — 50
Abbott/C.	Harper	1925	120 — 150
Spielmann/M.H.	A&C Black	1931	85 — 125
Mitchell/Silas W.	Century	[1897]	100 — 150
Mitchell/Silas W.	Century	1899	75 — 100
	Dillingham	(1903)	200 — 300
Pogany/N.	Unwin	(1913)	130 — 165
Pogany/Nandor	Stokes		75 — 100
Thompson/Ruth P.	Reilly & Lee	(1926)	200 — 300
Thompson/Ruth P.	Reilly & Lee	(1926)	150 — 200
Thompson/Ruth P.	Reilly & Lee	(1926)	40 — 60
Carroll/Lewis	Harper	1903	125 — 150
McCutcheon/George	Dodd	1908	25 — 30
Waugh/Ida	Sunshine	1890	50 — 75
Crane/Walter	G. Bell	1905	75 — 100
Weatherby/F.E.	Mack	1882	75 — 100
Lingwood/Lemmon	Jarrold	(1894)	100 — 150
Lingwood/Lemmon	Jarrold	(1910)	75 — 100
Holmes/Oliver W.	Houghton,Mifflin	1885	35 — 50
Ford/Julia E.	Duffield	1914	100 — 175
Ford/Julia E.	Dutton	1923	50 — 75
Ford/Julia E.	Duffield	1924	50 — 75
Janvier/Thomas	Harper	1894	20 — 30
Page/Thomas N.	Scribner	1896	25 — 35
Quiller-Couch/Arthur	Hodder & Stoughton	[1913]	700 — 900

LISTINGS BY TITLE

Title	Illustrator
In The Bishop's Carriage	Fisher/Harrison
In The Closed Room	Smith/Jessie Wilcox
In The Closed Room	Smith/Jessie Wilcox
In The Closed Room	Smith/Jessie Wilcox
In The Evening Of His Days	Rackham/Arthur
In The Valley	Pyle/Howard
Inca Princess (The)	Pyle/Howard
India Impressions	Crane/Walter
Indian History For Young Folks	Pyle/Howard
Ingoldsby Legends (The)	Rackham/Arthur
Ingoldsby Legends (The)	Rackham/Arthur
Ingoldsby Legends (The)	Rackham/Arthur
Ingoldsby Legends (The)	Rackham/Arthur
Ingoldsby Legends (The)	Rackham/Arthur
Ingoldsby Legends (The)	Rackham/Arthur
Ingoldsby Legends (The)	Rackham/Arthur
Irish Fairy Tales	Rackham/Arthur
Irish Fairy Tales	Rackham/Arthur
Irish Fairy Tales	Rackham/Arthur
Irish Fairy Tales	Rackham/Arthur
Isis Very Much Unveiled	Rackham/Arthur
Island Of Enchantment (The)	Pyle/Howard
Italian Villas & Their Gardens	Parrish/Maxfield

J

Title	Illustrator
J. Cole	Neill/John R.
Jack & The Bean-Stalk	Neill/John R.
Jack & The Beanstalk	Denslow/W.W.
Jack & The Beanstalk/Robinson Crusoe	Neill/John R.
Jack Pumpkinhead Of Oz	Neill/John R.
Jack Pumpkinhead Of Oz	Neill/John R.
Jack The Giant Killer	Thomson/Hugh
Jane Cable	Fisher/Harrison
Jane Eyre	Dulac/Edmund
Janice Meredith	Pyle/Howard
Japonette	Gibson/Charles D.
Jell-O Girl Entertains (The)	O'Neill/Rose
Jemima Puddle Duck's Painting Book	Potter/Beatrix
Jewel Weed	Fisher/Harrison
Jeweled Toad (The)	Denslow/W.W.
Jinglebob	Wyeth/N.C.
John Dough & The Cherub	Neill/John R.

LISTINGS BY TITLE

Author	Publisher	Year	Price Range
Michelson/M.	Bobbs-Merrill	(1904)	20 — 30
Burnett/Frances Hodgson	Grosset&Dunlap	(1904)	25 — 50
Burnett/Frances Hodgson	Hodder & Stoughton	1904	100 — 150
Burnett/Frances Hodgson	McClure,Phillips	1904	100 — 150
Friederichs/Hulda	Westminster Gazette	1896	200 — 300
Frederic/Harold	Scribner	1890	30 — 50
	Lippincott	1886	15 — 25
Crane/Walter	Macmillan	1907	100 — 125
Drake/Francis	Harper	1886	35 — 50
Ingoldsby/Thomas	Heinemann	(1909)	125 — 150
Ingoldsby/Thomas	Dent	1898	175 — 225
Ingoldsby/Thomas	Dent	1907	200 — 300
Ingoldsby/Thomas	Dent	1907	750 — 1000
Ingoldsby/Thomas	Dutton	1907	200 — 250
Ingoldsby/Thomas	Heinemann	1919	100 — 125
Ingoldsby/Thomas	Dent		125 — 150
Stephens/James	Macmillan	1920	850 — 1000
Stephens/James	Macmillan	1920	175 — 250
Stephens/James	Macmillan	1920	175 — 250
Stephens/James	Macmillan	1924	125 — 175
Garrett/Fydell E.	Westminster Gazette	[1894]	75 — 100
Forman/Justus M.	Harper	1905	25 — 35
Wharton/Edith	Century	1904	200 — 300
	Reilly & Britton	(1908)	75 — 100
	Reilly & Britton	(1908)	75 — 100
Denslow/W.W.	Dillingham	(1903)	150 — 200
	Reilly & Britton	(1908)	150 — 200
Thompson/Ruth P.	Reilly & Lee	(1929)	250 — 350
Thompson/Ruth P.	Reilly & Lee	(1929)	40 — 60
Thomson/Hugh	Macmillan	1898	160 — 200
McCutcheon/George	Dodd	1906	20 — 30
Bronte/Emily	Dutton		125 — 175
Ford/Paul Leicester	Dodd	1899	35 — 50
Chambers/R.	Appleton	1912	20 — 30
O'Neill/Rose	Jell-O Co.	[1920]	100 — 125
Potter/Beatrix	Warne	[1925]	100 — 150
Winter/A.A.	Bobbs-Merrill	(1910)	20 — 30
Johnston/I.M.	Bobbs-Merrill	(1907)	225 — 275
Rollins/P.A.	Scribner	1930	100 — 150
Baum/L. Frank	Reilly & Britton	(1906)	600 — 800

LISTINGS BY TITLE

Title	Illustrator
John Dough & The Cherub	Neill/John R.
John Dough & The Cherub	Neill/John R.
Johnny Gruelle's Golden Book	Gruelle/Johnny
Johnny Mouse/Wishing Stick	Gruelle/Johnny
Jolly Chinee	Cox/Palmer
Juvenile Budget	Cox/Palmer

K

Kabumpo In Oz	Neill/John R.
Kabumpo In Oz	Neill/John R.
Kabumpo In Oz	Neill/John R.
Kasidah Of Haji Abdu El-Yezdi	Pogany/Will
Kate Greenaway	Greenaway/Kate
Kate Greenaway Pictures	Greenaway/Kate
Kate Greenaway's Alphabet	Greenaway/Kate
Kate Greenaway's Birthday Book	Greenaway/Kate
Kate Greenaway's Book Of Games	Greenaway/Kate
Kate Greenaway's Book Of Games	Greenaway/Kate
Kate Greenaway's Carols	Greenaway/Kate
Kate Greenaway's Painting Book	Greenaway/Kate
Kate Greenaway: Sixteen Examples In Colour	Greenaway/Kate
Kate Greenaway: Sixteen Examples In Colour	Greenaway/Kate
Kenilworth	Ford/H.J.
Kenilworth	Ford/H.J.
Kentucky Cardinal Aftermath	Thomson/Hugh
Kewpie Kutouts (The)	O'Neill/Rose
Kewpie Primer	O'Neill/Rose
Kewpies & Dotty Darling (The)	O'Neill/Rose
Kewpies & Dotty Darling (The)	O'Neill/Rose
Kewpies & Runaway Baby	O'Neill/Rose
Kewpies: Their Book (The)	O'Neill/Rose
Kidnapped	Pyle/Howard
Kidnapped	Wyeth/N.C.
Kidnapped	Wyeth/N.C.
Kidnapped	Wyeth/N.C.
King Albert's Book	Crane/Walter
King Albert's Book	Dulac/Edmund
King Albert's Book	Fisher/Harrison
King Albert's Book	Gibson/Charles D.
King Albert's Book	Nielson/Kay
King Albert's Book	Parrish/Maxfield
King Albert's Book	Rackham/Arthur

LISTINGS BY TITLE

Author	Publisher	Year	Price Range
Baum/L. Frank	Reilly & Britton	(1906)	200 — 300
Baum/L. Frank	Reilly & Lee	(1906)	150 — 175
Gruelle/Johnny	Donohue	[1940]	75 — 150
Gruelle/Johnny	Bobbs-Merrill	(1922)	75 — 100
Cox/Palmer	Conkey	(1900)	75 — 100
Cox/Palmer	Donohue		30 — 50
Thompson/Ruth P.	Reilly & Lee	(1922)	200 — 300
Thompson/Ruth P.	Reilly & Lee	(1922)	125 — 175
Thompson/Ruth P.	Reilly & Lee	(1922)	40 — 60
Burton/R.	McKay	(1931)	65 — 100
Spielmann/M.H.	A&C Black	1905	75 — 150
	Warne	1921	150 — 200
Greenaway/Kate	Routledge	[1885]	150 — 200
Greenaway/Kate	Routledge	[1880]	175 — 250
Greenaway/Kate	Routledge	[1889]	200 — 250
Greenaway/Kate	Warne	[1890]	100 — 150
	Routledge	[1883]	100 — 150
	Warne		75 — 125
Spielmann/M.H.	A&C Black	1910	100 — 150
Spielmann/M.H.	A&C Black	1911	75 — 125
Scott/Sir Walter	Jack	(1920)	100 — 125
Scott/Sir Walter	McKay		50 — 75
Allen/J.L.	Macmillan	1900	60 — 80
O'Neill/Rose	Stokes	(1914)	700 — 900
O'Neill/Rose	Stokes	(1916)	150 — 200
O'Neill/Rose	Stokes	(1912)	200 — 300
O'Neill/Rose	Dent	1916	175 — 225
O'Neill/Rose	Doubleday	1928	175 — 225
O'Neill/Rose	Stokes	(1913)	225 — 325
Stevenson/Robert Louis	Scribner	1895	75 — 100
Stevenson/Robert Louis	Scribner	(1941)	35 — 50
Stevenson/Robert Louis	Scribner	1913	150 — 200
Stevenson/Robert Louis	Scribner	1940	40 — 65
	Daily Telegraph	[1914]	50 — 100
	Daily Telegraph	[1914]	50 — 100
	Daily Telegraph	[1914]	50 — 100
	Daily Telegraph	[1914]	50 — 100
	Daily Telegraph	[1914]	50 — 100
	Daily Telegraph	[1914]	50 — 100
	Daily Telegraph	[1914]	50 — 100

LISTINGS BY TITLE

Title	Illustrator
King Arthur & His Knights	Neill/John R.
King Arthur & His Knights	Neill/John R.
King Arthur's Nights	Crane/Walter
King Arthur's Nights	Crane/Walter
King Of Ireland's Son	Pogany/Will
King Of Ireland's Son	Pogany/Will
King Of Ireland's Son	Pogany/Will
King Of The Golden River	Rackham/Arthur
King Of The Golden River	Rackham/Arthur
King Of The Golden River	Rackham/Arthur
Kingdom Of The Pearl	Dulac/Edmund
Kingdom Of Why	Newell/Peter
Kingdoms Curious	Rackham/Arthur
Kingsway Shakespeare (The)	Rackham/Arthur
Kitchen Fun	Smith/Jessie Wilcox
Kitchen Fun	Smith/Jessie Wilcox
Knave Of Hearts (The)	Parrish/Maxfield
Knave Of Hearts (The)	Parrish/Maxfield
Knickerbocker's History Of Ny	Parrish/Maxfield
Knickerbocker's History Of Ny	Parrish/Maxfield
Knights Of The Round Table (The)	Crane/Walter

L

Lady In The White Vail	O'Neill/Rose
Lady Of Shalott (The)	Pyle/Howard
Lady Of The Lake	Christy/Howard Chandler
Land Of Enchantment (The)	Rackham/Arthur
Land Of Enchantment (The)	Rackham/Arthur
Land Of Oz (The)	Neill/John R.
Land Of Oz (The)	Neill/John R.
Land Of Oz (The)	Neill/John R.
Land Of Oz (The)	Neill/John R.
Land Of Oz (The)	Neill/John R.
Land Of Oz (The)	Neill/John R.
Langford Of The Three Bars	Wyeth/N.C.
Language Of Flowers	Greenaway/Kate
Language Of Flowers	Greenaway/Kate
Larger History Of The United States (A)	Pyle/Howard
Last Of The Mohicans	Wyeth/N.C.
Last Of The Mohicans	Wyeth/N.C.
Laugh & Learn	Barker/Cicely Mary
Legend Of Sleepy Hollow (The)	Rackham/Arthur

LISTINGS BY TITLE

Author	Publisher	Year	Price Range
Allen/Phillip S.	Rand Mcnally	(1924)	30 — 60
Allen/Phillip S.	Rand Mcnally	(1936)	20 — 30
Gilbert/Henry	Nelson	(1911)	125 —150
Gilbert/Henry	Jack	1911	175 — 225
Colum/Pedraic	Holt	1916	75 —100
Colum/Pedraic	Harrap	1920	75 —100
Colum/Pedraic	Macmillan	1921	50 — 75
Ruskin/John	Harrap	(1932)	150 —200
Ruskin/John	Harrap	(1932)	600 —800
Ruskin/John	Lippincott	1932	100 —150
Rosenthal/L.	Brentano's	[1920]	375 —475
Stone/S.B.	Bobbs-Merrill	(1913)	100 —150
Hamilton/Myra	Heinemann	1905	175 —250
	Harrap		125 —150
Bell/Louise P.	Harter	1932	50 — 75
Bell/Louise P.	Perks Publishing	1946	35 — 50
Saunders/Louise	Scribner	1925	750 —1000
Saunders/Louise	Scribner	1925	600 — 800
Irving/Washington	Russell	1900	125 —200
Irving/Washington	Dodd	1915	175 —250
Gilbert/Henry	Jack	1915	100 —150
O'Neill/Rose	Harper	1909	75 —100
Tennyson/Alfred	Dodd	(1881)	350 —450
Scott/Sir Walter	Bobbs-Merrill	(1910)	40 — 75
	Cassell	1907	175 —225
	Cassell	1907	200 —250
Baum/L. Frank	Reilly & Britton	(1904)	400 —600
Baum/L. Frank	Reilly & Britton	(1904)	175 —250
Baum/L. Frank	Reilly & Britton	(1904)	100 —150
Baum/L. Frank	Reilly & Lee	(1904)	75 —125
Baum/L. Frank	Reilly & Lee	(1904)	40 — 60
Baum/L. Frank	Reilly & Lee	(1904)	75 —125
Boyles/K.	McClurg	1907	40 — 60
Greenaway/Kate	Routledge	[1884]	125 —175
Greenaway/Kate	Warne	[1900]	75 —125
Higginson/Thomas W.	Harper	1886	40 — 60
Cooper/James Fenimore	Scribner	1919	150 —175
Cooper/James Fenimore	Scribner	1925	50 — 75
Humphreys/Jennett	Blackie & Sons	[1936]	50 — 75
Irving/Washington	Harrap	(1928)	200 —300

LISTINGS BY TITLE

Title	Illustrator
Legend Of Sleepy Hollow (The)	Rackham/Arthur
Legend Of Sleepy Hollow (The)	Rackham/Arthur
Legend Of Sleepy Hollow (The)	Rackham/Arthur
Legend Of Sleepy Hollow (The)	Rackham/Arthur
Legend Of The Tulip	Pogany/Will
Legends For Lionel	Crane/Walter
Legends Of Charlemagne	Wyeth/N.C.
Letters Of A Woman Homesteader	Wyeth/N.C.
Liberty Belles	Christy/Howard Chandler
Library (The)	Greenaway/Kate
Library Of Universal Adventure	Pyle/Howard
Life Of A Century (The)	Rackham/Arthur
Light Of Asia (The)	Pogany/Will
Light Princess	Humphrey/Maud
Lilac Fairy Book (The)	Ford/H.J.
Lilac Fairy Book (The)	Ford/H.J.
Lilac Fairy Book (The)	Ford/H.J.
Lincoln & The Sleeping Sentinel	Pyle/Howard
Line & Form	Crane/Walter
Line Of Love (The)	Pyle/Howard
Lion & The Unicorn (The)	Christy/Howard Chandler
Lions Of The Lord	O'Neill/Rose
Listen & Sing	Smith/Jessie Wilcox
Listen & Sing	Smith/Jessie Wilcox
Little Ann & Other Poems	Greenaway/Kate
Little Ann & Other Poems	Greenaway/Kate
Little Black Sambo	Neill/John R.
Little Black Sambo/Uncle Tom's Cabin	Neill/John R.
Little Book Of Old Rhymes (A)	Barker/Cicely Mary
Little Brother & Little Sister	Rackham/Arthur
Little Brother & Little Sister	Rackham/Arthur
Little Brother & Little Sister	Rackham/Arthur
Little Brown Bear	Gruelle/Johnny
Little Brown Bear	Gruelle/Johnny
Little Brown Bear	Gruelle/Johnny
Little Child's Book Of Stories (A)	Smith/Jessie Wilcox
Little Child's Book Of Stories (A)	Smith/Jessie Wilcox
Little Child's Book Of Stories (A)	Smith/Jessie Wilcox
Little Colonial Dame	Humphrey/Maud
Little Continentals	Humphrey/Maud
Little Folks	Greenaway/Kate
Little Folks Fairy Book (The)	Rackham/Arthur

LISTINGS BY TITLE

Author	Publisher	Year	Price Range
Irving/Washington	Harrap	(1928)	175 — 250
Irving/Washington	Harrap	(1928)	1000 — 1300
Irving/Washington	McKay	(1928)	150 — 200
Irving/Washington	McKay	(1928)	1000 — 1300
Newman/I.	Whitman	(1928)	30 — 40
Crane/Walter	Cassell	1887	150 — 200
Bullfinch/Thomas	Cosmopolitan	1924	125 — 200
Stewart/E.P.	Houghton,Mifflin	1914	40 — 60
	Bobbs-Merrill	(1912)	125 — 175
Lang/Andrew	Macmillan	1881	200 — 300
Howels/William & Perry/Thomas	Harper	1888	50 — 75
Hodder/Edwin	Newnes	1901	100 — 125
Arnold/Sir Edward	McKay	(1932)	75 — 100
	Putnam	1893	200 — 300
Lang/Andrew	Longmans	1910	200 — 250
Lang/Andrew	Longmans	1914	50 — 75
Lang/Andrew	Longmans	1919	50 — 75
Chittenden/Charles	Harper	1909	15 — 25
Crane/Walter	G. Bell	1900	125 — 175
Cabbell/James B.	Harper	1905	75 — 100
Davis/Richard Harding	Scribner	1899	15 — 30
Wilson/H.L.	Lothrop	(1903)	40 — 60
Glenn/Mabelle	Ginn	(1936)	35 — 50
Glenn/Mabelle	Ginn	(1943)	25 — 35
Taylor/Jane & Ann	Routledge	[1883]	150 — 200
Taylor/Jane & Ann	Warne	[1900]	100 — 150
	Reilly & Britton	(1908)	150 — 200
	Reilly & Britton	(1908)	150 — 200
Barker/Cicely Mary	Blackie & Sons		30 — 50
Grimm Brothers	Constable	(1917)	200 — 300
Grimm Brothers	Constable	(1917)	750 — 2000
Grimm Brothers	Dodd	(1917)	200 — 250
Gruelle/Johnny	Volland	(1920)	75 — 100
Gruelle/Johnny	Volland	(1920)	50 — 75
Gruelle/Johnny	Donohue	(1920)	35 — 50
Skinner/Ada & Eleanor	Dial Press	(1935)	50 — 75
Skinner/Ada & Eleanor	Duffield	1922	125 — 150
Skinner/Ada & Eleanor	Dial Press	1935	75 — 100
Sage/A.C.	Stokes	(1898)	50 — 70
	Stokes	1900	400 — 600
	Cassell	(1877)	75 — 100
Hamer/Sam H.	Cassell	1905	125 — 150

LISTINGS BY TITLE

Title	Illustrator
Little Folks Illustrated Annual	Smith/Jessie Wilcox
Little Folks Painting Book (The)	Greenaway/Kate
Little Folks Picture Album	Rackham/Arthur
Little Folks Plays (The)	Rackham/Arthur
Little Folks Plays (The)	Rackham/Arthur
Little Gift Book	Fisher/Harrison
Little Grownups	Humphrey/Maud
Little Heroes & Heroines	Humphrey/Maud
Little Homespun	Humphrey/Maud
Little Lamb Prince (The)	Neill/John R.
Little Miss Peggy	Crane/Walter
Little Miss Peggy	Crane/Walter
Little Mistress Goodhope	Smith/Jessie Wilcox
Little Mistress Goodhope	Smith/Jessie Wilcox
Little Mother Goose	Pogany/Will
Little Mother Goose (The)	Smith/Jessie Wilcox
Little Mother Goose (The)	Smith/Jessie Wilcox
Little Mother Goose (The)	Smith/Jessie Wilcox
Little Ones	Humphrey/Maud
Little Paul's Christ Child	Smith/Jessie Wilcox
Little Queen Anne & Her Majesty's Letters	Crane/Walter
Little Question Of Ladies' Rights	O'Neill/Rose
Little Red Riding Hood	Denslow/W.W.
Little Red Riding Hood	Neill/John R.
Little Red Riding Hood/Sleeping Beauty	Neill/John R.
Little Shepherd Of Kingdom Come (The)	Wyeth/N.C.
Little Shepherd Of Kingdom Come (The)	Wyeth/N.C.
Little Soldiers & Sailors	Humphrey/Maud
Little Sunny Stories	Gruelle/Johnny
Little Sunny Stories	Gruelle/Johnny
Little Sunny Stories	Gruelle/Johnny
Little Sunny Stories	Gruelle/Johnny
Little Taylor Of The Winding Way	Pogany/Will
Little White Bird	Rackham/Arthur
Little White Bird	Rackham/Arthur
Little Wizard Series	Neill/John R.
Little Wizard Series	Neill/John R.
Little Wizard Stories Of Oz	Neill/John R.
Little Wizard Stories Of Oz	Neill/John R.
Little Women	Humphrey/Maud
Little Women	Smith/Jessie Wilcox
Little Women	Smith/Jessie Wilcox

LISTINGS BY TITLE

Author	Publisher	Year	Price Range
Pratt/Charles & Ella	Small,Maynard	(1918)	75 — 100
Weatherly/George	Cassell	1879	125 — 175
Hamer/Sam H.	Cassell	1904	100 — 125
Hill & Browne	Cassell	1903	125 — 150
Hill & Browne	Cassell	1906	75 — 100
Fisher/Harrison	Scribner	1913	180 — 260
Tucker/E.S.	Stokes	1897	400 — 600
Humphrey/Maud	Stokes	1899	200 — 350
Ogden/R.	Stokes	(1897)	100 — 140
	Reilly & Britton	(1908)	75 — 100
Molesworth/Mrs.	Macmillan	1887	75 — 100
Molesworth/Mrs.	Macmillan	1912	40 — 60
Taylor/Mary I.	McClurg	(1902)	100 — 125
Taylor/Mary I.	McClurg	1902	150 — 175
	McBride	1915	165 — 190
Smith/Jessie Wilcox	Dodd	(1918)	125 — 160
Smith/Jessie Wilcox	Dodd	(1918)	100 — 125
Smith/Jessie Wilcox	Musson	1921	75 — 100
Tucker/E.S.	Stokes	1898	350 — 500
Bull/Kathryn J.	Np	1929	50 — 75
Crane/Walter	Marcus Ward	1885	150 — 250
Fillmore/P.H.	J. Lane	1916	50 — 75
Denslow/W.W.	Dillingham	(1903)	125 — 175
	Reilly & Britton	(1908)	100 — 125
	Reilly & Britton	(1908)	100 — 125
Fox/John	Scribner	1931	125 — 175
Fox/John	Scribner	1931	500 — 750
Humphrey/Maud	Stokes	(1899)	250 — 300
Gruelle/Johnny	Donohue	(1919)	35 — 50
Gruelle/Johnny	Volland	(1919)	75 — 100
Gruelle/Johnny	Volland	(1919)	65 — 85
Gruelle/Johnny	Laidlaw	(1924)	35 — 50
Crownfield/Gertrude	Macmillan		75 — 100
Barrie/J.M.	Scribner	1912	250 — 300
Barrie/J.M.	Scribner	1913	30 — 50
Baum/L. Frank	Reilly & Britton	(1913)	150 — 200
Baum/L. Frank	Reilly & Lee	(1913)	100 — 125
Baum/L. Frank	Reilly & Britton	(1914)	350 — 450
Baum/L. Frank	Reilly & Britton	(1914)	200 — 300
Alcott/Louisa May	Holiday	1906	75 — 100
Alcott/Louisa May	Little Brown	1915	125 — 150
Alcott/Louisa May	Little Brown	1917	100 — 125

LISTINGS BY TITLE

Title	Illustrator
Little Women	Smith/Jessie Wilcox
Little Women	Smith/Jessie Wilcox
Littledom Castle & Other Tales	Rackham/Arthur
Littledom Castle & Other Tales	Rackham/Arthur
Littledom Castle & Other Tales	Rackham/Arthur
Littlest Ones (The)	Humphrey/Maud
Lohengrin	Pogany/Will
Lohengrin	Pogany/Will
London	Gibson/Charles D.
London Garland (A)	Rackham/Arthur
London Garland (A)	Rackham/Arthur
Lonesomest Doll (The)	Rackham/Arthur
Long Roll (The)	Wyeth/N.C.
Long Roll (The)	Wyeth/N.C.
Lord Of The Rushie River (The)	Barker/Cicely Mary
Lost Boy (The)	Wyeth/N.C.
Lost King Of Oz (The)	Neill/John R.
Lost King Of Oz (The)	Neill/John R.
Lost King Of Oz (The)	Neill/John R.
Lost Princess Of Oz (The)	Neill/John R.
Lost Princess Of Oz (The)	Neill/John R.
Lost Princess Of Oz (The)	Neill/John R.
Lost Princess Of Oz (The)	Neill/John R.
Lost Princess Of Oz (The)	Neill/John R.
Love Of The Foolish Angel	Dulac/Edmund
Lovely Garden	Rae/John
Loves Of Edwy	O'Neill/Rose
Lucky Bucky In Oz	Neill/John R.
Lucky Bucky In Oz	Neill/John R.
Lucky Locket	Rae/John
Lullaby Book (The)	Smith/Jessie Wilcox
Lure Of The Garden	Parrish/Maxfield
Lyrics Pathetic & Humerous	Dulac/Edmund

M

Madame D'Aulnoy's Fairy Tales	Greenaway/Kate
Magic Bed (The)	Neill/John R.
Magic Cloak	Neill/John R.
Magic Horse	Dulac/Edmund
Magic Jaw Bone	Neill/John R.
Magic Of Kindness (The)	Crane/Walter
Magic Of Oz (The)	Neill/John R.

LISTINGS BY TITLE

Author	Publisher	Year	Price Range
Alcott/Louisa May	Little Brown	1922	50 — 75
Alcott/Louisa May	Little Brown	1930	25 — 50
Spielmann/Mrs. M.H.	Routledge	(1912)	75 —100
Spielmann/Mrs. M.H.	Routledge	1903	150 —200
Spielmann/Mrs. M.H.	Dutton	1903	125 —150
Tucker/Elizabeth	Stokes	1898	300 —400
Rolleston/T.	Harrap	(1913)	150 —200
Wagner/Richard	Crowell	(1913)	100 —150
Gibson/Charles D.	Scribner	1897	125 —175
Henley/W.E.	Macmillan	1895	175 —225
Henley/W.E.	Macmillan	1895	250 —350
Brown/Abbie F.	Houghton,Mifflin	(1928)	175 —250
Johnston/Mary	Houghton,Mifflin	1911	20 — 30
Johnston/Mary	Houghton,Mifflin	1911	20 — 40
Barker/Cicely Mary	Blackie & Sons	[1938]	50 — 75
Van Dyke/Henry	Harper	(1914)	20 — 30
Thompson/Ruth P.	Reilly & Lee	(1925)	200 —300
Thompson/Ruth P.	Reilly & Lee	(1925)	125 —175
Thompson/Ruth P.	Reilly & Lee	(1925)	40 — 60
Baum/L. Frank	Reilly & Britton	(1917)	500 —600
Baum/L. Frank	Reilly & Britton	(1917)	150 —250
Baum/L. Frank	Reilly & Lee	(1917)	100 —150
Baum/L. Frank	Reilly & Lee	(1917)	40 — 60
Baum/L. Frank	Reilly & Lee	(1917)	75 —125
Beauclerk/H.	Collins	1929	75 —100
Snyder/Fairmont	Volland	(1919)	50 — 75
O'Neill/Rose	Lothrop	(1904)	50 — 75
Neill/John R.	Reilly & Lee	(1942)	250 —350
Neill/John R.	Reilly & Lee	(1942)	40 — 60
Rae/John	Volland	(1928)	50 — 75
Shelby/Annie B.	Duffield	1921	50 — 75
Hawthorne/Hildegarde	Century	1911	50 —125
Dulac/Edmund	Warne	1908	300 —400
Greenaway/Kate	Gall & Inglis	1871	150 —175
Hartwell	Altemus	(1906)	50 — 75
Baum/L. Frank	Reilly & Lee	(1916)	500 —750
Housman/Laurence	Hodder & Stoughton	(1911)	200 —250
James/Hart	Altemus	(1906)	50 — 75
Mayhew Brothers	Cassell	1869	50 — 75
Baum/L. Frank	Reilly & Lee	(1919)	400 —600

LISTINGS BY TITLE

Title	Illustrator
Magic Of Oz (The)	Neill/John R.
Magic Of Oz (The)	Neill/John R.
Magical Land Of Noom (The)	Gruelle/Johnny
Magical Land Of Noom (The)	Gruelle/Johnny
Magical Land Of Noom (The)	Gruelle/Johnny
Magician/One Day	Neill/John R.
Magyar Fairy Tales	Pogany/Will
Maid Marian....	Thomson/Hugh
Maid-At-Arms	Christy/Howard Chandler
Maidens Fair	Fisher/Harrison
Make-Belive Men & Women	Humphrey/Maud
Man From Brodneys	Fisher/Harrison
Man In Moon Stories...	Gruelle/Johnny
Man In Moon Stories...	Gruelle/Johnny
Man In The Lower Ten	Christy/Howard Chandler
Man With The Hoe & Other Poems (The)	Pyle/Howard
Mansfield Park	Thomson/Hugh
Marcella Stories	Gruelle/Johnny
Marcella Stories	Gruelle/Johnny
Marcella Stories	Gruelle/Johnny
Marigold Garden	Greenaway/Kate
Marigold Garden	Greenaway/Kate
Market Place (The)	Fisher/Harrison
Marriage Of Cupid & Psyche	Dulac/Edmund
Marvelous Land Of Oz (The)	Neill/John R.
Mary Had A Little Lamb	Denslow/W.W.
Masque Of Comus (The)	Dulac/Edmund
Masque Of Comus (The)	Dulac/Edmund
Masque Of Days (A)	Crane/Walter
Master Simon's Garden	Rae/John
Master-Mistress	O'Neill/Rose
Masterman Ready	Rae/John
Me & Lawson	Denslow/W.W.
Memories And Garden	Smith/Jessie Wilcox
Men Of Concord	Wyeth/N.C.
Men Of Iron	Pyle/Howard
Men Of Iron	Pyle/Howard
Merry Adventures Of Robin Hood (The)	Pyle/Howard
Merry Adventures Of Robin Hood (The)	Pyle/Howard
Merry Adventures Of Robin Hood (The)	Pyle/Howard
Merry Men & Other Tales & Fables (The)	Pyle/Howard
Merry Wives Of Windsor	Thomson/Hugh

LISTINGS BY TITLE

Author	Publisher	Year	Price Range
Baum/L. Frank	Reilly & Lee	(1919)	150 — 200
Baum/L. Frank	Reilly & Lee	(1919)	40 — 60
Gruelle/Johnny	Donohue	(1922)	75 — 100
Gruelle/Johnny	Volland	(1922)	175 — 250
Gruelle/Johnny	Volland	(1922)	100 — 150
Jenks/Tudor	Altemus	(1905)	75 — 100
Pogany/N.	Dutton	(1930)	100 — 150
Peacock/T.L.	Macmillan	1895	50 — 75
Chambers/R.	Harper	1902	20 — 35
Fisher/Harrison	Dodd	1912	300 — 450
Tucker/Elizabeth	Stokes	(1897)	380 — 500
McCutcheon/George	Dodd	1908	20 — 35
Lawrence/Josephine	Cupples & Leon	(1922)	125 — 175
Lawrence/Josephine	Whitman	1930	35 — 50
Rinehart/M.R.	Bobbs-Merrill	(1909)	35 — 50
Markham/Edwin	McClure	1900	75 — 100
Austen/J.	Macmillan		50 — 75
Gruelle/Johnny	Donohue	(1929)	75 — 100
Gruelle/Johnny	Volland	(1929)	175 — 225
Gruelle/Johnny	Volland	(1929)	125 — 175
Greenaway/Kate	Routledge	[1885]	225 — 275
Greenaway/Kate	Warne	[1900]	100 — 150
Frederic/H.	Stokes	1899	30 — 40
			200 — 300
Baum/L. Frank	Reilly & Britton	(1904)	800 — 1000
Denslow/W.W.	Dillingham	(1903)	125 — 175
	Limited Editions Club	1954	125 — 175
	Heritage Press	1954	35 — 45
Crane/Walter	Cassell	1901	200 — 300
Meigs/C.	Macmillan	1929	50 — 75
O'Neill/Rose	Knopf	1922	50 — 75
Marryat	Harper	1928	35 — 50
Webb/R.	Dillingham	(1905)	75 — 100
Saville/Emily A.	Privately Printed	1924	100 — 150
Thoreau/Henry D.	Houghton,Mifflin	1936	175 — 225
Pyle/Howard	Harper	(1919)	40 — 60
Pyle/Howard	Harper	1892	150 — 200
Pyle/Howard	Scribner	(1911)	10 — 20
Pyle/Howard	Scribner	1884	150 — 175
Pyle/Howard	Scribner	1917	75 — 100
Stevfenson/Robert Louis	Scribner	1895	75 — 100
Shakespeare/William	Stokes	(1910)	100 — 140

LISTINGS BY TITLE

Title	Illustrator
Merry Wives Of Windsor	Thomson/Hugh
Merry Wives Of Windsor (The)	Crane/Walter
Merry-Go-Round	Newell/Peter
Michael Strogoff	Wyeth/N.C.
Midsummer Night's Dream	Rackham/Arthur
Midsummer Night's Dream	Rackham/Arthur
Midsummer Night's Dream	Rackham/Arthur
Midsummer Night's Dream	Rackham/Arthur
Midsummer Night's Dream	Rackham/Arthur
Midsummer Night's Dream	Rackham/Arthur
Militants (The)	Wyeth/N.C.
Miniature Under The Window	Greenaway/Kate
Modern Alladin (A)	Pyle/Howard
Modern Book Illustrators & Their Work	Rackham/Arthur
Modern Illustration	Pyle/Howard
Modern Pen Drawings	Pyle/Howard
Molly Bawn	Rackham/Arthur
Money-Spinner (The)	Rackham/Arthur
Money-Spinner (The)	Rackham/Arthur
Monster... (The)	Newell/Peter
More Really-So Stories	Rae/John
More Really-So Stories	Rae/John
More Tales From Arabian Nights	Pogany/Will
More Tales Of The Stumps	Rackham/Arthur
Mosses From An Old Manse	Smith/Jessie Wilcox
Mosses From An Old Manse	Smith/Jessie Wilcox
Mosses From An Old Manse	Smith/Jessie Wilcox
Mother	Rae/John
Mother Goose	Greenaway/Kate
Mother Goose	Greenaway/Kate
Mother Goose	Greenaway/Kate
Mother Goose	Humphrey/Maud
Mother Goose	Rackham/Arthur
Mother Goose	Rackham/Arthur
Mother Goose	Rackham/Arthur
Mother Goose	Rackham/Arthur
Mother Goose	Smith/Jessie Wilcox
Mother Goose	Smith/Jessie Wilcox
Mother Goose	Smith/Jessie Wilcox
Mother Goose	Smith/Jessie Wilcox
Mother Goose For Grownups	Newell/Peter
Mother Goose In Prose	Parrish/Maxfield

LISTINGS BY TITLE

Author	Publisher	Year	Price Range
Shakespeare/William	Heinemann	1910	120 — 160
Shakespeare/William	Dent	1896	100 — 150
Wells/Carolyn	Russell	1901	100 — 150
Verne/Jules	Scribner	1927	150 — 200
Shakespeare/William	Limited Editions Club	(1939)	250 — 350
Shakespeare/William	Heinemann	1908	225 — 325
Shakespeare/William	Heinemann	1908	750 —1000
Shakespeare/William	Doubleday	1908	200 — 250
Shakespeare/William	Heinemann	1911	125 — 175
Shakespeare/William	Heinemann	1920	175 — 250
Andrews/M.S.	Scribner	1907	25 — 40
	McLoughlin	[1883]	125 — 175
Pyle/Howard	Harper	1892	100 — 130
Salaman/M.C.	The Studio	1914	75 — 125
Pennell/Joseph	George Bell	1895	50 — 75
Holme/Charles	The Studio	1901	50 — 75
Hungerford/Margaret Wolfe	Newnesw	(1904)	300 — 500
Merriman/Henry S.	Smith,Elder	1896	150 — 250
Merriman/Henry S.	Smith,Elder	1897	100 — 150
Crane/S.	Harper	1899	150 — 200
Gordon/Elizabeth	Volland	(1929)	65 — 85
Gordon/Elizabeth	Wise-Parslow		25 — 50
Olcott/F.J.	Holt	1915	75 — 135
Bleackley/Horace	Ward,Lock	1902	175 — 225
Hawthorne/Nathaniel	Houghton,Mifflin	1900	750 —1000
Hawthorne/Nathaniel	Houghton,Mifflin	1900	75 — 100
Hawthorne/Nathaniel	Houghton,Mifflin	1903	50 — 60
Wister/O.	Dodd	1907	25 — 45
Greenaway/Kate	Routledge	[1881]	175 — 225
	McLoughlin	[1882]	150 — 175
Greenaway/Kate	Warne	[1900]	75 — 100
Humphrey/Maud	Stokes	1891	500 — 700
	Heinemann	(1913)	200 — 300
	Heinemann	[1913]	1000 —1500
	Century	1913	225 — 325
	Heinemann		75 — 100
Smith/Jessie Wilcox	Dodd	(1912)	175 — 250
Smith/Jessie Wilcox	Dodd	(1916)	125 — 150
Smith/Jessie Wilcox	Hodder & Stoughton	(1938)	75 — 100
Smith/Jessie Wilcox	Hodder & Stoughton	[1920]	125 — 150
Carryl/Guy W.	Harper	1900	100 — 125
Baum/L. Frank	Way/Williams	(1897)	4000 —5000

LISTINGS BY TITLE

Title	Illustrator
Mother Goose In Prose	Parrish/Maxfield
Mother Goose In Prose	Parrish/Maxfield
Mother Goose Nursery Tales	Neill/John R.
Mother Goose Rhymes & Jingles	Neill/John R.
Mother Goose's Menagerie	Newell/Peter
Mr. Munchausen	Newell/Peter
Mr. Twee Deedle	Gruelle/Johnny
Mr. Twee Deedle	Gruelle/Johnny
Mrs,. Mundi At Home	Crane/Walter
Mrs. John Vernon	Gibson/Charles D.
Mural Painting In America	Parrish/Maxfield
Music Master	Rae/John
My Country	Wyeth/N.C.
My Day With The Fairies	Dulac/Edmund
My Day With The Fairies	Dulac/Edmund
My Lady Peggy Goes To Town	Fisher/Harrison
My Own Set Of Sunny Books	Gruelle/Johnny
My Poetry Book	Pogany/Will
My Poetry Book	Pogany/Will
My Son & I	Thomson/Hugh
My Very Own Fairy Stories	Gruelle/Johnny
My Very Own Fairy Stories	Gruelle/Johnny
My Very Own Fairy Stories	Gruelle/Johnny
My Very Own Fairy Stories	Gruelle/Johnny
Mysteries Of Police & Crime	Rackham/Arthur
Mysteries Of Police & Crime	Rackham/Arthur
Mysterious Island	Wyeth/N.C.
Mysterious Island	Wyeth/N.C.
Mysterious Stranger (The)	Wyeth/N.C.
Mysterious Stranger (The)	Wyeth/N.C.

N

Nan Of Music Mountain	Wyeth/N.C.
Nan Of Music Mountain	Wyeth/N.C.
Nautical Lays Of A Landsman	Newell/Peter
Ne'er Do Well (The)	Christy/Howard Chandler
Necklace Of Princess Fiorimonde (The)	Crane/Walter
Nedra	Fisher/Harrison
New & True	Smith/Jessie Wilcox
New Adventures Of Alice	Rae/John
New Book Of Sense & Nonsense	Rackham/Arthur
New Book Of Sense & Nonsense	Rackham/Arthur

LISTINGS BY TITLE

Author	Publisher	Year	Price Range
Baum/L. Frank	Bobbs-Merrill	(1905)	500 — 750
Baum/L. Frank	Way/Williams	1901	500 — 750
	Altemus	(1904)	75 — 100
	Reilly & Britton	(1908)	75 — 100
Wells/Carolyn	Noyes	1901	175 — 225
Bangs/John K.	Noyes,Platt	1901	60 — 80
Gruelle/Johnny	Cupples & Leon	(1913)	150 — 175
Gruelle/Johnny	McKay		50 — 75
	Marcus Ward	1875	75 — 100
Addison/J.	Badger	1909	15 — 20
Blashfield/Edwin H.	Scribner	1913	25 — 50
Klein/C.	Dodd	1909	25 — 45
Turkington/Grace	Ginn	1923	15 — 25
Stawell/R.	Hodder & Stoughton	[1913]	225 — 325
Stawell/R.	Hodder & Stoughton	[1915]	150 — 200
Mathews/F.A.	Bowen	1901	20 — 30
	Donohue	[1940]	100 — 150
Ferris	Winston	(1934)	25 — 35
Ferris	Hufford	1934	25 — 35
Spielman/M.H.	G. Allen	1908	50 — 75
Gruelle/Johnny	Donohue	(1917)	50 — 75
Gruelle/Johnny	Volland	(1917)	125 — 175
Gruelle/Johnny	Volland	(1917)	100 — 125
Gruelle/Johnny	Johnny Gruelle Co.	(1940)	35 — 50
Griffiths&Gold	Cassell	[1901]	125 — 150
Griffiths&Gold	Cassell	[1904]	75 — 100
Verne/Jules	Scribner	1918	175 — 225
Verne/Jules	Scribner	1946	30 — 50
Twain/Mark	Harper	(1916)	100 — 150
Twain/Mark	Harper	(1916)	75 — 100
Spearman/Frank	Grosset&Dunlap	(1916)	15 — 25
Spearman/Frank	Scribner	1916	20 — 40
Irwin/Wallace	Dodd	1904	45 — 60
Beach/R.	Harper	1911	20 — 35
De Morgan/Mary	Macmillan	1880	175 — 225
McCutcheon/George	Dodd	1905	20 — 40
Staver/Mary Wiley	Lee & Shepard	1892	75 — 100
Rae/John	Volland	(1917)	100 — 150
Rhys/Ernest	Dent	(1928)	50 — 75
Rhys/Ernest	Dutton	(1928)	50 — 75

LISTINGS BY TITLE

Title	Illustrator
New England Bygones	Pyle/Howard
New Fiction & Other Papers	Rackham/Arthur
New Forest, Its History & Scenery (The)	Crane/Walter
New Wizard Of Oz (The)	Denslow/W.W.
New Wizard Of Oz (The)	Denslow/W.W.
New Wizard Of Oz (The)	Denslow/W.W.
Night Before Christmas	Denslow/W.W.
Night Before Christmas	Denslow/W.W.
Night Before Christmas (The)	Neill/John R.
Night Before Christmas (The)	Rackham/Arthur
Night Before Christmas (The)	Rackham/Arthur
Night Before Christmas (The)	Rackham/Arthur
Night Before Christmas (The)	Rackham/Arthur
Night Before Christmas/Mother Goose Rhymes	Neill/John R.
Nightingale (The)	Dulac/Edmund
Nobody's Boy	Gruelle/Johnny
Northanger Abbey	Thomson/Hugh
Not All The Truth	Rackham/Arthur
Not All The Truth	Rackham/Arthur
Now Then....	Rackham/Arthur
Now-A-Days Fairy Book (The)	Smith/Jessie Wilcox
Now-A-Days Fairy Book (The)	Smith/Jessie Wilcox
Now-A-Days Fairy Book (The)	Smith/Jessie Wilcox
Now-A-Days Fairy Book (The)	Smith/Jessie Wilcox
Now-A-Days Fairy Book (The)	Smith/Jessie Wilcox
Nursery Tales	Neill/John R.

O

Odd Volume (The)	Rackham/Arthur
Odes & Epodes Of Horace (The)	Pyle/Howard
Odysseus, The Hero Of Ithaca	Pyle/Howard
Odyssey Of Homer	Wyeth/N.C.
Of The Decorative Illustration Of Books Old & New	Crane/Walter
Ojo In Oz	Neill/John R.
Ojo In Oz	Neill/John R.
Ojo In Oz	Neill/John R.
Old Chester Tales	Pyle/Howard
Old English Songs	Thomson/Hugh
Old Garden (The)	Crane/Walter
Old Garden (The)	Crane/Walter
Old Gentlemen Of The Black Stock (The)	Christy/Howard Chandler
Old Homestead Poems	Pyle/Howard

LISTINGS BY TITLE

Author	Publisher	Year	Price Range
Arr/E.H.	Lippincott	1883	25 — 35
The Philistine	Westminster Gazette	1895	75 — 100
Wise/John	Smith,Elder	1863	150 — 200
Baum/L. Frank	Bobbs-Merrill	(1903)	400 — 1200
Baum/L. Frank	Bobbs-Merrill	(1903)	50 — 75
Baum/L. Frank	Bobbs-Merrill	(1939)	100 — 150
Denslow/W.W.	Dillingham	(1902)	300 — 500
Denslow/W.W.	Donohue	[1902]	150 — 200
	Reilly & Britton	(1908)	75 — 100
Moore/Clement C.	Harrap	[1931]	750 — 900
Moore/Clement C.	Harrap	[1931]	150 — 200
Moore/Clement C.	Lippincott	[1931]	750 — 900
Moore/Clement C.	Lippincott	[1931]	150 — 175
	Reilly & Britton	(1908)	75 — 100
Anderson/Hans Christian	Hodder & Stoughton	[1911]	225 — 275
Malot/Hector	Cupples & Leon	1916	60 — 80
Austin/J.	Macmillan	1897	50 — 75
Melville/Lewis	Jarrold	1928	50 — 75
Melville/Lewis	Doubleday,Page	1929	60 — 80
	Boy Scouts Appeal	[1927]	150 — 250
Chapin/Anna A.	Dodd	(1911)	150 — 175
Chapin/Anna A.	Prospect	(1913)	100 — 125
Chapin/Anna A.	Harrap	[1922]	100 — 125
Chapin/Anna A.	Coker	[1935]	75 — 100
Chapin/Anna A.	Dodd	1911	200 — 300
	Altemus	(1904)	50 — 75
Matz/B.W.	Simpkin,Marshall	1908	50 — 75
Smith/Clement	Bibliophile Society	1901	50 — 75
Burt/Mary E.	Scribner	1898	20 — 30
Palmer.George H.	Houghton,Mifflin	1929	150 — 200
Crane/Wlater	Bell	1896	100 — 150
Thompson/Ruth P.	Reilly & Lee	(1933)	200 — 300
Thompson/Ruth P.	Reilly & Lee	(1933)	40 — 60
Thompson/Ruth P.	Reilly & Lee	(1933)	100 — 150
Deland/Margaret	Harper	1899	25 — 50
	Macmillan	1894	50 — 75
Deland/Margaret	McIlvaine	1893	125 — 175
Deland/Margaret	Houghton,Mifflin	1894	75 — 100
Page/Thomas Nelson	Scribner	1900	30 — 45
Bruce/Wallace	Harper	1888	25 — 50

LISTINGS BY TITLE

Title	Illustrator
Old Mother Hubbard	Denslow/W.W.
Old Times In The Colonies	Pyle/Howard
Old Water -Colour Society's Club (The)	Rackham/Arthur
Old Water Colour Society (The)	Rackham/Arthur
Old Youngsters	Humphrey/Maud
Olive Fairy Book (The)	Ford/H.J.
Olive Fairy Book (The)	Ford/H.J.
On Hazardous Service	Pyle/Howard
One Ring Circus	Denslow/W.W.
One Way Out	Fisher/Harrison
One,Two Three Four	Humphrey/Maud
One-Hoss Shay (The)	Pyle/Howard
One-Hoss Shay (The)	Pyle/Howard
Orange Fairy Book (The)	Ford/H.J.
Oregon Trail	Wyeth/N.C.
Oriana	Humphrey/Maud
Orient Line Guide	Greenaway/Kate
Orphant Annie Story Book	Gruelle/Johnny
Otto Of The Silver Hand	Pyle/Howard
Our Girls	Christy/Howard Chandler
Our Neighbors	Gibson/Charles D.
Our Village	Thomson/Hugh
Out To Old Aunt Mary's	Christy/Howard Chandler
Outline Of Literature (The)	Rackham/Arthur
Oxted,Limpsfield & Neighbourhood	Rackham/Arthur
Oz Toy Book (The)	Neill/John R.
Ozma Of Oz	Neill/John R.
Ozma Of Oz	Neill/John R.
Ozma Of Oz	Neill/John R.
Ozoplanning With The Wizard Of Oz	Neill/John R.
Ozoplanning With The Wizard Of Oz	Neill/John R.

P

Painting Book (A)	Greenaway/Kate
Palmer Cox Brownie Printer (The)	Cox/Palmer
Palmer Cox's Funny Animals	Cox/Palmer
Pan Pipes	Crane/Walter
Pan Pipes	Crane/Walter
Pan Pipes	Crane/Walter
Paper Dragon	Gruelle/Johnny
Paper Dragon	Gruelle/Johnny
Parables Of Jesus	Wyeth/N.C.

LISTINGS BY TITLE

Author	Publisher	Year	Price Range
Denslow/W.W.	Dillingham	(1903)	125 — 150
Coffin/Charles C.	Harper	1881	25 — 50
Davies/Randall		1934	75 — 100
Holme/Charles	The Studio	1905	175 — 225
Tucker/Elizabeth S.	Stokes	(1897)	300 — 400
Lang/Andrew	Longmans	1907	175 — 225
Lang/Andrew	Longmans	1925	50 — 75
Beymer/William G.	Harper	1912	20 — 30
Denslow/W.W.	Dillingham	(1903)	200 — 250
Von Hutten/B.	Dodd	1906	30 — 40
	Stokes	[1890]	200 — 300
Holmes/Oliver W.	Houghton,Mifflin	1892	75 — 125
Holmes/Oliver W.	Houghton,Mifflin	1905	75 — 125
Lang/Andrew	Longmans	1906	175 — 225
Parkman/Francis	Little Brown	1925	75 — 100
	Estes & Lauriat	1888	40 — 60
Loftie/W.J.	Sampson Low	1888	100 — 150
Gruelle/Johnny	Bobbs-Merrill	(1921)	100 — 125
Pyle/Howard	Scribner	1888	175 — 250
Christy/Howard Chandler	Moffat	1907	75 — 100
Gibson/Charles D.	Scribner	1905	120 — 150
Mitford/M.R.	Macmillan	1893	50 — 65
Riley/James W.	Bobbs-Merrill	(1904)	25 — 40
Drinkwater/John	Newnes	[1930]	150 — 200
Fry/Lewis	W.&G. Godwin	(1932)	100 — 125
	Reilly & Britton	(1915)	600 — 800
Baum/L. Frank	Reilly & Britton	(1907)	500 — 750
Baum/L. Frank	Reilly & Britton	(1907)	150 — 200
Baum/L. Frank	Reilly & Lee	(1907)	75 — 100
Thompson/Ruth P.	Reilly & Lee	(1939)	175 — 250
Thompson/Ruth P.	Reilly & Lee	(1939)	40 — 60
Greenaway/Kate	Routledge	[1884]	200 — 275
	Century	1906	75 — 100
Cox/Palmer	Donohue		30 — 50
Marzials/Theo	Routledge	[1884]	100 — 150
Marzials/Theo	Routledge	1883	175 — 225
Marzials/Theo	Warne		100 — 150
Gruelle/Johnny	Volland	(1926)	75 — 100
Gruelle/Johnny	Volland	(1926)	50 — 75
Cadman/S.P.	McKay	1931	300 — 400

LISTINGS BY TITLE

Title	Illustrator
Parasite (The)	Pyle/Howard
Parsifal	Pogany/Will
Parson's Devil	Newell/Peter
Patchwork Girl Of Oz (The)	Neill/John R.
Patchwork Girl Of Oz (The)	Neill/John R.
Patchwork Girl Of Oz (The)	Neill/John R.
Peace At Any Price	Newell/Peter
Pearl & The Pumpkin	Denslow/W.W.
Pearl & The Pumpkin	Denslow/W.W.
Peer Gynt	Rackham/Arthur
Peer Gynt	Rackham/Arthur
Peer Gynt	Rackham/Arthur
Peer Gynt	Rackham/Arthur
Peg Woffington	Thomson/Hugh
Peg Woffington	Thomson/Hugh
Pen Drawing & Pen Draughtsmen	Pyle/Howard
Pen,Pencil & Chalk	Rackham/Arthur
Pepper & Salt	Pyle/Howard
Pepper & Salt	Pyle/Howard
Peradventures Of Private Pagett (The)	Rackham/Arthur
Peradventures Of Private Pagett (The)	Rackham/Arthur
Peter & The Princess	Neill/John R.
Peter Newell's Mother Goose	Newell/Peter
Peter Newell's Pictures & Rhymes	Newell/Peter
Peter Pan In Kensington Gardens	Rackham/Arthur
Peter Pan In Kensington Gardens	Rackham/Arthur
Peter Pan In Kensington Gardens	Rackham/Arthur
Peter Pan In Kensington Gardens	Rackham/Arthur
Peter Pan In Kensington Gardens	Rackham/Arthur
Peter Pan In Kensington Gardens	Rackham/Arthur
Peter Pan In Kensington Gardens	Rackham/Arthur
Peter Pan In Kensington Gardens	Rackham/Arthur
Peter Pan In Kensington Gardens	Rackham/Arthur
Peter Pan In Kensington Gardens	Rackham/Arthur
Peter Pan In Kensington Gardens	Rackham/Arthur
Peter Pan In Kensington Gardens	Rackham/Arthur
Peter Pan In Kensington Gardens	Rackham/Arthur
Peter Pan In Kensington Gardens	Rackham/Arthur
Peter Pan In Kensington Gardens	Rackham/Arthur
Peter Pan In Kensington Gardens	Rackham/Arthur
Peter Pan Portfolio	Rackham/Arthur
Peter Pan Portfolio	Rackham/Arthur

LISTINGS BY TITLE

Author	Publisher	Year	Price Range
Doyle/Arthur C.	Harper	1895	65 — 85
Rolleston/T.	Harrap	(1912)	180 — 220
Johnson/C.		(1927)	50 — 100
Baum/L. Frank	Reilly & Britton	(1913)	400 — 600
Baum/L. Frank	Reilly & Britton	(1913)	350 — 400
Baum/L. Frank	Reilly & Lee	(1913)	100 — 150
Browne/P.E.	Appleton	1916	75 — 100
West/P.	Dillingham	(1904)	200 — 250
West/P.	Donohue	[1911]	125 — 150
Ibsen/Henrik	Harrap	[1936]	850 — 1250
Ibsen/Henrik	Harrap	[1936]	100 — 150
Ibsen/Henrik	Harrap	[1936]	150 — 200
Ibsen/Henrik	Lippincott	[1936]	100 — 150
Reade/C.	G. Allen	1899	65 — 80
Reade/C.	Doubleday	1899	50 — 75
Pennell/Joseph	Macmillan	1889	100 — 150
Holme/Charles	The Studio	1911	50 — 75
Pyle/Howard	Harper	(1922)	50 — 75
Pyle/Howard	Harper	1886	275 — 400
Drury/W.P.	Chapman/Hall	(1911)	150 — 200
Drury/W.P.	Chapman/Hall	1904	200 — 300
Grabo/Carl H.	Reilly & Lee	(1920)	175 — 250
Bailey/C.S.	Holt	1905	75 — 100
Newell/Peter	Harper	1899	150 — 200
Barrie/J.M.	Hodder & Stoughton	(1910)	150 — 175
Barrie/J.M.	Hodder & Stoughton	(1910)	100 — 125
Barrie/J.M.	Hodder & Stoughton	(1912)	1250 — 1500
Barrie/J.M.	Hodder & Stoughton	(1912)	250 — 400
Byron/May	Hodder & Stoughton	(1929)	75 — 100
Byron/May	Scribner	(1929)	75 — 100
Barrie/J.M.	Hodder & Stoughton	1906	300 — 500
Barrie/J.M.	Hodder & Stoughton	1906	1250 — 2000
Barrie/J.M.	Scribner	1906	250 — 400
Barrie/J.M.	Scribner	1907	175 — 225
Barrie/J.M.	Scribner	1913	175 — 200
Barrie/J.M.	Scribner	1926	75 — 125
Barrie/J.M.	Scribner	1929	75 — 125
Barrie/J.M.	Scribner	1929	75 — 125
Byron/May	Scribner	1934	50 — 75
Barrie/J.M.	Scribner	1940	50 — 100
Rackham/Arthur	Hodder & Stoughton	(1912)	4000 — 6000
Rackham/Arthur	Brentano's	(1914)	2500 — 3500

LISTINGS BY TITLE

Title	Illustrator
Peter Rabbit's Almanac For 1929	Potter/Beatrix
Peter Rabbit's Almanac For 1929	Potter/Beatrix
Peter Rabbit's Painting Book	Potter/Beatrix
Peter Rabbit's Painting Book	Potter/Beatrix
Peter Rabbit/Dick Whittington	Neill/John R.
Peterkin	Parrish/Maxfield
Peterkin	Pogany/Will
Phaeton Rogers	Pyle/Howard
Picture Book/French Red Cross	Dulac/Edmund
Pictures & Rhymes	Newell/Peter
Pictures From The Wonderful Wizard Of Oz	Denslow/W.W.
Pictures In Color	Fisher/Harrison
Pictures Of People	Gibson/Charles D.
Pie & The Patty Pan (The)	Potter/Beatrix
Pie & The Patty Pan (The)	Potter/Beatrix
Pie & The Patty Pan (The)	Potter/Beatrix
Pied Piper Of Hamelin	Thomson/Hugh
Pied Piper Of Hamlin (The)	Rackham/Arthur
Pied Piper Of Hamlin (The)	Rackham/Arthur
Pied Piper Of Hamlin (The)	Rackham/Arthur
Pied Piper Of Hamlin(The)	Greenaway/Kate
Pied Piper Of Hamlin(The)	Greenaway/Kate
Pike County Ballads (The)	Wyeth/N.C.
Pilgrim's Progress	Ford/H.J.
Pilot & Other Stories	Ford/H.J.
Pink Fairy Book (The)	Ford/H.J.
Pink Fairy Book (The)	Ford/H.J.
Pioneer (The)	Fisher/Harrison
Pirates In Oz	Neill/John R.
Pirates In Oz	Neill/John R.
Playtime Story Book	Humphrey/Maud
Poems By Dobson, Locker & Praed	Humphrey/Maud
Poems Of American Patriotism	Wyeth/N.C.
Poems Of Childhood	Parrish/Maxfield
Poems Of Childhood	Parrish/Maxfield
Poems Of Childhood	Parrish/Maxfield
Poems Old & New	Smith/Jessie Wilcox
Poetical Works Of Poe	Dulac/Edmund
Pogany's Mother Goose	Pogany/Will
Polly Garden	Pogany/Will
Poor Cecco	Rackham/Arthur
Poor Cecco	Rackham/Arthur

LISTINGS BY TITLE

Author	Publisher	Year	Price Range
Potter/Beatrix	Warne	[1928]	150 — 200
Potter/Beatrix	Warne	[1928]	150 — 200
Potter/Beatrix	Warne	[1911]	100 — 150
Potter/Beatrix	Warne	[1917]	50 — 75
	Reilly & Britton	(1908)	75 — 100
Jackson/Gabrielle E.	Duffield	1912	75 — 125
Pogany/Will	McKay	1940	80 — 100
Johnson/Rossiter	Scribner	1881	25 — 50
Dulac/Edmund	Hodder & Stoughton	[1915]	200 — 300
Newell/Peter	Harper	(1899)	100 — 150
Russell/Thomas	Ogilvie	[1904]	300 — 400
Fisher/Harrison	Scribner	1910	350 — 500
Gibson/Charles D.	Russell	1896	100 — 165
Potter/Beatrix	Warne	(1933)	25 — 50
Potter/Beatrix	Warne	1905	225 — 350
Potter/Beatrix	Warne	1905	200 — 250
Buchanan/R.	Heinemann	1893	50 — 70
Browning/Robert	Harrap	[1934]	200 — 300
Browning/Robert	Lippincott	[1934]	100 — 200
Browning/Robert	Harrap	1934	750 — 1000
Browning/Robert	Routledge	[1888]	200 — 250
Browning/Robert	Warne	[1903]	100 — 150
Hay/John	Houghton,Mifflin	(1912)	75 — 125
Bunyan/John	Macmillan		50 — 75
Greene/H.P.	Macmillan	1916	125 — 175
Lang/Andrew	Longmans	1897	175 — 225
Lang/Andrew	Longmans	1906	50 — 75
Bonner/G.	Bobbs-Merrill	(1905)	30 — 40
Thompson/Ruth P.	Reilly & Lee	(1931)	200 — 300
Thompson/Ruth P.	Reilly & Lee	(1931)	40 — 60
	Hayes	1891	40 — 60
Dobson/L.	Stokes	1892	300 — 450
Matthews/B.	Scribner	1922	175 — 225
Field/Eugene	Lane	1904	150 — 225
Field/Eugene	Scribner	1904	150 — 225
Field/Eugene	Scribner	1929	100 — 150
Patten/William	Collier	(1918)	50 — 75
Poe/Edgar Allen	Doran	[1921]	225 — 300
Pogany/Will	Nelson	(1928)	130 — 170
Banks	Macmillan		75 — 100
Bianco/Margery W.	Chatto/Windus	(1925)	150 — 175
Bianco/Margery W.	Doran	(1925)	125 — 150

LISTINGS BY TITLE

Title	Illustrator
Poor Cecco	Rackham/Arthur
Poor Cecco	Rackham/Arthur
Poor Nelly	Greenaway/Kate
Portrait Of An Era	Gibson/Charles D.
Pothooks & Preseverance	Crane/Walter
Practice Of Water Colour Painting	Rackham/Arthur
Prayers/Little Men & Women	Rae/John
Price Of Blood (The)	Pyle/Howard
Pride & Prejudice	Thomson/Hugh
Prince & Fido	Humphrey/Maud
Princess & The Goblin (The)	Smith/Jessie Wilcox
Princess & The Goblin (The)	Smith/Jessie Wilcox
Princess & The Goblin (The)	Smith/Jessie Wilcox
Princess & The Goblin (The)	Smith/Jessie Wilcox
Princess (The)	Christy/Howard Chandler
Princess Badoura	Dulac/Edmund
Princess Mary's Gift Book	Rackham/Arthur
Prisoner Of Zenda (The)	Gibson/Charles D.
Prisoner Of Zenda (The)	Gibson/Charles D.
Puck & Blossom	Greenaway/Kate
Puck Of Pook's Hill	Rackham/Arthur
Puck Of Pook's Hill	Rackham/Arthur
Purple Parasol	Fisher/Harrison
Purple Prince Of Oz (The)	Neill/John R.
Purple Prince Of Oz (The)	Neill/John R.
Purple Prince Of Oz (The)	Neill/John R.
Pursuit Of The Houseboat	Newell/Peter

Q

Quacky Doodles/Danny Doodles	Gruelle/Johnny
Quality Street	Thomson/Hugh
Queen Bee (The)	Dulac/Edmund
Queen Mab's Fairy Realm	Rackham/Arthur
Queen Mab's Fairy Realm	Rackham/Arthur
Queen Of Pirate Isle	Greenaway/Kate
Queen Of Pirate Isle	Greenaway/Kate
Queen Summer	Crane/Walter
Queen Victoria's Jubilee Garland	Greenaway/Kate
Queen's Book Of The Red Cross	Dulac/Edmund
Queen's Gift Book	Rackham/Arthur
Queer People	Cox/Palmer
Queer People	Cox/Palmer

LISTINGS BY TITLE

Author	Publisher	Year	Price Range
Bianco/Margery W.	Doran	1925	6000 —8000
Bianco/Margery W.	Doubleday		100 — 125
Hunt/Mrs. Bonavia	Cassell	1878	150 — 175
Downey/Fairfax	Scribner	(1936)	20 — 50
Crane/Walter	Marcus Ward	1886	200 — 250
Baldry/A.L.	Macmillan	1911	75 — 100
Martin/J.	Harper	1912	50 — 75
Pyle/Howard	Badger	1899	150 — 225
Austin/J.	G. Allen	1894	65 — 90
	De Wolfe Fiske	(1885)	100 — 150
MacDonald/George	McKay	[1923]	50 — 75
MacDonald/George	McKay	1920	150 — 175
MacDonald/George	McKay	1920	125 — 150
MacDonald/George	McKay	1920	100 — 125
Tennyson/Alfred	Bobbs-Merrill	(1911)	75 — 100
Housman/Laurence	Hodder & Stoughton	[1913]	250 — 350
	Hodder & Stoughton	[1914]	50 — 75
Hope/Anthony	Grosset&Dunlap	(1898)	10 — 15
Hope/Anthony	Holt	1898	15 — 25
Mulholland/Rosa	Ward	1875	200 — 250
Kipling/Rudyard	Doubleday,Page	1906	60 — 100
Kipling/Rudyard	Doubleday	1916	25 — 50
McCutcheon/George	Dodd	1905	30 — 40
Thompson/Ruth P.	Reilly & Lee	(1932)	250 — 350
Thompson/Ruth P.	Reilly & Lee	(1932)	40 — 60
Thompson/Ruth P.	Reilly & Lee	(1932)	125 — 150
Bangs/John K.	Harper	1897	25 — 40
Hubbell/Rose Strong	Volland	(1916)	150 — 200
Barrie/J.M	Hodder & Stoughton	[1913]	130 — 170
Smith/C.M.	Nelson	1907	100 — 150
	Newnes	1901	225 — 300
	Newnes	1915	100 — 125
Harte/Bret	Chatto/Windus	[1886]	200 — 250
Harte/Bret	Houghton,Mifflin	1887	150 — 200
Crane/Walter	Cassell	1891	250 — 300
Greenaway/Kate	Routledge	[1887]	300 — 350
	Hodder & Stoughton	(1939)	50 — 75
	Hodder & Stoughton	[1915]	50 — 75
Cox/Palmer	Unwin	1896	125 — 175
Cox/Palmer	Hubbard	1899	125 — 175

LISTINGS BY TITLE

Title	Illustrator
Queer People With Paws And Claws....	Cox/Palmer
Queer People With Wings And Stings....	Cox/Palmer
Queerie Queers	Cox/Palmer
Quiver Of Love (The)	Crane/Walter
Quiver Of Love (The)	Greenaway/Kate
Quo Vadis	Pyle/Howard

R

Rab & His Friends	Neill/John R.
Rab & His Friends/J.Cole	Neill/John R.
Raggedy Andy Stories	Gruelle/Johnny
Raggedy Andy Stories	Gruelle/Johnny
Raggedy Andy Stories	Gruelle/Johnny
Raggedy Andy Stories	Gruelle/Johnny
Raggedy Andy's Number Book	Gruelle/Johnny
Raggedy Andy's Number Book	Gruelle/Johnny
Raggedy Ann & Andy/Camel	Gruelle/Johnny
Raggedy Ann & Andy/Camel	Gruelle/Johnny
Raggedy Ann & Andy/Camel	Gruelle/Johnny
Raggedy Ann & Andy/Camel	Gruelle/Johnny
Raggedy Ann Cut Out Paper Doll	Gruelle/Johnny
Raggedy Ann In Cookie Land	Gruelle/Johnny
Raggedy Ann In Cookie Land	Gruelle/Johnny
Raggedy Ann In Cookie Land	Gruelle/Johnny
Raggedy Ann In Cookie Land	Gruelle/Johnny
Raggedy Ann In Golden Meadow	Gruelle/Johnny
Raggedy Ann In The Deep Woods	Gruelle/Johnny
Raggedy Ann In The Deep Woods	Gruelle/Johnny
Raggedy Ann In The Deep Woods	Gruelle/Johnny
Raggedy Ann In The Deep Woods	Gruelle/Johnny
Raggedy Ann Stories	Gruelle/Johnny
Raggedy Ann Stories	Gruelle/Johnny
Raggedy Ann Stories	Gruelle/Johnny
Raggedy Ann Stories	Gruelle/Johnny
Raggedy Ann's Alphabet Book	Gruelle/Johnny
Raggedy Ann's Alphabet Book	Gruelle/Johnny
Raggedy Ann's Lucky Pennies	Gruelle/Johnny
Raggedy Ann's Lucky Pennies	Gruelle/Johnny
Raggedy Ann's Lucky Pennies	Gruelle/Johnny
Raggedy Ann's Magical Wishes	Gruelle/Johnny
Raggedy Ann's Magical Wishes	Gruelle/Johnny
Raggedy Ann's Magical Wishes	Gruelle/Johnny

LISTINGS BY TITLE

Author	Publisher	Year	Price Range
Cox/Palmer	Hubbard	(1888)	100 — 150
Cox/Palmer	Hubbard	(1888)	100 — 150
Cox/Palmer	Larkin	(1887)	125 — 150
Loftie/W.J.	Marcus Ward	1876	200 — 300
Loftie/W.J.	Marcus Ward	1876	200 — 300
Sienkiewicz/Henryk	Little Brown	1897	30 — 50
	Reilly & Britton	(1908)	75 — 100
	Reilly & Britton	(1908)	75 — 100
Gruelle/Johnny	Donohue	(1920)	50 — 75
Gruelle/Johnny	Volland	(1920)	150 — 200
Gruelle/Johnny	Volland	(1920)	100 — 150
Gruelle/Johnny	Johnny Gruelle Co.	(1940)	35 — 50
Gruelle/Johnny	Donohue	(1924)	20 — 30
Gruelle/Johnny	Volland	(1924)	50 — 75
Gruelle/Johnny	Donohue	(1924)	50 — 75
Gruelle/Johnny	Volland	(1924)	125 — 150
Gruelle/Johnny	Volland	(1924)	100 — 125
Gruelle/Johnny	Johnny Gruelle Co.	(1940)	35 — 50
Gruelle/Johnny	Whitman	1935	35 — 50
Gruelle/Johnny	Donohue	(1931)	50 — 75
Gruelle/Johnny	Volland	(1931)	125 — 150
Gruelle/Johnny	Volland	(1931)	100 — 125
Gruelle/Johnny	Johnny Gruelle Co.	(1940)	35 — 50
Gruelle/Johnny	Whitman	1935	75 — 100
Gruelle/Johnny	Donohue	(1930)	50 — 75
Gruelle/Johnny	Volland	(1930)	125 — 150
Gruelle/Johnny	Volland	(1930)	100 — 125
Gruelle/Johnny	Johnny Gruelle Co.	(1940)	35 — 50
Gruelle/Johnny	Donohue	(1918)	50 — 75
Gruelle/Johnny	Volland	(1918)	125 — 175
Gruelle/Johnny	Volland	(1918)	100 — 125
Gruelle/Johnny	Johnny Gruelle Co.	(1940)	35 — 50
Gruelle/Johnny	Donohue	(1925)	20 — 35
Gruelle/Johnny	Volland	(1925)	35 — 50
Gruelle/Johnny	Donohue	(1932)	50 — 75
Gruelle/Johnny	Volland	(1932)	125 — 150
Gruelle/Johnny	Volland	(1932)	100 — 125
Gruelle/Johnny	Donohue	(1928)	35 — 50
Gruelle/Johnny	Volland	(1928)	100 — 150
Gruelle/Johnny	Volland	(1928)	75 — 100

LISTINGS BY TITLE

Title	Illustrator
Raggedy Ann's Wishing Pebble	Gruelle/Johnny
Raggedy Ann's Wishing Pebble	Gruelle/Johnny
Raggedy Ann's Wishing Pebble	Gruelle/Johnny
Raggedy Ann's Wishing Pebble	Gruelle/Johnny
Raggedy Ann/Left Handed Pin	Gruelle/Johnny
Raggle-Taggle Adventures With A Fiddle	Rackham/Arthur
Raggle-Taggle Adventures With A Fiddle	Rackham/Arthur
Rainbow Book (The)	Rackham/Arthur
Rainbow Book (The)	Rackham/Arthur
Rainbow Book (The)	Thomson/Hugh
Rainbow Book (The)	Thomson/Hugh
Ramona	Wyeth/N.C.
Raven (The)	Neill/John R.
Really So Stories	Rae/John
Really So Stories	Rae/John
Recollections Of A Minister To France	Pyle/Howard
Rectory Children (The)	Crane/Walter
Red Book Of Animal Stories (The)	Ford/H.J.
Red Book Of True Stories (The)	Ford/H.J.
Red Fairy Book (The)	Ford/H.J.
Red Fairy Book (The)	Ford/H.J.
Red Magic	Nielson/Kay
Red Pottage	Rackham/Arthur
Red Pottage	Rackham/Arthur
Red Romance Book (The)	Ford/H.J.
Red True Story Book (The)	Ford/H.J.
Reminiscences Of The Old Chest Of Drawers	Smith/Jessie Wilcox
Renascene: A Book Of Verse	Crane/Walter
Rescue Syndicate	Neill/John R.
Return Of Peter Grimm	Rae/John
Reynard The Fox	Rae/John
Rhinegold & The Valkyrie (The)	Rackham/Arthur
Rhinegold & The Valkyrie (The)	Rackham/Arthur
Rhinegold & The Valkyrie (The)	Rackham/Arthur
Rhinegold & The Valkyrie (The)	Rackham/Arthur
Rhymes & Reminiscences	Smith/Jessie Wilcox
Rhymes For Kindly Children	Gruelle/Johnny
Rhymes For Kindly Children	Gruelle/Johnny
Rhymes For Kindly Children	Gruelle/Johnny
Rhymes For The Young Folks	Greenaway/Kate
Rhymes New & Old	Barker/Cicely Mary
Rhymes Of Real Children	Smith/Jessie Wilcox

LISTINGS BY TITLE

Author	Publisher	Year	Price Range
Gruelle/Johnny	Donohue	(1925)	35 — 50
Gruelle/Johnny	Volland	(1925)	75 — 100
Gruelle/Johnny	Volland	(1925)	65 — 85
Gruelle/Johnny	Johnny Gruelle Co.	(1940)	35 — 50
Gruelle/Johnny	Whitman	1935	50 — 75
Starkie/Walter	John Murray	(1933)	50 — 75
Starkie/Walter	Dutton	(1933)	40 — 60
Spielmann/Mrs. M.H.	Chatto/Windus	1909	150 — 175
Spielmann/Mrs. M.H.			125 — 150
Spielmann/Mrs. M.H.	Chatto/Windus	1909	150 — 175
Spielmann/Mrs. M.H.			125 — 150
Jackson/Helen Hunt	Little Brown	1945	35 — 50
Poe/Edgar Allen		(1910)	50 — 75
Gordon/Elizabeth	Volland	(1924)	50 — 75
Gordon/Elizabeth	Wise-Parslow	(1937)	25 — 50
Washburne/E.B.	Scribner	1889	30 — 60
Molesworth/Mrs.	Macmillan	1889	75 — 100
Lang/Andrew	Longmans	1899	75 — 125
Lang/Andrew	Longmans	1895	150 — 200
Lang/Andrew	Longmans	1890	175 — 225
Lang/Andrew	Longmans	1917	30 — 60
Wilson/R.	J. Cape	(1930)	400 — 600
Cholmondeley/Mary	Newnes	[1904]	200 — 300
Cholmondeley/Mary	Newnes	1904	400 — 550
Lang/Andrew	Longmans	1905	200 — 250
Lang/Andrew	Longmans	1895	75 — 125
Sill/Sarah Cauffman	Lippincott	1900	75 — 100
Crane/Walter	Elkin Mathews	1891	100 — 150
Jenks/Tudor	Altemus	(1905)	50 — 75
Belasco/David	Dodd	1912	25 — 40
Larned/W.T.	Volland	(1925)	65 — 100
Wagner/Richard	Heinemann	1910	200 — 300
Wagner/Richard	Heinemann	1910	750 — 1000
Wagner/Richard	Doubleday,Page	1910	150 — 175
Wagner/Richard	Garden City	1939	75 — 100
Saville/Henry M.	Stratford	(1929)	50 — 75
Snyder/Fairmont	Volland	(1916)	100 — 150
Fairmont/Ethel	Volland	(1928)	75 — 100
Fairmont/Ethel	Wise-Parslow	(1937)	50 — 75
Allingham/William	Cassell	(1887)	150 — 200
Barker/Cicely Mary	Blackie & Sons	[1936]	60 — 80
Sage/Betty	Duffield	1903	250 — 300

LISTINGS BY TITLE

Title	Illustrator
Rhymes Of Real Children	Smith/Jessie Wilcox
Rhymes Of Real Children	Smith/Jessie Wilcox
Riley's Roses	Christy/Howard Chandler
Rime/Ancient Mariner	Pogany/Will
Rime/Ancient Mariner	Pogany/Will
Rime/Ancient Mariner	Pogany/Will
Ring Of The Niblung (The)	Rackham/Arthur
Ring Of The Niblung (The)	Rackham/Arthur
Rinkitink In Oz	Neill/John R.
Rinkitink In Oz	Neill/John R.
Rinkitink In Oz	Neill/John R.
Rinkitink In Oz	Neill/John R.
Rip Van Winkle	Neill/John R.
Rip Van Winkle	Rackham/Arthur
Rip Van Winkle	Rackham/Arthur
Rip Van Winkle	Rackham/Arthur
Rip Van Winkle	Rackham/Arthur
Rip Van Winkle	Rackham/Arthur
Rip Van Winkle	Rackham/Arthur
Rip Van Winkle	Rackham/Arthur
Rip Van Winkle	Rackham/Arthur
Rip Van Winkle	Rackham/Arthur
Rip Van Winkle	Wyeth/N.C.
Rip Van Winkle	Wyeth/N.C.
Rise & Fall Of Prohibition (The)	Newell/Peter
River & Rainbow	Rackham/Arthur
River & Rainbow	Rackham/Arthur
Riverman (The)	Wyeth/N.C.
Road To Fairyland (A)	Rackham/Arthur
Road To Fairyland (A)	Rackham/Arthur
Road To Oz (The)	Neill/John R.
Road To Oz (The)	Neill/John R.
Road To Oz (The)	Neill/John R.
Robber Kitten	Neill/John R.
Robin Hood	Wyeth/N.C.
Robin Hood & His Merry Men	Crane/Walter
Robin Hood & The Men Of Greenwood	Crane/Walter
Robin Hood & The Men Of Greenwood	Crane/Walter
Robin Hood & The Men Of Greenwood	Crane/Walter
Robinson Crusoe	Wyeth/N.C.
Robinson Crusoe:His Man Friday	Neill/John R.
Rocket Book (The)	Newell/Peter

LISTINGS BY TITLE

Author	Publisher	Year	Price Range
Sage/Betty	D. Nutt	1905	150 — 200
Sage/Betty	Duffield	1906	150 — 200
Riley/James W.	Bobbs-Merrill	(1909)	75 — 100
Coleridge/S.T.	Harrap	(1910)	200 — 250
Coleridge/S.T.	Crowell	(1910)	150 — 200
Coleridge/S.T.	Doubleday	1928	75 — 100
Wagner/Richard	Garden City	(1939)	50 — 100
Wagner/Richard	Heinemann	(1939)	75 — 125
Baum/L. Frank	Reilly & Britton	(1916)	500 — 700
Baum/L. Frank	Reilly & Britton	(1916)	200 — 300
Baum/L. Frank	Reilly & Lee	(1916)	100 — 150
Baum/L. Frank	Reilly & Lee	(1916)	40 — 60
	Reilly & Britton	(1908)	75 — 100
Irving/Washington	Heinemann	(1916)	150 — 175
Irving/Washington	Doubleday,Page	(1916)	125 — 150
Irving/Washington	Heinemann	[1917]	75 — 100
Irving/Washington	Heinemann	1905	300 — 400
Irving/Washington	Heinemann	1905	1000 — 1500
Irving/Washington	Doubleday,Page	1905	200 — 250
Irving/Washington	Heinemann	1909	125 — 150
Irving/Washington	Heinemann	1919	200 — 300
Irving/Washington	Doubleday,Page	1919	200 — 300
Irving/Washington	McKay	(1921)	100 — 150
Irving/Washington	McKay	(1921)	75 — 100
	Macmillan	1923	50 — 75
Carroll/Walter	Forsyth	(1933)	125 — 150
Carroll/Walter	Forsyth	(1933)	75 — 100
White/S.E.	McClure	1908	40 — 60
Fay/Erica	Putnam	(1926)	100 — 150
Fay/Erica	Putnam	(1926)	100 — 150
Baum/L. Frank	Reilly & Britton	(1909)	400 — 600
Baum/L. Frank	Reilly & Britton	(1909)	125 — 175
Baum/L. Frank	Reilly & Lee	(1909)	40 — 60
	Altemus	(1904)	40 — 60
	McKay	1917	75 — 125
Gilbert/Henry	Jack	1915	75 — 100
Gilbert/Henry	Stokes	[1912]	100 — 125
Gilbert/Henry	Jack	1912	125 — 150
Gilbert/Henry	Nelson		75 — 100
Defoe/Daniel	Cosmopolitan	1920	125 — 150
	Reilly & Britton	(1908)	75 — 100
Newell/Peter	Harper	(1912)	175 — 225

LISTINGS BY TITLE

Title	Illustrator
Rocket Book (The)	Newell/Peter
Roly Poly Pudding (The)	Potter/Beatrix
Roly Poly Pudding (The)	Potter/Beatrix
Roly Poly Pudding (The)	Potter/Beatrix
Romance Of A Child	Denslow/W.W.
Romance Of King Arthur...(The)	Rackham/Arthur
Romance Of King Arthur...(The)	Rackham/Arthur
Romance Of King Arthur...(The)	Rackham/Arthur
Romance Of King Arthur...(The)	Rackham/Arthur
Romance Of King Arthur...(The)	Rackham/Arthur
Romance/Lohengrin	Pogany/Will
Romance/Three R's	Crane/Walter
Romantic America	Parrish/Maxfield
Rose (The)	Christy/Howard Chandler
Rose Of Paradise (The)	Pyle/Howard
Rosebud And Other Tales (The)	Crane/Walter
Rosebud Stories	Humphrey/Maud
Rosy	Crane/Walter
Rosy	Crane/Walter
Round Rabbit (The)	O'Neill/Rose
Royal Book Of Oz (The)	Neill/John R.
Royal Book Of Oz (The)	Neill/John R.
Royal Book Of Oz (The)	Neill/John R.
Royal Progress Of King Pepito (The)	Greenaway/Kate
Rubaiyat (The)	Dulac/Edmund
Rubaiyat (The)	Dulac/Edmund
Rubaiyat (The)	Dulac/Edmund
Rubaiyat (The)	Dulac/Edmund
Rubaiyat (The)	Dulac/Edmund
Rubaiyat (The)	Dulac/Edmund
Rubaiyat (The)	Dulac/Edmund
Rubaiyat (The)	Dulac/Edmund
Rubaiyat Of Omar Khayyam	Pogany/Will
Rubaiyat Of Omar Khayyam	Pogany/Will
Rubaiyat Of Omar Khayyam	Pogany/Will
Rubaiyat Of Omar Khayyam	Pogany/Will
Rubaiyat Of Omar Khayyam	Pogany/Will
Ruby Of Kishmoor (The)	Pyle/Howard
Ruby Story Book (The)	Parrish/Maxfield
Rudyard Kipling	Rackham/Arthur
Rumbo Rhymes	Crane/Walter
Runaway Equator	Newell/Peter

LISTINGS BY TITLE

Author	Publisher	Year	Price Range
Newell/Peter	Harper		75 — 100
Potter/Beatrix	Warne	(1908)	200 — 300
Potter/Beatrix	Warne	[1920]	50 — 75
Potter/Beatrix	Warne	1908	300 — 400
Loti/P.	Rand Mcnally	1897	50 — 75
Pollard/Alfred	Macmillan	1917	750 — 1250
Pollard/Alfred	Macmillan	1917	150 — 175
Pollard/Alfred	Macmillan	1917	150 — 175
Pollard/Alfred	Macmillan	1917	200 — 250
Pollard/Alfred	Macmillan	1926	40 — 60
Capes/B.	Dean	1905	125 — 150
Crane/Walter	Marcus Ward	1886	175 — 250
Schauffer/Robert Haven	Century	1913	75 — 100
Riley/James W.	Bobbs-Merrill	(1916)	30 — 45
Pyle/Howard	Harper	1888	75 — 100
Kelly/Arthur	Unwin	1909	175 — 225
Humphrey/Maud	Holiday	1906	150 — 200
Molesworth/Mrs.	Macmillan	1882	75 — 100
Molesworth/Mrs.	Macmillan	1896	30 — 50
Lee/A.	Copeland/Day	1898	150 — 250
Baum/L. Frank- Thompson/Ruth	Reilly & Lee	(1921)	250 — 350
Baum/L. Frank- Thompson/Ruth	Reilly & Lee	(1921)	100 — 150
Baum/L. Frank- Thompson/Ruth	Reilly & Lee	(1921)	40 — 60
Cresswell/Beatrice	Spck	[1889]	175 — 225
Fitzgerald/E.	Hodder & Stoughton	[1909]	200 — 300
Fitzgerald/E.	Hodder & Stoughton	[1914]	100 — 150
Fitzgerald/E.	Doran	[1920]	100 — 130
Fitzgerald/E.	Doran	1928	20 — 50
Fitzgerald/E.	Doubleday	1932	40 — 55
Fitzgerald/E.	Doubleday	1933	75 — 100
Fitzgerald/E.	Doubleday	1934	75 — 100
Fitzgerald/E.	Garden City	1937	20 — 40
Fitzgerald/E.	Harrap	(1909)	175 — 225
Fitzgerald/E.	Crowell	(1909)	125 — 175
Fitzgerald/E.	Crowell	(1930)	35 — 60
Fitzgerald/E.	Crowell	(1930)	600 — 800
Fitzgerald/E.	Crowell	[1933]	50 — 75
Pyle/Howard	Harper	1908	80 — 120
	Duffield	1921	75 — 125
Cooper/Anice P.	Doubleday,Page	1926	30 — 50
Calmour/Alfred C.	Harper	1911	150 — 175
Bell/L.	Stokes	(1911)	100 — 125

LISTINGS BY TITLE

Title	Illustrator

S

Title	Illustrator
Saint Joan Of Arc	Pyle/Howard
Sally Castleton/Southerner	Wyeth/N.C.
Salomy Jane	Fisher/Harrison
Sampo (The)	Wyeth/N.C.
Saphire Story Book (The)	Parrish/Maxfield
Scalawagons Of Oz (The)	Neill/John R.
Scalawagons Of Oz (The)	Neill/John R.
Scarecrow & The Tin Woodman Of Oz (The)	Neill/John R.
Scarecrow Of Oz (The)	Neill/John R.
Scarecrow Of Oz (The)	Neill/John R.
Scarecrow Of Oz (The)	Neill/John R.
Scarecrow Of Oz (The)	Neill/John R.
Scarlet Letter	Thomson/Hugh
Scars & Stripes	Newell/Peter
School For Scandal (The)	Thomson/Hugh
School For Scandal (The)	Thomson/Hugh
School History Of The United States (A)	Pyle/Howard
Scottish Chiefs	Wyeth/N.C.
Scottish Chiefs	Wyeth/N.C.
Sea Fairies	Neill/John R.
Sea Fairies	Neill/John R.
Seeker (The)	O'Neill/Rose
Sense & Sensibility	Thomson/Hugh
Seven Ages Of Childhood (The)	Smith/Jessie Wilcox
Seven Ages Of Childhood (The)	Smith/Jessie Wilcox
Seven Ages Of Childhood (The)	Smith/Jessie Wilcox
Shadow Show (A)	Newell/Peter
She Stoops To Conquer	Thomson/Hugh
Shepheard's Calander	Crane/Walter
Shirley	Dulac/Edmund
Siegfried & Twilight Of The Gods	Rackham/Arthur
Siegfried & Twilight Of The Gods	Rackham/Arthur
Siegfried & Twilight Of The Gods	Rackham/Arthur
Siegfried & Twilight Of The Gods	Rackham/Arthur
Siegfried & Twilight Of The Gods	Rackham/Arthur
Siegfried & Twilight Of The Gods	Rackham/Arthur
Silence & Other Stories	Pyle/Howard
Silver Princess In Oz	Neill/John R.
Silver Princess In Oz	Neill/John R.
Simple Simon	Denslow/W.W.

LISTINGS BY TITLE

Author	Publisher	Year	Price Range
Twain/Mark	Harper	1919	75 — 100
Marriott/C.	Lippincott	1913	25 — 50
Harte/Bret	Houghton,Mifflin	1910	50 — 75
Baldwin/J.	Scribner	1912	40 — 60
	Duffield	1919	75 — 125
Neill/John R.	Reilly & Lee	(1941)	250 — 350
Neill/John R.	Reilly & Lee	(1941)	40 — 60
Baum/L. Frank	Rand Mcnally	(1939)	25 — 50
Baum/L. Frank	Reilly & Britton	(1915)	400 — 600
Baum/L. Frank	Reilly & Britton	(1915)	125 — 175
Baum/L. Frank	Reilly & Lee	(1915)	100 — 150
Baum/L. Frank	Reilly & Lee	(1915)	40 — 60
Hawthorne/Nathaniel	Methuen	(1920)	150 — 200
Browne/P.E.	Doran	(1917)	25 — 35
Sheridan/Richard B.	Hodder & Stoughton	[1911]	100 — 145
Sheridan/Richard B.	Hodder & Stoughton	[1911]	200 — 300
Swinton/William	American Book Co.	1893	20 — 30
Wiggin/Kate Douglas	Scribner	1921	125 — 175
Wiggin/Kate Douglas	Scribner	1934	65 — 85
Baum/L. Frank	Reilly & Britton	(1911)	400 — 600
Baum/L. Frank	Reilly & Britton	(1911)	100 — 150
Wilson/H.L.	Doubleday	1904	25 — 40
Austen/Jane	Macmillan		50 — 75
Wells/Carolyn	Donohue	(1909)	100 — 125
Wells/Carolyn	Moffat	1909	250 — 350
Wells/Carolyn	Duffield	1921	100 — 125
Newell/Peter	Century	1896	250 — 300
Goldsmith/Oliver	Hodder & Stoughton	(1912)	120 — 160
Spenser/Edmund	Harper	1898	150 — 175
Bronte/Charlotte	Dent	1905	125 — 175
Wagner/Richard	Heinemann	(1911)	100 — 150
Wagner/Richard	Heinemann	1911	200 — 350
Wagner/Richard	Heinemann	1911	300 — 400
Wagner/Richard	Doubleday,Page	1911	175 — 275
Wagner/Richard	Heinemann	1911	800 — 1000
Wagner/Richard	Garden City	1930	75 — 125
Wilkins/Mary	Harper	1898	20 — 30
Thompson/Ruth P.	Reilly & Lee	(1938)	200 — 300
Thompson/Ruth P.	Reilly & Lee	(1938)	40 — 60
Denslow/W.W.	Dillingham	(1904)	100 — 150

LISTINGS BY TITLE

Title	Illustrator
Sinbad The Sailor	Dulac/Edmund
Sinbad The Sailor & Other Stories	Dulac/Edmund
Sing A Song Of Safety	O'Neill/Rose
Sir Christopher...	Pyle/Howard
Sirens Three	Crane/Walter
Sixpenny Toybooks	Crane/Walter
Sixpenny Toybooks	Crane/Walter
Sketch Book Of Geoffrey Crayon (The)	Rackham/Arthur
Sketch Book Of Geoffrey Crayon (The)	Rackham/Arthur
Sketch Book Of Geoffrey Crayon (The)	Rackham/Arthur
Sketches In Egypt	Gibson/Charles D.
Sky Island	Neill/John R.
Sky Island	Neill/John R.
Sky Island	Neill/John R.
Slant Book (The)	Newell/Peter
Slant Book (The)	Newell/Peter
Slatendpencilvania	Crane/Walter
Sleeping Beauty	Neill/John R.
Sleeping Beauty & Other Fairy Tales	Dulac/Edmund
Sleeping Beauty & Other Fairy Tales	Dulac/Edmund
Sleeping Beauty & Other Fairy Tales	Dulac/Edmund
Sleeping Beauty & Other Fairy Tales	Dulac/Edmund
Sleeping Beauty (The)	Rackham/Arthur
Sleeping Beauty (The)	Rackham/Arthur
Sleeping Beauty (The)	Rackham/Arthur
Sleepy-Time Stories	Humphrey/Maud
Sleepy-Time Stories	Humphrey/Maud
Snickerty Nick	Rackham/Arthur
Snickerty Nick & The Giant	Rackham/Arthur
Snickerty Nick & The Giant	Rackham/Arthur
Snow Bound	Pyle/Howard
Snow Queen & Other Stories	Dulac/Edmund
Snow White & Rose Red	Neill/John R.
Snowbound	Neill/John R.
Snowdrop & Other Tales	Rackham/Arthur
Snowdrop & Other Tales	Rackham/Arthur
Social Ladder	Gibson/Charles D.
Some American College Bookplates	Pyle/Howard
Some British Ballads	Rackham/Arthur
Some British Ballads	Rackham/Arthur
Some British Ballads	Rackham/Arthur
Some British Ballads	Rackham/Arthur

LISTINGS BY TITLE

Author	Publisher	Year	Price Range
	Hodder & Stoughton	[1914]	300 — 375
	Hodder & Stoughton	[1914]	250 — 350
Marks/Gerald		1937	30 — 50
Goodwin/Maud W.	Little Brown	1901	25 — 35
Crane/Walter	Macmillan	1886	175 — 200
	Warne	[1865]	50 — 75
	Routledge	[1867	50 — 75
Irving/Washington	Putnam	(1894)	125 — 150
Irving/Washington	Putnam	(1894)	250 — 300
Irving/Washington	Putnam	(1894)	100 — 125
Gibson/Charles D.	Doubleday	1899	80 — 100
Baum/L. Frank	Reilly & Britton	(1912)	500 — 750
Baum/L. Frank	Reilly & Britton	(1912)	150 — 250
Baum/L. Frank	Reilly & Lee	(1912)	100 — 150
Newell/Peter	Harper	(1910)	150 — 200
Newell/Peter	Harper		75 — 100
Crane/Walter	Marcus Ward	1885	125 — 150
	Reilly & Britton	(1908)	100 — 125
Quiller-Couch/Arthur	Garden City	(1915)	35 — 65
Quiller-Couch/Arthur	Hodder & Stoughton	[1910]	250 — 350
Quiller-Couch/Arthur	Doran	[1910]	125 — 225
Quiller-Couch/Arthur	Doubleday		125 — 225
Evans/C.S.	Heinemann	(1920)	150 — 200
Evans/C.S.	Heinemann	(1920)	750 — 1000
Evans/C.S.	Lippincott	(1920)	150 — 200
Booth/Maud B.	Putnam	1899	100 — 165
Booth/Maud B.	Putnam	1911	40 — 60
Ford/Julia E.	Moffat	1919	125 — 175
Ford/Julia E.	Sutton House	[1935]	35 — 50
Ford/Julia E.	Sutton House	1933	50 — 75
Whittier/John Greenleaf	Houghton, Mifflin	1906	60 — 80
Anderson/Hans Christian	Hodder & Stoughton		100 — 150
	Reilly & Britton	(1908)	75 — 100
Whittier/John G.	Reilly & Britton	(1909)	40 — 60
Grimm Brothers	Dutton	(1920)	150 — 175
Grimm Brothers	Constable	1920	150 — 200
Gibson/Charles D.	Russell	1902	120 — 150
Ward/Harry P.		1915	50 — 75
	Constable	[1919]	175 — 225
	Dodd	[1919]	150 — 175
	Heinemann	[1925]	150 — 175
	Constable	1919	750 — 1000

215

LISTINGS BY TITLE

Title	Illustrator
Some Merry Adventures Of Robin Hood	Pyle/Howard
Some Merry Adventures Of Robin Hood	Pyle/Howard
Song Of Hiawatha	Parrish/Maxfield
Song Of Hiawatha	Wyeth/N.C.
Songs Of Bilitis	Pogany/Will
Songs Of Father Goose	Denslow/W.W.
Songs Of Father Goose	Denslow/W.W.
Songs Of Sentiment	Christy/Howard Chandler
Songs/Jingles/Rhymes	Humphrey/Maud
Sonnets From The Portuguese	Pogany/Will
Sonnets From The Portuguese	Pogany/Will
Sonny's Father	Smith/Jessie Wilcox
Soul Of Melicent (The)	Pyle/Howard
Souvenir Of Sir Henry Irving	Rackham/Arthur
Spanish Raggle-Taggle......	Rackham/Arthur
Spanish Raggle-Taggle.......	Rackham/Arthur
Speedy In Oz	Neill/John R.
Speedy In Oz	Neill/John R.
Splendid Idle Forties	Fisher/Harrison
Spring Songs With Music....	Barker/Cicely Mary
Springtide Of Life	Rackham/Arthur
Springtide Of Life	Rackham/Arthur
Springtide Of Life	Rackham/Arthur
Springtide Of Life	Rackham/Arthur
Springtide Of Life	Rackham/Arthur
Squibs Of California	Cox/Palmer
St. Joan Of Arc	Pyle/Howard
Star Bearer (The)	Pyle/Howard
Stealers Of Light	Dulac/Edmund
Stolen Treasure	Pyle/Howard
Stops Of Various Quills	Pyle/Howard
Storied Holidays	Pyle/Howard
Stories From ...	Dulac/Edmund
Stories From ...	Dulac/Edmund
Stories From ...	Dulac/Edmund
Stories From ...	Dulac/Edmund
Stories From Arabian Nights	Dulac/Edmund
Stories From Arabian Nights	Dulac/Edmund
Stories From Arabian Nights	Dulac/Edmund
Stories From Arabian Nights	Dulac/Edmund
Stories From Arabian Nights	Dulac/Edmund
Stories From Arabian Nights	Dulac/Edmund

LISTINGS BY TITLE

Author	Publisher	Year	Price Range
Pyle/Howard	Scribner	(1911)	20 — 30
Pyle/Howard	Scribner	1902	100 — 150
Longfellow/Henry W.	Houghton, Mifflin	1911	200 — 400
Longfellow/Henry W.	Houghton, Mifflin	1911	200 — 350
Louys/P.	Macy		125 — 150
Baum/L. Frank	Bobbs-Merrill	(1909)	125 — 175
Baum/L. Frank	Geo Hill	1900	400 — 600
Christy/Howard Chandler	Moffat	1910	75 — 100
Thomas/E.	Stokes	(1894)	250 — 350
Browning/Elizabeth Barrett	Crowell	(1936)	50 — 75
Browning/Elizabeth Barrett	Crowell	(1945)	40 — 60
Stuart/Ruth M.	Century	1910	70 — 90
Cabbell/James B.	Stokes	(1913)	90 — 130
Calvert/Walter	Chant, Drane	(1895)	75 — 100
Starkie/Walter	John Murray	(1934)	75 — 100
Starkie/Walter	Dutton	1934	50 — 75
Thompson/Ruth P.	Reilly & Lee	(1934)	200 — 300
Thompson/Ruth P.	Reilly & Lee	(1934)	40 — 60
Atherton/G.	Macmillan	1902	30 — 45
Linnell/Olive	Blackie & Sons	[1920]	75 — 125
Swinburne/Algernon C.	Heinemann	(1818)	250 — 300
Swinburne/Algernon C.	Heinemann	(1918)	200 — 250
Swinburne/Algernon C.	Heinemann	(1918)	750 — 1000
Swinburne/Algernon C.	Heinemann	(1918)	50 — 75
Swinburne/Algernon C.	Lippincott	(1918)	100 — 150
	Mutual	1874	100 — 150
Twain/Mark	Harper	(1919)	75 — 125
Stedman/Edmund C.	Lothrop	[1888]	100 — 125
	Hodder & Stoughton	1916	125 — 150
Pyle/Howard	Harper	1907	100 — 125
Howells/W.D.	Harper	1895	50 — 75
Brooks/Elbridge S.	Lothrop	[1887]	150 — 175
Anderson/Hans Christian	Hodder & Stoughton	(1911)	350 — 500
Anderson/Hans Christian	Hodder & Stoughton	[1915]	125 — 175
Anderson/Hans Christian	Doran		200 — 250
Anderson/Hans Christian	Doubleday		125 — 150
Housman/Laurence	Hodder & Stoughton	(1907)	300 — 400
Housman/Laurence	Scribner	(1907)	175 — 225
Housman/Laurence	Hodder & Stoughton	[1911]	100 — 150
Housman/Laurence	Hodder & Stoughton	[1920]	100 — 125
Housman/Laurence	Doran	[1920]	125 — 175
Housman/Laurence	Garden City	[1932]	50 — 75

LISTINGS BY TITLE

Title	Illustrator
Stories From Arabian Nights	Dulac/Edmund
Stories From Memel For The Young	Crane/Walter
Stories Of King Arthur	Rackham/Arthur
Stories Of King Arthur	Rackham/Arthur
Stories Of Later American History	Pyle/Howard
Stories That Never Grow Old	Gruelle/Johnny
Stories To Tell The Littlest Ones	Pogany/Will
Stories To Tell The Littlest Ones	Pogany/Will
Stories To Tell The Littlest Ones	Pogany/Will
Story Of A Fierce Bad Rabbit (The)	Potter/Beatrix
Story Of A Fierce Bad Rabbit (The)	Potter/Beatrix
Story Of A Fierce Bad Rabbit (The)	Potter/Beatrix
Story Of A Fierce Bad Rabbit (The)	Potter/Beatrix
Story Of Canterbury Pilgrims (The)	Thomson/Hugh
Story Of Champions Of The Round Table (The)	Pyle/Howard
Story Of Glittering Plain (The)	Crane/Walter
Story Of Greece (The)	Crane/Walter
Story Of Hiawatha (The)	Pogany/Will
Story Of Jack Ballister's Fortunes (The)	Pyle/Howard
Story Of King Arthur & Knights (The)	Pyle/Howard
Story Of King Arthur & Knights (The)	Pyle/Howard
Story Of Louise	Denslow/W.W.
Story Of Mince Pie	Rae/John
Story Of Miss Moppet (The)	Potter/Beatrix
Story Of Miss Moppet (The)	Potter/Beatrix
Story Of Miss Moppet (The)	Potter/Beatrix
Story Of Miss Moppet (The)	Potter/Beatrix
Story Of Miss Moppet (The)	Potter/Beatrix
Story Of Peter Rabbit	Neill/John R.
Story Of Peter Rabbit (The)	Neill/John R.
Story Of Rosina	Thomson/Hugh
Story Of Siegfried (The)	Pyle/Howard
Story Of Siegfried (The)	Pyle/Howard
Story Of Sir Launcelot (The)	Pyle/Howard
Story Of The Golden Age	Pyle/Howard
Story Of The Golden Age (A)	Pyle/Howard
Story Of The Grail....(The)	Pyle/Howard
Story Of The Grail....(The)	Pyle/Howard
Story Of The Revolution (The)	Pyle/Howard
Story Teller's Pack	Newell/Peter
Story/Dogie Told To Me	Rae/John
Strange Story Book (The)	Ford/H.J.

Listings By Title

Author	Publisher	Year	Price Range
Housman/Laurence	Doubleday		125 — 175
Havilland/Agnes De	Hunt	1864	100 — 125
Haydon/A.L.	Cassell	1910	175 — 225
Haydon/A.L.	Cassell	1918	100 — 125
Gordy/Wilbur	Scribner	1915	15 — 20
	Cupples & Leon	(1918)	75 — 100
Bryant/Sara C.	Houghton,Mifflin	(1916)	50 — 75
Bryant/Sara C.	Harrap	1918	75 — 100
Bryant/Sara C.	Harrap	1919	25 — 50
Potter/Beatrix	Warne	[1906]	400 — 500
Potter/Beatrix	Warne	[1914]	300 — 400
Potter/Beatrix	Warne	[1914]	200 — 300
Potter/Beatrix	Warne	[1933]	100 — 150
Darton/Frederick J.	Stokes		40 — 60
Pyle/Howard	Scribner	1905	75 — 100
Morris/William	Kelmscott Press	1894	100 — 150
MacGregor/Mary	Jack	1913	125 — 150
Elias/Edith L.	Harrap	[1914]	75 — 100
Pyle/Howard	Century	1895	150 — 200
Pyle/Howard	Scribner	(1933)	40 — 60
Pyle/Howard	Scribner	1903	100 — 175
Welch/D.		1901	50 — 75
Gates/J.S.	Dodd	1916	50 — 75
Potter/Beatrix	Warne	[1906]	400 — 600
Potter/Beatrix	Warne	[1913]	350 — 450
Potter/Beatrix	Warne	[1925]	250 — 350
Potter/Beatrix	Warne	[1933]	100 — 125
Potter/Beatrix	Warne	[1933]	100 — 125
Potter/Beatrix	Reilly & Britton	(1911)	100 — 125
	Reilly & Britton	(1908)	125 — 150
Dobson/A.	Kegan	1895	65 — 80
Baldwin/James	Scribner	1882	150 — 200
Baldwin/James	Scribner	1929	75 — 100
Pyle/Howard	Scribner	1907	175 — 225
Baldwin/J.	Scribner	1887	180 — 230
Baldwin/James	Scribner	1887	75 — 100
Pyle/Howard	Scribner	1910	175 — 225
Pyle/Howard	Scribner	1927	50 — 75
Lodge/Henry C.	Scribner	1898	25 — 35
Stockton/F.	Copp	1897	50 — 75
Barbour/R.H.	Dodd	1914	35 — 50
Lang/Andrew	Longmans	1913	200 — 250

219

Listings By Title

Title	Illustrator
Stray Birds	Pogany/Will
Streets Of Ascalon	Gibson/Charles D.
Struggle For A Continent (The)	Pyle/Howard
Studies & Stories	Crane/Walter
Summer Songs With Music...	Barker/Cicely Mary
Sun Princess (The)	Rackham/Arthur
Sunny Bunny	Gruelle/Johnny
Sunny Bunny	Gruelle/Johnny
Sunny Bunny	Gruelle/Johnny
Sunny-Book Readers	Gruelle/Johnny
Sunrise-Land	Rackham/Arthur
Sunrise-Land	Rackham/Arthur
Sunshine For Little Children	Humphrey/Maud
Surprising Adventures Of Tuppy & Tue (The)	Rackham/Arthur
Susanna & Sue	Wyeth/N.C.
Swinton's Advanced Third Reader	Pyle/Howard
Swiss Family Robinson (The)	Neill/John R.
Sword Of Dundee	Rae/John

T

Title	Illustrator
Tailor Of Gloucester	Potter/Beatrix
Tailor Of Gloucester	Potter/Beatrix
Tailor Of Gloucester	Potter/Beatrix
Tailor Of Gloucester	Potter/Beatrix
Tale Of Benjamin Bunny (The)	Potter/Beatrix
Tale Of Benjamin Bunny (The)	Potter/Beatrix
Tale Of Benjamin Bunny (The)	Potter/Beatrix
Tale Of Flopsy Bunnies (The)	Potter/Beatrix
Tale Of Flopsy Bunnies (The)	Potter/Beatrix
Tale Of Flopsy Bunnies (The)	Potter/Beatrix
Tale Of Flopsy Bunnies (The)	Potter/Beatrix
Tale Of Jemima Puddle Duck (The)	Potter/Beatrix
Tale Of Jemima Puddle Duck (The)	Potter/Beatrix
Tale Of Jemima Puddle Duck (The)	Potter/Beatrix
Tale Of Jemima Puddle Duck (The)	Potter/Beatrix
Tale Of Johnny Town Mouse (The)	Potter/Beatrix
Tale Of Johnny Town Mouse (The)	Potter/Beatrix
Tale Of Johnny Town Mouse (The)	Potter/Beatrix
Tale Of Little Pig Robinson (The)	Potter/Beatrix
Tale Of Little Pig Robinson (The)	Potter/Beatrix
Tale Of Little Pig Robinson (The)	Potter/Beatrix
Tale Of Mr. Jeremy Fisher (The)	Potter/Beatrix

LISTINGS BY TITLE

Author	Publisher	Year	Price Range
Tagore/Rabindranth	Macmillan	1917	30 — 40
Chambers/R.	Appleton	1912	25 — 35
Parkman/Francis	Little Brown	1902	40 — 60
Molesworth/Mrs.	A.D. Innes	1893	125 —150
Linnell/Olive	Blackie & Sons	[1920]	75 — 125
Millar/H.R.	Shaw	[1930]	40 — 60
Putnam/Nina Wilcox	Volland	(1918)	125 —150
Putnam/Nina Wilcox	Volland	(1918)	100 — 125
Putnam/Nina Wilcox	Algonquin	(1918)	40 — 60
	Laidlaw	1924	25 — 35
Berlyn/Mrs. Alfred	Jarrold	1894	175 —225
Berlyn/Mrs. Alfred	Jarrold	1898	100 —125
	Sunshine	1888	150 —200
Brown/Maggie	Cassell	1904	250 —350
Wiggin/Kate Douglas	Houghton,Mifflin	1909	40 — 60
	Ivison	1886	15 — 25
	Reilly & Britton	(1908)	75 —100
Peck/T.	Duffield	1908	25 — 35
Potter/Beatrix	Warne	(1903)	500 —650
Potter/Beatrix	Warne	[1903]	350 —500
Potter/Beatrix	Warne	[1909]	75 — 100
Potter/Beatrix	Privately Printed	1902	1000 —2000
Potter/Beatrix	Warne	(1932)	50 — 75
Potter/Beatrix	Warne	[1908]	250 —300
Potter/Beatrix	Warne	1904	400 —500
Potter/Beatrix	Warne	(1937)	25 — 50
Potter/Beatrix	Warne	[1909]	200 —300
Potter/Beatrix	Warne	[1915]	50 — 75
Potter/Beatrix	Warne	1909	300 —500
Potter/Beatrix	Warne	(1908)	75 — 125
Potter/Beatrix	Warne	(1908)	125 —175
Potter/Beatrix	Warne	[1920]	50 — 75
Potter/Beatrix	Warne	1908	350 —450
Potter/Beatrix	Warne	(1918)	200 —300
Potter/Beatrix	Warne	(1918)	100 — 150
Potter/Beatrix	Warne	(1946)	25 — 50
Potter/Beatrix	Warne	(1930)	100 — 150
Potter/Beatrix	Warne	(1930)	225 —275
Potter/Beatrix	McKay	(1930)	200 —250
Potter/Beatrix	Warne	(1934)	25 — 50

LISTINGS BY TITLE

Title	Illustrator
Tale Of Mr. Jeremy Fisher (The)	Potter/Beatrix
Tale Of Mr. Jeremy Fisher (The)	Potter/Beatrix
Tale Of Mr. Jeremy Fisher (The)	Potter/Beatrix
Tale Of Mr. Tod (The)	Potter/Beatrix
Tale Of Mr. Tod (The)	Potter/Beatrix
Tale Of Mrs. Tiggy Winkle (The)	Potter/Beatrix
Tale Of Mrs. Tiggy Winkle (The)	Potter/Beatrix
Tale Of Mrs. Tittlemouse (The)	Potter/Beatrix
Tale Of Mrs. Tittlemouse (The)	Potter/Beatrix
Tale Of Mrs. Tittlemouse (The)	Potter/Beatrix
Tale Of Peter Rabbit (The)	Neill/John R.
Tale Of Peter Rabbit (The)	Potter/Beatrix
Tale Of Peter Rabbit (The)	Potter/Beatrix
Tale Of Peter Rabbit (The)	Potter/Beatrix
Tale Of Peter Rabbit (The)	Potter/Beatrix
Tale Of Peter Rabbit (The)	Potter/Beatrix
Tale Of Peter Rabbit (The)	Potter/Beatrix
Tale Of Pigling Bland (The)	Potter/Beatrix
Tale Of Pigling Bland (The)	Potter/Beatrix
Tale Of Pigling Bland (The)	Potter/Beatrix
Tale Of Squirrel Nutkin (The)	Potter/Beatrix
Tale Of Squirrel Nutkin (The)	Potter/Beatrix
Tale Of Squirrel Nutkin (The)	Potter/Beatrix
Tale Of Squirrel Nutkin (The)	Potter/Beatrix
Tale Of Timmy Tiptoes (The)	Potter/Beatrix
Tale Of Timmy Tiptoes (The)	Potter/Beatrix
Tale Of Timmy Tiptoes (The)	Potter/Beatrix
Tale Of Tom Kitten (The)	Potter/Beatrix
Tale Of Tom Kitten (The)	Potter/Beatrix
Tale Of Tom Kitten (The)	Potter/Beatrix
Tale Of Two Bad Mice (The)	Potter/Beatrix
Tale Of Two Bad Mice (The)	Potter/Beatrix
Tale Of Two Bad Mice (The)	Potter/Beatrix
Tale/Beatrix Potter	Potter/Beatrix
Tales & Sketches	Smith/Jessie Wilcox
Tales & Sketches	Smith/Jessie Wilcox
Tales & Talks About Animals	Rackham/Arthur
Tales From Maria Edgeworth	Thomson/Hugh
Tales From Shakespeare	Rackham/Arthur
Tales From Shakespeare	Rackham/Arthur
Tales From Shakespeare	Rackham/Arthur
Tales From Shakespeare	Rackham/Arthur

LISTINGS BY TITLE

Author	Publisher	Year	Price Range
Potter/Beatrix	Warne	[1908]	250 — 350
Potter/Beatrix	Warne	[1915]	75 — 100
Potter/Beatrix	Warne	1906	450 — 600
Potter/Beatrix	Warne	[1912]	200 — 250
Potter/Beatrix	Warne	1912	280 — 350
Potter/Beatrix	Warne	[1915]	75 — 100
Potter/Beatrix	Warne	1905	450 — 600
Potter/Beatrix	Warne	(1938)	20 — 30
Potter/Beatrix	Warne	[1915]	100 — 150
Potter/Beatrix	Warne	1910	300 — 375
Potter/Beatrix	Altemus	(1904)	100 — 150
Potter/Beatrix	Platt & Munk	(1938)	25 — 35
Potter/Beatrix	Privately Printed	[1901]	3000 — 5000
Potter/Beatrix	Warne	[1902]	700 — 1000
Potter/Beatrix	Warne	[1902]	500 — 800
Potter/Beatrix	Warne	[1906]	50 — 100
Potter/Beatrix	Altemus	1904	350 — 500
Potter/Beatrix	Warne	(1941)	25 — 50
Potter/Beatrix	Warne	[1913]	200 — 250
Potter/Beatrix	Warne	1913	275 — 325
Potter/Beatrix	Warne	(1903)	250 — 350
Potter/Beatrix	Warne	(1905)	150 — 200
Potter/Beatrix	Warne	(1931)	25 — 50
Potter/Beatrix	Warne	1903	350 — 500
Potter/Beatrix	Warne	(1911)	200 — 300
Potter/Beatrix	Warne	[1919]	100 — 150
Potter/Beatrix	Warne	1911	350 — 500
Potter/Beatrix	Warne	(1935)	30 — 50
Potter/Beatrix	Warne	[1909]	100 — 150
Potter/Beatrix	Warne	1907	300 — 500
Potter/Beatrix	Warne	(1932)	25 — 50
Potter/Beatrix	Warne	[1908]	150 — 300
Potter/Beatrix	Warne	1904	300 — 450
Lane/Margaret	Warne	(1946)	50 — 75
Hawthorne/Nathaniel	Houghton,Mifflin	1900	750 — 1000
Hawthorne/Nathaniel	Houghton,Mifflin	1900	75 — 100
	Blackie & Sons	(1907)	125 — 150
Edgeworth/Maria	Stokes		40 — 60
Lamb/Charles & Mary	Dent	1899	150 — 200
Lamb/Charles & Mary	Dent	1909	200 — 275
Lamb/Charles & Mary	Dent	1909	750 — 1000
Lamb/Charles & Mary	Dutton	1909	175 — 225

LISTINGS BY TITLE

Title	Illustrator
Tales Of A Traveler	Rackham/Arthur
Tales Of A Traveler	Rackham/Arthur
Tales Of Mystery & Imagination	Rackham/Arthur
Tales Of Mystery & Imagination	Rackham/Arthur
Tales Of Mystery & Imagination	Rackham/Arthur
Tales Of Mystery & Imagination	Rackham/Arthur
Tales Of Troy & Greece	Ford/H.J.
Tales/Persian Genii	Pogany/Will
Tanglewood Tales	Dulac/Edmund
Tanglewood Tales	Pogany/Will
Tannhauser	Pogany/Will
Tannhauser	Pogany/Will
Tapestry Room (The)	Crane/Walter
Tapestry Room (The)	Crane/Walter
Tempest (The)	Crane/Walter
Tempest (The)	Dulac/Edmund
Tempest (The)	Rackham/Arthur
Tempest (The)	Rackham/Arthur
Tempest (The)	Rackham/Arthur
Ten To Seventeen	Smith/Jessie Wilcox
That Stanley	Cox/Palmer
The Light Princess	Humphrey/Maud
Theatrical Bookplates	Pyle/Howard
Their First Formal Call	Newell/Peter
Their Hearts Desire	Fisher/Harrison
Third Annual Of Advertising Art	Rackham/Arthur
Thirty Favorite Paintings	Christy/Howard Chandler
Thirty Favorite Paintings	Fisher/Harrison
Thirty Favorite Paintings	Gibson/Charles D.
Thirty Favorite Paintings	Parrish/Maxfield
Thirty Favorite Paintings	Parrish/Maxfield
Thirty Favorite Paintings	Smith/Jessie Wilcox
This & That	Thomson/Hugh
Three Bears (The)	Neill/John R.
Three Little Frogs	Rae/John
Three Men On Wheels	Fisher/Harrison
Through A Glass Lightly	Rackham/Arthur
Through The Gates/Old Romance	Rae/John
Through The Looking Glass	Gutmann/Bessie Pease
Through The Looking Glass	Newell/Peter
Through The Looking Glass;Humpty Dumpty	Neill/John R.
Throwback (The)	Wyeth/N.C.

LISTINGS BY TITLE

Author	Publisher	Year	Price Range
Irving/Washington	Putnam	1895	100 — 150
Irving/Washington	Putnam	1895	250 — 350
Poe/Edgar Allan	Harrap	(1935)	200 — 250
Poe/Edgar Allan	Harrap	(1935)	250 — 300
Poe/Edgar Allan	Harrap	[1935]	1500 — 2500
Poe/Edgar Allan	Lippincott	[1935]	175 — 250
Lang/Andrew	Longmans	1907	150 — 175
Olcott/F.J.	Harrap	1919	70 —
Hawthorne/Nathaniel	Hodder & Stoughton	(1938)	150 — 200
Hawthorne/Nathaniel	Unwin	[1910]	100 — 130
Wagner/Richard	Harrap	(1911)	175 — 250
Wagner/Richard	Brentano's		75 — 100
Molesworth/Mrs.	Macmillan	1879	75 — 100
Molesworth/Mrs.	Macmillan	1906	25 — 50
Shakespeare/William	Dent	1892	100 — 150
Shakespeare/William	Hodder & Stoughton	[1908]	350 — 500
Shakespeare/William	Heinemann	(1926)	175 — 250
Shakespeare/William	Heinemann	(1926)	1000 — 1250
Shakespeare/William	Doubleday,Page	(1926)	150 — 200
Bacon/Josephine D.	Harper	1908	40 — 60
	Art Printing	1878	50 — 100
MacDonald/George	Putnam	(1893)	140 — 175
Pope/A. Winthrop	Fowler	1914	75 — 100
Cooke/G.M.	Harper	1906	50 — 100
Perry/F.F.	Dodd	1909	65 — 80
Art Directors Club	Book Service Co.	1924	75 — 100
	Collier	1909	300 — 500
	Collier	1909	300 — 500
	Collier	1909	300 — 500
	P.F. Collier	1908	100 — 150
	Collier	1909	300 — 500
	Collier	1909	300 — 500
Molesworth/Mrs.	Macmillan	1899	50 — 65
	Reilly & Britton	(1908)	75 — 100
Mee/J.	Volland	(1924)	40 — 60
Jerome/J.K.	Dodd	1900	35 — 50
Greg/T.T.	Dent	1897	175 — 200
Mills/W.J.	Lippincott	1903	25 — 40
Carroll/Lewis	Dodge	(1909)	125 — 175
Carroll/Lewis	Harper	1902	150 — 200
	Reilly & Britton	(1908)	100 — 125
Lewis/A.H.	Outing	1906	35 — 50

LISTINGS BY TITLE

Title	Illustrator
Tik-Tok Of Oz	Neill/John R.
Tik-Tok Of Oz	Neill/John R.
Tik-Tok Of Oz	Neill/John R.
Tik-Tok Of Oz	Neill/John R.
Tin Woodsman Of Oz (The)	Neill/John R.
Tin Woodsman Of Oz (The)	Neill/John R.
Tin Woodsman Of Oz (The)	Neill/John R.
Tin Woodsman Of Oz (The)	Neill/John R.
Tiny Folk/Wintery Days	Humphrey/Maud
Tiny Todlers	Humphrey/Maud
Tiny Todlers	Humphrey/Maud
Tisza Tales	Pogany/Will
To Have & To Hold	Pyle/Howard
To The Other Side	Rackham/Arthur
Told To The Little Tot	Gutmann/Bessie Pease
Tom Brown's School Days	Thomson/Hugh
Tom Kitten's Painting Book	Potter/Beatrix
Tommy Toodles	Newell/Peter
Tomorrow's House	O'Neill/Rose
Topaz Story Book (The)	Parrish/Maxfield
Topo	Greenaway/Kate
Topsys & Turveys	Newell/Peter
Topsys & Turveys #2	Newell/Peter
Tour Around New York (A)	Pyle/Howard
Treasure Island	Dulac/Edmund
Treasure Island	Dulac/Edmund
Treasure Island	Dulac/Edmund
Treasure Island	Wyeth/N.C.
Treasure Island	Wyeth/N.C.
Treasury Of Stones,Jingles & Rhymes	Humphrey/Maud
Treasury Of Verse	Pogany/Will
Treasury Of Verse For Little Children	Pogany/Will
Treasury Of Verse For Little Children	Pogany/Will
Treatment/Drapery In Art	Crane/Walter
Trending Into Maine	Wyeth/N.C.
Triplets	Crane/Walter
Trot's Journey	Greenaway/Kate
Troubadour Tales	Parrish/Maxfield
Troubadour Tales	Parrish/Maxfield
True Story Of George Washington (The)	Pyle/Howard
True Story Of Unites States Of America (The)	Pyle/Howard
Trusty John & Other Stories	Ford/H.J.

LISTINGS BY TITLE

Author	Publisher	Year	Price Range
Baum/L.Frank	Reilly & Britton	(1914)	500 — 700
Baum/L.Frank	Reilly & Britton	(1914)	150 — 200
Baum/L.Frank	Reilly & Lee	(1914)	100 — 150
Baum/L.Frank	Reilly & Lee	(1914)	40 — 60
Baum/L.Frank	Reilly & Britton	(1918)	400 — 600
Baum/L.Frank	Reilly & Lee	(1918)	50 — 75
Baum/L.Frank	Reilly & Lee	(1918)	100 — 150
Baum/L.Frank	Reilly & Lee	(1918)	40 — 60
Thomas/E.	Stokes	1889	500 — 650
Humphrey/Maud	Dean	[1890]	450 — 500
Humphrey/Maud	Stokes	1890	650 — 800
Schwimmer/R.	Doubleday	1928	85 — 100
Johnston/Mary	Houghton,Mifflin	1900	20 — 30
Rhodes/Thomas	George Philip	1893	300 — 400
Cooke/E.V.	Dodge	(1906)	125 — 175
Hughes/Thomas	Ginn		50 — 75
	Warne	[1917]	500 — 700
Lee/Al	Harper	1896	150 — 200
O'Neill/G.	Dutton	1930	40 — 60
Skinner/Ada & Eleanor	Duffield	1917	75 — 125
Brunefille/G.	Marcus Ward	1878	200 — 250
Newell/Peter	Century	1893	225 — 300
Newell/Peter	Century	1894	200 — 225
Mines/John F.	Harper	1893	50 — 75
Stevenson/Robert Louis	Doran	[1927]	125 — 175
Stevenson/Robert Louis	Garden City	[1939]	40 — 60
Stevenson/Robert Louis	Doubleday		125 — 175
Stevenson/Robert Louis	Scribner	(1939)	50 — 75
Stevenson/Robert Louis	Scribner	1911	175 — 225
	Stokes	1894	250 — 350
Edgar/M.G.	Crowell	(1908)	100 — 135
Edgar/Madalen G.	Crowell	1923	10 — 20
Edgar/Madalen G.	Macmillan		30 — 50
Rhead/G.W.	G. Bell	1904	75 — 125
Roberts/Kenneth	Little Brown	1938	75 — 100
Crane/Walter	Routledge	1894	350 — 400
Greenaway/Kate	Worthington	(1882)	100 — 125
Stein/Evaleen	Bobbs-Merrill	(1903)	75 — 100
Stein/Evaleen	Bobbs-Merrill	1929	25 — 40
Brooks/Elbridge	Lothrop	1895	15 — 25
Brooks/Elbridge	Lothrop	1891	15 — 25
Lang/Andrew	Longmans	1906	75 — 100

LISTINGS BY TITLE

Title	Illustrator
Truth Dexter	Smith/Jessie Wilcox
Truth Dexter	Smith/Jessie Wilcox
Tuning Up	Smith/Jessie Wilcox
Tuning Up	Smith/Jessie Wilcox
Turquoise Cup	Parrish/Maxfield
Turquoise Cup	Parrish/Maxfield
Turquoise Story Book (The)	Parrish/Maxfield
Turtle Dove's Nest (The)	Crane/Walter
Twas The Night Before Christmas	Smith/Jessie Wilcox
Twas The Night Before Christmas	Smith/Jessie Wilcox
Twelve Dancing Princesses	Nielson/Kay
Twelve Dancing Princesses	Nielson/Kay
Twelve Dancing Princesses	Nielson/Kay
Twilight Land	Pyle/Howard
Twilight Land	Pyle/Howard
Twilight Land	Pyle/Howard
Two Gentlemen Of Verona	Crane/Walter
Two Little Waifs	Crane/Walter
Two Old Ladies,Two Foolish Fairies & A Tom Cat	Rackham/Arthur
Two Old Ladies,Two Foolish Fairies & A Tom Cat	Rackham/Arthur
Two Years Before The Mast	Rackham/Arthur
Two Years Before The Mast	Rackham/Arthur
Two Years Before The Mast	Rackham/Arthur
Two Years Before The Mast	Rackham/Arthur

U

Title	Illustrator
Ugly Duckling/Rip Van Winkle	Neill/John R.
Uncle Davie's Children	Pogany/Will
Uncle Tom's Cabin;The Story Of Topsy	Neill/John R.
Uncrowned King	Neill/John R.
Under Green Apple Boughs	Pyle/Howard
Under The Rose	Christy/Howard Chandler
Under The Southern Cross	Rae/John
Under The Window	Greenaway/Kate
Under The Window	Greenaway/Kate
Under The Window	Greenaway/Kate
Under The Window	Greenaway/Kate
Undine	Rackham/Arthur
Undine	Rackham/Arthur
Undine	Rackham/Arthur
Undine	Rackham/Arthur
Undine	Rackham/Arthur

LISTINGS BY TITLE

Author	Publisher	Year	Price Range
McCall/Sidney	Little Brown	1903	25 — 50
McCall/Sidney	Little Brown	1906	15 — 25
Glenn/Mabelle	Ginn	(1936)	35 — 50
Glenn/Mabelle	Ginn	(1943)	25 — 35
Smith/Arthur Coslett	Scribner	1903	50 — 80
Smith/Arthur Coslett	Scribner	1910	25 — 40
Skinner/Ada & Eleanor	Duffield	1918	90 — 140
	Routledge	1890	50 — 75
Moore/Clement C.	Houghton,Mifflin	(1912)	160 — 220
Moore/Clement C.	Houghton,Mifflin	[1914]	100 — 150
Quiller-Couch/Arthur	Doran	[1913]	300 — 400
Quiller-Couch/Arthur	Doubleday	1930	75 — 125
Quiller-Couch/Arthur	Doran		150 — 200
Pyle/Howard	Harper	(1894)	40 — 60
Pyle/Howard	Harper	(1922)	25 — 40
Pyle/Howard	Harrap	1895	75 — 100
Shakespeare/William	Dent	1894	300 — 500
Molesworth/Mrs.	Macmillan	(1883)	100 — 125
Brown/Maggie	Cassell	1897	500 — 750
Brown/Maggie	Cassell	1904	100 — 150
Dana/Richard Henry	Collins	(1904)	100 — 150
Dana/Richard Henry	Collins	(1904)	75 — 100
Dana/Richard Henry	Monarch	[1904]	75 — 100
Dana/Richard Henry	Winston	1904	50 — 75
	Reilly & Britton	(1908)	75 — 100
Daulton	Macmillan		75 — 100
	Reilly & Britton	(1908)	100 — 125
Wright/H.B.	Book Supply Co.	1910	50 — 75
Campbell/Helen	Fords, Howard	1882	35 — 50
Isham/Frederick S.	Bobbs-Merrill	(1903)	15 — 25
Robbins/E.	Stokes	(1907)	25 — 40
Greenaway/Kate	Routledge	[1878]	200 — 250
Greenaway/Kate	McLoughlin	[1879]	175 — 225
Greenaway/Kate	Routledge	[1879]	150 — 175
Greenaway/Kate	Warne	[1900]	100 — 150
Fouque/De La Motte	Heinemann	1909	250 — 300
Fouque/De La Motte	Heinemann	1909	750 — 1000
Fouque/De La Motte	Doubleday,Page	1909	200 — 250
Fouque/De La Motte	Heinemann	1911	100 — 125
Fouque/De La Motte	Doubleday	1919	100 — 150

LISTINGS BY TITLE

Title	Illustrator
University Press Shakespeare	Rackham/Arthur
Us:An Old Fashioned Story	Crane/Walter
Us:An Old Fashioned Story	Crane/Walter

V

Vacation Joys	Humphrey/Maud
Valentine & Orson	Crane/Walter
Van Bibber & Others	Gibson/Charles D.
Van Rensselaers/Old Manhattan	Rae/John
Vandermark's Folly	Wyeth/N.C.
Venture (The) Annual Of Art & Literature	Rackham/Arthur
Venture (The) Annual Of Art & Literature	Rackham/Arthur
Very Little Child's Book Of Stories (A)	Smith/Jessie Wilcox
Very Little Child's Book Of Stories (A)	Smith/Jessie Wilcox
Very Little Child's Book Of Stories (A)	Smith/Jessie Wilcox
Very Little Person	O'Neill/Rose
Vicar Of Wakefield	Thomson/Hugh
Vicar Of Wakefield (The)	Rackham/Arthur
Vicar Of Wakefield (The)	Rackham/Arthur
Vicar Of Wakefield (The)	Rackham/Arthur
Vicar Of Wakefield (The)	Rackham/Arthur
Vicar Of Wakefield (The)	Rackham/Arthur
Violet Fairy Book (The)	Ford/H.J.
Violet Fairy Book (The)	Ford/H.J.
Vision Of Dante (The)	Crane/Walter

W

Walter Crane Reader (The)	Crane/Walter
Walter Crane's Picture Book	Crane/Walter
Walter Crane's Picture Book	Crane/Walter
Walter Crane's Picture Book	Crane/Walter
Wanted A Matchmaker	Christy/Howard Chandler
Wanted, A Chaperone	Christy/Howard Chandler
War	Wyeth/N.C.
Water Babies (The)	Smith/Jessie Wilcox
Water Babies (The)	Smith/Jessie Wilcox
Water Babies (The)	Smith/Jessie Wilcox
Water Babies (The)	Smith/Jessie Wilcox
Water Babies (The)	Smith/Jessie Wilcox
Water Babies (The)	Smith/Jessie Wilcox
Water Babies (The)	Smith/Jessie Wilcox
Water Babies (The)	Smith/Jessie Wilcox

LISTINGS BY TITLE

Author	Publisher	Year	Price Range
Shakespeare/William	Harrap	1908	75 — 100
Molesworth/Mrs.	Macmillan	1886	100 — 125
Molesworth/Mrs.	Macmillan		75 — 100
	Donohue	1889	50 — 75
Crane/Walter	Routledge	(1873)	125 — 150
Davis/Richard Harding	Harper	1892	20 — 30
Mills/W.J.	Stokes	(1907)	25 — 40
Quick/H.	Bobbs-Merrill	(1922)	20 — 40
	John Baillie	1903	100 — 125
	John Baillie	1905	75 — 100
Skinner/Ada & Eleanor	Dial Press	(1935)	50 — 75
Skinner/Ada & Eleanor	Duffield	1923	125 — 150
Skinner/Ada & Eleanor	Dial Press	1935	75 — 100
Vorse/M.H.	Houghton,Mifflin	1911	40 — 60
Goldsmith/Oliver	Macmillan	1890	75 — 100
Goldsmith/Oliver	Harrap	[1929]	175 — 225
Goldsmith/Oliver	Harrap	[1929]	200 — 250
Goldsmith/Oliver	Harrap	[1929]	750 — 1000
Goldsmith/Oliver	McKay	[1929]	125 — 150
Goldsmith/Oliver	Lippincott	1929	75 — 100
Lang/Andrew	Longmans	1901	200 — 275
Lang/Andrew	Longmans	1933	25 — 50
Harrison/Elizabeth	Chicago Kindergarten College	1895	75 — 100
Dale/Nellie	Dent	1899	40 — 60
Crane/Walter	Cupples & Leon	(1903)	75 — 125
Crane/Walter	J. Lane	[1895]	200 — 300
Crane/Walter	Dodd		75 — 100
Ford/Paul L.	Dodd	1900	25 — 40
Ford/Paul L.	Dodd	1902	25 — 50
Long/John L.	Bobbs-Merrill	(1913)	50 — 75
Kingsley/Charles	Dodd	(1916)	100 — 175
Kingsley/Charles	Dodd	(1916)	75 — 150
Kingsley/Charles	Dodd	(1916)	200 — 300
Kingsley/Charles	Dodd	(1916)	225 — 325
Kingsley/Charles	Dodd	(1916)	175 — 250
Kingsley/Charles	Garden City	(1937)	35 — 50
Kingsley/Charles	Hodder & Stoughton	(1938)	100 — 150
Kingsley/Charles	Boots	[1919]	150 — 250

LISTINGS BY TITLE

Title	Illustrator
Water Babies (The)	Smith/Jessie Wilcox
Water Babies (The)	Smith/Jessie Wilcox
Water Babies (The)	Smith/Jessie Wilcox
Water Color Rendering Sugg.	Parrish/Maxfield
Waters Of Caney Fork	Denslow/W.W.
Way To Wonderland (The)	Smith/Jessie Wilcox
Way To Wonderland (The)	Smith/Jessie Wilcox
Way To Wonderland (The)	Smith/Jessie Wilcox
Wayfarer's Love	Crane/Walter
Welsh Fairy Book	Pogany/Will
Westward Ho	Wyeth/N.C.
Westward Ho	Wyeth/N.C.
Westward Ho	Wyeth/N.C.
Westward Ho	Wyeth/N.C.
When Christmas Comes Around	Smith/Jessie Wilcox
When Christmas Comes Around	Smith/Jessie Wilcox
When I Grow Up	Denslow/W.W.
When Mother Lets Us Make Paper Box Furniture	Smith/Jessie Wilcox
Where Flies The Flag	Rackham/Arthur
Where Flies The Flag	Rackham/Arthur
Where The Blue Begins	Rackham/Arthur
Where The Blue Begins	Rackham/Arthur
Where The Blue Begins	Rackham/Arthur
Where The Blue Begins	Rackham/Arthur
Where The Blue Begins	Rackham/Arthur
Whilomville Stories	Newell/Peter
Whispering Smith	Wyeth/N.C.
Whispering Smith	Wyeth/N.C.
Whispering Smith	Wyeth/N.C.
Whist Reference Book	Parrish/Maxfield
White Company (The)	Wyeth/N.C.
Why...	Rae/John
Widow & Her Friends (A)	Gibson/Charles D.
Wild Life In Hampshire Highlands	Rackham/Arthur
Wildflowers Of America	Humphrey/Maud
Wind In The Rose Bush	Newell/Peter
Wind In The Willows (The)	Rackham/Arthur
Wind In The Willows (The)	Rackham/Arthur
Wind In The Willows (The)	Rackham/Arthur
Wind In The Willows (The)	Rackham/Arthur
Windmill (The)	Rackham/Arthur
Windmill (The)	Rackham/Arthur

LISTINGS BY TITLE

Author	Publisher	Year	Price Range
Kingsley/Charles	Hodder & Stoughton	[1919]	175 — 250
Kingsley/Charles	Boots	[1925]	125 — 150
Kingsley/Charles	Dodd	[1936]	25 — 35
	J.H. Jansen	1917	150 — 200
Read/Opie	Rand Mcnally	1898	40 — 60
Stewart/Mary	Dodd	(1917)	170 — 240
Stewart/Mary	Dodd	(1917)	150 — 200
Stewart/Mary	Hodder & Stoughton	[1920]	200 — 250
Various	Constable	1904	50 — 75
Jenkyn-Thomas	Unwin	(1907)	150 — 200
Kingsley/Charles	Scribner	(1948)	20 — 35
Kingsley/Charles	Scribner	1920	75 — 150
Kingsley/Charles	Scribner	1935	30 — 50
Kingsley/Charles	Scribner	1947	20 — 50
Underwood/Priscilla	Chatto/Windus	1915	175 — 200
Underwood/Priscilla	Duffield	1915	175 — 200
Denslow/W.W.	Century	1909	175 — 225
Rich/G. Ellingwood	Dodd	1925	50 — 75
Harbour/Henry	Collins	(1904)	150 — 200
Harbour/Henry	Collins	[1904]	50 — 75
Morley/Christopher	Doubleday,Page	(1922)	1000 — 1250
Morley/Christopher	Heinemann	[1922]	750 — 1000
Morley/Christopher	Heinemann	[1925]	100 — 125
Morley/Christopher	Doubleday,Page	[1925]	100 — 125
Morley/Christopher	Lippincott	[1925]	50 — 100
Crane/S.	Harper	1900	175 — 225
Spearman/Frank	Scribner	1906	35 — 55
Spearman/Frank	Scribner	1908	15 — 25
Spearman/Frank	Grosset&Dunlap		15 — 25
Butler	John C. Yorston	1897	175 — 250
Doyle/Arthur C.	Cosmopolitan	1922	175 — 225
Rae/John	Dodd	1910	75 — 100
Gibson/Charles D.	Harper	1901	120 — 150
Dewar/George A.B.	Dent	1899	150 — 200
	Buer		40 — 60
Wilkins/M.E.	Doubleday	1903	50 — 75
Grahame/Kenneth	Heritage Press	(1940)	50 — 75
Grahame/Kenneth	Methuen	(1950)	40 — 60
Grahame/Kenneth	Methuen	(1951)	250 — 500
Grahame/Kenneth	Limited Editions Club	1940	400 — 600
Callender/L.	Heinemann	1923	75 — 100
Callender/L.	Heinemann	1923	125 — 150

LISTINGS BY TITLE

Title	Illustrator
Wishing Horse Of Oz (The)	Neill/John R.
Wishing Horse Of Oz (The)	Neill/John R.
Witch's Kitchen	Pogany/Will
Witch's Kitchen	Pogany/Will
Within The Capes	Pyle/Howard
Wm. Morris To Whistler	Crane/Walter
Wonder Book	Pogany/Will
Wonder Book & Tangelwood Tales	Parrish/Maxfield
Wonder Book & Tangelwood Tales	Parrish/Maxfield
Wonder Book & Tanglewood Tales	Crane/Walter
Wonder Book (A)	Rackham/Arthur
Wonder Book (A)	Rackham/Arthur
Wonder Book (A)	Rackham/Arthur
Wonder Book For Boys & Girls	Crane/Walter
Wonder Book For Boys & Girls	Crane/Walter
Wonder Book For Boys & Girls	Crane/Walter
Wonder Book For Boys & Girls	Crane/Walter
Wonder City Of Oz (The)	Neill/John R.
Wonder City Of Oz (The)	Neill/John R.
Wonder Clock (The)	Pyle/Howard
Wonder Clock (The)	Pyle/Howard
Wonder Clock (The)	Pyle/Howard
Wonderful Visit (The)	Rackham/Arthur
Wonderful Wizard Of Oz	Denslow/W.W.
Wooden Willie	Gruelle/Johnny
Wooden Willie	Gruelle/Johnny
Wooden Willie	Gruelle/Johnny
Works Of William Makepeace Thackery	Pyle/Howard
World In A Garden (A)	Rackham/Arthur

Y

Yankee Doodle	Pyle/Howard
Yearling (The)	Wyeth/N.C.
Yearling (The)	Wyeth/N.C.
Yearling (The)	Wyeth/N.C.
Yearling (The)	Wyeth/N.C.
Yellow Fairy Book (The)	Ford/H.J.
Yellow Fairy Book (The)	Ford/H.J.
Yellow Fairy Book (The)	Ford/H.J.
Yellow Knight Of Oz (The)	Neill/John R.
Yellow Knight Of Oz (The)	Neill/John R.
Yellow Knight Of Oz (The)	Neill/John R.

LISTINGS BY TITLE

Author	Publisher	Year	Price Range
Thompson/Ruth P.	Reilly & Lee	(1935)	250 — 350
Thompson/Ruth P.	Reilly & Lee	(1935)	40 — 60
Young/G.	Crowell	(1912)	120 — 160
Young/G.	Harrap	1910	150 — 180
Pyle/Howard	Int'l Assoc Of Newspapers	1901	15 — 30
Crane/Walter	G. Bell	1911	75 — 100
Hawthorne/Nathaniel	Jacobs	(1909)	100 — 150
Palgrave/Francis Turner	Duffield	1910	125 — 200
Palgrave/Francis Turner	Duffield	1928	100 — 150
Hawthorne/Nathaniel	Houghton,Mifflin	1898	175 — 225
Hawthorne/Nathaniel	Hodder & Stoughton	(1922)	225 — 300
Hawthorne/Nathaniel	Hodder & Stoughton	(1922)	750 — 1000
Hawthorne/Nathaniel	Doran	(1922)	200 — 250
Hawthorne/Nathaniel	Osgood	1892	170 — 220
Hawthorne/Nathaniel	Houghton,Mifflin	1893	140 — 180
Hawthorne/Nathaniel	Riverside Press	1893	250 — 350
Hawthorne/Nathaniel	Houghton,Mifflin	1905	40 — 65
Neill/John R.	Reilly & Lee	(1940)	250 — 350
Neill/John R.	Reilly & Lee	(1940)	40 — 60
Pyle/Howard	Harper	1888	200 — 300
Pyle/Howard	Harper	1899	100 — 125
Pyle/Howard	Harper	1915	25 — 35
Wells/H.G.	Dent	1895	125 — 150
Baum/L. Frank	Geo Hill	1900	5M — 10M
Gruelle/Johnny	Donohue	(1927)	35 — 50
Gruelle/Johnny	Volland	(1927)	100 — 125
Gruelle/Johnny	Volland	(1927)	75 — 100
Ritchie/Lady	Harper	1910	30 — 50
Neish/R.	Dent	1899	75 — 100
Pyle/Howard	Dodd	1881	250 — 300
Rawlings/M.K.	Scribner	1938	100 — 150
Rawlings/M.K.	Scribner	1940	75 — 100
Rawlings/M.K.	Scribner	1942	50 — 75
Rawlings/M.K.	Scribner	1945	25 — 50
Lang/Andrew	Longmans	1894	175 — 225
Lang/Andrew	Longmans	1895	100 — 150
Lang/Andrew	Longmans	1897	100 — 150
Thompson/Ruth P.	Reilly & Lee	(1930)	350 — 500
Thompson/Ruth P.	Reilly & Lee	(1930)	100 — 150
Thompson/Ruth P.	Reilly & Lee	(1930)	40 — 60

LISTINGS BY TITLE

Title	Illustrator
Youma: The Story Of A West Indian Slave	Pyle/Howard
Young American Speaker	Humphrey/Maud
Young Puritans In Captivity (The)	Smith/Jessie Wilcox
Young Puritans In Captivity (The)	Smith/Jessie Wilcox
Zankiwank & The Bletherwitch	Rackham/Arthur
Zankiwank & The Bletherwitch	Rackham/Arthur
Zankiwank & The Bletherwitch	Rackham/Arthur

LISTINGS BY TITLE

Author	Publisher	Year	Price Range
Hearn/Lafcadio	Harper	1890	250 — 350
	Donohue	1890	75 — 100
Smith/Mary P. Wells	Little Brown	1899	100 — 160
Smith/Mary P. Wells	Little Brown	1907	50 — 75
Fitzgerald/S.J.	Dent	1896	600 — 750
Fitzgerald/S.J.	Dutton	1896	300 — 450
Fitzgerald/S.J.	Stokes	1896	250 — 350

LISTINGS BY AUTHOR

Author	Title	Illustrator	Publisher	Year	Price Range
		A			
Abbott/C.	Howard Pyle/A Chronicle	Pyle/H.	Harper	1925	120 — 150
Addison/J.	Mrs. John Vernon	Gibson/C.D.	Badger	1909	15 — 20
Aesop	Aesop's Fables	Rackham/A.	Bell & Cockb.	1912	150 — 175
Aesop	Aesop's Fables	Rackham/A.	Dbl.,Page	1912	175 — 225
Aesop	Aesop's Fables	Rackham/A.	Heinemann	1912	225 — 300
Aesop	Aesop's Fables	Rackham/A.	Heinemann	1912	800 —1200
Aesop	Aesop's Fables	Rackham/A.	Doubleday	1926	50 — 100
Aitken/R.	Golden Horshoe (The)	Fisher/H.	G&D	(1907)	20 — 30
Alcott/L.M.	An Old-Fashioned Girl	Smith/J.W.	Little Brown	1902	100 — 150
Alcott/L.M.	An Old-Fashioned Girl	Smith/J.W.	Little Brown	1904	75 — 100
Alcott/L.M.	An Old-Fashioned Girl	Smith/J.W.	Sampson.Low	1907	75 — 100
Alcott/L.M.	An Old-Fashioned Girl	Smith/J.W.	Little Brown	1915	85 — 100
Alcott/L.M.	Little Women	Humphrey/M.	Holiday	1906	75 — 100
Alcott/L.M.	Little Women	Smith/J.W.	Little Brown	1915	125 — 150
Alcott/L.M.	Little Women	Smith/J.W.	Little Brown	1917	100 — 125
Alcott/L.M.	Little Women	Smith/J.W.	Little Brown	1922	50 — 75
Alcott/L.M.	Little Women	Smith/J.W.	Little Brown	1930	25 — 50
Allen/H.	Anthony Adverse	Wyeth/N.C.	F&R	1934	75 — 100
Allen/J.L.	Flute & Violin/Other Tales	Pyle/H.	Harper	1891	20 — 40
Allen/J.L.	Kentucky Cardinal Aftermath	Thomson/H.	Macmillan	1900	60 — 80
Allen/P.S.	King Arthur & His Knights	Neill/J.R.	Rand Mcnally	(1924)	30 — 60
Allen/P.S.	King Arthur & His Knights	Neill/J.R.	Rand Mcnally	(1936)	20 — 30
Allingham/W.	Rhymes For The Young Folks	Greenaway/K.	Cassell	(1887)	150 — 200
Anderson/H.C.	Fairy Tales	Nielson/K.	Doran	(1924)	275 — 450
Anderson/H.C.	Fairy Tales	Nielson/K.	H&S	[1924]	600 — 800
Anderson/H.C.	Fairy Tales	Nielson/K.	H&S	[1924]	1000 —1250
Anderson/H.C.	Fairy Tales	Nielson/K.	Garden City	[1932]	70 — 100
Anderson/H.C.	Fairy Tales	Nielson/K.	Doubleday		75 — 125
Anderson/H.C.	Fairy Tales By H. Anderson	Rackham/A.	Harrap	(1932)	125 — 150
Anderson/H.C.	Fairy Tales By H. Anderson	Rackham/A.	Harrap	(1932)	150 — 175
Anderson/H.C.	Fairy Tales By H. Anderson	Rackham/A.	McKay	(1932)	75 — 100
Anderson/H.C.	Fairy Tales By H. Anderson	Rackham/A.	Harrap	[1932]	900 —1250
Anderson/H.C.	Fairy Tales By..	Neill/J.R.	Cupples	(1923)	50 — 75
Anderson/H.C.	Nightingale (The)	Dulac/E.	H&S	[1911]	225 — 275
Anderson/H.C.	Snow Queen & Other Stories	Dulac/E.	H&S		100 — 150
Anderson/H.C.	Stories From ...	Dulac/E.	H&S	(1911)	350 — 500
Anderson/H.C.	Stories From ...	Dulac/E.	H&S	[1915]	125 — 175
Anderson/H.C.	Stories From ...	Dulac/E.	Doran		200 — 250
Anderson/H.C.	Stories From ...	Dulac/E.	Doubleday		125 — 150
Andrews/B.	History Of The United States	Pyle/H.	Scribner	1895	20 — 30

LISTINGS BY AUTHOR

Author	Title	Illustrator	Publisher	Year	Price Range
Andrews/B.	History Of/Last Century	Pyle/H.	Scribner	1896	20 — 30
Andrews/M.S.	Militants (The)	Wyeth/N.C.	Scribner	1907	25 — 40
Arnold/E.	Light Of Asia (The)	Pogany/W.	McKay	(1932)	75 — 100
Arr/E.H.	New England Bygones	Pyle/H.	Lippincott	1883	25 — 35
Art Dir.Club	Fourth Annual Of Adv. Art	Rackham/A.	Book Service Co.	1925	50 — 75
Art Dir.Club	Third Annual/Advertising Art	Rackham/A.	Book Service Co.	1924	75 — 100
Asbjornsen	East Of The Sun West Of Moon	Nielson/K.	Doran	[1914]	250 — 350
Asbjornsen	East Of The Sun West Of Moon	Nielson/K.	H&S	[1914]	500 — 700
Asbjornsen	East Of The Sun West Of Moon	Nielson/K.	Garden City	[1930]	50 — 100
Asbjornsen	East Of The Sun West Of Moon	Nielson/K.	Doran		100 — 150
Asbjornsen	East Of The Sun West Of Moon	Nielson/K.	Doubleday		75 — 100
Atherton/G.	Splendid Idle Forties	Fisher/H.	Macmillan	1902	30 — 45
Austen/J.	Emma	Thomson/H.	Macmillan		50 — 75
Austen/J.	Mansfield Park	Thomson/H.	Macmillan		50 — 75
Austen/J.	Northanger Abbey	Thomson/H.	Macmillan	1897	50 — 75
Austen/J.	Pride & Prejudice	Thomson/H.	G. Allen	1894	65 — 90
Austen/J.	Sense & Sensibility	Thomson/H.	Macmillan		50 — 75

B

Author	Title	Illustrator	Publisher	Year	Price Range
Bacon/J.D.	Biography Of A Boy	O'Neill/R.	Harper	1910	50 — 75
Bacon/J.D.	Ten To Seventeen	Smith/J.W.	Harper	1908	40 — 60
Bailey/C.S.	Peter Newell's Mother Goose	Newell/P.	Holt	1905	75 — 100
Baker/F.T.	Everyday Classics	Pogany/W.	Macmillan	1923	25 — 50
Baldry/A.L.	Practice/W. Colour Painting	Rackham/A.	Macmillan	1911	75 — 100
Baldwin/J.	Sampo (The)	Wyeth/N.C.	Scribner	1912	40 — 60
Baldwin/J.	Story Of Seigfried (The)	Pyle/H.	Scribner	1882	150 — 200
Baldwin/J.	Story Of Seigfried (The)	Pyle/H.	Scribner	1929	75 — 100
Baldwin/J.	Story Of The Golden Age	Pyle/H.	Scribner	1887	180 — 230
Baldwin/J.	Story Of The Golden Age (A)	Pyle/H.	Scribner	1887	75 — 100
Bangs/J.K.	Bikey The Skycycle	Newell/P.	Riggs	1902	35 — 50
Bangs/J.K.	Booming Of Acre Hill	Gibson/C.D.	Harper	1900	20 — 30
Bangs/J.K.	Enchanted Typewriter (The)	Newell/P.	Harper	1899	25 — 50
Bangs/J.K.	From Pillar To Post	Neill/J.R.	Century	1916	50 — 75
Bangs/J.K.	House Boat On The Styx	Newell/P.	Harper	1896	25 — 50
Bangs/J.K.	Mr. Munchausen	Newell/P.	Noyes,Platt	1901	60 — 80
Bangs/J.K.	Pursuit Of The Houseboat	Newell/P.	Harper	1897	25 — 40
Banks	Polly Garden	Pogany/W.	Macmillan		75 — 100
Bannerman/H.	All About Little Black Sambo	Gruelle/J.	Cupples	(1917)	125 — 175
Bannerman/H.	All About Little Black Sambo	Gruelle/J.	Cupples	(1929)	50 — 75
Barbour/R.H.	Story/Dogie Told To Me	Rae/J.	Dodd	1914	35 — 50
Barker/C.M.	Book Of Flower Fairies	Barker/C.M.	Blackie	[1927]	150 — 250
Barker/C.M.	Book Of Flower Fairies	Barker/C.M.	Blackie	[1940]	50 — 75

LISTINGS BY AUTHOR

Author	Title	Illustrator	Publisher	Year	Price Range
Barker/C.M.	Children's Book Of Hymns	Barker/C.M.	Blackie		50 — 75
Barker/C.M.	Children's Book Of Hymns	Barker/C.M.	Blackie		15 — 20
Barker/C.M.	Fairies Of The Flowers/Trees	Barker/C.M.	Blackie		50 — 75
Barker/C.M.	Flower Fairies Of Autumn	Barker/C.M.	Blackie	[1927]	75 — 125
Barker/C.M.	Flower Fairies Of Summer	Barker/C.M.	Blackie	(1923)	75 — 125
Barker/C.M.	Flower Fairy Alphabet (A)	Barker/C.M.	Blackie	(1934)	75 — 125
Barker/C.M.	Flower Songs/Seasons	Barker/C.M.	Blackie	[1915]	100 — 150
Barker/C.M.	Little Book Of Old Rhymes (A)	Barker/C.M.	Blackie		30 — 50
Barker/C.M.	Lord Of The Rushie River (The)	Barker/C.M.	Blackie	[1938]	50 — 75
Barker/C.M.	Rhymes New & Old	Barker/C.M.	Blackie	[1936]	60 — 80
Barker/Mrs. S.	Birthday Book For Children	Greenaway/K.	Routledge	[1880]	200 — 275
Barker/Mrs. S.	Birthday Book For Children	Greenaway/K.	Warne	[1900]	100 — 125
Barrie/J.M	Quality Street	Thomson/H.	H&S	[1913]	130 — 170
Barrie/J.M.	Admirable Crichton	Thomson/H.	H&S	[1914]	125 — 165
Barrie/J.M.	Little White Bird	Rackham/A.	Scribner	1912	250 — 300
Barrie/J.M.	Little White Bird	Rackham/A.	Scribner	1913	30 — 50
Barrie/J.M.	Peter Pan/Kensington Gardens	Rackham/A.	H&S	(1910)	150 — 175
Barrie/J.M.	Peter Pan/Kensington Gardens	Rackham/A.	H&S	(1910)	100 — 125
Barrie/J.M.	Peter Pan/Kensington Gardens	Rackham/A.	H&S	(1912)	1250 — 1500
Barrie/J.M.	Peter Pan/Kensington Gardens	Rackham/A.	H&S	(1912)	250 — 400
Barrie/J.M.	Peter Pan/Kensington Gardens	Rackham/A.	H&S	1906	300 — 500
Barrie/J.M.	Peter Pan/Kensington Gardens	Rackham/A.	H&S	1906	1250 — 2000
Barrie/J.M.	Peter Pan/Kensington Gardens	Rackham/A.	Scribner	1906	250 — 400
Barrie/J.M.	Peter Pan/Kensington Gardens	Rackham/A.	Scribner	1907	175 — 225
Barrie/J.M.	Peter Pan/Kensington Gardens	Rackham/A.	Scribner	1913	175 — 200
Barrie/J.M.	Peter Pan/Kensington Gardens	Rackham/A.	Scribner	1926	75 — 125
Barrie/J.M.	Peter Pan/Kensington Gardens	Rackham/A.	Scribner	1929	75 — 125
Barrie/J.M.	Peter Pan/Kensington Gardens	Rackham/A.	Scribner	1929	75 — 125
Barrie/J.M.	Peter Pan/Kensington Gardens	Rackham/A.	Scribner	1940	50 — 100
Barritt/L.	How To Draw	Pyle/H.	Harper	1904	30 — 50
Bartruse/G.	Children In Japan	Pogany/W.	McBride	1915	130 — 180
Baum/L.F.	Dorothy & The Wizard Of Oz	Neill/J.R.	R&B	(1908)	500 — 750
Baum/L.F.	Dorothy & The Wizard Of Oz	Neill/J.R.	R&B	(1908)	125 — 200
Baum/L.F.	Dorothy & The Wizard Of Oz	Neill/J.R.	R&L	(1908)	75 — 125
Baum/L.F.	Dorothy & The Wizard Of Oz	Neill/J.R.	R&L	(1908)	40 — 60
Baum/L.F.	Dorothy & The Wizard Of Oz	Neill/J.R.	R&L	(1908)	75 — 100
Baum/L.F.	Dot & Tot In Merryland	Denslow/W.W.	Bobbs-Merrill	(1903)	200 — 300
Baum/L.F.	Dot & Tot In Merryland	Denslow/W.W.	Geo Hill	1901	600 — 800
Baum/L.F.	Emerald City Of Oz (The)	Neill/J.R.	R&B	(1910)	500 — 750
Baum/L.F.	Emerald City Of Oz (The)	Neill/J.R.	R&B	(1910)	175 — 250
Baum/L.F.	Emerald City Of Oz (The)	Neill/J.R.	R&L	(1910)	100 — 125
Baum/L.F.	Emerald City Of Oz (The)	Neill/J.R.	R&L	(1910)	40 — 60

Listings By Author

Author	Title	Illustrator	Publisher	Year	Price Range
Baum/L.F.	Father Goose His Book	Denslow/W.W.	Geo Hill	(1899)	200 — 700
Baum/L.F.	Father Goose His Book	Denslow/W.W.	Geo Hill	(1899)	2000 — 4000
Baum/L.F.	Father Goose His Book	Denslow/W.W.	Donohue	[1913]	100 — 150
Baum/L.F.	Father Goose His Book	Denslow/W.W.	Donohue	1910	150 — 200
Baum/L.F.	Gingerbread Man	Neill/J.R.	R&B	(1917)	200 — 300
Baum/L.F.	Glinda Of Oz	Neill/J.R.	R&L	(1920)	250 — 350
Baum/L.F.	Glinda Of Oz	Neill/J.R.	R&L	(1920)	100 — 150
Baum/L.F.	Glinda Of Oz	Neill/J.R.	R&L	(1920)	40 — 60
Baum/L.F.	John Dough & The Cherub	Neill/J.R.	R&B	(1906)	600 — 800
Baum/L.F.	John Dough & The Cherub	Neill/J.R.	R&B	(1906)	200 — 300
Baum/L.F.	John Dough & The Cherub	Neill/J.R.	R&L	(1906)	150 — 175
Baum/L.F.	Land Of Oz (The)	Neill/J.R.	R&B	(1904)	400 — 600
Baum/L.F.	Land Of Oz (The)	Neill/J.R.	R&B	(1904)	175 — 250
Baum/L.F.	Land Of Oz (The)	Neill/J.R.	R&B	(1904)	100 — 150
Baum/L.F.	Land Of Oz (The)	Neill/J.R.	R&L	(1904)	75 — 125
Baum/L.F.	Land Of Oz (The)	Neill/J.R.	R&L	(1904)	40 — 60
Baum/L.F.	Land Of Oz (The)	Neill/J.R.	R&L	(1904)	75 — 125
Baum/L.F.	Little Wizard Series	Neill/J.R.	R&B	(1913)	150 — 200
Baum/L.F.	Little Wizard Series	Neill/J.R.	R&L	(1913)	100 — 125
Baum/L.F.	Little Wizard Stories Of Oz ·	Neill/J.R.	R&B	(1914)	350 — 450
Baum/L.F.	Little Wizard Stories Of Oz	Neill/J.R.	R&B	(1914)	200 — 300
Baum/L.F.	Lost Princess Of Oz (The)	Neill/J.R.	R&B	(1917)	500 — 600
Baum/L.F.	Lost Princess Of Oz (The)	Neill/J.R.	R&B	(1917)	150 — 250
Baum/L.F.	Lost Princess Of Oz (The)	Neill/J.R.	R&L	(1917)	100 — 150
Baum/L.F.	Lost Princess Of Oz (The)	Neill/J.R.	R&L	(1917)	40 — 60
Baum/L.F.	Lost Princess Of Oz (The)	Neill/J.R.	R&L	(1917)	75 — 125
Baum/L.F.	Magic Cloak	Neill/J.R.	R&L	(1916)	500 — 750
Baum/L.F.	Magic Of Oz (The)	Neill/J.R.	R&L	(1919)	400 — 600
Baum/L.F.	Magic Of Oz (The)	Neill/J.R.	R&L	(1919)	150 — 200
Baum/L.F.	Magic Of Oz (The)	Neill/J.R.	R&L	(1919)	40 — 60
Baum/L.F.	Marvelous Land Of Oz (The)	Neill/J.R.	R&B	(1904)	800 — 1000
Baum/L.F.	Mother Goose In Prose	Parrish/M.	Way/Williams	(1897)	4000 — 5000
Baum/L.F.	Mother Goose In Prose	Parrish/M.	Bobbs-Merrill	(1905)	500 — 750
Baum/L.F.	Mother Goose In Prose	Parrish/M.	Way/Williams	1901	500 — 750
Baum/L.F.	New Wizard Of Oz (The)	Denslow/W.W.	Bobbs-Merrill	(1903)	400 — 1200
Baum/L.F.	New Wizard Of Oz (The)	Denslow/W.W.	Bobbs-Merrill	(1903)	50 — 75
Baum/L.F.	New Wizard Of Oz (The)	Denslow/W.W.	Bobbs-Merrill	(1939)	100 — 150
Baum/L.F.	Ozma Of Oz	Neill/J.R.	R&B	(1907)	500 — 750
Baum/L.F.	Ozma Of Oz	Neill/J.R.	R&B	(1907)	150 — 200
Baum/L.F.	Ozma Of Oz	Neill/J.R.	R&L	(1907)	75 — 100
Baum/L.F.	Patchwork Girl Of Oz (The)	Neill/J.R.	R&B	(1913)	400 — 600
Baum/L.F.	Patchwork Girl Of Oz (The)	Neill/J.R.	R&B	(1913)	350 — 400

LISTINGS BY AUTHOR

Author	Title	Illustrator	Publisher	Year	Price Range
Baum/L.F.	Patchwork Girl Of Oz (The)	Neill/J.R.	R&L	(1913)	100 — 150
Baum/L.F.	Rinkitink In Oz	Neill/J.R.	R&B	(1916)	500 — 700
Baum/L.F.	Rinkitink In Oz	Neill/J.R.	R&B	(1916)	200 — 300
Baum/L.F.	Rinkitink In Oz	Neill/J.R.	R&L	(1916)	100 — 150
Baum/L.F.	Rinkitink In Oz	Neill/J.R.	R&L	(1916)	40 — 60
Baum/L.F.	Road To Oz (The)	Neill/J.R.	R&B	(1909)	400 — 600
Baum/L.F.	Road To Oz (The)	Neill/J.R.	R&B	(1909)	125 — 175
Baum/L.F.	Road To Oz (The)	Neill/J.R.	R&L	(1909)	40 — 60
Baum/L.F.	Scarecrow Of Oz (The)	Neill/J.R.	R&B	(1915)	400 — 600
Baum/L.F.	Scarecrow Of Oz (The)	Neill/J.R.	R&B	(1915)	125 — 175
Baum/L.F.	Scarecrow Of Oz (The)	Neill/J.R.	R&L	(1915)	100 — 150
Baum/L.F.	Scarecrow Of Oz (The)	Neill/J.R.	R&L	(1915)	40 — 60
Baum/L.F.	Scarecrow/Tin Woodman Of Oz	Neill/J.R.	Rand Mcnally	(1939)	25 — 50
Baum/L.F.	Sea Fairies	Neill/J.R.	R&B	(1911)	400 — 600
Baum/L.F.	Sea Fairies	Neill/J.R.	R&B	(1911)	100 — 150
Baum/L.F.	Sky Island	Neill/J.R.	R&B	(1912)	500 — 750
Baum/L.F.	Sky Island	Neill/J.R.	R&B	(1912)	150 — 250
Baum/L.F.	Sky Island	Neill/J.R.	R&L	(1912)	100 — 150
Baum/L.F.	Songs Of Father Goose	Denslow/W.W.	Bobbs-Merrill	(1909)	125 — 175
Baum/L.F.	Songs Of Father Goose	Denslow/W.W.	Geo Hill	1900	400 — 600
Baum/L.F.	Tik-Tok Of Oz	Neill/J.R.	R&B	(1914)	500 — 700
Baum/L.F.	Tik-Tok Of Oz	Neill/J.R.	R&B	(1914)	150 — 200
Baum/L.F.	Tik-Tok Of Oz	Neill/J.R.	R&L	(1914)	100 — 150
Baum/L.F.	Tik-Tok Of Oz	Neill/J.R.	R&L	(1914)	40 — 60
Baum/L.F.	Tin Woodsman Of Oz (The)	Neill/J.R.	R&B	(1918)	400 — 600
Baum/L.F.	Tin Woodsman Of Oz (The)	Neill/J.R.	R&L	(1918)	50 — 75
Baum/L.F.	Tin Woodsman Of Oz (The)	Neill/J.R.	R&L	(1918)	100 — 150
Baum/L.F.	Tin Woodsman Of Oz (The)	Neill/J.R.	R&L	(1918)	40 — 60
Baum/L.F.	Wonderful Wizard Of Oz	Denslow/W.W.	Geo Hill	1900	5M — 10M
Beach/R.	Ne'er Do Well (The)	Christy/H.C.	Harper	1911	20 — 35
Beauclerk/H.	Green Lacquer Pavillion	Dulac/E.	Doran	(1926)	50 — 75
Beauclerk/H.	Green Lacquer Pavillion	Dulac/E.	Collins	1926	75 — 100
Beauclerk/H.	Love Of The Foolish Angel	Dulac/E.	Collins	1929	75 — 100
Beeching/H.C.	Book Of Christmas Verse	Crane/W.	Methuen	1895	75 — 100
Beeching/H.C.	Book Of Christmas Verse	Crane/W.	Methuen	1895	300 — 500
Belasco/D.	Return Of Peter Grimm	Rae/J.	Dodd	1912	25 — 40
Bell/L.	Runaway Equator	Newell/P.	Stokes	(1911)	100 — 125
Bell/L.P.	Kitchen Fun	Smith/J.W.	Harter	1932	50 — 75
Bell/L.P.	Kitchen Fun	Smith/J.W.	Perks Pub.	1946	35 — 50
Benjamin/S.G.W.	Art In America	Pyle/H.	Harper	1880	75 — 100
Benoit/C.F.	Childrens St./Never Grow Old	Neill/J.R.	R&B	(1908)	75 — 100
Benson/A.C.	Book Of Queen's Doll House	Rackham/A.	Methuen	(1924)	50 — 75

Listings By Author

Author	Title	Illustrator	Publisher	Year	Price Range
Benson/A.C.	Book Of Queen's Doll House	Rackham/A.	Methuen	(1924)	150 — 200
Benson/E.F.	David Blaize & The Blue Door	Ford/H.J.	Doubleday		75 — 100
Berlyn/Mrs.	Sunrise-Land	Rackham/A.	Jarrold	1894	175 — 225
Berlyn/Mrs.	Sunrise-Land	Rackham/A.	Jarrold	1898	100 — 125
Beymer/W.G.	On Hazardous Service	Pyle/H.	Harper	1912	20 — 30
Bianco/M.W.	Poor Cecco	Rackham/A.	Chatto/Windus	(1925)	150 — 175
Bianco/M.W.	Poor Cecco	Rackham/A.	Doran	(1925)	125 — 150
Bianco/M.W.	Poor Cecco	Rackham/A.	Doran	1925	6000 — 8000
Bianco/M.W.	Poor Cecco	Rackham/A.	Doubleday		100 — 125
Bicknell/W.H.	Etchings	Pyle/H.	Biblio. Soc.	1903	75 — 100
Bicknell/W.H.	Etchings	Pyle/H.	Biblio. Soc.	1913	50 — 75
Bingham/C.	Faithful Friends	Rackham/A.	Blackie	(1902)	350 — 450
Bingham/C.	Faithful Friends	Rackham/A.	Blackie	[1913]	250 — 300
Blashfield/E.H.	Mural Painting In America	Parrish/M.	Scribner	1913	25 — 50
Bleackley/H.	More Tales Of The Stumps	Rackham/A.	Ward,Lock	1902	175 — 225
Bonner/G.	Pioneer (The)	Fisher/H.	Bobbs-Merrill	(1905)	30 — 40
Booth/M.B.	Sleepy-Time Stories	Humphrey/M.	Putnam	1899	100 — 165
Booth/M.B.	Sleepy-Time Stories	Humphrey/M.	Putnam	1911	40 — 60
Bowen/B.	Eclogues Of Vergil (The)	Pyle/H.	Priv. Prnt	1904	100 — 150
Boyd/J.	Drums	Wyeth/N.C.	Scribner	1928	100 — 150
Boyd/J.	Drums	Wyeth/N.C.	Scribner	1928	500 — 750
Boyd/J.	Drums	Wyeth/N.C.	Scribner	1930	50 — 75
Boyles/K.	Langford Of The Three Bars	Wyeth/N.C.	McClurg	1907	40 — 60
Brainerd/E.H.	For Love Of Mary Ellen	O'Neill/R.	Harper	1912	30 — 50
Briscoe/M.	Harper's Book Of Little Plays	Pyle/H.	Harper	1910	30 — 50
Bronte/C.	Shirley	Dulac/E.	Dent	1905	125 — 175
Bronte/E.	Jane Eyre	Dulac/E.	Dutton		125 — 175
Brooks/E.	Great Men's Sons	Pyle/H.	Putnam	1895	30 — 50
Brooks/E.	Storied Holidays	Pyle/H.	Lothrop	[1887]	150 — 175
Brooks/E.	True Story Of G.Washington	Pyle/H.	Lothrop	1895	15 — 25
Brooks/E.	True Story Of U.S.Of America	Pyle/H.	Lothrop	1891	15 — 25
Brown/A.F.	Lonesomest Doll (The)	Rackham/A.	Houghton	(1928)	175 — 250
Brown/M.	Book Of Betty Barber (The)	Rackham/A.	Duckworth	(1910)	250 — 350
Brown/M.	Book Of Betty Barber (The)	Rackham/A.	Badger	[1910]	250 — 350
Brown/M.	Surprising Adv.Of Tuppy & Tue	Rackham/A.	Cassell	1904	250 — 350
Brown/M.	Two Old Ladies,Two Foolish........	Rackham/A.	Cassell	1897	500 — 750
Brown/M.	Two Old Ladies,Two Foolish........	Rackham/A.	Cassell	1904	100 — 150
Browne/P.E.	Peace At Any Price	Newell/P.	Appleton	1916	75 — 100
Browne/P.E.	Scars & Stripes	Newell/P.	Doran	(1917)	25 — 35
Browning/E.	Sonnets From The Portuguese	Pogany/W.	Crowell	(1936)	50 — 75
Browning/E.	Sonnets From The Portuguese	Pogany/W.	Crowell	(1945)	40 — 60
Browning/R.	Pied Piper Of Hamlin (The)	Rackham/A.	Harrap	[1934]	200 — 300

LISTINGS BY AUTHOR

Author	Title	Illustrator	Publisher	Year	Price Range
Browning/R.	Pied Piper Of Hamlin (The)	Rackham/A.	Lippincott	[1934]	100 — 200
Browning/R.	Pied Piper Of Hamlin (The)	Rackham/A.	Harrap	1934	750 — 1000
Browning/R.	Pied Piper Of Hamlin(The)	Greenaway/K.	Routledge	[1888]	200 — 250
Browning/R.	Pied Piper Of Hamlin(The)	Greenaway/K.	Warne	[1903]	100 — 150
Bruce/W.	Old Homestead Poems	Pyle/H.	Harper	1888	25 — 50
Brunefille/G.	Topo	Greenaway/K.	Marcus Ward	1878	200 — 250
Bryant/L.M.	American Pictures & Painters	Parrish/M.	J. Lane	1917	40 — 80
Bryant/S.C.	Stories To Tell/Littlest Ones	Pogany/W.	Houghton	(1916)	50 — 75
Bryant/S.C.	Stories To Tell/Littlest Ones	Pogany/W.	Harrap	1918	75 — 100
Bryant/S.C.	Stories To Tell/Littlest Ones	Pogany/W.	Harrap	1919	25 — 50
Buchanan/R.	Pied Piper Of Hamelin	Thomson/H.	Heinemann	1893	50 — 70
Bull/K.J.	Little Paul's Christ Child	Smith/J.W.	Np	1929	50 — 75
Bullfinch/T.	Legends Of Charlemagne	Wyeth/N.C.	Cosmopolitan	1924	125 — 200
Bunyan/J.	Pilgrim's Progress	Ford/H.J.	Macmillan		50 — 75
Burnett/F.H.	In The Closed Room	Smith/J.W.	G&D	(1904)	25 — 50
Burnett/F.H.	In The Closed Room	Smith/J.W.	H&S	1904	100 — 150
Burnett/F.H.	In The Closed Room	Smith/J.W.	McClure	1904	100 — 150
Burney/F.	Evelina	Rackham/A.	Newnes	[1900]	100 — 150
Burney/F.	Evelina	Rackham/A.	Newnes	1898	175 — 225
Burney/F.	Evelina	Thomson/H.	Macmillan		40 — 60
Burnham/C.L.	Clever Betsy	O'Neill/R.	Houghton	1910	30 — 50
Burns/R.	Cotter's Saturday Night (The)	Rackham/A.	Heweston	[1908]	125 — 150
Burt/M.E.	Odysseus, The Hero Of Ithaca	Pyle/H.	Scribner	1898	20 — 30
Burton/R.	Kasidah Of Haji Abdu El-Yezdi	Pogany/W.	McKay	(1931)	65 — 100
Butler	Whist Reference Book	Parrish/M.	Yorston	1897	175 — 250
Butt/G.	Esther...	Greenaway/K.	Marcus Ward	1878	200 — 250
Byron/M.	Featherweights	Rackham/A.	H&S	(1908)	150 — 250
Byron/M.	Peter Pan/Kensington Gardens	Rackham/A.	H&S	(1929)	75 — 100
Byron/M.	Peter Pan/Kensington Gardens	Rackham/A.	Scribner	(1929)	75 — 100
Byron/M.	Peter Pan/Kensington Gardens	Rackham/A.	Scribner	1934	50 — 75

C

Cabbell/J.B.	Chivalry	Pyle/H.	Harper	1909	90 — 125
Cabbell/J.B.	Gallantry	Pyle/H.	Harper	1907	100 — 145
Cabbell/J.B.	Line Of Love (The)	Pyle/H.	Harper	1905	75 — 100
Cabbell/J.B.	Soul Of Melicent (The)	Pyle/H.	Stokes	(1913)	90 — 130
Cable/G.	Cavalier (The)	Christy/H.C.	Scribner	1901	40 — 60
Cadman/S.P.	Parables Of Jesus	Wyeth/N.C.	McKay	1931	300 — 400
Caine/R.H.	Children's Hour (The)	Rackham/A.	Newnes	(1906)	75 — 100
Callender/L.	Windmill (The)	Rackham/A.	Heinemann	1923	75 — 100
Callender/L.	Windmill (The)	Rackham/A.	Heinemann	1923	125 — 150
Calmour/A.C.	Rumbo Rhymes	Crane/W.	Harper	1911	150 — 175

Listings By Author

Author	Title	Illustrator	Publisher	Year	Price Range
Calvert/W.	Souvenir Of Sir Henry Irving	Rackham/A.	Chant,Drane	(1895)	75 — 100
Campbell/H.	Under Green Apple Boughs	Pyle/H.	Fords,Howard	1882	35 — 50
Capes/B.	Romance/Lohengrin	Pogany/W.	Dean	1905	125 — 150
Carleton/W.	City Ballads	Pyle/H.	Harper	1886	25 — 35
Carleton/W.	Farm Ballads	Pyle/H.	Harper	1882	25 — 35
Carroll/L.	Alice In Wonderland	Gutmann/B.P.	Dodge	(1907)	150 — 200
Carroll/L.	Alice In Wonderland	Gutmann/B.P.	Coker	[1915]	100 — 150
Carroll/L.	Alice In Wonderland	Gutmann/B.P.	Lippincott	1923	150 — 200
Carroll/L.	Alice's/Wonderland	Newell/P.	Harper	(1901)	125 — 150
Carroll/L.	Alice's/Wonderland	Newell/P.	Harper	(1901)	30 — 50
Carroll/L.	Alice's/Wonderland	Pogany/W.	Dutton	(1929)	100 — 150
Carroll/L.	Alice's/Wonderland	Rackham/A.	Doubleday	[1907]	125 — 175
Carroll/L.	Alice's/Wonderland	Rackham/A.	Doubleday	[1907]	400 — 600
Carroll/L.	Alice's/Wonderland	Rackham/A.	Heinemann	[1907]	500 — 700
Carroll/L.	Alice's/Wonderland	Rackham/A.	Heinemann	[1907]	150 — 200
Carroll/L.	Hunting Of The Snark (The)	Newell/P.	Harper	1903	125 — 150
Carroll/L.	Through The Looking Glass	Gutmann/B.P.	Dodge	(1909)	125 — 175
Carroll/L.	Through The Looking Glass	Newell/P.	Harper	1902	150 — 200
Carroll/W.	River & Rainbow	Rackham/A.	Forsyth	(1933)	125 — 150
Carroll/W.	River & Rainbow	Rackham/A.	Forsyth	(1933)	75 — 100
Carryl/G.W.	Fables For The Frivolous	Newell/P.	Harper	1898	75 — 100
Carryl/G.W.	Far From The Maddening Girls	Newell/P.	McClure	1904	50 — 75
Carryl/G.W.	Garden Of Years	Parrish/M.	Putnam	1904	45 — 75
Carryl/G.W.	Mother Goose For Grownups	Newell/P.	Harper	1900	100 — 125
Chabot/A.	Dancing-Master	Smith/J.W.	Lippincott	1901	150 — 175
Chambers/R.	Japonette	Gibson/C.D.	Appleton	1912	20 — 30
Chambers/R.	Maid-At-Arms	Christy/H.C.	Harper	1902	20 — 35
Chambers/R.	Streets Of Ascalon	Gibson/C.D.	Appleton	1912	25 — 35
Chapin/A.A.	Everyday & Now-A-Day Fairy Bk	Smith/J.W.	Coker	[1935]	100 — 150
Chapin/A.A.	Everyday & Now-A-Day Fairy Bk	Smith/J.W.	Coker	[1935]	75 — 100
Chapin/A.A.	Everyday Fairy Book (The)	Smith/J.W.	Harrap	(1919)	100 — 150
Chapin/A.A.	Everyday Fairy Book (The)	Smith/J.W.	Coker	[1935]	100 — 150
Chapin/A.A.	Everyday Fairy Book (The)	Smith/J.W.	Coker	[1935]	75 — 100
Chapin/A.A.	Everyday Fairy Book (The)	Smith/J.W.	Dodd	1915	175 — 250
Chapin/A.A.	Everyday Fairy Book (The)	Smith/J.W.	Harrap	1917	150 — 225
Chapin/A.A.	Now-A-Days Fairy Book (The)	Smith/J.W.	Dodd	(1911)	150 — 175
Chapin/A.A.	Now-A-Days Fairy Book (The)	Smith/J.W.	Prospect	(1913)	100 — 125
Chapin/A.A.	Now-A-Days Fairy Book (The)	Smith/J.W.	Harrap	[1922]	100 — 125
Chapin/A.A.	Now-A-Days Fairy Book (The)	Smith/J.W.	Coker	[1935]	75 — 100
Chapin/A.A.	Now-A-Days Fairy Book (The)	Smith/J.W.	Dodd	1911	200 — 300
Cheney/W.	Challenge (The)	Wyeth/N.C.	Bobbs-Merrill	(1906)	20 — 35
Chittenden/C.	Lincoln/Sleeping Sentinel	Pyle/H.	Harper	1909	15 — 25

Listings By Author

Author	Title	Illustrator	Publisher	Year	Price Range
Cholmondeley/M.	Red Pottage	Rackham/A.	Newnes	[1904]	200 — 300
Cholmondeley/M.	Red Pottage	Rackham/A.	Newnes	1904	400 — 550
Christy/H.C.	American Girl (The)	Christy/H.C.	Moffat	1906	100 — 150
Christy/H.C.	Christy Girl (The)	Christy/H.C.	Bobbs-Merrill	(1906)	75 — 100
Christy/H.C.	Drawings	Christy/H.C.	Moffat	1905	125 — 175
Christy/H.C.	Drawings	Christy/H.C.	Rev. Of Rev.	1913	75 — 100
Christy/H.C.	Our Girls	Christy/H.C.	Moffat	1907	75 — 100
Christy/H.C.	Songs Of Sentiment	Christy/H.C.	Moffat	1910	75 — 100
Churchill/W.	Crossing ...(The)	Rae/J.	Macmillan	1930	25 — 50
Cobb/I.S.	Cobb's Anatomy	Newell/P.	Doran	(1912)	35 — 45
Cobb/I.S.	Cobb's Bill Of Fare	Newell/P.	Doran	(1913)	35 — 45
Coe/F.	Founders Of Our Country	Pyle/H.	Am. Book Co	1912	15 — 20
Coffin/C.C.	Abraham Lincoln	Pyle/H.	Harper	1893	30 — 50
Coffin/C.C.	Building The Nation	Pyle/H.	Harper	1883	25 — 35
Coffin/C.C.	Old Times In The Colonies	Pyle/H.	Harper	1881	25 — 50
Coleridge/S.T.	Rime/Ancient Mariner	Pogany/W.	Crowell	(1910)	150 — 200
Coleridge/S.T.	Rime/Ancient Mariner	Pogany/W.	Harrap	(1910)	200 — 250
Coleridge/S.T.	Rime/Ancient Mariner	Pogany/W.	Doubleday	1928	75 — 100
Colum/P.	Adventures Of Odysseus	Pogany/W.	Macmillan	(1927)	25 — 50
Colum/P.	Adventures Of Odysseus	Pogany/W.	Macmillan	1918	50 — 75
Colum/P.	Children Of Odin (The)	Pogany/W.	Macmillan	(1929)	25 — 35
Colum/P.	Children Of Odin (The)	Pogany/W.	Macmillan	1920	35 — 50
Colum/P.	Frenzied Prince	Pogany/W.	McKay	(1943)	75 — 100
Colum/P.	Goldon Fleece (The)	Pogany/W.	Macmillan	(1921)	50 — 60
Colum/P.	Goldon Fleece (The)	Pogany/W.	Macmillan		15 — 25
Colum/P.	Gulliver's Travels	Pogany/W.	Macmillan	1917	75 — 100
Colum/P.	Gulliver's Travels	Pogany/W.	Harrap	1919	50 — 75
Colum/P.	King Of Ireland's Son	Pogany/W.	Holt	1916	75 — 100
Colum/P.	King Of Ireland's Son	Pogany/W.	Harrap	1920	75 — 100
Colum/P.	King Of Ireland's Son	Pogany/W.	Macmillan	1921	50 — 75
Cone/H.G.	Baby Sweethearts	Humphrey/M.	Stokes	1890	400 — 600
Cone/H.G.	Bonnie Little People	Humphrey/M.	Stokes	1890	400 — 550
Connolly/J.B.	Crested Seas (The)	Wyeth/N.C.	Scribner	1907	20 — 40
Cooke/E.V.	Biography Of Our Baby	Gutmann/B.P.	Dodge	(1906)	175 — 225
Cooke/E.V.	Chronicles/Little Tot	Gutmann/B.P.	Dodge	(1905)	150 — 175
Cooke/E.V.	Told To The Little Tot	Gutmann/B.P.	Dodge	(1906)	125 — 175
Cooke/G.M.	Their First Formal Call	Newell/P.	Harper	1906	50 — 100
Coolidge/S.	Guernsey Lily	Greenaway/K.	Roberts	1881	125 — 175
Cooper/A.P.	Rudyard Kipling	Rackham/A.	Dbl.,Page	1926	30 — 50
Cooper/J.F.	Deerslayer (The)	Wyeth/N.C.	Scribner	1925	100 — 150
Cooper/J.F.	Deerslayer (The)	Wyeth/N.C.	Scribner	1925	100 — 150
Cooper/J.F.	Deerslayer (The)	Wyeth/N.C.	Scribner	1927	45 — 75

LISTINGS BY AUTHOR

Author	Title	Illustrator	Publisher	Year	Price Range
Cooper/J.F.	Deerslayer (The)	Wyeth/N.C.	Scribner	1929	20 — 50
Cooper/J.F.	Last Of The Mohicans	Wyeth/N.C.	Scribner	1919	150 — 175
Cooper/J.F.	Last Of The Mohicans	Wyeth/N.C.	Scribner	1925	50 — 75
Coussens/P.	Child's Book Of Stories (A)	Smith/J.W.	Duffield	1911	250 — 300
Coussens/P.	Child's Book Of Stories (A)	Smith/J.W.	Chatto/Windus	1913	125 — 150
Coussens/P.	Child's Book Of Stories (A)	Smith/J.W.	Duffield	1914	150 — 175
Coussens/P.	Child's Book Of Stories (A)	Smith/J.W.	Dial Press	1935	75 — 100
Coussens/P.	Child's Book/Famous Stories	Smith/J.W.	Garden City	(1940)	40 — 60
Cox/F.T.	Chronicles Of Rhoda (The)	Smith/J.W.	Small.Maynard	(1909)	75 — 125
Cox/F.T.	Epic Of Ebenezer (The)	Rae/J.	Dodd	1912	25 — 35
Cox/P.	Another Brownie Book	Cox/P.	Century	(1890)	175 — 225
Cox/P.	Another Brownie Book	Cox/P.	Unwin	(1890)	175 — 225
Cox/P.	Brownie Clown/Brownie Town	Cox/P.	Century	[1908]	175 — 225
Cox/P.	Brownie Year Book	Cox/P.	McLoughlin	[1895]	175 — 225
Cox/P.	Brownies & Other Stories	Cox/P.	Donohue		40 — 70
Cox/P.	Brownies & Prince Florimel	Cox/P.	Century	(1918)	100 — 130
Cox/P.	Brownies Abroad (The)	Cox/P.	Century	(1899)	175 — 225
Cox/P.	Brownies Abroad (The)	Cox/P.	Unwin	(1899)	150 — 185
Cox/P.	Brownies Around The World	Cox/P.	Century	(1894)	175 — 225
Cox/P.	Brownies Around The World	Cox/P.	Unwin	(1894)	150 — 200
Cox/P.	Brownies At Home (The)	Cox/P.	Century	(1893)	175 — 225
Cox/P.	Brownies At Home (The)	Cox/P.	Unwin	(1893)	175 — 225
Cox/P.	Brownies In Fairyland (The)	Cox/P.	Century	(1925)	125 — 150
Cox/P.	Brownies In Fairyland (The)	Cox/P.	Harms	1894	175 — 225
Cox/P.	Brownies In The Philippines	Cox/P.	Century	(1904)	175 — 225
Cox/P.	Brownies In The Philippines	Cox/P.	Unwin	(1904)	175 — 225
Cox/P.	Brownies Many More Nights	Cox/P.	Century	(1913)	150 — 200
Cox/P.	Brownies Through The Union	Cox/P.	Century	(1895)	175 — 225
Cox/P.	Brownies Through The Union	Cox/P.	Unwin	(1895)	175 — 225
Cox/P.	Brownies' Latest Adventure	Cox/P.	Century	(1910)	175 — 225
Cox/P.	Brownies' Latest Adventure	Cox/P.	Unwin	(1910)	175 — 225
Cox/P.	Brownies: Their Book	Cox/P.	Century	(1887)	225 — 300
Cox/P.	Brownies: Their Book	Cox/P.	Century	(1887)	125 — 175
Cox/P.	Brownies: Their Book	Cox/P.	Unwin	1888	175 — 225
Cox/P.	Children's Funny Book	Cox/P.	Lothrop	(1879)	75 — 100
Cox/P.	Comic Yarns In Verse	Cox/P.	Hubbard	(1889)	75 — 100
Cox/P.	Frontier Humor	Cox/P.	Hubbard	(1895)	50 — 75
Cox/P.	Jolly Chinee	Cox/P.	Conkey	(1900)	75 — 100
Cox/P.	Juvenile Budget	Cox/P.	Donohue		30 — 50
Cox/P.	Palmer Cox's Funny Animals	Cox/P.	Donohue		30 — 50
Cox/P.	Queer People	Cox/P.	Unwin	1896	125 — 175
Cox/P.	Queer People	Cox/P.	Hubbard	1899	125 — 175

LISTINGS BY AUTHOR

Author	Title	Illustrator	Publisher	Year	Price Range
Cox/P.	Queer People With Paws	Cox/P.	Hubbard	(1888)	100 — 150
Cox/P.	Queer People With Wings	Cox/P.	Hubbard	(1888)	100 — 150
Cox/P.	Queerie Queers	Cox/P.	Larkin	(1887)	125 — 150
Crane/L.	Grimm's Animal Stories	Rae/J.	Duffield	1911	75 — 125
Crane/S.	Monster... (The)	Newell/P.	Harper	1899	150 — 200
Crane/S.	Whilomville Stories	Newell/P.	Harper	1900	175 — 225
Crane/W.	Aladdin's Picture Book	Crane/W.	Routledge	(1875)	125 — 150
Crane/W.	An Artist's Reminiscences	Crane/W.	Methuen		100 — 150
Crane/W.	Baby's Bouquet	Crane/W.	Routledge	[1878]	200 — 250
Crane/W.	Baby's Bouquet	Crane/W.	Warne	[1890]	50 — 100
Crane/W.	Baby's Opera	Crane/W.	Routledge	[1877]	175 — 225
Crane/W.	Baby's Opera	Crane/W.	Warne	1900	100 — 125
Crane/W.	Baby's Own Aesop	Crane/W.	Routledge	1887	125 — 150
Crane/W.	Baby's Own Aesop	Crane/W.	Warne		75 — 100
Crane/W.	Bases Of Design	Crane/W.	G. Bell	1898	150 — 200
Crane/W.	Blue Beard's Picture Book	Crane/W.	Routledge	1875	150 — 200
Crane/W.	Cinderella's Picture Book	Crane/W.	J. Lane	(1897)	125 — 150
Crane/W.	Cinderella's Picture Book	Crane/W.	Dodd		30 — 50
Crane/W.	Columbia's Courtship	Crane/W.	Prang Co.	(1892)	200 — 250
Crane/W.	Flora's Feast	Crane/W.	Cassell	1889	200 — 250
Crane/W.	Floral Fantasy/Eng. Garden	Crane/W.	Harper	1899	125 — 225
Crane/W.	Flower Wedding (A)	Crane/W.	Cassell	1905	200 — 250
Crane/W.	Flowers/Shakesp.Garden	Crane/W.	Cassell	1906	150 — 200
Crane/W.	Forty Thieves	Crane/W.	Routledge	1873	100 — 150
Crane/W.	Goody Two Shoes	Crane/W.	J. Lane	(1901)	175 — 200
Crane/W.	Grammer In Rhyme	Crane/W.	Routledge	(1868)	75 — 100
Crane/W.	Ideals In Art	Crane/W.	G. Bell	1905	75 — 100
Crane/W.	India Impressions	Crane/W.	Macmillan	1907	100 — 125
Crane/W.	Legends For Lionel	Crane/W.	Cassell	1887	150 — 200
Crane/W.	Line & Form	Crane/W.	G. Bell	1900	125 — 175
Crane/W.	Little/ Anne/Majesty's Letters	Crane/W.	Marcus Ward	1885	150 — 250
Crane/W.	Masque Of Days (A)	Crane/W.	Cassell	1901	200 — 300
Crane/W.	Of The Dec. Ill.Of Books	Crane/W.	Bell	1896	100 — 150
Crane/W.	Pothooks & Preserverance	Crane/W.	Marcus Ward	1886	200 — 250
Crane/W.	Queen Summer	Crane/W.	Cassell	1891	250 — 300
Crane/W.	Renascene: A Book Of Verse	Crane/W.	Elkin Mathews	1891	100 — 150
Crane/W.	Romance/Three R's	Crane/W.	Marcus Ward	1886	175 — 250
Crane/W.	Sirens Three	Crane/W.	Macmillan	1886	175 — 200
Crane/W.	Slatendpencilvania	Crane/W.	Marcus Ward	1885	125 — 150
Crane/W.	Triplets	Crane/W.	Routledge	1894	350 — 400
Crane/W.	Valentine & Orson	Crane/W.	Routledge	(1873)	125 — 150
Crane/W.	Walter Crane's Picture Book	Crane/W.	Cupples	(1903)	75 — 125

LISTINGS BY AUTHOR

Author	Title	Illustrator	Publisher	Year	Price Range
Crane/W.	Walter Crane's Picture Book	Crane/W.	J. Lane	[1895]	200 — 300
Crane/W.	Walter Crane's Picture Book	Crane/W.	Dodd		75 — 100
Crane/W.	Wm. Morris To Whistler	Crane/W.	G. Bell	1911	75 — 100
Crane/W.& L.	Art & Formation Of Taste	Crane/W.	Macmillan	1882	125 — 175
Crary/M.	Daughters Of The Stars	Dulac/E.	Hatchard	1939	100 — 150
Cresswell/B.	Royal Progress/King Pepito	Greenaway/K.	Spck	[1889]	175 — 225
Crothers/S.M.	Children Of Dickens (The)	Smith/J.W.	Scribner	1925	100 — 150
Crothers/S.M.	Children Of Dickens (The)	Smith/J.W.	Scribner	1933	35 — 50
Crothers/S.M.	Children Of Dickens (The)	Smith/J.W.	Scribner	1940	25 — 40
Crothers/S.M.	Children Of Dickens (The)	Smith/J.W.	Scribner	1944	25 — 35
Crownfield/G.	Little Taylor/Winding Way	Pogany/W.	Macmillan		75 — 100

D

Author	Title	Illustrator	Publisher	Year	Price Range
D'aulnoy	Fairy Tales Of ...	Crane/W.	Lawrence	1892	175 — 225
Dale/N.	Dale Readers Book 2 (The)	Crane/W.	Philip	1907	50 — 75
Dale/N.	Walter Crane Reader (The)	Crane/W.	Dent	1899	40 — 60
Dana/R.H.	Two Years Before The Mast	Rackham/A.	Collins	(1904)	100 — 150
Dana/R.H.	Two Years Before The Mast	Rackham/A.	Collins	(1904)	75 — 100
Dana/R.H.	Two Years Before The Mast	Rackham/A.	Monarch	[1904]	75 — 100
Dana/R.H.	Two Years Before The Mast	Rackham/A.	Winston	1904	50 — 75
Darton/F.J.	Story Of Canterbury Pilgrims	Thomson/H.	Stokes		40 — 60
Daulton	Uncle Davie's Children	Pogany/W.	Macmillan		75 — 100
Davies/R.	Old Watercolour Society Club	Rackham/A.		1934	75 — 100
Davis/R.H.	About Paris	Gibson/C.D.	Harper	1895	20 — 30
Davis/R.H.	Her First Appearance	Gibson/C.D.	Harper	1901	15 — 25
Davis/R.H.	Lion & The Unicorn (The)	Christy/H.C.	Scribner	1899	15 — 30
Davis/R.H.	Van Bibber & Others	Gibson/C.D.	Harper	1892	20 — 30
Dawe/C.	Captain Castle	Rackham/A.	Smith,Elder	1897	50 — 75
De Morgan/M.	Necklace/Princess Fiorimonde	Crane/W.	Macmillan	1880	175 — 225
Defoe/D.	Robinson Crusoe	Wyeth/N.C.	Cosmopolitan	1920	125 — 150
Deland/M.	Around Old Chester	Pyle/H.	Harper	1915	20 — 30
Deland/M.	Good For The Soul	Pyle/H.	Harper	1899	25 — 35
Deland/M.	Old Chester Tales	Pyle/H.	Harper	1899	25 — 50
Deland/M.	Old Garden (The)	Crane/W.	McIlvaine	1893	125 — 175
Deland/M.	Old Garden (The)	Crane/W.	Houghton	1894	75 — 100
Denslow/W.W.	Billy Bounce	Denslow/W.W.	Dillingham	(1906)	300 — 400
Denslow/W.W.	Denslow's Animal Fair	Denslow/W.W.	Dillingham	1904	175 — 225
Denslow/W.W.	Denslow's Five Little Pigs	Denslow/W.W.	Dillingham	(1903)	100 — 125
Denslow/W.W.	Denslow's Mother Goose	Denslow/W.W.	McClure	1901	400 — 600
Denslow/W.W.	Denslow's Mother Goose	Denslow/W.W.	Chambers	1902	250 — 300
Denslow/W.W.	Denslow's Scarecrow/Tin-Man	Denslow/W.W.	Dillingham	[1904]	200 — 300
Denslow/W.W.	Denslow's Scarecrow/Tin-Man	Denslow/W.W.	Dillingham	[1904]	150 — 200

LISTINGS BY AUTHOR

Author	Title	Illustrator	Publisher	Year	Price Range
Denslow/W.W.	Denslow's Scarecrow/Tin-Man	Denslow/W.W.	Unwin	[1904]	150 — 200
Denslow/W.W.	Denslow's Scarecrow/Tin-Man	Denslow/W.W.	Donohue	[1913]	50 — 100
Denslow/W.W.	Denslow's Scarecrow/Tin-Man	Denslow/W.W.	Donohue	[1913]	50 — 100
Denslow/W.W.	Denslow's Tom Thumb	Denslow/W.W.	Dillingham	(1903)	100 — 150
Denslow/W.W.	Denslow's Zoo	Denslow/W.W.	Dillingham	(1903)	75 — 125
Denslow/W.W.	House That Jack Built	Denslow/W.W.	Dillingham	(1903)	150 — 200
Denslow/W.W.	Jack & The Beanstalk	Denslow/W.W.	Dillingham	(1903)	150 — 200
Denslow/W.W.	Little Red Riding Hood	Denslow/W.W.	Dillingham	(1903)	125 — 175
Denslow/W.W.	Mary Had A Little Lamb	Denslow/W.W.	Dillingham	(1903)	125 — 175
Denslow/W.W.	Night Before Christmas	Denslow/W.W.	Dillingham	(1902)	300 — 500
Denslow/W.W.	Night Before Christmas	Denslow/W.W.	Donohue	[1902]	150 — 200
Denslow/W.W.	Old Mother Hubbard	Denslow/W.W.	Dillingham	(1903)	125 — 150
Denslow/W.W.	One Ring Circus	Denslow/W.W.	Dillingham	(1903)	200 — 250
Denslow/W.W.	Simple Simon	Denslow/W.W.	Dillingham	(1904)	100 — 150
Denslow/W.W.	When I Grow Up	Denslow/W.W.	Century	1909	175 — 225
Dewar/G.A.B.	Wild Life/Hampshire Highlands	Rackham/A.	Dent	1899	150 — 200
Dibdin/T.F.	Bibliomanis Or Book Madness	Pyle/H.	Biblio. Soc.	1903	50 — 75
Dickens/C.	Chimes (The)	Thomson/H.	H&S	(1920)	50 — 75
Dickens/C.	Chimes (The)	Rackham/A.	Lec	1931	350 — 600
Dickens/C.	Christmas Carol (A)	Rackham/A.	Heinemann	(1915)	1000 — 1250
Dickens/C.	Christmas Carol (A)	Rackham/A.	Heinemann	(1915)	150 — 200
Dickens/C.	Christmas Carol (A)	Rackham/A.	Heinemann	(1915)	175 — 225
Dickens/C.	Christmas Carol (A)	Rackham/A.	Lippincott	(1915)	1000 — 1250
Dickens/C.	Christmas Carol (A)	Rackham/A.	Lippincott	(1915)	100 — 150
Dickens/C.	Christmas Carol (A)	Rackham/A.	Lippincott	(1923)	75 — 100
Dickens/C.	Christmas Carol (A)	Rackham/A.	Heinemann	[1923]	75 — 100
Dobson/A.	Story Of Rosina	Thomson/H.	Kegan	1895	65 — 80
Dobson/L.	Poems By Dobson......	Humphrey/M.	Stokes	1892	300 — 450
Dodge/M.M.	Golden Gate (The)	Cox/P.		(1903)	35 — 50
Douglas/A.M.	Clover's Princess	Neill/J.R.	Altemus	(1904)	50 — 75
Downey/F.	Portrait Of An Era	Gibson/C.D.	Scribner	(1936)	20 — 50
Doyle/A.C.	Parasite (The)	Pyle/H.	Harper	1895	65 — 85
Doyle/A.C.	White Company (The)	Wyeth/N.C.	Cosmopolitan	1922	175 — 225
Drake/F.	Indian History/Young Folks	Pyle/H.	Harper	1886	35 — 50
Drinkwater/J.	Outline Of Literature (The)	Rackham/A.	Newnes	[1930]	150 — 200
Drury/W.P.	Peradventures Of Pr. Pagett	Rackham/A.	Chapman/Hall	(1911)	150 — 200
Drury/W.P.	Peradventures Of Pr. Pagett	Rackham/A.	Chapman/Hall	1904	200 — 300
Dulac/E.	Edmund Dulac's Fairy Book	Dulac/E.	Doran	(1916)	250 — 300
Dulac/E.	Fairy Garland (A)	Dulac/E.	Cassell	(1928)	150 — 200
Dulac/E.	Fairy Garland (A)	Dulac/E.	Cassell	(1928)	600 — 800
Dulac/E.	Fairy Garland (A)	Dulac/E.	Cassell	(1928)	500 — 650
Dulac/E.	Fairy Garland (A)	Dulac/E.	Scribner	(1929)	100 — 150

LISTINGS BY AUTHOR

Author	Title	Illustrator	Publisher	Year	Price Range
Dulac/E.	Fairy Tales Of Allied Nations	Dulac/E.	H&S	[1916]	250 — 350
Dulac/E.	Lyrics Pathetic & Humerous	Dulac/E.	Warne	1908	300 — 400
Dulac/E.	Picture Book/Red Cross	Dulac/E.	H&S	[1915]	200 — 300
Dunham/E.	Diary Of A Mouse	Gutmann/B.P.	Dodge	(1907)	75 — 125

E

Author	Title	Illustrator	Publisher	Year	Price Range
Edgar/M.G.	Treasury Of Verse	Pogany/W.	Crowell	(1908)	100 — 135
Edgar/M.G.	Treasury Of Verse For.....	Pogany/W.	Crowell	1923	10 — 20
Edgar/M.G.	Treasury Of Verse For.....	Pogany/W.	Macmillan		30 — 50
Edgeworth/M.	Tales From Maria Edgeworth	Thomson/H.	Stokes		40 — 60
Elias/E.	Cinderella	Pogany/W.	McBride	1915	175 — 200
Elias/E.	Story Of Hiawatha (The)	Pogany/W.	Harrap	[1914]	75 — 100
Ellis/F.S.	History Of Reynard The Fox	Crane/W.	D. Nutt	1895	175 — 225
Ellis/F.S.	History Of Reynard The Fox	Crane/W.	D. Nutt	1897	100 — 125
Evans/C.S.	Cinderella	Rackham/A.	Heinemann	(1919)	750 — 1000
Evans/C.S.	Cinderella	Rackham/A.	Heinemann	(1919)	200 — 250
Evans/C.S.	Cinderella	Rackham/A.	Lippincott	(1919)	175 — 250
Evans/C.S.	Sleeping Beauty (The)	Rackham/A.	Heinemann	(1920)	150 — 200
Evans/C.S.	Sleeping Beauty (The)	Rackham/A.	Heinemann	(1920)	750 — 1000
Evans/C.S.	Sleeping Beauty (The)	Rackham/A.	Lippincott	(1920)	150 — 200

F

Author	Title	Illustrator	Publisher	Year	Price Range
Fable/L.	Gingerbread Man	Pogany/W.	McBride	1915	100 — 130
Fairmont/E.	Rhymes For Kindly Children	Gruelle/J.	Volland	(1928)	75 — 100
Fairmont/E.	Rhymes For Kindly Children	Gruelle/J.	Wise-Parslow	(1937)	50 — 75
Farrow/G.E.	Adventures Of A Dodo	Pogany/W.	Unwin	(1907)	150 — 200
Fay/E.	Road To Fairyland (A)	Rackham/A.	Putnam	(1926)	100 — 150
Fay/E.	Road To Fairyland (A)	Rackham/A.	Putnam	(1926)	100 — 150
Ferris	My Poetry Book	Pogany/W.	Winston	(1934)	25 — 35
Ferris	My Poetry Book	Pogany/W.	Hufford	1934	25 — 35
Fesenden/L.D.	Colonial Dame	Denslow/W.W.	Rand Mcnally	1897	50 — 75
Field/E.	Poems Of Childhood	Parrish/M.	Lane	1904	150 — 225
Field/E.	Poems Of Childhood	Parrish/M.	Scribner	1904	150 — 225
Field/E.	Poems Of Childhood	Parrish/M.	Scribner	1929	100 — 150
Fillmore/P.H.	Hickory Limb(The)	O'Neill/R.	J. Lane	1910	40 — 60
Fillmore/P.H.	Little Question/Ladies' Rights	O'Neill/R.	J. Lane	1916	50 — 75
Fisher/H.	American Beauties	Fisher/H.	Bobbs-Merrill	(1909)	200 — 250
Fisher/H.	American Beauties	Fisher/H.	G&D	(1909)	150 — 200
Fisher/H.	American Belles	Fisher/H.	Dodd	1911	200 — 250
Fisher/H.	American Girl	Fisher/H.	Scribner	1909	250 — 350
Fisher/H.	Bachelor Belles	Fisher/H.	G&D	(1908)	50 — 75
Fisher/H.	Bachelor Belles	Fisher/H.	Dodd	1908	175 — 225

LISTINGS BY AUTHOR

Author	Title	Illustrator	Publisher	Year	Price Range
Fisher/H.	Dream Of Fair Women	Fisher/H.	G&D	(1907)	125 — 175
Fisher/H.	Dream Of Fair Women	Fisher/H.	Bobbs-Merrill	(1909)	180 — 250
Fisher/H.	Fair Americans	Fisher/H.	Scribner	1911	180 — 220
Fisher/H.	Garden Of Girls (A)	Fisher/H.	Dodd	1910	300 — 450
Fisher/H.	Garden Of Girls (A)	Fisher/H.		1910	200 — 250
Fisher/H.	Girl's Life & Other Pictures	Fisher/H.			250 — 350
Fisher/H.	Harrison Fisher Book	Fisher/H.	Scribner	1907	160 — 230
Fisher/H.	Little Gift Book	Fisher/H.	Scribner	1913	180 — 260
Fisher/H.	Maidens Fair	Fisher/H.	Dodd	1912	300 — 450
Fisher/H.	Pictures In Color	Fisher/H.	Scribner	1910	350 — 500
Fitzgerald/E.	Rubaiyat (The)	Dulac/E.	H&S	[1909]	200 — 300
Fitzgerald/E.	Rubaiyat (The)	Dulac/E.	H&S	[1914]	100 — 150
Fitzgerald/E.	Rubaiyat (The)	Dulac/E.	Doran	[1920]	100 — 130
Fitzgerald/E.	Rubaiyat (The)	Dulac/E.	Doran	1928	20 — 50
Fitzgerald/E.	Rubaiyat (The)	Dulac/E.	Doubleday	1932	40 — 55
Fitzgerald/E.	Rubaiyat (The)	Dulac/E.	Doubleday	1933	75 — 100
Fitzgerald/E.	Rubaiyat (The)	Dulac/E.	Doubleday	1934	75 — 100
Fitzgerald/E.	Rubaiyat (The)	Dulac/E.	Garden City	1937	20 — 40
Fitzgerald/E.	Rubaiyat Of Omar Khayyam	Pogany/W.	Crowell	(1909)	125 — 175
Fitzgerald/E.	Rubaiyat Of Omar Khayyam	Pogany/W.	Harrap	(1909)	175 — 225
Fitzgerald/E.	Rubaiyat Of Omar Khayyam	Pogany/W.	Crowell	(1930)	35 — 60
Fitzgerald/E.	Rubaiyat Of Omar Khayyam	Pogany/W.	Crowell	(1930)	600 — 800
Fitzgerald/E.	Rubaiyat Of Omar Khayyam	Pogany/W.	Crowell	[1933]	50 — 75
Fitzgerald/S.J.	Zankiwank & The Bletherwitch	Rackham/A.	Dent	1896	600 — 750
Fitzgerald/S.J.	Zankiwank & The Bletherwitch	Rackham/A.	Dutton	1896	300 — 450
Fitzgerald/S.J.	Zankiwank & The Bletherwitch	Rackham/A.	Stokes	1896	250 — 350
Ford/J.E.	Imagina	Rackham/A.	Duffield	1914	100 — 175
Ford/J.E.	Imagina	Rackham/A.	Dutton	1923	50 — 75
Ford/J.E.	Imagina	Rackham/A.	Duffield	1924	50 — 75
Ford/J.E.	Snickerty Nick	Rackham/A.	Moffat	1919	125 — 175
Ford/J.E.	Snickerty Nick & The Giant	Rackham/A.	Sutton House	[1935]	35 — 50
Ford/J.E.	Snickerty Nick & The Giant	Rackham/A.	Sutton House	1933	50 — 75
Ford/P.L.	Checked Love Affair	Fisher/H.	Dodd	1903	30 — 45
Ford/P.L.	Janice Meredith	Pyle/H.	Dodd	1899	35 — 50
Ford/P.L.	Wanted A Matchmaker	Christy/H.C.	Dodd	1900	25 — 40
Ford/P.L.	Wanted, A Chaperone	Christy/H.C.	Dodd	1902	25 — 50
Forman/J.M.	Island Of Enchantment (The)	Pyle/H.	Harper	1905	25 — 35
Foster/M.B.	Day In A Child's Life (A)	Greenaway/K.	Routledge	[1881]	175 — 225
Fouque/D.	Undine	Rackham/A.	Dbl.,Page	1909	200 — 250
Fouque/D.	Undine	Rackham/A.	Heinemann	1909	250 — 300
Fouque/D.	Undine	Rackham/A.	Heinemann	1909	750 — 1000
Fouque/D.	Undine	Rackham/A.	Heinemann	1911	100 — 125

LISTINGS BY AUTHOR

Author	Title	Illustrator	Publisher	Year	Price Range
Fouque/D.	Undine	Rackham/A.	Doubleday	1919	100 — 150
Fox/J.	Little Shepherd/Kingdom Come	Wyeth/N.C.	Scribner	1931	125 — 175
Fox/J.	Little Shepherd/Kingdom Come	Wyeth/N.C.	Scribner	1931	500 — 750
Franchot/A.W.	Bobs, King/Fortunate Isle	Smith/J.W.	Dutton	(1928)	50 — 75
Franchot/A.W.	Bugs & Wings & Other Things	Smith/J.W.	Dutton	(1918)	50 — 75
Frederic/H.	In The Valley	Pyle/H.	Scribner	1890	30 — 50
Frederic/H.	Market Place (The)	Fisher/H.	Stokes	1899	30 — 40
Freshfield/Mrs.	Aesop's Fables/Little Readers	Ford/H.J.	Unwin	[1888]	150 — 200
Friederichs/H.	In The Evening Of His Days	Rackham/A.	West. Gaz.	1896	200 — 300
Fry/L.	Oxted,Limpsfield.....	Rackham/A.	W.&G. Godwin	(1932)	100 — 125

G

Author	Title	Illustrator	Publisher	Year	Price Range
Garnett/L.A.	Creature Songs...	Newell/P.	Ditson	(1912)	125 — 175
Garrett/F.	Isis Very Much Unveiled	Rackham/A.	West. Gaz.	[1894]	75 — 100
Gask/L.	Fairies & Christmas Child	Pogany/W.	Crowell	(1910)	140 — 185
Gask/L.	Fairy Tales From Many Lands	Pogany/W.		1933	25 — 30
Gask/L.	Folk Tales Of Many Lands	Pogany/W.	Crowell	(1910)	75 — 100
Gask/L.	Folk Tales Of Many Lands	Pogany/W.	Harrap	1910	100 — 125
Gask/L.	Folk Tales Of Many Lands	Pogany/W.	Harrap	1929	20 — 40
Gaskell/E.C.	Cranford	Thomson/H.	Macmillan		40 — 60
Gates/E.	Good Night	Rackham/A.	Crowell	(1907)	350 — 500
Gates/J.S.	Story Of Mince Pie	Rae/J.	Dodd	1916	50 — 75
Gibson/C.D.	80 Drawings/Weaker Sex	Gibson/C.D.	Scribner	1903	100 — 150
Gibson/C.D.	Americans	Gibson/C.D.	Russell	1903	75 — 100
Gibson/C.D.	Drawings	Gibson/C.D.	Russell	1897	120 — 150
Gibson/C.D.	Education Of Mr. Pipp	Gibson/C.D.	Russell	1899	120 — 150
Gibson/C.D.	Everyday People	Gibson/C.D.	Scribner	1904	120 — 150
Gibson/C.D.	Gibson Book (The)	Gibson/C.D.	Scribner	1906	150 — 200
Gibson/C.D.	London	Gibson/C.D.	Scribner	1897	125 — 175
Gibson/C.D.	Our Neighbors	Gibson/C.D.	Scribner	1905	120 — 150
Gibson/C.D.	Pictures Of People	Gibson/C.D.	Russell	1896	100 — 165
Gibson/C.D.	Sketches In Egypt	Gibson/C.D.	Doubleday	1899	80 — 100
Gibson/C.D.	Social Ladder	Gibson/C.D.	Russell	1902	120 — 150
Gibson/C.D.	Widow & Her Friends (A)	Gibson/C.D.	Harper	1901	120 — 150
Gilbert/H.	King Arthur's Nights	Crane/W.	Nelson	(1911)	125 — 150
Gilbert/H.	King Arthur's Nights	Crane/W.	Jack	1911	175 — 225
Gilbert/H.	Knights Of The Round Table	Crane/W.	Jack	1915	100 — 150
Gilbert/H.	Robin Hood & His Merry Men	Crane/W.	Jack	1915	75 — 100
Gilbert/H.	Robin Hood/Men Of Greenwood	Crane/W.	Stokes	[1912]	100 — 125
Gilbert/H.	Robin Hood/Men Of Greenwood	Crane/W.	Jack	1912	125 — 150
Gilbert/H.	Robin Hood/Men Of Greenwood	Crane/W.	Nelson		75 — 100
Glenn/M.	Listen & Sing	Smith/J.W.	Ginn	(1936)	35 — 50

LISTINGS BY AUTHOR

Author	Title	Illustrator	Publisher	Year	Price Range
Glenn/M.	Listen & Sing	Smith/J.W.	Ginn	(1943)	25 — 35
Glenn/M.	Tuning Up	Smith/J.W.	Ginn	(1936)	35 — 50
Glenn/M.	Tuning Up	Smith/J.W.	Ginn	(1943)	25 — 35
Goethe	Faust	Pogany/W.	Hutchinson	(1908)	150 — 200
Goethe	Faust	Pogany/W.	Musson	[1908]	350 — 500
Goldsmith/O.	She Stoops To Conquer	Thomson/H.	H&S	(1912)	120 — 160
Goldsmith/O.	Vicar Of Wakefield	Thomson/H.	Macmillan	1890	75 — 100
Goldsmith/O.	Vicar Of Wakefield (The)	Rackham/A.	Harrap	[1929]	175 — 225
Goldsmith/O.	Vicar Of Wakefield (The)	Rackham/A.	Harrap	[1929]	200 — 250
Goldsmith/O.	Vicar Of Wakefield (The)	Rackham/A.	Harrap	[1929]	750 — 1000
Goldsmith/O.	Vicar Of Wakefield (The)	Rackham/A.	McKay	[1929]	125 — 150
Goldsmith/O.	Vicar Of Wakefield (The)	Rackham/A.	Lippincott	1929	75 — 100
Goodloe/A.C.	College Girls	Gibson/C.D.	Scribner	1895	20 — 30
Goodwin/M.W.	Head Of A Hundred (The)	Smith/J.W.	Little Brown	1897	85 — 100
Goodwin/M.W.	Head Of A Hundred (The)	Smith/J.W.	Little Brown	1899	70 — 80
Goodwin/M.W.	Head Of A Hundred (The)	Smith/J.W.	Little Brown	1900	75 — 100
Goodwin/M.W.	Sir Christopher...	Pyle/H.	Little Brown	1901	25 — 35
Gordon/E.	Buddy Jim	Rae/J.	Volland	(1922)	40 — 70
Gordon/E.	Buddy Jim	Rae/J.	Wise-Parslow	(1935)	20 — 35
Gordon/E.	More Really-So Stories	Rae/J.	Volland	(1929)	65 — 85
Gordon/E.	More Really-So Stories	Rae/J.	Wise-Parslow		25 — 50
Gordon/E.	Really So Stories	Rae/J.	Volland	(1924)	50 — 75
Gordon/E.	Really So Stories	Rae/J.	Wise-Parslow	(1937)	25 — 50
Gordy/W.	History Of The United States	Pyle/H.	Scribner	1904	20 — 30
Gordy/W.	Stories Of Later Am. History	Pyle/H.	Scribner	1915	15 — 20
Gosse/E.	Allies' Fairy Book (The)	Rackham/A.	Heinemann	(1916)	850 — 1250
Gosse/E.	Allies' Fairy Book (The)	Rackham/A.	Heinemann	(1918)	100 — 125
Gosse/E.	Allies' Fairy Book (The)	Rackham/A.	Heinemann	[1916]	175 — 275
Gosse/E.	Allies' Fairy Book (The)	Rackham/A.	Lippincott	[1916]	125 — 225
Gould/E.J.	Children's Plutarch (The)	Crane/W.	Watts	1906	100 — 125
Gould/E.J.	Children's Plutarch (The)	Crane/W.	Harper	1910	75 — 100
Grabo/C.H.	Peter & The Princess	Neill/J.R.	R&L	(1920)	175 — 250
Grahame/K.	Dream Days	Parrish/M.	J. Lane	[1902]	75 — 150
Grahame/K.	Golden Age (The)	Parrish/M.	J. Lane	(1904)	75 — 125
Grahame/K.	Golden Age (The)	Parrish/M.	J. Lane	1900	100 — 200
Grahame/K.	Wind In The Willows (The)	Rackham/A.	Heritage	(1940)	50 — 75
Grahame/K.	Wind In The Willows (The)	Rackham/A.	Methuen	(1950)	40 — 60
Grahame/K.	Wind In The Willows (The)	Rackham/A.	Methuen	(1951)	250 — 500
Grahame/K.	Wind In The Willows (The)	Rackham/A.	Lec	1940	400 — 600
Greenaway/K.	A Apple Pie	Greenaway/K.	Routledge	[1886]	200 — 250
Greenaway/K.	A Apple Pie	Greenaway/K.	Warne	[1890]	75 — 100
Greenaway/K.	A Apple Pie	Greenaway/K.	Saalfield	1907	75 — 100

LISTINGS BY AUTHOR

Author	Title	Illustrator	Publisher	Year	Price Range
Greenaway/K.	Almanack For 1884	Greenaway/K.	Routledge	1884	100 — 150
Greenaway/K.	Almanack For 1885	Greenaway/K.	Routledge	1885	100 — 150
Greenaway/K.	Almanack For 1886	Greenaway/K.	Routledge	1886	100 — 150
Greenaway/K.	Almanack For 1887	Greenaway/K.	Routledge	1887	100 — 150
Greenaway/K.	Almanack For 1888	Greenaway/K.	Routledge	1888	100 — 150
Greenaway/K.	Almanack For 1889	Greenaway/K.	Routledge	1889	100 — 150
Greenaway/K.	Almanack For 1890	Greenaway/K.	Routledge	1890	100 — 150
Greenaway/K.	Almanack For 1891	Greenaway/K.	Routledge	1891	100 — 150
Greenaway/K.	Almanack For 1892	Greenaway/K.	Routledge	1892	100 — 150
Greenaway/K.	Almanack For 1893	Greenaway/K.	Routledge	1893	100 — 150
Greenaway/K.	Almanack For 1894	Greenaway/K.	Routledge	1894	100 — 150
Greenaway/K.	Almanack For 1895	Greenaway/K.	Routledge	1895	100 — 150
Greenaway/K.	Almanack For 1897	Greenaway/K.	Dent	1897	100 — 150
Greenaway/K.	English Spelling Book (The)	Greenaway/K.	Routledge	[1885]	200 — 250
Greenaway/K.	Greenaway's Babies	Greenaway/K.	Saalfield	1907	100 — 150
Greenaway/K.	K.Greenaway's Birthday Book	Greenaway/K.	Routledge	[1880]	175 — 250
Greenaway/K.	K.Greenaway's Book Of Games	Greenaway/K.	Routledge	[1889]	200 — 250
Greenaway/K.	K.Greenaway's Book Of Games	Greenaway/K.	Warne	[1890]	100 — 150
Greenaway/K.	Kate Greenaway's Alphabet	Greenaway/K.	Routledge	[1885]	150 — 200
Greenaway/K.	Language Of Flowers	Greenaway/K.	Routledge	[1884]	125 — 175
Greenaway/K.	Language Of Flowers	Greenaway/K.	Warne	[1900]	75 — 125
Greenaway/K.	Madame D'aulnoy''s Fairy Tales	Greenaway/K.	Gall & Inglis	1871	150 — 175
Greenaway/K.	Marigold Garden	Greenaway/K.	Routledge	[1885]	225 — 275
Greenaway/K.	Marigold Garden	Greenaway/K.	Warne	[1900]	100 — 150
Greenaway/K.	Mother Goose	Greenaway/K.	Routledge	[1881]	175 — 225
Greenaway/K.	Mother Goose	Greenaway/K.	Warne	[1900]	75 — 100
Greenaway/K.	Painting Book (A)	Greenaway/K.	Routledge	[1884]	200 — 275
Greenaway/K.	Queen Victoria's/Garland	Greenaway/K.	Routledge	[1887]	300 — 350
Greenaway/K.	Trot's Journey	Greenaway/K.	Worthington	(1882)	100 — 125
Greenaway/K.	Under The Window	Greenaway/K.	Routledge	[1878]	200 — 250
Greenaway/K.	Under The Window	Greenaway/K.	McLoughlin	[1879]	175 — 225
Greenaway/K.	Under The Window	Greenaway/K.	Routledge	[1879]	150 — 175
Greenaway/K.	Under The Window	Greenaway/K.	Warne	[1900]	100 — 150
Greene/H.P.	Pilot & Other Stories	Ford/H.J.	Macmillan	1916	125 — 175
Greene/Mrs.	Grey House On The Hill (The)	Rackham/A.	Nelson	[1903]	150 — 175
Greene/Mrs.	Grey House On The Hill (The)	Rackham/A.	Nelson	[1905]	100 — 125
Greg/T.T.	Through A Glass Lightly	Rackham/A.	Dent	1897	175 — 200
Griffiths&Gold	Mysteries Of Police & Crime	Rackham/A.	Cassell	[1901]	125 — 150
Griffiths&Gold	Mysteries Of Police & Crime	Rackham/A.	Cassell	[1904]	75 — 100
Grimm Bros.	Fairy Tales Of Bros. Grimm	Rackham/A.	Freemantle	[1900]	150 — 200
Grimm Bros.	Fairy Tales Of Bros. Grimm	Rackham/A.	Freemantle	[1900]	125 — 175
Grimm Bros.	Fairy Tales Of Bros. Grimm	Rackham/A.	Lippincott	[1900]	75 — 100

LISTINGS BY AUTHOR

Author	Title	Illustrator	Publisher	Year	Price Range
Grimm Bros.	Fairy Tales Of Bros. Grimm	Rackham/A.	Partridge	[1904]	75 — 125
Grimm Bros.	Fairy Tales Of Bros. Grimm	Rackham/A.	Constable	[1907]	100 — 125
Grimm Bros.	Fairy Tales Of Bros. Grimm	Rackham/A.	Constable	1909	300 — 400
Grimm Bros.	Fairy Tales Of Bros. Grimm	Rackham/A.	Constable	1909	1000 — 1500
Grimm Bros.	Fairy Tales Of Bros. Grimm	Rackham/A.	Doubleday	1909	350 — 450
Grimm Bros.	Grimm's Fairy Tales	Crane/W.	Worthington	(1888)	75 — 100
Grimm Bros.	Grimm's Fairy Tales	Gruelle/J.	Cupples	(1914)	150 — 200
Grimm Bros.	Grimm's Fairy Tales	Rackham/A.	Heinemann	(1925)	150 — 200
Grimm Bros.	Grimm's Fairy Tales	Smith/J.W.	G&D	[1940]	15 — 25
Grimm Bros.	Hansel & Gretel	Nielson/K.	Doran	(1925)	250 — 350
Grimm Bros.	Hansel & Gretel	Nielson/K.	Doran	(1925)	125 — 175
Grimm Bros.	Hansel & Gretel	Nielson/K.	H&S	[1925]	750 — 1000
Grimm Bros.	Hansel & Gretel	Nielson/K.	Doubleday		100 — 125
Grimm Bros.	Hansel & Grethel/Other Tales	Rackham/A.	Constable	(1920)	175 — 250
Grimm Bros.	Hansel & Grethel/Other Tales	Rackham/A.	Dutton	(1920)	175 — 225
Grimm Bros.	Household Stories	Crane/W.	Am.Publishing	[1894]	75 — 100
Grimm Bros.	Household Stories	Crane/W.	Macmillan	1882	175 — 250
Grimm Bros.	Household Stories	Crane/W.	Macmillan	1914	75 — 100
Grimm Bros.	Household Stories	Crane/W.	Macmillan	1941	25 — 35
Grimm Bros.	Little Brother & Little Sister	Rackham/A.	Constable	(1917)	200 — 300
Grimm Bros.	Little Brother & Little Sister	Rackham/A.	Constable	(1917)	750 — 2000
Grimm Bros.	Little Brother & Little Sister	Rackham/A.	Dodd	(1917)	200 — 250
Grimm Bros.	Snowdrop & Other Tales	Rackham/A.	Dutton	(1920)	150 — 175
Grimm Bros.	Snowdrop & Other Tales	Rackham/A.	Constable	1920	150 — 200
Gruelle/J.	All About Cinderella	Gruelle/J.	Cupples	(1916)	75 — 125
Gruelle/J.	All About Cinderella	Gruelle/J.	Cupples	(1929)	25 — 35
Gruelle/J.	All About/Red Riding Hood	Gruelle/J.	Cupples	(1916)	75 — 100
Gruelle/J.	All About/Red Riding Hood	Gruelle/J.	Cupples	(1929)	25 — 35
Gruelle/J.	Beloved Belindy	Gruelle/J.	Donohue	(1926)	50 — 75
Gruelle/J.	Beloved Belindy	Gruelle/J.	Volland	(1926)	150 — 200
Gruelle/J.	Beloved Belindy	Gruelle/J.	Volland	(1926)	100 — 150
Gruelle/J.	Beloved Belindy	Gruelle/J.	J.Gruelle Co.	(1940)	50 — 75
Gruelle/J.	Cheery Scarcrow	Gruelle/J.	Donohue	(1929)	40 — 60
Gruelle/J.	Cheery Scarcrow	Gruelle/J.	Volland	(1929)	100 — 125
Gruelle/J.	Cheery Scarcrow	Gruelle/J.	Volland	(1929)	75 — 100
Gruelle/J.	Eddie Elephant	Gruelle/J.	Donohue	(1921)	40 — 60
Gruelle/J.	Eddie Elephant	Gruelle/J.	Volland	(1921)	100 — 125
Gruelle/J.	Eddie Elephant	Gruelle/J.	Volland	(1921)	75 — 100
Gruelle/J.	Friendly Fairies	Gruelle/J.	Donohue	(1919)	45 — 60
Gruelle/J.	Friendly Fairies	Gruelle/J.	Volland	(1919)	125 — 175
Gruelle/J.	Friendly Fairies	Gruelle/J.	Volland	(1919)	100 — 125
Gruelle/J.	Friendly Fairies	Gruelle/J.	J.Gruelle Co.	(1940)	35 — 50

LISTINGS BY AUTHOR

Author	Title	Illustrator	Publisher	Year	Price Range
Gruelle/J.	Funny Little Book	Gruelle/J.	Donohue	(1918)	35 — 50
Gruelle/J.	Funny Little Book	Gruelle/J.	Volland	(1918)	100 — 125
Gruelle/J.	Funny Little Book	Gruelle/J.	Volland	(1918)	75 — 100
Gruelle/J.	Johnny Gruelle's Golden Book	Gruelle/J.	Donohue	[1940]	75 — 150
Gruelle/J.	Johnny Mouse/Wishing Stick	Gruelle/J.	Bobbs-Merrill	(1922)	75 — 100
Gruelle/J.	Little Brown Bear	Gruelle/J.	Donohue	(1920)	35 — 50
Gruelle/J.	Little Brown Bear	Gruelle/J.	Volland	(1920)	75 — 100
Gruelle/J.	Little Brown Bear	Gruelle/J.	Volland	(1920)	50 — 75
Gruelle/J.	Little Sunny Stories	Gruelle/J.	Donohue	(1919)	35 — 50
Gruelle/J.	Little Sunny Stories	Gruelle/J.	Volland	(1919)	75 — 100
Gruelle/J.	Little Sunny Stories	Gruelle/J.	Volland	(1919)	65 — 85
Gruelle/J.	Little Sunny Stories	Gruelle/J.	Laidlaw	(1924)	35 — 50
Gruelle/J.	Magical Land Of Noom (The)	Gruelle/J.	Donohue	(1922)	75 — 100
Gruelle/J.	Magical Land Of Noom (The)	Gruelle/J.	Volland	(1922)	175 — 250
Gruelle/J.	Magical Land Of Noom (The)	Gruelle/J.	Volland	(1922)	100 — 150
Gruelle/J.	Marcella Stories	Gruelle/J.	Donohue	(1929)	75 — 100
Gruelle/J.	Marcella Stories	Gruelle/J.	Volland	(1929)	175 — 225
Gruelle/J.	Marcella Stories	Gruelle/J.	Volland	(1929)	125 — 175
Gruelle/J.	Mr. Twee Deedle	Gruelle/J.	Cupples	(1913)	150 — 175
Gruelle/J.	Mr. Twee Deedle	Gruelle/J.	McKay		50 — 75
Gruelle/J.	My Very Own Fairy Stories	Gruelle/J.	Donohue	(1917)	50 — 75
Gruelle/J.	My Very Own Fairy Stories	Gruelle/J.	Volland	(1917)	125 — 175
Gruelle/J.	My Very Own Fairy Stories	Gruelle/J.	Volland	(1917)	100 — 125
Gruelle/J.	My Very Own Fairy Stories	Gruelle/J.	J.Gruelle Co.	(1940)	35 — 50
Gruelle/J.	Orphant Annie Story Book	Gruelle/J.	Bobbs-Merrill	(1921)	100 — 125
Gruelle/J.	Paper Dragon	Gruelle/J.	Volland	(1926)	75 — 100
Gruelle/J.	Paper Dragon	Gruelle/J.	Volland	(1926)	50 — 75
Gruelle/J.	Raggedy Andy Stories	Gruelle/J.	Donohue	(1920)	50 — 75
Gruelle/J.	Raggedy Andy Stories	Gruelle/J.	Volland	(1920)	150 — 200
Gruelle/J.	Raggedy Andy Stories	Gruelle/J.	Volland	(1920)	100 — 150
Gruelle/J.	Raggedy Andy Stories	Gruelle/J.	J.Gruelle Co.	(1940)	35 — 50
Gruelle/J.	Raggedy Andy's Number Book	Gruelle/J.	Donohue	(1924)	20 — 30
Gruelle/J.	Raggedy Andy's Number Book	Gruelle/J.	Volland	(1924)	50 — 75
Gruelle/J.	Raggedy Ann & Andy/Camel	Gruelle/J.	Donohue	(1924)	50 — 75
Gruelle/J.	Raggedy Ann & Andy/Camel	Gruelle/J.	Volland	(1924)	125 — 150
Gruelle/J.	Raggedy Ann & Andy/Camel	Gruelle/J.	Volland	(1924)	100 — 125
Gruelle/J.	Raggedy Ann & Andy/Camel	Gruelle/J.	J.Gruelle Co.	(1940)	35 — 50
Gruelle/J.	Raggedy Ann Cut Out/Doll	Gruelle/J.	Whitman	1935	35 — 50
Gruelle/J.	Raggedy Ann In Cookie Land	Gruelle/J.	Donohue	(1931)	50 — 75
Gruelle/J.	Raggedy Ann In Cookie Land	Gruelle/J.	Volland	(1931)	125 — 150
Gruelle/J.	Raggedy Ann In Cookie Land	Gruelle/J.	Volland	(1931)	100 — 125
Gruelle/J.	Raggedy Ann In Cookie Land	Gruelle/J.	J.Gruelle Co.	(1940)	35 — 50

Listings By Author

Author	Title	Illustrator	Publisher	Year	Price Range
Gruelle/J.	Raggedy Ann Stories	Gruelle/J.	Donohue	(1918)	50 — 75
Gruelle/J.	Raggedy Ann Stories	Gruelle/J.	Volland	(1918)	125 — 175
Gruelle/J.	Raggedy Ann Stories	Gruelle/J.	Volland	(1918)	100 — 125
Gruelle/J.	Raggedy Ann Stories	Gruelle/J.	J.Gruelle Co.	(1940)	35 — 50
Gruelle/J.	Raggedy Ann's Alphabet Book	Gruelle/J.	Donohue	(1925)	20 — 35
Gruelle/J.	Raggedy Ann's Alphabet Book	Gruelle/J.	Volland	(1925)	35 — 50
Gruelle/J.	Raggedy Ann's Lucky Pennies	Gruelle/J.	Donohue	(1932)	50 — 75
Gruelle/J.	Raggedy Ann's Lucky Pennies	Gruelle/J.	Volland	(1932)	125 — 150
Gruelle/J.	Raggedy Ann's Lucky Pennies	Gruelle/J.	Volland	(1932)	100 — 125
Gruelle/J.	Raggedy Ann's Magical Wishes	Gruelle/J.	Donohue	(1928)	35 — 50
Gruelle/J.	Raggedy Ann's Magical Wishes	Gruelle/J.	Volland	(1928)	100 — 150
Gruelle/J.	Raggedy Ann's Magical Wishes	Gruelle/J.	Volland	(1928)	75 — 100
Gruelle/J.	Raggedy Ann's Wishing Pebble	Gruelle/J.	Donohue	(1925)	35 — 50
Gruelle/J.	Raggedy Ann's Wishing Pebble	Gruelle/J.	Volland	(1925)	75 — 100
Gruelle/J.	Raggedy Ann's Wishing Pebble	Gruelle/J.	Volland	(1925)	65 — 85
Gruelle/J.	Raggedy Ann's Wishing Pebble	Gruelle/J.	J.Gruelle Co.	(1940)	35 — 50
Gruelle/J.	Raggedy Ann/Deep Woods	Gruelle/J.	Donohue	(1930)	50 — 75
Gruelle/J.	Raggedy Ann/Deep Woods	Gruelle/J.	Volland	(1930)	125 — 150
Gruelle/J.	Raggedy Ann/Deep Woods	Gruelle/J.	Volland	(1930)	100 — 125
Gruelle/J.	Raggedy Ann/Deep Woods	Gruelle/J.	J.Gruelle Co.	(1940)	35 — 50
Gruelle/J.	Raggedy Ann/Golden Meadow	Gruelle/J.	Whitman	1935	75 — 100
Gruelle/J.	Raggedy Ann/Left Handed Pin	Gruelle/J.	Whitman	1935	50 — 75
Gruelle/J.	Wooden Willie	Gruelle/J.	Donohue	(1927)	35 — 50
Gruelle/J.	Wooden Willie	Gruelle/J.	Volland	(1927)	100 — 125
Gruelle/J.	Wooden Willie	Gruelle/J.	Volland	(1927)	75 — 100

H

Author	Title	Illustrator	Publisher	Year	Price Range
Hamer/S.H.	Little Folks Fairy Book (The)	Rackham/A.	Cassell	1905	125 — 150
Hamer/S.H.	Little Folks Picture Album	Rackham/A.	Cassell	1904	100 — 125
Hamerton/P.	Art/American Wood Engraver	Pyle/H.	Scribner	1894	50 — 75
Hamilton/M.	Kingdoms Curious	Rackham/A.	Heinemann	1905	175 — 250
Harbour/H.	Where Flies The Flag	Rackham/A.	Collins	(1904)	150 — 200
Harbour/H.	Where Flies The Flag	Rackham/A.	Collins	[1904]	50 — 75
Harris/A.V.	Favorites Of Fairyland	Newell/P.	Harper	1911	75 — 100
Harrison/B.	Bric-A-Brac Stories	Crane/W.	Scribner	1885	125 — 150
Harrison/B.	Folk & Fairy Tales	Crane/W.	Marcus Ward	1885	150 — 250
Harrison/E.	Vision Of Dante (The)	Crane/W.	Chi.Kind.Co.	1895	75 — 100
Harte/B.	Queen Of Pirate Isle	Greenaway/K.	Chatto/Windus	[1886]	200 — 250
Harte/B.	Queen Of Pirate Isle	Greenaway/K.	Houghton	1887	150 — 200
Harte/B.	Salomy Jane	Fisher/H.	Houghton	1910	50 — 75
Hartmann/S.	History Of American Art (A)	Pyle/H.	L.C. Page	1901	50 — 75
Hartwell	Magic Bed (The)	Neill/J.R.	Altemus	(1906)	50 — 75

LISTINGS BY AUTHOR

Author	Title	Illustrator	Publisher	Year	Price Range
Havilland/A.	Stories From Memel/Young	Crane/W.	Hunt	1864	100 — 125
Hawthorne/H.	Lure Of The Garden	Parrish/M.	Century	1911	50 — 125
Hawthorne/N.	Mosses From An Old Manse	Smith/J.W.	Houghton	1900	750 — 1000
Hawthorne/N.	Mosses From An Old Manse	Smith/J.W.	Houghton	1900	75 — 100
Hawthorne/N.	Mosses From An Old Manse	Smith/J.W.	Houghton	1903	50 — 60
Hawthorne/N.	Scarlet Letter	Thomson/H.	Methuen	(1920)	150 — 200
Hawthorne/N.	Tales & Sketches	Smith/J.W.	Houghton	1900	750 — 1000
Hawthorne/N.	Tales & Sketches	Smith/J.W.	Houghton	1900	75 — 100
Hawthorne/N.	Tanglewood Tales	Dulac/E.	H&S	(1938)	150 — 200
Hawthorne/N.	Tanglewood Tales	Pogany/W.	Unwin	[1910]	100 — 130
Hawthorne/N.	Wonder Bk/Tanglewood Tales	Crane/W.	Houghton	1898	175 — 225
Hawthorne/N.	Wonder Book	Pogany/W.	Jacobs	(1909)	100 — 150
Hawthorne/N.	Wonder Book (A)	Rackham/A.	Doran	(1922)	200 — 250
Hawthorne/N.	Wonder Book (A)	Rackham/A.	H&S	(1922)	225 — 300
Hawthorne/N.	Wonder Book (A)	Rackham/A.	H&S	(1922)	750 — 1000
Hawthorne/N.	Wonder Book For Boys & Girls	Crane/W.	Osgood	1892	170 — 220
Hawthorne/N.	Wonder Book For Boys & Girls	Crane/W.	Houghton	1893	140 — 180
Hawthorne/N.	Wonder Book For Boys & Girls	Crane/W.	Riverside	1893	250 — 350
Hawthorne/N.	Wonder Book For Boys & Girls	Crane/W.	Houghton	1905	40 — 65
Hay/J.	Pike County Ballads (The)	Wyeth/N.C.	Houghton	(1912)	75 — 125
Haydon/A.L.	Stories Of King Arthur	Rackham/A.	Cassell	1910	175 — 225
Haydon/A.L.	Stories Of King Arthur	Rackham/A.	Cassell	1918	100 — 125
Hearn/L.	Youma:/West Indian Slave	Pyle/H.	Harper	1890	250 — 350
Heine/H.	Atta Troll	Pogany/W.	Sidgwick	1913	90 — 130
Heine/H.	Atta Troll	Pogany/W.	Huebsch	1914	75 — 100
Henley/W.E.	London Garland (A)	Rackham/A.	Macmillan	1895	175 — 225
Henley/W.E.	London Garland (A)	Rackham/A.	Macmillan	1895	250 — 350
Henty/G.A	Brains & Bravery	Rackham/A.	Chambers	1903	75 — 125
Henty/G.A	Brains & Bravery	Rackham/A.	Chambers	1905	50 — 75
Herbertson/A.G.	Bee-Blowaways (The)	Rackham/A.	Cassell	[1900]	100 — 150
Higgins/A.C.	Dream Blocks	Smith/J.W.	Duffield	(1908)	275 — 375
Higgins/A.C.	Dream Blocks	Smith/J.W.	Chatto/Windus	1911	200 — 250
Higginson/T.W.	History Of The United States	Pyle/H.	Harper	1905	20 — 30
Higginson/T.W.	Larger History Of The U.S.	Pyle/H.	Harper	1886	40 — 60
Hill & Browne	Little Folks Plays (The)	Rackham/A.	Cassell	1903	125 — 150
Hill & Browne	Little Folks Plays (The)	Rackham/A.	Cassell	1906	75 — 100
Hodder/E.	Life Of A Century (The)	Rackham/A.	Newnes	1901	100 — 125
Holme/C.	Modern Pen Drawings	Pyle/H.	The Studio	1901	50 — 75
Holme/C.	Old Watercolour Society Club	Rackham/A.	The Studio	1905	175 — 225
Holme/C.	Pen,Pencil & Chalk	Rackham/A.	The Studio	1911	50 — 75
Holme/G.	British Book Illustration	Rackham/A.	The Studio	1923	75 — 100
Holmes/O.W.	Autocrat/Breakfast Table	Pyle/H.	Houghton	1894	125 — 150

LISTINGS BY AUTHOR

Author	Title	Illustrator	Publisher	Year	Price Range
Holmes/O.W.	Dorothy Q.	Pyle/H.	Houghton	1893	75 — 100
Holmes/O.W.	Ill.Poems Of Oliver W. Holmes	Pyle/H.	Houghton	1885	35 — 50
Holmes/O.W.	One-Hoss Shay (The)	Pyle/H.	Houghton	1892	75 — 125
Holmes/O.W.	One-Hoss Shay (The)	Pyle/H.	Houghton	1905	75 — 125
Holt/A.	Fancy Dresses Described	Greenaway/K.		[1882]	125 — 175
Hope/A.	Dolly Dialogues	Christy/H.C.	Russell	1901	30 — 45
Hope/A.	Dolly Dialogues (The)	Rackham/A.	Holt	1894	50 — 100
Hope/A.	Dolly Dialogues (The)	Rackham/A.	West. Gaz.	1894	150 — 250
Hope/A.	Dolly Dialogues (The)	Rackham/A.	West. Gaz.	1894	125 — 175
Hope/A.	Prisoner Of Zenda (The)	Gibson/C.D.	G&D	(1898)	10 — 15
Hope/A.	Prisoner Of Zenda (The)	Gibson/C.D.	Holt	1898	15 — 25
Housman/L.	Magic Horse	Dulac/E.	H&S	(1911)	200 — 250
Housman/L.	Princess Badoura	Dulac/E.	H&S	[1913]	250 — 350
Housman/L.	Stories From Arabian Nights	Dulac/E.	H&S	(1907)	300 — 400
Housman/L.	Stories From Arabian Nights	Dulac/E.	Scribner	(1907)	175 — 225
Housman/L.	Stories From Arabian Nights	Dulac/E.	H&S	[1911]	100 — 150
Housman/L.	Stories From Arabian Nights	Dulac/E.	Doran	[1920]	125 — 175
Housman/L.	Stories From Arabian Nights	Dulac/E.	H&S	[1920]	100 — 125
Housman/L.	Stories From Arabian Nights	Dulac/E.	Garden City	[1932]	50 — 75
Housman/L.	Stories From Arabian Nights	Dulac/E.	Doubleday		125 — 175
Howells/W.D.	Stops Of Various Quills	Pyle/H.	Harper	1895	50 — 75
Howels/W.& Perry/T.	Library/Universal Adventure	Pyle/H.	Harper	1888	50 — 75
Hubbell/R.S.	Quacky Doodles/D. Doodles	Gruelle/J.	Volland	(1916)	150 — 200
Hughes/T.	Tom Brown's School Days	Thomson/H.	Ginn		50 — 75
Humphrey/M.	Babes Of The Year	Humphrey/M.	Stokes	1888	300 — 500
Humphrey/M.	Book Of Fairy Tales	Humphrey/M.	Stokes	1892	500 — 700
Humphrey/M.	Children Of The Revolution	Humphrey/M.	Stokes	1900	400 — 500
Humphrey/M.	Gallant Little Patriots	Humphrey/M.	Stokes	1899	450 — 650
Humphrey/M.	Golf Girl	Humphrey/M.	Stokes	(1899)	300 — 400
Humphrey/M.	Little Heroes & Heroines	Humphrey/M.	Stokes	1899	200 — 350
Humphrey/M.	Little Soldiers & Sailors	Humphrey/M.	Stokes	(1899)	250 — 300
Humphrey/M.	Mother Goose	Humphrey/M.	Stokes	1891	500 — 700
Humphrey/M.	Rosebud Stories	Humphrey/M.	Holiday	1906	150 — 200
Humphrey/M.	Tiny Todlers	Humphrey/M.	Dean	[1890]	450 — 500
Humphrey/M.	Tiny Todlers	Humphrey/M.	Stokes	1890	650 — 800
Humphrey/Mbl.	Book Of The Child (The)	Smith/J.W.	Stokes	(1903)	600 — 750
Humphreys/J.	Laugh & Learn	Barker/C.M.	Blackie	[1936]	50 — 75
Hungerford/M.	Molly Bawn	Rackham/A.	Newnes	(1904)	300 — 500
Hunt/Mrs. B.	Poor Nelly	Greenaway/K.	Cassell	1878	150 — 175
Hutton/E.	Children's Christmas Treasury	Rackham/A.	Dent	(1905)	250 — 300
Hutton/E.	Children's Christmas Treasury	Rackham/A.	Dutton	(1905)	225 — 275

LISTINGS BY AUTHOR

Author	Title	Illustrator	Publisher	Year	Price Range

I

Author	Title	Illustrator	Publisher	Year	Price Range
Ibsen/H.	Peer Gynt	Rackham/A.	Harrap	[1936]	850 — 1250
Ibsen/H.	Peer Gynt	Rackham/A.	Harrap	[1936]	100 — 150
Ibsen/H.	Peer Gynt	Rackham/A.	Harrap	[1936]	150 — 200
Ibsen/H.	Peer Gynt	Rackham/A.	Lippincott	[1936]	100 — 150
Ingersoll/E.	Book Of The Ocean (The)	Pyle/H.	Century	1898	50 — 75
Ingoldsby/T.	Ingoldsby Legends (The)	Rackham/A.	Heinemann	(1909)	125 — 150
Ingoldsby/T.	Ingoldsby Legends (The)	Rackham/A.	Dent	1898	175 — 225
Ingoldsby/T.	Ingoldsby Legends (The)	Rackham/A.	Dent	1907	200 — 300
Ingoldsby/T.	Ingoldsby Legends (The)	Rackham/A.	Dent	1907	750 — 1000
Ingoldsby/T.	Ingoldsby Legends (The)	Rackham/A.	Dutton	1907	200 — 250
Ingoldsby/T.	Ingoldsby Legends (The)	Rackham/A.	Heinemann	1919	100 — 125
Ingoldsby/T.	Ingoldsby Legends (The)	Rackham/A.	Dent		125 — 150
Irving/W.	Bracebridge Hall	Rackham/A.	Putnam	1896	100 — 150
Irving/W.	Bracebridge Hall	Rackham/A.	Putnam	1896	200 — 300
Irving/W.	Knickerbocker's History Of Ny	Parrish/M.	Russell	1900	125 — 200
Irving/W.	Knickerbocker's History Of Ny	Parrish/M.	Dodd	1915	175 — 250
Irving/W.	Legend Of Sleepy Hollow	Rackham/A.	Harrap	(1928)	200 — 300
Irving/W.	Legend Of Sleepy Hollow	Rackham/A.	Harrap	(1928)	175 — 250
Irving/W.	Legend Of Sleepy Hollow	Rackham/A.	Harrap	(1928)	1000 — 1300
Irving/W.	Legend Of Sleepy Hollow	Rackham/A.	McKay	(1928)	150 — 200
Irving/W.	Legend Of Sleepy Hollow	Rackham/A.	McKay	(1928)	1000 — 1300
Irving/W.	Rip Van Winkle	Rackham/A.	Dbl.,Page	(1916)	125 — 150
Irving/W.	Rip Van Winkle	Rackham/A.	Heinemann	(1916)	150 — 175
Irving/W.	Rip Van Winkle	Wyeth/N.C.	McKay	(1921)	100 — 150
Irving/W.	Rip Van Winkle	Wyeth/N.C.	McKay	(1921)	75 — 100
Irving/W.	Rip Van Winkle	Rackham/A.	Heinemann	[1917]	75 — 100
Irving/W.	Rip Van Winkle	Rackham/A.	Dbl.,Page	1905	200 — 250
Irving/W.	Rip Van Winkle	Rackham/A.	Heinemann	1905	300 — 400
Irving/W.	Rip Van Winkle	Rackham/A.	Heinemann	1905	1000 — 1500
Irving/W.	Rip Van Winkle	Rackham/A.	Heinemann	1909	125 — 150
Irving/W.	Rip Van Winkle	Rackham/A.	Dbl.,Page	1919	200 — 300
Irving/W.	Rip Van Winkle	Rackham/A.	Heinemann	1919	200 — 300
Irving/W.	Sketch Book/Geoffrey Crayon	Rackham/A.	Putnam	(1894)	125 — 150
Irving/W.	Sketch Book/Geoffrey Crayon	Rackham/A.	Putnam	(1894)	250 — 300
Irving/W.	Sketch Book/Geoffrey Crayon	Rackham/A.	Putnam	(1894)	100 — 125
Irving/W.	Tales Of A Traveler	Rackham/A.	Putnam	1895	100 — 150
Irving/W.	Tales Of A Traveler	Rackham/A.	Putnam	1895	250 — 350
Irwin/W.	Nautical Lays Of A Landsman	Newell/P.	Dodd	1904	45 — 60
Isham/F.S.	Black Friday	Fisher/H.	Bobbs-Merrill	(1904)	25 — 30
Isham/F.S.	Under The Rose	Christy/H.C.	Bobbs-Merrill	(1903)	15 — 25

Listings By Author

Author	Title	Illustrator	Publisher	Year	Price Range

J

Author	Title	Illustrator	Publisher	Year	Price Range
Jackson/G.E.	Peterkin	Parrish/M.	Duffield	1912	75 — 125
Jackson/H.H.	Ramona	Wyeth/N.C.	Little Brown	1945	35 — 50
James/H.	Magic Jaw Bone	Neill/J.R.	Altemus	(1906)	50 — 75
Janvier/T.	In Old New York	Pyle/H.	Harper	1894	20 — 30
Jenks/T.	Magician/One Day	Neill/J.R.	Altemus	(1905)	75 — 100
Jenks/T.	Rescue Syndicate	Neill/J.R.	Altemus	(1905)	50 — 75
Jenkyn-Thomas	Welsh Fairy Book	Pogany/W.	Unwin	(1907)	150 — 200
Jerome/J.K.	Three Men On Wheels	Fisher/H.	Dodd	1900	35 — 50
Jerrold/A.	Cruise In The Acorn	Greenaway/K.	Marcus Ward	1875	300 — 350
Johnson	20 Years Of Hus'ling	Denslow/W.W.	Thompson	1900	100 — 150
Johnson/C.	Parson's Devil	Newell/P.		(1927)	50 — 100
Johnson/E.	Anthology/Children's Lit.	Wyeth/N.C.	Houghton	1940	125 — 150
Johnson/E.	Anthology/Children's Lit.	Wyeth/N.C.	Houghton	1948	50 — 100
Johnson/R.	Phaeton Rogers	Pyle/H.	Scribner	1881	25 — 50
Johnston/I.M.	Jeweled Toad (The)	Denslow/W.W.	Bobbs-Merrill	(1907)	225 — 275
Johnston/M.	Cease Firing	Wyeth/N.C.	Houghton	1912	20 — 35
Johnston/M.	Long Roll (The)	Wyeth/N.C.	Houghton	1911	20 — 30
Johnston/M.	Long Roll (The)	Wyeth/N.C.	Houghton	1911	20 — 40
Johnston/M.	To Have & To Hold	Pyle/H.	Houghton	1900	20 — 30

K

Author	Title	Illustrator	Publisher	Year	Price Range
Kelly/A.	Rosebud And Other Tales (The)	Crane/W.	Unwin	1909	175 — 225
Kenyon/C.R.	Argonauts Of The Amazon	Rackham/A.	W.R. Chambers	1901	175 — 250
Kenyon/C.R.	Argonauts Of The Amazon	Rackham/A.	Dutton	1901	125 — 175
Keyes/A.M.	Five Senses (The)	Smith/J.W.	Moffat,Yard	1911	180 — 250
Kingsley/C.	Water Babies (The)	Smith/J.W.	Dodd	(1916)	100 — 175
Kingsley/C.	Water Babies (The)	Smith/J.W.	Dodd	(1916)	75 — 150
Kingsley/C.	Water Babies (The)	Smith/J.W.	Dodd	(1916)	200 — 300
Kingsley/C.	Water Babies (The)	Smith/J.W.	Dodd	(1916)	225 — 325
Kingsley/C.	Water Babies (The)	Smith/J.W.	Dodd	(1916)	175 — 250
Kingsley/C.	Water Babies (The)	Smith/J.W.	Garden City	(1937)	35 — 50
Kingsley/C.	Water Babies (The)	Smith/J.W.	H&S	(1938)	100 — 150
Kingsley/C.	Water Babies (The)	Smith/J.W.	Boots	[1919]	150 — 250
Kingsley/C.	Water Babies (The)	Smith/J.W.	H&S	[1919]	175 — 250
Kingsley/C.	Water Babies (The)	Smith/J.W.	Boots	[1925]	125 — 150
Kingsley/C.	Water Babies (The)	Smith/J.W.	Dodd	[1936]	25 — 35
Kingsley/C.	Westward Ho	Wyeth/N.C.	Scribner	(1948)	20 — 35
Kingsley/C.	Westward Ho	Wyeth/N.C.	Scribner	1920	75 — 150
Kingsley/C.	Westward Ho	Wyeth/N.C.	Scribner	1935	30 — 50
Kingsley/C.	Westward Ho	Wyeth/N.C.	Scribner	1947	20 — 50

LISTINGS BY AUTHOR

Author	Title	Illustrator	Publisher	Year	Price Range
Kipling/R.	Puck Of Pook's Hill	Rackham/A.	Dbl.,Page	1906	60 — 100
Kipling/R.	Puck Of Pook's Hill	Rackham/A.	Doubleday	1916	25 — 50
Klein/C.	Music Master	Rae/J.	Dodd	1909	25 — 45
Knickerbocker/D.	History Of New York...... (A)	Pyle/H.	Grolier Club	1886	50 — 75
Knox/K.	Fairy Gifts	Greenaway/K.	Dutton	(1874)	125 — 175
Knox/K.	Fairy Gifts	Greenaway/K.	G&F	1874	125 — 175
Konody/P.G.	Art Of Walter Crane	Crane/W.	G. Bell	1902	300 — 400
Kunos/I.	44 Turkish Tales	Pogany/W.	Harrap	(1913)	150 — 200

L

Author	Title	Illustrator	Publisher	Year	Price Range
La Fontaine	Fables In Rhyme/Little Folk	Rae/J.	Volland	(1918)	50 — 75
La Fontaine	Fables In Rhyme/Little Folk	Rae/J.	Wise-Parslow	1950	25 — 50
Lamb/C.&M.	Tales From Shakespeare	Rackham/A.	Dent	1899	150 — 200
Lamb/C.&M.	Tales From Shakespeare	Rackham/A.	Dent	1909	200 — 275
Lamb/C.&M.	Tales From Shakespeare	Rackham/A.	Dent	1909	750 — 1000
Lamb/C.&M.	Tales From Shakespeare	Rackham/A.	Dutton	1909	175 — 225
Lane/M.	Tale/Beatrix Potter	Potter/B.	Warne	(1946)	50 — 75
Lang/A.	Animal Story Book (The)	Ford/H.J.	Longmans	1896	100 — 150
Lang/A.	Arabian Nights Entertainments	Ford/H.J.	Longmans	1898	150 — 175
Lang/A.	Blue Fairy Book (The)	Ford/H.J.	Longmans	1890	50 — 100
Lang/A.	Blue Fairy Book (The)	Ford/H.J.	Longmans	1903	50 — 100
Lang/A.	Blue Fairy Book (The)	Ford/H.J.	Longmans		150 — 200
Lang/A.	Blue Poetry Book (The)	Ford/H.J.	Longmans	1891	150 — 200
Lang/A.	Book Of Romance (The)	Ford/H.J.	Longmans	1902	175 — 225
Lang/A.	Brown Fairy Book (The)	Ford/H.J.	Longmans	1904	200 — 250
Lang/A.	Brown Fairy Book (The)	Ford/H.J.	Longmans	1908	150 — 200
Lang/A.	Crimson Fairy Book (The)	Ford/H.J.	Longmans	1903	200 — 250
Lang/A.	Crimson Fairy Book (The)	Ford/H.J.	Longmans	1914	50 — 75
Lang/A.	Disentanglers	Ford/H.J.	Longmans	1902	100 — 150
Lang/A.	Green Fairy Book (The)	Ford/H.J.	Longmans	1892	175 — 225
Lang/A.	Green Fairy Book (The)	Ford/H.J.	Longmans	1898	75 — 100
Lang/A.	Green Fairy Book (The)	Ford/H.J.	Longmans	1916	50 — 75
Lang/A.	Green Fairy Book (The)	Ford/H.J.	Longmans	1924	25 — 50
Lang/A.	Grey Fairy Book (The)	Ford/H.J.	Longmans	1900	175 — 225
Lang/A.	Grey Fairy Book (The)	Ford/H.J.	Longmans	1924	25 — 50
Lang/A.	Library (The)	Greenaway/K.	Macmillan	1881	200 — 300
Lang/A.	Lilac Fairy Book (The)	Ford/H.J.	Longmans	1910	200 — 250
Lang/A.	Lilac Fairy Book (The)	Ford/H.J.	Longmans	1914	50 — 75
Lang/A.	Lilac Fairy Book (The)	Ford/H.J.	Longmans	1919	50 — 75
Lang/A.	Olive Fairy Book (The)	Ford/H.J.	Longmans	1907	175 — 225
Lang/A.	Olive Fairy Book (The)	Ford/H.J.	Longmans	1925	50 — 75
Lang/A.	Orange Fairy Book (The)	Ford/H.J.	Longmans	1906	175 — 225

LISTINGS BY AUTHOR

Author	Title	Illustrator	Publisher	Year	Price Range
Lang/A.	Pink Fairy Book (The)	Ford/H.J.	Longmans	1897	175 — 225
Lang/A.	Pink Fairy Book (The)	Ford/H.J.	Longmans	1906	50 — 75
Lang/A.	Red Book Of Animal Stories	Ford/H.J.	Longmans	1899	75 — 125
Lang/A.	Red Book Of True Stories	Ford/H.J.	Longmans	1895	150 — 200
Lang/A.	Red Fairy Book (The)	Ford/H.J.	Longmans	1890	175 — 225
Lang/A.	Red Fairy Book (The)	Ford/H.J.	Longmans	1917	30 — 60
Lang/A.	Red Romance Book (The)	Ford/H.J.	Longmans	1905	200 — 250
Lang/A.	Red True Story Book (The)	Ford/H.J.	Longmans	1895	75 — 125
Lang/A.	Strange Story Book (The)	Ford/H.J.	Longmans	1913	200 — 250
Lang/A.	Tales Of Troy & Greece	Ford/H.J.	Longmans	1907	150 — 175
Lang/A.	Trusty John & Other Stories	Ford/H.J.	Longmans	1906	75 — 100
Lang/A.	Violet Fairy Book (The)	Ford/H.J.	Longmans	1901	200 — 275
Lang/A.	Violet Fairy Book (The)	Ford/H.J.	Longmans	1933	25 — 50
Lang/A.	Yellow Fairy Book (The)	Ford/H.J.	Longmans	1894	175 — 225
Lang/A.	Yellow Fairy Book (The)	Ford/H.J.	Longmans	1895	100 — 150
Lang/A.	Yellow Fairy Book (The)	Ford/H.J.	Longmans	1897	100 — 150
Lang/L.B.	All Sorts Of Stories Book	Ford/H.J.	Longmans	1911	100 — 150
Lang/Mrs.	Book Of Princes & Princesses	Ford/H.J.	Longmans	1908	175 — 225
Lang/Mrs.	Book Of Princes & Princesses	Ford/H.J.	Longmans	1908	125 — 150
Lang/Mrs.	Book Of Saints & Heroes (The)	Ford/H.J.	Longmans	1912	150 — 175
Lanier/S.	Boy's King Arthur	Wyeth/N.C.	Scribner	1917	125 — 150
Lanier/S.	Boy's King Arthur	Wyeth/N.C.	Scribner	1926	50 — 75
Larned/W.T.	American Indian Fairy Tales	Rae/J.	Volland	(1921)	75 — 100
Larned/W.T.	American Indian Fairy Tales	Rae/J.	Wise-Parslow	(1935)	35 — 50
Larned/W.T.	Fairy Tales From France	Rae/J.	Volland	(1920)	50 — 75
Larned/W.T.	Reynard The Fox	Rae/J.	Volland	(1925)	65 — 100
Latimore/S.B.	Arthur Rackham/Bibliography	Rackham/A.	Suttonhouse	1936	100 — 150
Latimore/S.B.	Arthur Rackham/Bibliography	Rackham/A.	Suttonhouse	1936	50 — 75
Lawrence/J.	Gingerbread Man (The)	Gruelle/J.	Whitman	1930	25 — 35
Lawrence/J.	Man In Moon Stories...	Gruelle/J.	Cupples	(1922)	125 — 175
Lawrence/J.	Man In Moon Stories...	Gruelle/J.	Whitman	1930	35 — 50
Lee/A.	Round Rabbit (The)	O'Neill/R.	Copeland/Day	1898	150 — 250
Lee/A.	Tommy Toodles	Newell/P.	Harper	1896	150 — 200
Lever/C.	C.O'Malley/Irish Dragoon	Rackham/A.	Nesbit	[1899]	100 — 125
Lever/C.	C.O'Malley/Irish Dragoon	Rackham/A.	Putnam	1897	100 — 125
Lever/C.	C.O'Malley/Irish Dragoon	Rackham/A.	Service	1897	125 — 150
Lewis/A.H.	Throwback (The)	Wyeth/N.C.	Outing	1906	35 — 50
Leyland/J.	Gardens Old & New	Rackham/A.	Newnes	[1900]	175 — 225
Lingwood/L.	Ill.Guide/Wells-Next-The-Sea	Rackham/A.	Jarrold	(1894)	100 — 150
Lingwood/L.	Ill.Guide/Wells-Next-The-Sea	Rackham/A.	Jarrold	(1910)	75 — 100
Linnell/O.	Autumn Song With Music	Barker/C.M.	Blackie	[1920]	75 — 125
Linnell/O.	Autumn Song With Music	Barker/C.M.	Blackie	[1930]	50 — 75

Listings By Author

Author	Title	Illustrator	Publisher	Year	Price Range
Linnell/O.	Spring Songs With Music....	Barker/C.M.	Blackie	[1920]	75 — 125
Linnell/O.	Summer Songs With Music...	Barker/C.M.	Blackie	[1920]	75 — 125
Lodge/H.C.	Story Of The Revolution (The)	Pyle/H.	Scribner	1898	25 — 35
Loftie/W.J.	Orient Line Guide	Greenaway/K.	Sampson Low	1888	100 — 150
Loftie/W.J.	Quiver Of Love (The)	Crane/W.	Marcus Ward	1876	200 — 300
Loftie/W.J.	Quiver Of Love (The)	Greenaway/K.	Marcus Ward	1876	200 — 300
Long/J.L.	Billy Boy	Smith/J.W.	Dodd	(1906)	100 — 150
Long/J.L.	Billy Boy	Smith/J.W.	Dodd	1906	150 — 200
Long/J.L.	War	Wyeth/N.C.	Bobbs-Merrill	(1913)	50 — 75
Longfellow/H.W.	Courtship Of Miles Standish	Christy/H.C.	Bobbs-Merrill	(1903)	25 — 50
Longfellow/H.W.	Courtship Of Miles Standish	Wyeth/N.C.	Houghton	1920	100 — 150
Longfellow/H.W.	Evangeline	Christy/H.C.	Bobbs-Merrill	(1905)	30 — 50
Longfellow/H.W.	Evangeline	Neill/J.R.	R&B	(1909)	75 — 100
Longfellow/H.W.	Evangeline	Smith/J.W.	Gay & Bird	1897	150 — 200
Longfellow/H.W.	Evangeline	Smith/J.W.	Houghton	1897	150 — 200
Longfellow/H.W.	Evangeline	Smith/J.W.	Houghton	1897	125 — 150
Longfellow/H.W.	Evangeline	Smith/J.W.	Houghton	1916	50 — 75
Longfellow/H.W.	Hiawatha	Fisher/H.	Bobbs-Merrill	(1906)	80 — 120
Longfellow/H.W.	Hiawatha	Neill/J.R.	R&B	(1909)	75 — 100
Longfellow/H.W.	Hiawatha	Parrish/M.	Harrap	[1911]	175 — 225
Longfellow/H.W.	Hiawatha	Wyeth/N.C.	Harrap	[1911]	175 — 225
Longfellow/H.W.	Song Of Hiawatha	Parrish/M.	Houghton	1911	200 — 400
Longfellow/H.W.	Song Of Hiawatha	Wyeth/N.C.	Houghton	1911	200 — 350
Lossing/B.	Harper's/Cyclopaedia......	Pyle/H.	Harper	1881	75 — 100
Loti/P.	Romance Of A Child	Denslow/W.W.	Rand Mcnally	1897	50 — 75
Louys/P.	Songs Of Bilitis	Pogany/W.	Macy		125 — 150
Lucas/Mrs. E.	Fairy Tales Of Bros. Grimm	Rackham/A.	Constable		35 — 60

M

Author	Title	Illustrator	Publisher	Year	Price Range
MacDonald/G.	At The Back Of The North Wind	Smith/J.W.	McKay	(1919)	100 — 150
MacDonald/G.	At The Back Of The North Wind	Smith/J.W.	McKay	1919	125 — 175
MacDonald/G.	Princess & The Goblin (The)	Smith/J.W.	McKay	[1923]	50 — 75
MacDonald/G.	Princess & The Goblin (The)	Smith/J.W.	McKay	1920	150 — 175
MacDonald/G.	Princess & The Goblin (The)	Smith/J.W.	McKay	1920	125 — 150
MacDonald/G.	Princess & The Goblin (The)	Smith/J.W.	McKay	1920	100 — 125
MacDonald/G.	The Light Princess	Humphrey/M.	Putnam	(1893)	140 — 175
MacGrath/H.	Half A Rogue	Fisher/H.	Bobbs-Merrill	(1906)	15 — 25
MacGregor/M.	Story Of Greece (The)	Crane/W.	Jack	1913	125 — 150
MacKaye/P.	Far Familiar (The)	Rackham/A.	Richards	(1938)	75 — 100
Major/C.	Dorothy Vernon/Hoddon Hall	Christy/H.C.	Macmillan	1902	20 — 30
Malot/H.	Nobody's Boy	Gruelle/J.	Cupples	1916	60 — 80
Markham/E.	Man With The Hoe/Other Poems	Pyle/H.	McClure	1900	75 — 100

LISTINGS BY AUTHOR

Author	Title	Illustrator	Publisher	Year	Price Range
Marks/G.	Sing A Song Of Safety	O'Neill/R.		1937	30 — 50
Marriott/C.	Sally Castleton/Southerner	Wyeth/N.C.	Lippincott	1913	25 — 50
Marryat	Masterman Ready	Rae/J.	Harper	1928	35 — 50
Martin/J.	Prayers/Little Men & Women	Rae/J.	Harper	1912	50 — 75
Martineau/H.	Feats Of The Fjord	Rackham/A.	Dent	(1910)	50 — 75
Martineau/H.	Feats Of The Fjord	Rackham/A.	Dutton	(1910)	50 — 75
Martineau/H.	Feats Of The Fjord	Rackham/A.	Dent	(1914)	75 — 100
Martineau/H.	Feats Of The Fjord	Rackham/A.	Dutton	(1914)	75 — 125
Martineau/H.	Feats Of The Fjord	Rackham/A.	Dent	1899	150 — 250
Martineau/H.	Feats Of The Fjord	Rackham/A.	Dent		50 — 75
Martineau/H.	Feats Of The Fjord	Rackham/A.	Dutton		50 — 75
Marzials/T.	Pan Pipes	Crane/W.	Routledge	[1884]	100 — 150
Marzials/T.	Pan Pipes	Crane/W.	Routledge	1883	175 — 225
Marzials/T.	Pan Pipes	Crane/W.	Warne		100 — 150
Masson/T.	Corner In Women (A)	Gibson/C.D.	Moffat	1905	20 — 40
Mathews/F.A.	My Lady Peggy Goes To Town	Fisher/H.	Bowen	1901	20 — 30
Matthews/B.	Poems Of American Patriotism	Wyeth/N.C.	Scribner	1922	175 — 225
Matz/B.W.	Odd Volume (The)	Rackham/A.	Simpkin,Marsh.	1908	50 — 75
Mayhew Bros.	Magic Of Kindness (The)	Crane/W.	Cassell	1869	50 — 75
McCall/S.	Truth Dexter	Smith/J.W.	Little Brown	1903	25 — 50
McCall/S.	Truth Dexter	Smith/J.W.	Little Brown	1906	15 — 25
McCutcheon/G.	Alternative (The)	Fisher/H.	Dodd	1909	20 — 30
McCutcheon/G.	Beverly Of Graustark	Fisher/H.	Dodd	1904	15 — 30
McCutcheon/G.	Beverly Of Graustark	Fisher/H.	Dodd	1906	10 — 25
McCutcheon/G.	Butterfly Man	Fisher/H.	Dodd	1910	25 — 30
McCutcheon/G.	Day Of The Dog	Fisher/H.	Dodd	1904	35 — 50
McCutcheon/G.	Husbands Of Edith	Fisher/H.	Dodd	1908	25 — 30
McCutcheon/G.	Jane Cable	Fisher/H.	Dodd	1906	20 — 30
McCutcheon/G.	Man From Brodneys	Fisher/H.	Dodd	1908	20 — 35
McCutcheon/G.	Nedra	Fisher/H.	Dodd	1905	20 — 40
McCutcheon/G.	Purple Parasol	Fisher/H.	Dodd	1905	30 — 40
McEvoy/J.P.	Bam Bam Clock	Gruelle/J.	Volland	(1920)	75 — 100
McEvoy/J.P.	Bam Bam Clock	Gruelle/J.	Algonquin	(1936)	35 — 50
Meadon/J.	Graphic Arts/Crafts Yearbook	Parrish/M.	Rep.Pub	1907	40 — 60
Mee/J.	Three Little Frogs	Rae/J.	Volland	(1924)	40 — 60
Meigs/C.	Master Simon's Garden	Rae/J.	Macmillan	1929	50 — 75
Meiklejohn	Golden Primer	Crane/W.	Meiklejohn	1884	125 — 150
Melville/L.	Not All The Truth	Rackham/A.	Jarrold	1928	50 — 75
Melville/L.	Not All The Truth	Rackham/A.	Dbl.,Page	1929	60 — 80
Merriman/H.S.	Grey Lady (The)	Rackham/A.	Smith,Elder	1897	125 — 150
Merriman/H.S.	Grey Lady (The)	Rackham/A.	Smith,Elder	1898	75 — 100
Merriman/H.S.	Money-Spinner (The)	Rackham/A.	Smith,Elder	1896	150 — 250

Listings By Author

Author	Title	Illustrator	Publisher	Year	Price Range
Merriman/H.S.	Money-Spinner (The)	Rackham/A.	Smith,Elder	1897	100 — 150
Michelson/M.	In The Bishop's Carriage	Fisher/H.	Bobbs-Merrill	(1904)	20 — 30
Millar/H.R.	Sun Princess (The)	Rackham/A.	Shaw	[1930]	40 — 60
Mills/W.J.	Girl I Left Behind Me	Rae/J.	Dodd	1910	75 — 100
Mills/W.J.	Through/Gates/Old Romance	Rae/J.	Lippincott	1903	25 — 40
Mills/W.J.	Van Rensselaers/Manhattan	Rae/J.	Stokes	(1907)	25 — 40
Milton/J.	Comus	Dulac/E.		(1954)	40 — 75
Milton/J.	Comus	Rackham/A.	Dbl.,Page	[1921]	175 — 225
Milton/J.	Comus	Rackham/A.	Heinemann	[1921]	500 — 800
Milton/J.	Comus	Rackham/A.	Heinemann	[1921]	175 — 250
Mines/J.F.	Tour Around New York (A)	Pyle/H.	Harper	1893	50 — 75
Mitchell/S.W.	Hugh Wynne,Free Quaker	Pyle/H.	Century	[1897]	100 — 150
Mitchell/S.W.	Hugh Wynne,Free Quaker	Pyle/H.	Century	1899	75 — 100
Mitford/M.R.	Our Village	Thomson/H.	Macmillan	1893	50 — 65
Molesworth/Mrs.	Adventures Of Her Baby (The)	Crane/W.	Macmillan	1881	150 — 175
Molesworth/Mrs.	Adventures Of Her Baby (The)	Crane/W.	Macmillan	1886	100 — 125
Molesworth/Mrs.	An Old Fashioned Story	Crane/W.	Macmillan	1923	25 — 35
Molesworth/Mrs.	Carrots: Just A Little Boy	Crane/W.	Macmillan	1921	35 — 50
Molesworth/Mrs.	Carrots: Just A Little Boy	Crane/W.	Macmillan	1929	25 — 35
Molesworth/Mrs.	Children Of The Castle (The)	Crane/W.	Macmillan	1890	75 — 100
Molesworth/Mrs.	Christmas Child (A)	Crane/W.	Macmillan	1880	125 — 150
Molesworth/Mrs.	Christmas Posy (A)	Crane/W.	Macmillan	1888	75 — 100
Molesworth/Mrs.	Christmas-Tree Land	Crane/W.	Macmillan	1884	100 — 125
Molesworth/Mrs.	Cuckoo Clock/Tapestry Room	Crane/W.	Macmillan	(1877)	125 — 175
Molesworth/Mrs.	Cuckoo Clock/Tapestry Room	Crane/W.	Macmillan	1919	50 — 75
Molesworth/Mrs.	Four Winds Farm	Crane/W.	Macmillan	1887	75 — 100
Molesworth/Mrs.	Grandmother Dear	Crane/W.	Macmillan	(1878)	75 — 100
Molesworth/Mrs.	Little Miss Peggy	Crane/W.	Macmillan	1887	75 — 100
Molesworth/Mrs.	Little Miss Peggy	Crane/W.	Macmillan	1912	40 — 60
Molesworth/Mrs.	Rectory Children (The)	Crane/W.	Macmillan	1889	75 — 100
Molesworth/Mrs.	Rosy	Crane/W.	Macmillan	1882	75 — 100
Molesworth/Mrs.	Rosy	Crane/W.	Macmillan	1896	30 — 50
Molesworth/Mrs.	Studies & Stories	Crane/W.	A.D. Innes	1893	125 — 150
Molesworth/Mrs.	Tapestry Room (The)	Crane/W.	Macmillan	1879	75 — 100
Molesworth/Mrs.	Tapestry Room (The)	Crane/W.	Macmillan	1906	25 — 50
Molesworth/Mrs.	This & That	Thomson/H.	Macmillan	1899	50 — 65
Molesworth/Mrs.	Two Little Waifs	Crane/W.	Macmillan	(1883)	100 — 125
Molesworth/Mrs.	Us:An Old Fashioned Story	Crane/W.	Macmillan	1886	100 — 125
Molesworth/Mrs.	Us:An Old Fashioned Story	Crane/W.	Macmillan		75 — 100
Montague/G.	Art Of Pen Drawing (The)	Rackham/A.	B.T. Batsford	(1927)	50 — 75
Moore/A.C.	Century Of Kate Greenaway	Greenaway/K.	Warne	1946	15 — 30
Moore/C.C.	Night Before Christmas (The)	Rackham/A.	Harrap	[1931]	750 — 900

LISTINGS BY AUTHOR

Author	Title	Illustrator	Publisher	Year	Price Range
Moore/C.C.	Night Before Christmas (The)	Rackham/A.	Harrap	[1931]	150 — 200
Moore/C.C.	Night Before Christmas (The)	Rackham/A.	Lippincott	[1931]	750 — 900
Moore/C.C.	Night Before Christmas (The)	Rackham/A.	Lippincott	[1931]	150 — 175
Moore/C.C.	Twas/Night Before Christmas	Smith/J.W.	Houghton	(1912)	160 — 220
Moore/C.C.	Twas/Night Before Christmas	Smith/J.W.	Houghton	[1914]	100 — 150
Morley/C.	Where The Blue Begins	Rackham/A.	Dbl.,Page	(1922)	1000 — 1250
Morley/C.	Where The Blue Begins	Rackham/A.	Heinemann	[1922]	750 — 1000
Morley/C.	Where The Blue Begins	Rackham/A.	Dbl.,Page	[1925]	100 — 125
Morley/C.	Where The Blue Begins	Rackham/A.	Heinemann	[1925]	100 — 125
Morley/C.	Where The Blue Begins	Rackham/A.	Lippincott	[1925]	50 — 100
Morris/W.	Story Of Glittering Plain (The)	Crane/W.	Kelmscott	1894	100 — 150
Mulford/C.	Bar 20	Wyeth/N.C.	A.L. Burt	(1907)	10 — 20
Mulford/C.	Bar 20	Wyeth/N.C.	Outing	1907	25 — 45
Mulholland/R.	Puck & Blossom	Greenaway/K.	Ward	1875	200 — 250

N

Author	Title	Illustrator	Publisher	Year	Price Range
Neill/J.R.	Lucky Bucky In Oz	Neill/J.R.	R&L	(1942)	250 — 350
Neill/J.R.	Lucky Bucky In Oz	Neill/J.R.	R&L	(1942)	40 — 60
Neill/J.R.	Scalawagons Of Oz (The)	Neill/J.R.	R&L	(1941)	250 — 350
Neill/J.R.	Scalawagons Of Oz (The)	Neill/J.R.	R&L	(1941)	40 — 60
Neill/J.R.	Wonder City Of Oz (The)	Neill/J.R.	R&L	(1940)	250 — 350
Neill/J.R.	Wonder City Of Oz (The)	Neill/J.R.	R&L	(1940)	40 — 60
Neish/R.	World In A Garden (A)	Rackham/A.	Dent	1899	75 — 100
Neuhaus/E.	History & Ideals Of Amer. Art	Parrish/M.	Stanford U. Pr.	1931	20 — 35
Newell/P.	Hole Book (The)	Newell/P.	Harper	(1908)	175 — 225
Newell/P.	Hole Book (The)	Newell/P.	Harper		75 — 100
Newell/P.	P.Newell's Pictures & Rhymes	Newell/P.	Harper	1899	150 — 200
Newell/P.	Pictures & Rhymes	Newell/P.	Harper	(1899)	100 — 150
Newell/P.	Rocket Book (The)	Newell/P.	Harper	(1912)	175 — 225
Newell/P.	Rocket Book (The)	Newell/P.	Harper		75 — 100
Newell/P.	Shadow Show (A)	Newell/P.	Century	1896	250 — 300
Newell/P.	Slant Book (The)	Newell/P.	Harper	(1910)	150 — 200
Newell/P.	Slant Book (The)	Newell/P.	Harper		75 — 100
Newell/P.	Topsys & Turveys	Newell/P.	Century	1893	225 — 300
Newell/P.	Topsys & Turveys #2	Newell/P.	Century	1894	200 — 225
Newman/I.	Fairy Flowers	Pogany/W.	H. Milford	(1926)	160 — 200
Newman/I.	Fairy Flowers	Pogany/W.	Holt	(1926)	130 — 180
Newman/I.	Legend Of The Tulip	Pogany/W.	Whitman	(1928)	30 — 40
Nicholson/M.	House Of A Thousand Candles	Christy/H.C.	Bobbs-Merrill	(1905)	15 — 30
Niebuhr	Greek Heroes (The)	Rackham/A.	Cassell	1903	250 — 275
Niebuhr	Greek Heroes (The)	Rackham/A.	Cassell	1910	175 — 225
Niebuhr	Greek Heroes (The)	Rackham/A.	Cassell		75 — 125

LISTINGS BY AUTHOR

Author	Title	Illustrator	Publisher	Year	Price Range
Nordhoff & Hall	Botany Bay	Wyeth/N.C.	Little Brown	1941	100 — 150
Nordhoff & Hall	Bounty Trilogy	Wyeth/N.C.	Little Brown	1940	150 — 200

O

Author	Title	Illustrator	Publisher	Year	Price Range
O'Neill/G.	Tomorrow's House	O'Neill/R.	Dutton	1930	40 — 60
O'Neill/R.	Garda	O'Neill/R.	Doubleday	1929	40 — 60
O'Neill/R.	Goblin Woman	O'Neill/R.	Doubleday	1930	40 — 60
O'Neill/R.	Jell-O Girl Entertains (The)	O'Neill/R.	Jell-O Co.	[1920]	100 — 125
O'Neill/R.	Kewpie Kutouts (The)	O'Neill/R.	Stokes	(1914)	700 — 900
O'Neill/R.	Kewpie Primer	O'Neill/R.	Stokes	(1916)	150 — 200
O'Neill/R.	Kewpies & Dotty Darling (The)	O'Neill/R.	Stokes	(1912)	200 — 300
O'Neill/R.	Kewpies & Dotty Darling (The)	O'Neill/R.	Dent	1916	175 — 225
O'Neill/R.	Kewpies & Runaway Baby	O'Neill/R.	Doubleday	1928	175 — 225
O'Neill/R.	Kewpies: Their Book (The)	O'Neill/R.	Stokes	(1913)	225 — 325
O'Neill/R.	Lady In The White Vail	O'Neill/R.	Harper	1909	75 — 100
O'Neill/R.	Loves Of Edwy	O'Neill/R.	Lothrop	(1904)	50 — 75
O'Neill/R.	Master-Mistress	O'Neill/R.	Knopf	1922	50 — 75
Ogden/R.	Little Homespun	Humphrey/M.	Stokes	(1897)	100 — 140
Olcott/F.J.	Bible Stories/Read And Tell	Pogany/W.	Houghton	1916	50 — 75
Olcott/F.J.	More Tales/Arabian Nights	Pogany/W.	Holt	1915	75 — 135
Olcott/F.J.	Tales/Persian Genii	Pogany/W.	Harrap	1919	70 —

P

Author	Title	Illustrator	Publisher	Year	Price Range
Page/T.N.	Bred In The Bone	Fisher/H.	Scribner	1904	25 — 35
Page/T.N.	In Ole Virginia	Pyle/H.	Scribner	1896	25 — 35
Page/T.N.	Old Gentlemen/Black Stock	Christy/H.C.	Scribner	1900	30 — 45
Palgrave/F.T.	Golden Treasury Of Songs..	Parrish/M.	Duffield	1911	150 — 225
Palgrave/F.T.	Golden Treasury Of Songs..	Parrish/M.	Duffield	1941	50 — 80
Palgrave/F.T.	Golden Treasury Of Songs..	Parrish/M.	Scribner		100 — 125
Palgrave/F.T.	Wonder Bk/Tanglewood Tales	Parrish/M.	Duffield	1910	125 — 200
Palgrave/F.T.	Wonder Bk/Tanglewood Tales	Parrish/M.	Duffield	1928	100 — 150
Palmer.G.H.	Odyssey Of Homer	Wyeth/N.C.	Houghton	1929	150 — 200
Parkman/F.	Oregon Trail	Wyeth/N.C.	Little Brown	1925	75 — 100
Parkman/F.	Struggle For A Continent (The)	Pyle/H.	Little Brown	1902	40 — 60
Parrish/R.	Beth Norvell	Wyeth/N.C.	McClurg	1907	25 — 40
Parry/J.	Don Quixote	Crane/W.	Blackie	1900	175 — 225
Parry/J.	Don Quixote	Crane/W.	J. Lane	1900	100 — 125
Parry/J.	Don Quixote	Crane/W.	Dodd	1926	75 — 100
Patten/W.	Fairy & Wonder Tales	Smith/J.W.	Collier	(1918)	50 — 75
Patten/W.	Poems Old & New	Smith/J.W.	Collier	(1918)	50 — 75
Peacock/T.L.	Maid Marian....	Thomson/H.	Macmillan	1895	50 — 75
Peck/T.	Sword Of Dundee	Rae/J.	Duffield	1908	25 — 35

LISTINGS BY AUTHOR

Author	Title	Illustrator	Publisher	Year	Price Range
Pennell/J.	Modern Illustration	Pyle/H.	George Bell	1895	50 — 75
Pennell/J.	Pen Drawing/Pen Draughtsmen	Pyle/H.	Macmillan	1889	100 — 150
Perry/F.F.	Their Hearts Desire	Fisher/H.	Dodd	1909	65 — 80
Peterson/H.	Dulcibel	Pyle/H.	Winston	1907	50 — 75
Phillips/D.G.	Cost (The)	Fisher/H.	G&D	(1904)	15 — 25
Phillips/D.G.	Cost (The)	Fisher/H.	Bobbs-Merrill	1904	35 — 50
Phillpotts/E.	Dish Of Apples (A)	Rackham/A.	H&S	(1921)	600 — 800
Phillpotts/E.	Dish Of Apples (A)	Rackham/A.	H&S	[1921]	175 — 225
Phillpotts/E.	Dish Of Apples (A)	Rackham/A.	H&S	[1921]	150 — 175
Pier/A.S.	Boys Of St. Timothy's	Wyeth/N.C.	Scribner	1904	50 — 75
Poe/E.A.	Bells & Other Poems	Dulac/E.	H&S		200 — 400
Poe/E.A.	Bells (The)	Dulac/E.	H&S	(1912)	250 — 300
Poe/E.A.	Poetical Works Of Poe	Dulac/E.	Doran	[1921]	225 — 300
Poe/E.A.	Raven (The)	Neill/J.R.		(1910)	50 — 75
Poe/E.A.	Tales Of Mystery & Imagination	Rackham/A.	Harrap	(1935)	200 — 250
Poe/E.A.	Tales Of Mystery & Imagination	Rackham/A.	Harrap	(1935)	250 — 300
Poe/E.A.	Tales Of Mystery & Imagination	Rackham/A.	Harrap	[1935]	1500 — 2500
Poe/E.A.	Tales Of Mystery & Imagination	Rackham/A.	Lippincott	[1935]	175 — 250
Pogany/E.	Golden Cockerel	Pogany/W.	Nelson	1938	80 — 110
Pogany/N.	Hungarian Fairy Book	Pogany/W.	Unwin	(1913)	130 — 165
Pogany/N.	Hungarian Fairy Book	Pogany/W.	Stokes		75 — 100
Pogany/N.	Magyar Fairy Tales	Pogany/W.	Dutton	(1930)	100 — 150
Pogany/W.	Peterkin	Pogany/W.	McKay	1940	80 — 100
Pogany/W.	Pogany's Mother Goose	Pogany/W.	Nelson	(1928)	130 — 170
Pollard/A.	Romance Of King Arthur...(The)	Rackham/A.	Macmillan	1917	750 — 1250
Pollard/A.	Romance Of King Arthur...(The)	Rackham/A.	Macmillan	1917	150 — 175
Pollard/A.	Romance Of King Arthur...(The)	Rackham/A.	Macmillan	1917	150 — 175
Pollard/A.	Romance Of King Arthur...(The)	Rackham/A.	Macmillan	1917	200 — 250
Pollard/A.	Romance Of King Arthur...(The)	Rackham/A.	Macmillan	1926	40 — 60
Pollock/W.H.	Amateur Theatricals	Greenaway/K.	Macmillan	1879	100 — 150
Pope/A.W.	Theatrical Bookplates	Pyle/H.	Fowler	1914	75 — 100
Potter/B.	Appley Dapply's/Rhymes	Potter/B.	Warne	(1917)	50 — 75
Potter/B.	Appley Dapply's/Rhymes	Potter/B.	Warne	[1917]	300 — 400
Potter/B.	Appley Dapply's/Rhymes	Potter/B.	Warne	[1919]	150 — 200
Potter/B.	C. Parsley's Nursery Rhymes	Potter/B.	Warne	(1922)	150 — 300
Potter/B.	C. Parsley's Nursery Rhymes	Potter/B.	Warne	[1922]	500 — 750
Potter/B.	Fairy Caravan (The)	Potter/B.	McKay	(1929)	125 — 175
Potter/B.	Ginger & Pickles	Potter/B.	Warne	(1909)	150 — 200
Potter/B.	Ginger & Pickles	Potter/B.	Warne	[1920]	100 — 150
Potter/B.	Ginger & Pickles	Potter/B.	Warne	1909	350 — 450
Potter/B.	Jemima Puddle Duck's/Book	Potter/B.	Warne	[1925]	100 — 150
Potter/B.	Peter Rabbit's Almanac/1929	Potter/B.	Warne	[1928]	150 — 200

Listings By Author

Author	Title	Illustrator	Publisher	Year	Price Range
Potter/B.	Peter Rabbit's Almanac/1929	Potter/B.	Warne	[1928]	150 — 200
Potter/B.	Peter Rabbit's Painting Book	Potter/B.	Warne	[1911]	100 — 150
Potter/B.	Peter Rabbit's Painting Book	Potter/B.	Warne	[1917]	50 — 75
Potter/B.	Pie & The Patty Pan (The)	Potter/B.	Warne	(1933)	25 — 50
Potter/B.	Pie & The Patty Pan (The)	Potter/B.	Warne	1905	225 — 350
Potter/B.	Pie & The Patty Pan (The)	Potter/B.	Warne	1905	200 — 250
Potter/B.	Roly Poly Pudding (The)	Potter/B.	Warne	(1908)	200 — 300
Potter/B.	Roly Poly Pudding (The)	Potter/B.	Warne	[1920]	50 — 75
Potter/B.	Roly Poly Pudding (The)	Potter/B.	Warne	1908	300 — 400
Potter/B.	Story Of A Fierce Bad Rabbit	Potter/B.	Warne	[1906]	400 — 500
Potter/B.	Story Of A Fierce Bad Rabbit	Potter/B.	Warne	[1914]	300 — 400
Potter/B.	Story Of A Fierce Bad Rabbit	Potter/B.	Warne	[1914]	200 — 300
Potter/B.	Story Of A Fierce Bad Rabbit	Potter/B.	Warne	[1933]	100 — 150
Potter/B.	Story Of Miss Moppet (The)	Potter/B.	Warne	[1906]	400 — 600
Potter/B.	Story Of Miss Moppet (The)	Potter/B.	Warne	[1913]	350 — 450
Potter/B.	Story Of Miss Moppet (The)	Potter/B.	Warne	[1925]	250 — 350
Potter/B.	Story Of Miss Moppet (The)	Potter/B.	Warne	[1933]	100 — 125
Potter/B.	Story Of Miss Moppet (The)	Potter/B.	Warne	[1933]	100 — 125
Potter/B.	Story Of Peter Rabbit	Neill/J.R.	R&B	(1911)	100 — 125
Potter/B.	Tailor Of Gloucester	Potter/B.	Warne	(1903)	500 — 650
Potter/B.	Tailor Of Gloucester	Potter/B.	Warne	[1903]	350 — 500
Potter/B.	Tailor Of Gloucester	Potter/B.	Warne	[1909]	75 — 100
Potter/B.	Tailor Of Gloucester	Potter/B.	Priv. Prnt	1902	1000 — 2000
Potter/B.	Tale Of Benjamin Bunny (The)	Potter/B.	Warne	(1932)	50 — 75
Potter/B.	Tale Of Benjamin Bunny (The)	Potter/B.	Warne	[1908]	250 — 300
Potter/B.	Tale Of Benjamin Bunny (The)	Potter/B.	Warne	1904	400 — 500
Potter/B.	Tale Of Flopsy Bunnies (The)	Potter/B.	Warne	(1937)	25 — 50
Potter/B.	Tale Of Flopsy Bunnies (The)	Potter/B.	Warne	[1909]	200 — 300
Potter/B.	Tale Of Flopsy Bunnies (The)	Potter/B.	Warne	[1915]	50 — 75
Potter/B.	Tale Of Flopsy Bunnies (The)	Potter/B.	Warne	1909	300 — 500
Potter/B.	Tale Of Jemima Puddle Duck	Potter/B.	Warne	(1908)	75 — 125
Potter/B.	Tale Of Jemima Puddle Duck	Potter/B.	Warne	(1908)	125 — 175
Potter/B.	Tale Of Jemima Puddle Duck	Potter/B.	Warne	[1920]	50 — 75
Potter/B.	Tale Of Jemima Puddle Duck	Potter/B.	Warne	1908	350 — 450
Potter/B.	Tale Of Johnny Town Mouse	Potter/B.	Warne	(1918)	200 — 300
Potter/B.	Tale Of Johnny Town Mouse	Potter/B.	Warne	(1918)	100 — 150
Potter/B.	Tale Of Johnny Town Mouse	Potter/B.	Warne	(1946)	25 — 50
Potter/B.	Tale Of Little Pig Robinson	Potter/B.	McKay	(1930)	200 — 250
Potter/B.	Tale Of Little Pig Robinson	Potter/B.	Warne	(1930)	100 — 150
Potter/B.	Tale Of Little Pig Robinson	Potter/B.	Warne	(1930)	225 — 275
Potter/B.	Tale Of Mr. Jeremy Fisher	Potter/B.	Warne	(1934)	25 — 50
Potter/B.	Tale Of Mr. Jeremy Fisher	Potter/B.	Warne	[1908]	250 — 350

LISTINGS BY AUTHOR

Author	Title	Illustrator	Publisher	Year	Price Range
Potter/B.	Tale Of Mr. Jeremy Fisher	Potter/B.	Warne	[1915]	75 — 100
Potter/B.	Tale Of Mr. Jeremy Fisher	Potter/B.	Warne	1906	450 — 600
Potter/B.	Tale Of Mr. Tod (The)	Potter/B.	Warne	[1912]	200 — 250
Potter/B.	Tale Of Mr. Tod (The)	Potter/B.	Warne	1912	280 — 350
Potter/B.	Tale Of Mrs. Tiggy Winkle (The)	Potter/B.	Warne	[1915]	75 — 100
Potter/B.	Tale Of Mrs. Tiggy Winkle (The)	Potter/B.	Warne	1905	450 — 600
Potter/B.	Tale Of Mrs. Tittlemouse (The)	Potter/B.	Warne	(1938)	20 — 30
Potter/B.	Tale Of Mrs. Tittlemouse (The)	Potter/B.	Warne	[1915]	100 — 150
Potter/B.	Tale Of Mrs. Tittlemouse (The)	Potter/B.	Warne	1910	300 — 375
Potter/B.	Tale Of Peter Rabbit (The)	Neill/J.R.	Altemus	(1904)	100 — 150
Potter/B.	Tale Of Peter Rabbit (The)	Potter/B.	Platt & Munk	(1938)	25 — 35
Potter/B.	Tale Of Peter Rabbit (The)	Potter/B.	Priv. Prnt	[1901]	3000 —5000
Potter/B.	Tale Of Peter Rabbit (The)	Potter/B.	Warne	[1902]	700 —1000
Potter/B.	Tale Of Peter Rabbit (The)	Potter/B.	Warne	[1902]	500 — 800
Potter/B.	Tale Of Peter Rabbit (The)	Potter/B.	Warne	[1906]	50 — 100
Potter/B.	Tale Of Peter Rabbit (The)	Potter/B.	Altemus	1904	350 — 500
Potter/B.	Tale Of Pigling Bland (The)	Potter/B.	Warne	(1941)	25 — 50
Potter/B.	Tale Of Pigling Bland (The)	Potter/B.	Warne	[1913]	200 — 250
Potter/B.	Tale Of Pigling Bland (The)	Potter/B.	Warne	1913	275 — 325
Potter/B.	Tale Of Squirrel Nutkin (The)	Potter/B.	Warne	(1903)	250 — 350
Potter/B.	Tale Of Squirrel Nutkin (The)	Potter/B.	Warne	(1905)	150 — 200
Potter/B.	Tale Of Squirrel Nutkin (The)	Potter/B.	Warne	(1931)	25 — 50
Potter/B.	Tale Of Squirrel Nutkin (The)	Potter/B.	Warne	1903	350 — 500
Potter/B.	Tale Of Timmy Tiptoes (The)	Potter/B.	Warne	(1911)	200 — 300
Potter/B.	Tale Of Timmy Tiptoes (The)	Potter/B.	Warne	[1919]	100 — 150
Potter/B.	Tale Of Timmy Tiptoes (The)	Potter/B.	Warne	1911	350 — 500
Potter/B.	Tale Of Tom Kitten (The)	Potter/B.	Warne	(1935)	30 — 50
Potter/B.	Tale Of Tom Kitten (The)	Potter/B.	Warne	[1909]	100 — 150
Potter/B.	Tale Of Tom Kitten (The)	Potter/B.	Warne	1907	300 — 500
Potter/B.	Tale Of Two Bad Mice (The)	Potter/B.	Warne	(1932)	25 — 50
Potter/B.	Tale Of Two Bad Mice (The)	Potter/B.	Warne	[1908]	150 — 300
Potter/B.	Tale Of Two Bad Mice (The)	Potter/B.	Warne	1904	300 — 450
Pratt/C.E.	Little Folks Ill. Annual	Smith/J.W.	Small.Maynard	(1918)	75 — 100
Pushkin/A.	Golden Cockerel (The)	Dulac/E.	Heritage		40 — 60
Pushkin/A.	Golden Cockerel (The)	Dulac/E.	Lec		350 — 400
Putnam/N.W.	Sunny Bunny	Gruelle/J.	Algonquin	(1918)	40 — 60
Putnam/N.W.	Sunny Bunny	Gruelle/J.	Volland	(1918)	125 — 150
Putnam/N.W.	Sunny Bunny	Gruelle/J.	Volland	(1918)	100 — 125
Pyle/H.	Book Of American Spirit	Pyle/H.	Harper	(1923)	100 — 125
Pyle/H.	Book Of American Spirit	Pyle/H.	Harper	1923	140 — 185
Pyle/H.	Book Of Pirates	Pyle/H.	Harper	(1921)	50 — 75
Pyle/H.	Book Of Pirates	Pyle/H.	Harper	1921	150 — 185

LISTINGS BY AUTHOR

Author	Title	Illustrator	Publisher	Year	Price Range
Pyle/H.	Champions/Round Table (The)	Pyle/H.	Scribner	1905	175 — 225
Pyle/H.	Garden Behind The Moon (The)	Pyle/H.	Scribner	1895	125 — 175
Pyle/H.	Men Of Iron	Pyle/H.	Harper	(1919)	40 — 60
Pyle/H.	Men Of Iron	Pyle/H.	Harper	1892	150 — 200
Pyle/H.	Merry Adv. Of Robin Hood	Pyle/H.	Scribner	(1911)	10 — 20
Pyle/H.	Merry Adv. Of Robin Hood	Pyle/H.	Scribner	1884	150 — 175
Pyle/H.	Merry Adv. Of Robin Hood	Pyle/H.	Scribner	1917	75 — 100
Pyle/H.	Modern Alladin (A)	Pyle/H.	Harper	1892	100 — 130
Pyle/H.	Otto Of The Silver Hand	Pyle/H.	Scribner	1888	175 — 250
Pyle/H.	Pepper & Salt	Pyle/H.	Harper	(1922)	50 — 75
Pyle/H.	Pepper & Salt	Pyle/H.	Harper	1886	275 — 400
Pyle/H.	Price Of Blood (The)	Pyle/H.	Badger	1899	150 — 225
Pyle/H.	Rose Of Paradise (The)	Pyle/H.	Harper	1888	75 — 100
Pyle/H.	Ruby Of Kishmoor (The)	Pyle/H.	Harper	1908	80 — 120
Pyle/H.	Some Merry Adv./Robin Hood	Pyle/H.	Scribner	(1911)	20 — 30
Pyle/H.	Some Merry Adv./Robin Hood	Pyle/H.	Scribner	1902	100 — 150
Pyle/H.	Stolen Treasure	Pyle/H.	Harper	1907	100 — 125
Pyle/H.	Story Of Champ./Round Table	Pyle/H.	Scribner	1905	75 — 100
Pyle/H.	Story Of King Arthur&Knights	Pyle/H.	Scribner	(1933)	40 — 60
Pyle/H.	Story Of King Arthur&Knights	Pyle/H.	Scribner	1903	100 — 175
Pyle/H.	Story Of Sir Launcelot (The)	Pyle/H.	Scribner	1907	175 — 225
Pyle/H.	Story Of The Grail....(The)	Pyle/H.	Scribner	1910	175 — 225
Pyle/H.	Story Of The Grail....(The)	Pyle/H.	Scribner	1927	50 — 75
Pyle/H.	Story/J.Ballister's Fortunes	Pyle/H.	Century	1895	150 — 200
Pyle/H.	Twilight Land	Pyle/H.	Harper	(1894)	40 — 60
Pyle/H.	Twilight Land	Pyle/H.	Harper	(1922)	25 — 40
Pyle/H.	Twilight Land	Pyle/H.	Harrap	1895	75 — 100
Pyle/H.	Within The Capes	Pyle/H.	Int'l Assoc/Np	1901	15 — 30
Pyle/H.	Wonder Clock (The)	Pyle/H.	Harper	1888	200 — 300
Pyle/H.	Wonder Clock (The)	Pyle/H.	Harper	1899	100 — 125
Pyle/H.	Wonder Clock (The)	Pyle/H.	Harper	1915	25 — 35
Pyle/H.	Yankee Doodle	Pyle/H.	Dodd	1881	250 — 300

Q

Author	Title	Illustrator	Publisher	Year	Price Range
Queen Marie	Dreamer Of Dreams	Dulac/E.	H&S	(1915)	250 — 300
Quick/H.	Vandermark's Folly	Wyeth/N.C.	Bobbs-Merrill	(1922)	20 — 40
Quiller-Couch/A.	In Powder & Crinoline	Nielson/K.	H&S	[1913]	700 — 900
Quiller-Couch/A.	Sleeping Beauty/Other Fairy Tales	Dulac/E.	Garden City	(1915)	35 — 65
Quiller-Couch/A.	Sleeping Beauty /Other Fairy Tales	Dulac/E.	Doran	[1910]	125 — 225
Quiller-Couch/A.	Sleeping Beauty/Other Fairy Tales	Dulac/E.	H&S	[1910]	250 — 350
Quiller-Couch/A.	Sleeping Beauty/Other Fairy Tales	Dulac/E.	Doubleday		125 — 225
Quiller-Couch/A.	Twelve Dancing Princesses	Nielson/K.	Doran	[1913]	300 — 400

LISTINGS BY AUTHOR

Author	Title	Illustrator	Publisher	Year	Price Range
Quiller-Couch/A.	Twelve Dancing Princesses	Nielson/K.	Doubleday	1930	75 — 125
Quiller-Couch/A.	Twelve Dancing Princesses	Nielson/K.	Doran		150 — 200

R

Author	Title	Illustrator	Publisher	Year	Price Range
Rackham/A.	A.Rackham's Book Of Pictures	Rackham/A.	Century	(1913)	175 — 250
Rackham/A.	A.Rackham's Book Of Pictures	Rackham/A.	Heinemann	(1913)	300 — 400
Rackham/A.	A.Rackham's Book Of Pictures	Rackham/A.	Heinemann	(1913)	750 — 1000
Rackham/A.	A.Rackham's Book Of Pictures	Rackham/A.	Heinemann		100 — 150
Rackham/A.	Arthur Rackham Fairy Book	Rackham/A.	Harrap	(1933)	175 — 250
Rackham/A.	Arthur Rackham Fairy Book	Rackham/A.	Lippincott	(1933)	100 — 150
Rackham/A.	Arthur Rackham Fairy Book	Rackham/A.	Harrap	1933	1000 — 1500
Rackham/A.	Costume Through The Ages	Rackham/A.	Maggs	1938	125 — 150
Rackham/A.	Fairy Book (A)	Rackham/A.	Dbl.,Page	(1923)	125 — 175
Rackham/A.	Peter Pan Portfolio	Rackham/A.	H&S	(1912)	4000 — 6000
Rackham/A.	Peter Pan Portfolio	Rackham/A.	Brentano's	(1914)	2500 — 3500
Rae/J.	Big Family (The)	Rae/J.	Dodd	1916	50 — 75
Rae/J.	Granny Goose	Rae/J.	Volland	(1926)	100 — 150
Rae/J.	Grasshopper Green &	Rae/J.	Algonquin	(1922)	25 — 35
Rae/J.	Grasshopper Green &	Rae/J.	Volland	(1922)	40 — 60
Rae/J.	Lucky Locket	Rae/J.	Volland	(1928)	50 — 75
Rae/J.	New Adventures Of Alice	Rae/J.	Volland	(1917)	100 — 150
Rae/J.	Why...	Rae/J.	Dodd	1910	75 — 100
Ranking/B.M.	Flowers & Fancies	Greenaway/K.	Marcus Ward	1882	200 — 250
Rawlings/M.K.	Yearling (The)	Wyeth/N.C.	Scribner	1938	100 — 150
Rawlings/M.K.	Yearling (The)	Wyeth/N.C.	Scribner	1940	75 — 100
Rawlings/M.K.	Yearling (The)	Wyeth/N.C.	Scribner	1942	50 — 75
Rawlings/M.K.	Yearling (The)	Wyeth/N.C.	Scribner	1945	25 — 50
Raynor/E.	Free To Serve	Parrish/M.	Copeland/Day	1897	100 — 150
Read/O.	Arkansas Planter	Denslow/W.W.	Rand Mcnally	(1896)	75 — 100
Read/O.	Bolanyo	Parrish/M.	Way/Williams	1897	150 — 200
Read/O.	Waters Of Caney Fork	Denslow/W.W.	Rand Mcnally	1898	40 — 60
Read/T.B.	Closing Scene (The)	Pyle/H.	Lippincott	1887	25 — 35
Reade/C.	Peg Woffington	Thomson/H.	Doubleday	1899	50 — 75
Reade/C.	Peg Woffington	Thomson/H.	G. Allen	1899	65 — 80
Reed/H.L.	Brenda's Summer At Rockley	Smith/J.W.	Little Brown	1901	175 — 225
Reed/H.L.	Brenda's Summer At Rockley	Smith/J.W.	Little Brown	1904	75 — 100
Reed/H.L.	Brenda, Her School/Her Club	Smith/J.W.	Little Brown	1900	175 — 225
Reed/M.	Book Of Clever Beasts (The)	Newell/P.	Putnam	1904	50 — 75
Reid/K.E.J.	Book Of Wedding Days	Crane/W.	Longmans	1889	250 — 300
Rhead/G.W.	Treatment/Drapery In Art	Crane/W.	G. Bell	1904	75 — 125
Rhodes/T.	To The Other Side	Rackham/A.	George Philip	1893	300 — 400
Rhys/E.	Book Of The Titmarsh Club	Rackham/A.	J. Davy	1925	125 — 175

Listings By Author

Author	Title	Illustrator	Publisher	Year	Price Range
Rhys/E.	New Book/Sense & Nonsense	Rackham/A.	Dent	(1928)	50 — 75
Rhys/E.	New Book/Sense & Nonsense	Rackham/A.	Dutton	(1928)	50 — 75
Rich/G. E.	When Mother Lets Us.....	Smith/J.W.	Dodd	1925	50 — 75
Riley/J.W.	An Old Sweetheart Of Mine	Christy/H.C.	Bobbs-Merrill	(1902)	25 — 50
Riley/J.W.	An Old Sweetheart Of Mine	Christy/H.C.	Bobbs-Merrill	(1902)	250 — 350
Riley/J.W.	An Old Sweetheart Of Mine	Christy/H.C.	G&D	(1902)	15 — 25
Riley/J.W.	Home Again	Christy/H.C.	Bobbs-Merrill	(1908)	40 — 75
Riley/J.W.	Home Again With Me	Christy/H.C.	Bobbs-Merrill	(1908)	35 — 60
Riley/J.W.	Out To Old Aunt Mary's	Christy/H.C.	Bobbs-Merrill	(1904)	25 — 40
Riley/J.W.	Riley's Roses	Christy/H.C.	Bobbs-Merrill	(1909)	75 — 100
Riley/J.W.	Rose (The)	Christy/H.C.	Bobbs-Merrill	(1916)	30 — 45
Rinehart/M.R.	Man In The Lower Ten	Christy/H.C.	Bobbs-Merrill	(1909)	35 — 50
Ritchie/L.	Works Of William M.Thackery	Pyle/H.	Harper	1910	30 — 50
Robbins/E.	Under The Southern Cross	Rae/J.	Stokes	(1907)	25 — 40
Roberts/K.	Trending Into Maine	Wyeth/N.C.	Little Brown	1938	75 — 100
Robertson/W.G.	Golden Book Of Sonnets	Pogany/W.	Harrap	1903	100 — 125
Rolleston/T.	Lohengrin	Pogany/W.	Harrap	(1913)	150 — 200
Rolleston/T.	Parsifal	Pogany/W.	Harrap	(1912)	180 — 220
Rollins/P.A.	Jinglebob	Wyeth/N.C.	Scribner	1930	100 — 150
Rosenthal/L.	Kingdom Of The Pearl	Dulac/E.	Brentano's	[1920]	375 — 475
Rossetti/C.	Goblin Market	Rackham/A.	Harrap	(1933)	200 — 250
Rossetti/C.	Goblin Market	Rackham/A.	Lippincott	[1933]	150 — 175
Rossetti/C.	Goblin Market	Rackham/A.	Harrap	1933	750 — 900
Rowland/H.	Countess Diane	Rae/J.	Dodd	1908	35 — 50
Ruskin/J.	Dame Wiggins Of Lee	Greenaway/K.	George Allen	1885	150 — 200
Ruskin/J.	Dame Wiggins Of Lee	Greenaway/K.	George Allen	1897	100 — 125
Ruskin/J.	Dame Wiggins Of Lee	Greenaway/K.	Dutton		75 — 100
Ruskin/J.	Fors Clavigera	Greenaway/K.	George Allen	[1895]	125 — 150
Ruskin/J.	Fors Clavigera	Greenaway/K.	George Allen	1883	200 — 300
Ruskin/J.	King Of The Golden River	Rackham/A.	Harrap	(1932)	150 — 200
Ruskin/J.	King Of The Golden River	Rackham/A.	Harrap	(1932)	600 — 800
Ruskin/J.	King Of The Golden River	Rackham/A.	Lippincott	1932	100 — 150
Russell/M.	April Baby's Book Of Tunes	Greenaway/K.	Macmillan	1900	175 — 225
Russell/T.	Pictures From/Wizard Of Oz	Denslow/W.W.	Ogilvie	[1904]	300 — 400

S

Author	Title	Illustrator	Publisher	Year	Price Range
Sage/A.C.	Little Colonial Dame	Humphrey/M.	Stokes	(1898)	50 — 70
Sage/B.	Rhymes Of Real Children	Smith/J.W.	Duffield	1903	250 — 300
Sage/B.	Rhymes Of Real Children	Smith/J.W.	D. Nutt	1905	150 — 200
Sage/B.	Rhymes Of Real Children	Smith/J.W.	Duffield	1906	150 — 200
Salaman/M.C.	Modern Book Ill.&Their Work	Rackham/A.	The Studio	1914	75 — 125
Saunders/L.	Knave Of Hearts (The)	Parrish/M.	Scribner	1925	750 —1000

LISTINGS BY AUTHOR

Author	Title	Illustrator	Publisher	Year	Price Range
Saunders/L.	Knave Of Hearts (The)	Parrish/M.	Scribner	1925	600 — 800
Saville/E.A.	Memories And Garden	Smith/J.W.	Priv. Prnt	1924	100 — 150
Saville/H.M.	Rhymes & Reminiscences	Smith/J.W.	Stratford	(1929)	50 — 75
Savory/H.	Auld Acquaintance	Rackham/A.	Dent	1907	75 — 100
Schauffer/R.H.	Romantic America	Parrish/M.	Century	1913	75 — 100
Schwimmer/R.	Tisza Tales	Pogany/W.	Doubleday	1928	85 — 100
Scott/Sir W.	Kenilworth	Ford/H.J.	Jack	(1920)	100 — 125
Scott/Sir W.	Kenilworth	Ford/H.J.	McKay		50 — 75
Scott/Sir W.	Lady Of The Lake	Christy/H.C.	Bobbs-Merrill	(1910)	40 — 75
Scudder/H.	Children's Book (The)	Parrish/M.	Houghton	1907	75 — 100
Scudder/H.	History Of The United States	Pyle/H.	Sheldon	1884	25 — 35
Seawell/M.E.	Francezka	Fisher/H.	Bobbs-Merrill	(1902)	30 — 45
Seitz/D.	Bucaneers (The)	Pyle/H.	Harper	1912	50 — 75
Sewell/A.	Black Beauty	Neill/J.R.	R&B	1908	50 — 75
Shakespeare/W.	As You Like It	Thomson/H.	H&S	[1909]	130 — 165
Shakespeare/W.	Merry Wives Of Windsor	Thomson/H.	Stokes	(1910)	100 — 140
Shakespeare/W.	Merry Wives Of Windsor	Crane/W.	Dent	1896	100 — 150
Shakespeare/W.	Merry Wives Of Windsor	Thomson/H.	Heinemann	1910	120 — 160
Shakespeare/W.	Midsummer Night's Dream	Rackham/A.	Lec	(1939)	250 — 350
Shakespeare/W.	Midsummer Night's Dream	Rackham/A.	Doubleday	1908	200 — 250
Shakespeare/W.	Midsummer Night's Dream	Rackham/A.	Heinemann	1908	225 — 325
Shakespeare/W.	Midsummer Night's Dream	Rackham/A.	Heinemann	1908	750 — 1000
Shakespeare/W.	Midsummer Night's Dream	Rackham/A.	Heinemann	1911	125 — 175
Shakespeare/W.	Midsummer Night's Dream	Rackham/A.	Heinemann	1920	175 — 250
Shakespeare/W.	Tempest (The)	Rackham/A.	Dbl.,Page	(1926)	150 — 200
Shakespeare/W.	Tempest (The)	Rackham/A.	Heinemann	(1926)	175 — 250
Shakespeare/W.	Tempest (The)	Rackham/A.	Heinemann	(1926)	1000 — 1250
Shakespeare/W.	Tempest (The)	Dulac/E.	H&S	[1908]	350 — 500
Shakespeare/W.	Tempest (The)	Crane/W.	Dent	1892	100 — 150
Shakespeare/W.	Two Gentlemen Of Verona	Crane/W.	Dent	1894	300 — 500
Shakespeare/W.	Univ.Press Shakespeare	Rackham/A.	Harrap	1908	75 — 100
Shelby/A.B.	Lullaby Book (The)	Smith/J.W.	Duffield	1921	50 — 75
Sheridan/R.B.	School For Scandal (The)	Thomson/H.	H&S	[1911]	100 — 145
Sheridan/R.B.	School For Scandal (The)	Thomson/H.	H&S	[1911]	200 — 300
Sheringham/G.	Drawings In Pen & Pencil	Rackham/A.	The Studio	1922	50 — 75
Sheringham/G.	Drawings In Pen & Pencil	Rackham/A.	The Studio	1922	150 — 200
Sienkiewicz/H.	Quo Vadis	Pyle/H.	Little Brown	1897	30 — 50
Sill/S.C.	Reminiscences/ Of Drawers	Smith/J.W.	Lippincott	1900	75 — 100
Sketchley/R.E.D.	English Book Ill. Of Today	Rackham/A.	Kegan	1903	75 — 100
Sketchley/R.E.D.	English Book Ill. Of Today	Rackham/A.	Kegan	1903	100 — 125
Skinner/A.&E.	Child's Book/Country Stories	Smith/J.W.	Dial Press	(1935)	50 — 75
Skinner/A.&E.	Child's Book/Country Stories	Smith/J.W.	Duffield	1925	175 — 225

LISTINGS BY AUTHOR

Author	Title	Illustrator	Publisher	Year	Price Range
Skinner/A.&E.	Child's Book/Country Stories	Smith/J.W.	Dial Press	1935	75 — 100
Skinner/A.&E.	Child's Book/Modern Stories	Smith/J.W.	Duffield	1920	175 — 225
Skinner/A.&E.	Child's Book/Modern Stories	Smith/J.W.	Dial Press	1935	100 — 125
Skinner/A.&E.	Emerald Story Book (The)	Parrish/M.	Duffield	1917	75 — 150
Skinner/A.&E.	Little Child's Book Of Stories	Smith/J.W.	Dial Press	(1935)	50 — 75
Skinner/A.&E.	Little Child's Book Of Stories	Smith/J.W.	Duffield	1922	125 — 150
Skinner/A.&E.	Little Child's Book Of Stories	Smith/J.W.	Dial Press	1935	75 — 100
Skinner/A.&E.	Topaz Story Book (The)	Parrish/M.	Duffield	1917	75 — 125
Skinner/A.&E.	Turquoise Story Book (The)	Parrish/M.	Duffield	1918	90 — 140
Skinner/A.&E.	Very Little Child's/Stories	Smith/J.W.	Dial Press	(1935)	50 — 75
Skinner/A.&E.	Very Little Child's/Stories	Smith/J.W.	Duffield	1923	125 — 150
Skinner/A.&E.	Very Little Child's/Stories	Smith/J.W.	Dial Press	1935	75 — 100
Smith/A.C.	Turquoise Cup	Parrish/M.	Scribner	1903	50 — 80
Smith/A.C.	Turquoise Cup	Parrish/M.	Scribner	1910	25 — 40
Smith/C.	Odes & Epodes Of Horace (The)	Pyle/H.	Biblio. Soc.	1901	50 — 75
Smith/C.M.	Queen Bee (The)	Dulac/E.	Nelson	1907	100 — 150
Smith/E.S.	Book Of Lullabies (A)	Smith/J.W.	Lothrop	(1925)	25 — 50
Smith/F.H.	American Illustrators	Pyle/H.	Scribner	1892	75 — 100
Smith/J.W.	Baby's Red Letter Days	Smith/J.W.	Just Foods	(1906)	100 — 200
Smith/J.W.	Baby's Red Letter Days	Smith/J.W.	Just Foods	[1901]	200 — 300
Smith/J.W.	Child's Book Of Old Verses (A)	Smith/J.W.	Duffield	(1910)	125 — 150
Smith/J.W.	Child's Book Of Old Verses (A)	Smith/J.W.	Dial Press	(1935)	50 — 75
Smith/J.W.	Child's Book Of Old Verses (A)	Smith/J.W.	Duffield	1910	175 — 225
Smith/J.W.	Child's Book Of Old Verses (A)	Smith/J.W.	Dial Press	1935	75 — 100
Smith/J.W.	Child's Book Of Verses (A)	Smith/J.W.	Chatto/Windus	1912	100 — 125
Smith/J.W.	Child's Stamp Book/Old Verses	Smith/J.W.	Duffield	1915	125 — 175
Smith/J.W.	Dickens's Children	Smith/J.W.	Chatto/Windus	1912	125 — 175
Smith/J.W.	Dickens's Children	Smith/J.W.	Scribner	1912	125 — 175
Smith/J.W.	Dickens's Children	Smith/J.W.	Scribner	1912	100 — 150
Smith/J.W.	Dickens's Children	Smith/J.W.	Chatto/Windus	1913	100 — 125
Smith/J.W.	Little Mother Goose (The)	Smith/J.W.	Dodd	(1918)	125 — 160
Smith/J.W.	Little Mother Goose (The)	Smith/J.W.	Dodd	(1918)	100 — 125
Smith/J.W.	Little Mother Goose (The)	Smith/J.W.	Musson	1921	75 — 100
Smith/J.W.	Mother Goose	Smith/J.W.	Dodd	(1912)	175 — 250
Smith/J.W.	Mother Goose	Smith/J.W.	Dodd	(1916)	125 — 150
Smith/J.W.	Mother Goose	Smith/J.W.	H&S	(1938)	75 — 100
Smith/J.W.	Mother Goose	Smith/J.W.	H&S	[1920]	125 — 150
Smith/M.P.W.	Young Puritans In Captivity	Smith/J.W.	Little Brown	1899	100 — 160
Smith/M.P.W.	Young Puritans In Captivity	Smith/J.W.	Little Brown	1907	50 — 75
Smith/N.	Boys & Girls Of Bookland	Smith/J.W.	McKay	(1923)	100 — 150
Smith/N.	Boys & Girls Of Bookland	Smith/J.W.	McKay	(1923)	75 — 100
Smith/N.	Boys & Girls Of Bookland	Smith/J.W.	Cosmopolitan	1923	150 — 175

LISTINGS BY AUTHOR

Author	Title	Illustrator	Publisher	Year	Price Range
Snyder/F.	Lovely Garden	Rae/J.	Volland	(1919)	50 — 75
Snyder/F.	Rhymes For Kindly Children	Gruelle/J.	Volland	(1916)	100 — 150
Sousa/J.P.	Fifth String (The)	Christy/H.C.	Bowen/M	(1902)	10 — 20
Spearman/F.	Nan Of Music Mountain	Wyeth/N.C.	G&D	(1916)	15 — 25
Spearman/F.	Nan Of Music Mountain	Wyeth/N.C.	Scribner	1916	20 — 40
Spearman/F.	Whispering Smith	Wyeth/N.C.	Scribner	1906	35 — 55
Spearman/F.	Whispering Smith	Wyeth/N.C.	Scribner	1908	15 — 25
Spearman/F.	Whispering Smith	Wyeth/N.C.	G&D		15 — 25
Spenser/E.	Faerie Queen (The)	Crane/W.	George Allen	1895	150 — 200
Spenser/E.	Shepheard's Calander	Crane/W.	Harper	1898	150 — 175
Spielman/M.H.	My Son & I	Thomson/H.	G. Allen	1908	50 — 75
Spielmann/M.H.	Hugh Thomson: His Art	Thomson/H.	A&C Black	1931	85 — 125
Spielmann/M.H.	K.Greenaway: 16 Examples......	Greenaway/K.	A&C Black	1910	100 — 150
Spielmann/M.H.	K.Greenaway: 16 Examples......	Greenaway/K.	A&C Black	1911	75 — 125
Spielmann/M.H.	Kate Greenaway	Greenaway/K.	A&C Black	1905	75 — 150
Spielmann/Mrs.	Littledom Castle/Other Tales	Rackham/A.	Routledge	(1912)	75 — 100
Spielmann/Mrs.	Littledom Castle/Other Tales	Rackham/A.	Dutton	1903	125 — 150
Spielmann/Mrs.	Littledom Castle/Other Tales	Rackham/A.	Routledge	1903	150 — 200
Spielmann/Mrs.	Rainbow Book (The)	Rackham/A.	Chatto/Windus	1909	150 — 175
Spielmann/Mrs.	Rainbow Book (The)	Thomson/H.	Chatto/Windus	1909	150 — 175
Spielmann/Mrs.	Rainbow Book (The)	Rackham/A.			125 — 150
Spielmann/Mrs.	Rainbow Book (The)	Thomson/H.			125 — 150
Spyri/J.	Heidi	Smith/J.W.	McKay	(1922)	100 — 150
Spyri/J.	Heidi	Smith/J.W.	McKay	1922	125 — 175
Spyri/J.	Heidi	Smith/J.W.	Dial Press	1935	75 — 100
Stacpoole/H.	Blue Lagoon	Pogany/W.	Unwin	1910	150 — 180
Starkie/W.	Don Gypsy	Rackham/A.	John Murray	(1936)	40 — 80
Starkie/W.	Raggle-Taggle Adv./A Fiddle	Rackham/A.	Dutton	(1933)	40 — 60
Starkie/W.	Raggle-Taggle Adv./A Fiddle	Rackham/A.	John Murray	(1933)	50 — 75
Starkie/W.	Spanish Raggle-Taggle......	Rackham/A.	John Murray	(1934)	75 — 100
Starkie/W.	Spanish Raggle-Taggle........	Rackham/A.	Dutton	1934	50 — 75
Staver/M.W.	New & True	Smith/J.W.	Lee & Shepard	1892	75 — 100
Stawell/R.	Fairies I Have Met	Dulac/E.	J. Lane	(1907)	250 — 300
Stawell/R.	Fairies I Have Met	Dulac/E.	H&S	[1910]	225 — 275
Stawell/R.	My Day With The Fairies	Dulac/E.	H&S	[1913]	225 — 325
Stawell/R.	My Day With The Fairies	Dulac/E.	H&S	[1915]	150 — 200
Stedman/E.C.	Star Bearer (The)	Pyle/H.	Lothrop	[1888]	100 — 125
Steele/F.A.	English Fairy Tales	Rackham/A.	Macmillan	1918	750 — 900
Steele/F.A.	English Fairy Tales	Rackham/A.	Macmillan	1918	200 — 250
Steele/F.A.	English Fairy Tales	Rackham/A.	Macmillan	1918	175 — 250
Steele/F.A.	English Fairy Tales	Rackham/A.	Macmillan	1918	250 — 350
Steele/F.A.	English Fairy Tales	Rackham/A.	Macmillan	1919	125 — 175

Listings By Author

Author	Title	Illustrator	Publisher	Year	Price Range
Steele/F.A.	English Fairy Tales	Rackham/A.	Macmillan	1930	50 — 75
Stein/E.	Troubadour Tales	Parrish/M.	Bobbs-Merrill	(1903)	75 — 100
Stein/E.	Troubadour Tales	Parrish/M.	Bobbs-Merrill	1929	25 — 40
Stephens/J.	Irish Fairy Tales	Rackham/A.	Macmillan	1920	850 — 1000
Stephens/J.	Irish Fairy Tales	Rackham/A.	Macmillan	1920	175 — 250
Stephens/J.	Irish Fairy Tales	Rackham/A.	Macmillan	1920	175 — 250
Stephens/J.	Irish Fairy Tales	Rackham/A.	Macmillan	1924	125 — 175
Stephens/R.N.	Captain Ravenshaw	Pyle/H.	L.C. Page	1901	20 — 30
Stevenson/B.E.	Home Book Of Verse/Folks	Pogany/W.	Holt	(1922)	25 — 50
Stevenson/R.L.	Black Arrow (The)	Wyeth/N.C.	Scribner	1916	150 — 175
Stevenson/R.L.	Black Arrow (The)	Wyeth/N.C.	Scribner	1927	60 — 90
Stevenson/R.L.	Child's Garden Of Verses	Gutmann/B.P.	Dodge	(1905)	100 — 150
Stevenson/R.L.	Child's Garden Of Verses	Gutmann/B.P.	Dodge	(1908)	75 — 100
Stevenson/R.L.	Child's Garden Of Verses (A)	Smith/J.W.	Longmans	1905	125 — 250
Stevenson/R.L.	Child's Garden Of Verses (A)	Smith/J.W.	Scribner	1905	125 — 250
Stevenson/R.L.	Child's Garden Of Verses (A)	Smith/J.W.	Scribner	1925	75 — 100
Stevenson/R.L.	Child's Garden Of Verses (A)	Smith/J.W.	Scribner	1944	30 — 75
Stevenson/R.L.	Child's Garden Of Verses (A)	Smith/J.W.	Scribner	1945	30 — 75
Stevenson/R.L.	David Balfour	Pyle/H.	Scribner	1895	25 — 50
Stevenson/R.L.	David Balfour	Wyeth/N.C.	Scribner	1924	100 — 150
Stevenson/R.L.	David Balfour	Wyeth/N.C.	Scribner	1927	45 — 75
Stevenson/R.L.	Kidnapped	Wyeth/N.C.	Scribner	(1941)	35 — 50
Stevenson/R.L.	Kidnapped	Pyle/H.	Scribner	1895	75 — 100
Stevenson/R.L.	Kidnapped	Wyeth/N.C.	Scribner	1913	150 — 200
Stevenson/R.L.	Kidnapped	Wyeth/N.C.	Scribner	1940	40 — 65
Stevenson/R.L.	Merry Men/Other Tales....	Pyle/H.	Scribner	1895	75 — 100
Stevenson/R.L.	Treasure Island	Wyeth/N.C.	Scribner	(1939)	50 — 75
Stevenson/R.L.	Treasure Island	Dulac/E.	Doran	[1927]	125 — 175
Stevenson/R.L.	Treasure Island	Dulac/E.	Garden City	[1939]	40 — 60
Stevenson/R.L.	Treasure Island	Wyeth/N.C.	Scribner	1911	175 — 225
Stevenson/R.L.	Treasure Island	Dulac/E.	Doubleday		125 — 175
Stewart/E.P.	Letters/Woman Homesteader	Wyeth/N.C.	Houghton	1914	40 — 60
Stewart/M.	Way To Wonderland (The)	Smith/J.W.	Dodd	(1917)	170 — 240
Stewart/M.	Way To Wonderland (The)	Smith/J.W.	Dodd	(1917)	150 — 200
Stewart/M.	Way To Wonderland (The)	Smith/J.W.	H&S	[1920]	200 — 250
Stockton/F.	Afield & Afloat	Newell/P.	Scribner	1900	40 — 60
Stockton/F.	Great Stone Of Sardis	Newell/P.	Harper	1898	50 — 75
Stockton/F.	Story Teller's Pack	Newell/P.	Copp	1897	50 — 75
Stone/S.B.	Kingdom Of Why	Newell/P.	Bobbs-Merrill	(1913)	100 — 150
Stuart/R.M.	Sonny's Father	Smith/J.W.	Century	1910	70 — 90
Swift/J.	Gulliver's Travels	Rackham/A.	Dent	(1904)	75 — 125
Swift/J.	Gulliver's Travels	Rackham/A.	Dent	[1912]	100 — 125

LISTINGS BY AUTHOR

Author	Title	Illustrator	Publisher	Year	Price Range
Swift/J.	Gulliver's Travels	Rackham/A.	Temple Press	[1937]	40 — 60
Swift/J.	Gulliver's Travels	Rackham/A.	Dent	1900	150 — 200
Swift/J.	Gulliver's Travels	Rackham/A.	Dent	1901	50 — 100
Swift/J.	Gulliver's Travels	Rackham/A.	Dent	1909	250 — 300
Swift/J.	Gulliver's Travels	Rackham/A.	Dent	1909	750 — 1000
Swift/J.	Gulliver's Travels	Rackham/A.	Dutton	1909	175 — 225
Swift/J.	Gulliver's Travels	Rackham/A.	Temple Press	1939	30 — 50
Swinburne/A.C.	Springtide Of Life	Rackham/A.	Heinemann	(1918)	250 — 300
Swinburne/A.C.	Springtide Of Life	Rackham/A.	Heinemann	(1918)	200 — 250
Swinburne/A.C.	Springtide Of Life	Rackham/A.	Heinemann	(1918)	750 — 1000
Swinburne/A.C.	Springtide Of Life	Rackham/A.	Heinemann	(1918)	50 — 75
Swinburne/A.C.	Springtide Of Life	Rackham/A.	Lippincott	(1918)	100 — 150
Swinton/W.	First Lessons/History	Pyle/H.	Am. Book Co	1894	20 — 30
Swinton/W.	School History Of The U.S.	Pyle/H.	Am. Book Co	1893	20 — 30

T

Author	Title	Illustrator	Publisher	Year	Price Range
Tagore/R.	Stray Birds	Pogany/W.	Macmillan	1917	30 — 40
Tate/W.J.	East Coast Scenery	Rackham/A.	Jarrold	1899	100 — 150
Taylor/J.	Ann & Other Poems	Greenaway/K.	Routledge	[1882]	200 — 225
Taylor/J.&A.	Little Ann & Other Poems	Greenaway/K.	Routledge	[1883]	150 — 200
Taylor/J.&A.	Little Ann & Other Poems	Greenaway/K.	Warne	[1900]	100 — 150
Taylor/M.I.	Little Mistress Goodhope	Smith/J.W.	McClurg	(1902)	100 — 125
Taylor/M.I.	Little Mistress Goodhope	Smith/J.W.	McClurg	1902	150 — 175
Tennant/P.	Children & Pictures (The)	Rackham/A.	Heinemann	1907	100 — 150
Tennant/P.	Children & Pictures (The)	Rackham/A.	Macmillan	1907	100 — 150
Tennyson/A.	Lady Of Shalott (The)	Pyle/H.	Dodd	(1881)	350 — 450
Tennyson/A.	Princess (The)	Christy/H.C.	Bobbs-Merrill	(1911)	75 — 100
Thackeray/W.M.	Chronicle Of The Drum (The)	Pyle/H.	Scribner	1882	25 — 35
Thackeray/W.M.	Henry Esmond	Thomson/H.	Macmillan		50 — 75
Thackeray/W.M.	History/Henry Esmond	Thomson/H.	Macmillan	1905	50 — 75
The Philistine	New Fiction & Other Papers	Rackham/A.	West. Gaz.	1895	75 — 100
Thomas	G.W.Lincoln Goes/World	Pogany/W.	Nelson		50 — 75
Thomas/E.	Songs/Jingles/Rhymes	Humphrey/M.	Stokes	(1894)	250 — 350
Thomas/E.	Tiny Folk/Wintery Days	Humphrey/M.	Stokes	1889	500 — 650
Thomas/E.M.	Babes Of The Nations	Humphrey/M.	Stokes	1889	400 — 600
Thompson/R.P.	Captain Salt In Oz	Neill/J.R.	R&L	(1936)	200 — 300
Thompson/R.P.	Captain Salt In Oz	Neill/J.R.	R&L	(1936)	40 — 60
Thompson/R.P.	Cowardly Lion Of Oz (The)	Neill/J.R.	R&L	(1923)	300 — 400
Thompson/R.P.	Cowardly Lion Of Oz (The)	Neill/J.R.	R&L	(1923)	100 — 150
Thompson/R.P.	Cowardly Lion Of Oz (The)	Neill/J.R.	R&L	(1923)	40 — 60
Thompson/R.P.	Curious Cruise/Captain Santa	Neill/J.R.	R&L	(1926)	200 — 300
Thompson/R.P.	Giant Horse Of Oz (The)	Neill/J.R.	R&L	(1928)	200 — 250

LISTINGS BY AUTHOR

Author	Title	Illustrator	Publisher	Year	Price Range
Thompson/R.P.	Giant Horse Of Oz (The)	Neill/J.R.	R&L	(1928)	125 — 175
Thompson/R.P.	Giant Horse Of Oz (The)	Neill/J.R.	R&L	(1928)	40 — 60
Thompson/R.P.	Gnome King Of Oz (The)	Neill/J.R.	R&L	(1927)	400 — 600
Thompson/R.P.	Gnome King Of Oz (The)	Neill/J.R.	R&L	(1927)	40 — 60
Thompson/R.P.	Handy Mandy In Oz	Neill/J.R.	R&L	(1937)	150 — 200
Thompson/R.P.	Handy Mandy In Oz	Neill/J.R.	R&L	(1937)	40 — 60
Thompson/R.P.	Hungry Tiger Of Oz (The)	Neill/J.R.	R&L	(1926)	200 — 300
Thompson/R.P.	Hungry Tiger Of Oz (The)	Neill/J.R.	R&L	(1926)	150 — 200
Thompson/R.P.	Hungry Tiger Of Oz (The)	Neill/J.R.	R&L	(1926)	40 — 60
Thompson/R.P.	Jack Pumpkinhead Of Oz	Neill/J.R.	R&L	(1929)	250 — 350
Thompson/R.P.	Jack Pumpkinhead Of Oz	Neill/J.R.	R&L	(1929)	40 — 60
Thompson/R.P.	Kabumpo In Oz	Neill/J.R.	R&L	(1922)	200 — 300
Thompson/R.P.	Kabumpo In Oz	Neill/J.R.	R&L	(1922)	125 — 175
Thompson/R.P.	Kabumpo In Oz	Neill/J.R.	R&L	(1922)	40 — 60
Thompson/R.P.	Lost King Of Oz (The)	Neill/J.R.	R&L	(1925)	200 — 300
Thompson/R.P.	Lost King Of Oz (The)	Neill/J.R.	R&L	(1925)	125 — 175
Thompson/R.P.	Lost King Of Oz (The)	Neill/J.R.	R&L	(1925)	40 — 60
Thompson/R.P.	Ojo In Oz	Neill/J.R.	R&L	(1933)	200 — 300
Thompson/R.P.	Ojo In Oz	Neill/J.R.	R&L	(1933)	40 — 60
Thompson/R.P.	Ojo In Oz	Neill/J.R.	R&L	(1933)	100 — 150
Thompson/R.P.	Ozoplanning/Wizard Of Oz	Neill/J.R.	R&L	(1939)	175 — 250
Thompson/R.P.	Ozoplanning/Wizard Of Oz	Neill/J.R.	R&L	(1939)	40 — 60
Thompson/R.P.	Pirates In Oz	Neill/J.R.	R&L	(1931)	200 — 300
Thompson/R.P.	Pirates In Oz	Neill/J.R.	R&L	(1931)	40 — 60
Thompson/R.P.	Purple Prince Of Oz (The)	Neill/J.R.	R&L	(1932)	250 — 350
Thompson/R.P.	Purple Prince Of Oz (The)	Neill/J.R.	R&L	(1932)	40 — 60
Thompson/R.P.	Purple Prince Of Oz (The)	Neill/J.R.	R&L	(1932)	125 — 150
Thompson/R.P.	Royal Book Of Oz (The)	Neill/J.R.	R&L	(1921)	250 — 350
Thompson/R.P.	Royal Book Of Oz (The)	Neill/J.R.	R&L	(1921)	100 — 150
Thompson/R.P.	Royal Book Of Oz (The)	Neill/J.R.	R&L	(1921)	40 — 60
Thompson/R.P.	Silver Princess In Oz	Neill/J.R.	R&L	(1938)	200 — 300
Thompson/R.P.	Silver Princess In Oz	Neill/J.R.	R&L	(1938)	40 — 60
Thompson/R.P.	Speedy In Oz	Neill/J.R.	R&L	(1934)	200 — 300
Thompson/R.P.	Speedy In Oz	Neill/J.R.	R&L	(1934)	40 — 60
Thompson/R.P.	Wishing Horse Of Oz (The)	Neill/J.R.	R&L	(1935)	250 — 350
Thompson/R.P.	Wishing Horse Of Oz (The)	Neill/J.R.	R&L	(1935)	40 — 60
Thompson/R.P.	Yellow Knight Of Oz (The)	Neill/J.R.	R&L	(1930)	350 — 500
Thompson/R.P.	Yellow Knight Of Oz (The)	Neill/J.R.	R&L	(1930)	100 — 150
Thompson/R.P.	Yellow Knight Of Oz (The)	Neill/J.R.	R&L	(1930)	40 — 60
Thomson/H.	Jack The Giant Killer	Thomson/H.	Macmillan	1898	160 — 200
Thoreau/H.D.	Men Of Concord	Wyeth/N.C.	Houghton	1936	175 — 225
Thorpe/J.	English Illustration:Nineties	Rackham/A.	Faber	1935	50 — 75

LISTINGS BY AUTHOR

Author	Title	Illustrator	Publisher	Year	Price Range
Toogood/C.C.	Child's Prayer (A)	Smith/J.W.	McKay	(1925)	40 — 60
Toogood/C.C.	Child's Prayer (A)	Smith/J.W.	McKay	(1925)	30 — 50
Tucker/E.S.	Book Of Pets	Humphrey/M.	Gardner	1897	400 — 600
Tucker/E.S.	Little Grownups	Humphrey/M.	Stokes	1897	400 — 600
Tucker/E.S.	Little Ones	Humphrey/M.	Stokes	1898	350 — 500
Tucker/E.S.	Littlest Ones (The)	Humphrey/M.	Stokes	1898	300 — 400
Tucker/E.S.	Make-Belive Men & Women	Humphrey/M.	Stokes	(1897)	380 — 500
Tucker/E.S.	Old Youngsters	Humphrey/M.	Stokes	(1897)	300 — 400
Turkington/G.	My Country	Wyeth/N.C.	Ginn	1923	15 — 25
Twain/M.	Adventure Of Tom Sawyer	Wyeth/N.C.	Winston	1931	25 — 50
Twain/M.	Mysterious Stranger (The)	Wyeth/N.C.	Harper	(1916)	100 — 150
Twain/M.	Mysterious Stranger (The)	Wyeth/N.C.	Harper	(1916)	75 — 100
Twain/M.	Saint Joan Of Arc	Pyle/H.	Harper	1919	75 — 100
Twain/M.	St. Joan Of Arc	Pyle/H.	Harper	(1919)	75 — 125

U

Underwood/P.	When Christmas Comes Around	Smith/J.W.	Chatto/Windus	1915	175 — 200
Underwood/P.	When Christmas Comes Around	Smith/J.W.	Duffield	1915	175 — 200

V

Van Dyke/H.	Blue Flower (The)	Pyle/H.	Scribner	1902	25 — 50
Van Dyke/H.	Blue Flower (The)	Pyle/H.	Scribner	1909	15 — 25
Van Dyke/H.	Even Unto Bethlehem	Wyeth/N.C.	Scribner	1928	30 — 50
Van Dyke/H.	First Christmas Tree (The)	Pyle/H.	Scribner	1897	35 — 50
Van Dyke/H.	Lost Boy (The)	Wyeth/N.C.	Harper	(1914)	20 — 30
Various	Wayfarer's Love	Crane/W.	Constable	1904	50 — 75
Veale/E.	Captivating Stories Of Animals	Cox/P.	Juv. Pub.	(1908)	75 — 125
Verne/J.	Michael Strogoff	Wyeth/N.C.	Scribner	1927	150 — 200
Verne/J.	Mysterious Island	Wyeth/N.C.	Scribner	1918	175 — 225
Verne/J.	Mysterious Island	Wyeth/N.C.	Scribner	1946	30 — 50
Viele/H.K.	Heartbreak Hill	Rae/J.	Duffield	1908	40 — 60
Von Hutten/B.	One Way Out	Fisher/H.	Dodd	1906	30 — 40
Vorse/M.H.	Very Little Person	O'Neill/R.	Houghton	1911	40 — 60

W

Wagner/R.	Lohengrin	Pogany/W.	Crowell	(1913)	100 — 150
Wagner/R.	Rhinegold & The Valkyrie (The)	Rackham/A.	Dbl.,Page	1910	150 — 175
Wagner/R.	Rhinegold & The Valkyrie (The)	Rackham/A.	Heinemann	1910	200 — 300
Wagner/R.	Rhinegold & The Valkyrie (The)	Rackham/A.	Heinemann	1910	750 — 1000
Wagner/R.	Rhinegold & The Valkyrie (The)	Rackham/A.	Garden City	1939	75 — 100
Wagner/R.	Ring Of The Niblung (The)	Rackham/A.	Garden City	(1939)	50 — 100
Wagner/R.	Ring Of The Niblung (The)	Rackham/A.	Heinemann	(1939)	75 — 125

LISTINGS BY AUTHOR

Author	Title	Illustrator	Publisher	Year	Price Range
Wagner/R.	Siegfried/Twilight Of The Gods	Rackham/A.	Heinemann	(1911)	100 — 150
Wagner/R.	Siegfried/Twilight Of The Gods	Rackham/A.	Dbl.,Page	1911	175 — 275
Wagner/R.	Siegfried/Twilight Of The Gods	Rackham/A.	Heinemann	1911	200 — 350
Wagner/R.	Siegfried/Twilight Of The Gods	Rackham/A.	Heinemann	1911	300 — 400
Wagner/R.	Siegfried/Twilight Of The Gods	Rackham/A.	Heinemann	1911	800 — 1000
Wagner/R.	Siegfried/Twilight Of The Gods	Rackham/A.	Garden City	1930	75 — 125
Wagner/R.	Tannhauser	Pogany/W.	Harrap	(1911)	175 — 250
Wagner/R.	Tannhauser	Pogany/W.	Brentano's		75 — 100
Walton/I.	Compleat Angler (The)	Rackham/A.	Harrap	(1931)	225 — 275
Walton/I.	Compleat Angler (The)	Rackham/A.	Harrap	(1931)	250 — 300
Walton/I.	Compleat Angler (The)	Rackham/A.	Harrap	[1931]	750 — 1000
Walton/I.	Compleat Angler (The)	Rackham/A.	McKay	[1931]	125 — 175
Ward/H.P.	Some Am.College Bookplates	Pyle/H.		1915	50 — 75
Washburne/E.B.	Recollect./Minister To France	Pyle/H.	Scribner	1889	30 — 60
Waterman	Ben King's Verse	Denslow/W.W.		1894	75 — 100
Waugh/I.	Ideal Heads	Smith/J.W.	Sunshine	1890	50 — 75
Weatherby/F.E.	Ill.Children's Birthday Book	Greenaway/K.	Mack	1882	75 — 100
Weatherly/G.	Little Folks Painting Book	Greenaway/K.	Cassell	1879	125 — 175
Webb/R.	Me & Lawson	Denslow/W.W.	Dillingham	(1905)	75 — 100
Welch/D.	Story Of Louise	Denslow/W.W.		1901	50 — 75
Wells/C.	Beauties	Fisher/H.	Dodd	1913	225 — 300
Wells/C.	Merry-Go-Round	Newell/P.	Russell	1901	100 — 150
Wells/C.	Mother Goose's Menagerie	Newell/P.	Noyes	1901	175 — 225
Wells/C.	Seven Ages Of Childhood (The)	Smith/J.W.	Donohue	(1909)	100 — 125
Wells/C.	Seven Ages Of Childhood (The)	Smith/J.W.	Moffat	1909	250 — 350
Wells/C.	Seven Ages Of Childhood (The)	Smith/J.W.	Duffield	1921	100 — 125
Wells/H.G.	Wonderful Visit (The)	Rackham/A.	Dent	1895	125 — 150
West/P.	Pearl & The Pumpkin	Denslow/W.W.	Dillingham	(1904)	200 — 250
West/P.	Pearl & The Pumpkin	Denslow/W.W.	Donohue	[1911]	125 — 150
Weyman/S.	Castle Inn (The)	Rackham/A.	Smith,Elder	[1900]	50 — 75
Weyman/S.	Castle Inn (The)	Rackham/A.	Smith,Elder	1898	100 — 125
Wharton/E.	Italian Villas & Their Gardens	Parrish/M.	Century	1904	200 — 300
White/S.E.	Arizona Nights	Wyeth/N.C.	G&D	(1907)	10 — 20
White/S.E.	Arizona Nights	Wyeth/N.C.	McClure	1907	50 — 75
White/S.E.	Riverman (The)	Wyeth/N.C.	McClure	1908	40 — 60
Whitford/W.G.	Art Stories - Book One	Smith/J.W.	Scott,Fore.	[1933]	35 — 50
Whitney/H.H.	Bed-Time Book (The)	Smith/J.W.	Chatto/Windus	1907	225 — 275
Whitney/H.H.	Bed-Time Book (The)	Smith/J.W.	Duffield	1907	225 — 275
Whittier/J.G.	Captain's Well (The)	Pyle/H.	N Y Ledger	1890	50 — 75
Whittier/J.G.	Snow Bound	Pyle/H.	Houghton	1906	60 — 80
Whittier/J.G.	Snowbound	Neill/J.R.	R&B	(1909)	40 — 60
Wiggin/K.D.	Arabian Nights (The)	Parrish/M.	Scribner	(1937)	50 — 90

Listings By Author

Author	Title	Illustrator	Publisher	Year	Price Range
Wiggin/K.D.	Arabian Nights (The)	Parrish/M.	Scribner	1909	125 — 200
Wiggin/K.D.	Arabian Nights (The)	Parrish/M.	Scribner	1919	100 — 175
Wiggin/K.D.	Arabian Nights (The)	Parrish/M.	Scribner	1935	50 — 90
Wiggin/K.D.	Scottish Chiefs	Wyeth/N.C.	Scribner	1921	125 — 175
Wiggin/K.D.	Scottish Chiefs	Wyeth/N.C.	Scribner	1934	65 — 85
Wiggin/K.D.	Susanna & Sue	Wyeth/N.C.	Houghton	1909	40 — 60
Wilde/O.	Happy Prince (The)	Crane/W.	D. Nutt	1888	300 — 400
Wilkins/M.E.	Giles Corey, Yeoman	Pyle/H.	Harper	1893	25 — 50
Wilkins/M.E.	Silence & Other Stories	Pyle/H.	Harper	1898	20 — 30
Wilkins/M.E.	Wind In The Rose Bush	Newell/P.	Doubleday	1903	50 — 75
Williamson/H.	Gods & Mortals In Love	Dulac/E.	Country Life	(1935)	75 — 100
Wilson/H.	Boss Of The Little Arcady	O'Neill/R.	L.L. & S.	1905	30 — 50
Wilson/H.L.	Lions Of The Lord	O'Neill/R.	Lothrop	(1903)	40 — 60
Wilson/H.L.	Seeker (The)	O'Neill/R.	Doubleday	1904	25 — 40
Wilson/R.	Red Magic	Nielson/K.	J. Cape	(1930)	400 — 600
Wilson/W.	George Washington	Pyle/H.	Harper	1897	50 — 75
Wilson/W.	History Of/American People	Pyle/H.	Harper	1902	75 — 100
Wilson/W.	History Of/American People	Pyle/H.	Harper	1918	50 — 75
Winter/A.A.	Jewel Weed	Fisher/H.	Bobbs-Merrill	(1910)	20 — 30
Wise/J.	New Forest/History & Scenery	Crane/W.	Smith,Elder	1863	150 — 200
Wise/J.R.	First Of May (The)	Crane/W.	Southeran	1881	100 — 150
Wise/J.R.	First Of May (The)	Crane/W.	Southeran	1881	350 — 500
Wister/O.	Mother	Rae/J.	Dodd	1907	25 — 45
Wright/H.B.	Uncrowned King	Neill/J.R.	Book Supply	1910	50 — 75

Y

Yeats/W.B.	Four Plays/Dancers	Dulac/E.	Macmillan	1921	100 — 150
Yonge/C.	Heartsease/Brothers Wife	Greenaway/K.	Macmillan	(1902)	100 — 125
Yonge/C.	Heartsease/Brothers Wife	Greenaway/K.	Macmillan	1879	125 — 175
Yonge/C.	Heartsease/Brothers Wife	Greenaway/K.	Macmillan	1897	50 — 75
Yonge/C.	Heir Of Redclyffe (The)	Greenaway/K.	Macmillan	1881	75 — 100
Yonge/C.	Heir Of Redclyffe (The)	Greenaway/K.	Macmillan	1881	100 — 150
Yonge/C.	Heir Of Redclyffe (The)	Greenaway/K.	Macmillan	1902	50 — 75
Young/G.	Witch's Kitchen	Pogany/W.	Crowell	(1912)	120 — 160
Young/G.	Witch's Kitchen	Pogany/W.	Harrap	1910	150 — 180

DEALER LIST

DEALER LIST

The following is a list of Booksellers that specialize in Children's or Illustrated Books. This is by no means a recommendation of these dealers by the author. If we have not included any dealer that should be listed, please let us know and we will include them in the next edition.

There is no charge for these listings.

It is recommended that you call as some of these dealers are by appointment or catalogue only and some may have unusual hours.

DEALER	STREET
A. Dalrymple, Bookseller	1791 Graefield
Aleph-Bet Books	218 Waters Edge
Ann Dumler Books	645 Melrose
Banbury Cross	992 Oakdale Road N.E.
Barbara Stone Rare Books	135 Kings Rd.
Barnaby Rudge Bookseller	1475 Glenneyre St.
Bleak House Books	P.O. Box 1465
Book Baron (The)	1236 S. Magnolia Ave.
Book Gallery	1181 N. "E" St.
Book Lady	P.O. box 2544
Bookstall (The)	570 Sutter St.
C.M. Lee fine Books	224 Ridgway Ave.
Caravan Books Annex	P.O. Box 861
Carol Docheff Bookseller	1390 Reliez Valley Rd.
Cattermole Books	9880 Fairmount Rd.
Charlotte F. Safir	1349 Lexington Ave. 9B
Children's Book Adoption Agency	P.O. Box 643
Children's Bookshop (The)	Toll Cottage, Pontvaen
D.R. Friedlander,Antiques	1341 Bardstown Rd.
Deirdre's Books	8110 Northfield Rd.
Dorothy G. Cook	80 Hollins Dr.
Dorothy J. Sawyer Books	P.O. Box 44
Dorothy Meyer	10751 S. Hoyne Ave.
Dower House	P.O. Box 76
Drusilla's Books	859 N. Howard St.
Edward T. Pollack	236 Beacon St.
Elaine Woodford	P.O. Box 68
Elaine's Upper Story	1234 Larke Ave.
Enchanted Books	2435 Ocean Ave. #6J
Garcia-Garst Booksellers	2857 Geer Suite C
Heritage Book Shop	8540 Melrose Ave.
Hobby Horse Books	P.O. Box 591
Jane Adams Bookshop	208 N. Neil St.
Jo Ann Reisler, Ltd.	360 Glyndon St. NE
Justin G. Schiller	135 E. 57th St. 12th Floor
Linda E. Strike	36 Portuguese Rd.

DEALER LIST

CITY	STATE	ZIP	PHONE
Birmingham	MI	48009	(810)649-2149
Valley Cottage	NY	10989	(914)268-7410
Kenilworth,	IL	60043	(708)251-2035
Atlanta,	GA	30307	(404)373-3511
Chelsea	London	SW3 4PW	(071)351-0963
Laguna Beach	CA	92651	(714)497-4079
Thousand Oaks	CA	91358	
Anaheim	CA	92804	(714)527-7022
San Bernardino	CA	92410	
Atherton	CA	94025	(415)324-1201
San Francisco	CA	94102	(415)362-6353
Santa Rosa	CA	95401	(707)526-4546
Stillwater	OK	74076	
Lafayette	CA	94549	(510)935-9595
Newbury	OH	44065	(216)338-3253
New York	NY	10128	(212)534-7933
Kensington	MD	20895	(301)565-2834
Hay-On-Wye, Hereford	Great Britain	HR3 5EW	(0497)821-083
Louisville	KY	40204	(502)459-5729
Clarence Centre	NY	14032	(716)741-9236
Santa Cruz	CA	95060	(408)426-1119
Webster	NY	14580	
Chicago	IL	60643	(312)233-3368
Athol	MA	01331	(508)249-2335
Baltimore	MD	21201	(410)225-0277
Boston	MA	02116	
Haddonfield	NJ	08033	(609)354-9158
Rogers City	MI	49779	
Brooklyn	NY	11229	(718)891-5241
Turlock	CA	95380	(209)632-5054
Los Angeles	CA	90069	(310)659-3674
Ho-Ho-Kus	NJ	07423	(201)327-4717
Champaign	IL	61820	(217)356-2555
Vienna	VA	22180	(703)938-2967
New York	NY	10022	(212)832-8231
Rolling Hills	CA	90274	(310)377-8511

DEALER LIST

DEALER	STREET
M & D Reeve Children Books	P.O. Box 16 Wheatley
Marion F. Adler	P.O. Box 627
Page Books	Rt. 65 Box 233
Petersons (The)	6324 Langdon St.
Pictus Orbis	42031 Main St.
Prince & The Pauper (The)	3201 Adams Ave.
R.H. Shove	87 Orlin Ave. S.E.
Ramelle Onstott, Books	6489 South Land Park Dr.
Rebecca Of Sunny Brook Farm	P.O. Box 209
Richard Dix Illustrated Books	13660 S.W. Brightood
Room with A View	635 Camino De Los Mares #106
RPM Books	104-20 Jamaica Ave.
Thomas & Mary Jo Barron	120 Lismore Ave.
Treasures From The Castle	1720 N. Livernois
Unicorn Bookshop	P.O. Box 154 Rt 50
Ursula Davidson	134 Linden Lane
Windy Hill Books	3806 Whittier Rd.
Wonderland Books	1824 Wilton Rd.

DEALER LIST

CITY	STATE	ZIP	PHONE
Oxford	England	OX33 1RD	(011 44)865-874383
Stockbridge	MA	01262	(413)298-3559
Kingston	AR	72742	(501)861-5831
Philadelphia	PA	19111	(215)744-5671
Temecula	CA	92590	(909)695-3139
San Diego	CA	92116	(619)283-4380
Minneapolis	MN	55414	
Sacramento	CA	95831	(916)428-2863
Hershey	PA	17033	(717)533-3039
Beaverton	OR	97005	(503)646-1780
San Clemente	CA	92673	(714)240-4333
Richmond Hill	NY	11418	
Glenside	PA	19038	
Rochester	MI	48306	(810)651-7317
Trappe	MD	21673	(410)476-3838
San Rafael	CA	94901	(415)454-3939
Central City	IA	52214	
Cleveland Heights	OH	44118	(216)464-0120

BIBLIOGRAPHY

BIBLIOGRAPHY

TITLE OF BOOK	AUTHOR
1993 Price Guide For Books Illustrated By Arthur Rackham	Gary Overmann
A New Bibliography Of Arthur Rackham	Richard Riall
Ab Bookman's Weekly	Jacob Chernofsky
American Book Prices Current Vol 97	Katharine Leab
American Book Prices Current Vol 98	Katharine Leab
American Book Prices Current Vol 99	Katharine Leab
Annual Register Of Book Values -Children's Books	Michael Cole
Arthur Rackham A Biography	James Hamilton
Beatrix Potter A Bibliographical Checklist	Quinby/Jane
Bibliographia Oziana	Doug Greene & Peter Hanff
Book Illustrators Of The Twentieth Century	Brigid Peppin & Lucy Micklethwait
Book Prices Used & Rare 1993	Edward Zempel&Linda Verkler
Collected Books The Guide To Values	Allen & Patricia Ahearn
Contemporary Illustrators Of Children's Books	Bertha Mahony & Elinor Whitney
English Children's Books	Percy Muir
Howard Pyle	Henry C. Pitz
Illustrators A Finding List	Louise P. Latimer
Jessie Wilcox Smith A Biography	Edward D. Nudelman
Jessie Wilcox Smith American Illustrator	Edward D. Nudelman
Johnny Gruelle Creator Of Raggedy Ann & Andy	Patricia Hall
Kate Greenaway	M.H. Spielmann & G.S. Layard
Maxfield Parrish	Coy Ludwig
N.C. Wyeth	Kate F. Jennings
Of The Decorative Illustration Of Books	Walter Crane
Price Guide For Children's & Illustrated Books	E. Lee Baumgarten
The Art Of Kate Greenaway	Ina Taylor
The Collectors Book Of Children's Books	Eric Quayle
The Illustartor In America 1900-1960's	Walt Reed
The Maxfield Parrish Identification & Price Guide	Richard Perry
Twentieth-Century Children's Writers	D.L. Kirkpatrick
Walter Crane As A Book Illustrator	Rodney K. Engen

BIBLIOGRAPHY

PUBLISHER	DATE	CITY
Gary Overmann	1993	Batavia
Ross Press	1994	Bath
	1993-94	Clifton
Bancroft-Parkman Inc.	1992	Washington
Bancroft-Parkman Inc.	1993	Washington
Bancroft-Parkman Inc.	1994	Washington
The Clique	1994	York
Arcade Publishing	1990	New York
Stroud	1983	
International Wizard Of Oz Club	1988	
Arco Publishing	1984	New York
Spoon River Press	1993	Peoria
G.P. Putnam's Sons	1991	New York
The Bookshop For Boys & Girls	1930	Boston
B.T. Batsford	1985	London
Bramhall House	1965	New York
F.W. Faxon Co.	1929	Boston
Pelican Publishing	1989	Gretna
Pelican Publishing	1990	Gretna
Pelican Publishing	1993	Gretna
Adam & Charles Black	1905	London
Watson-Guptill Publications	1973	New York
Crescent Books	1992	New York
Bracken Books	1984	London
E. Lee Baumgarten	1993	Martinsburg Wv
Pelican Publishing	1991	Gretna
Clarkson N. Potter Inc.	1971	New York
Reinhold Publishing Corp	1966	New York
Starbound Publishing Co.	1993	Portland
St. Martin's Press	1983	New York
St. Martin's Press	1975	New York